BEYOND THE ⟨ NARRATIV

Politics, Sex, and Manuscripts
in the Haitian Revolution

Deborah Jenson

LIVERPOOL UNIVERSITY PRESS

First published 2011 by
Liverpool University Press
4 Cambridge Street
Liverpool
L69 7ZU

British Library Cataloguing-in-Publication data

A British Library CIP record is available

ISBN 978-1-84631-497-1 cased
ISBN 978-1-84631-760-6 paperback

Typeset by Carnegie Book Production, Lancaster
Printed and bound by CPI Group (UK) Ltd, Croydon, CR0 4YY

BEYOND THE SLAVE NARRATIVE

POLITICS, SEX, AND MANUSCRIPTS
IN THE HAITIAN REVOLUTION

Contents

Acknowledgments

When I encountered two poems in a French/Creole hybrid by the French Romantic poet Marceline Desbordes-Valmore almost a decade ago, I never imagined that my quest to decipher their meaning and historical *raison d'être* would lead me far afield from French Romanticism, through years of studying Haitian Creole (*Kreyòl*) and researching the literary products of the Haitian Revolution. As a result of the scope of the engagements represented in this research trajectory, including not only a new linguistic field but historiographical methodology and archival research in France, the U.S., and the Caribbean, it is difficult to adequately thank the array of individuals and groups who have welcomed my work and provided incisive contributions to its development. Those cited here, and many others besides, have made assembling and interpreting a field of Haitian Revolutionary literary evidence into an unforgettable adventure.

Beginning in the present moment and working backward, I would like to thank my colleague Laurent Dubois for his galvanizing intellectual presence and friendship. Due to the visionary contributions of Ian Baucom, with Laurent and additional colleagues Guy-Uriel Charles, Jacques Pierre, Victoria Szabo, and Kathy Walmer, the finalization of this book coincided with an opportunity to test the limits of Haitian Studies, and of cultural engagement in the humanities more generally, in Duke University's Franklin Humanities Institute "Haiti Lab." I'm grateful to numerous Duke Caribbeanist/postcolonialist colleagues including Esther Gabara, Pedro Lasch, Walter Mignolo, Richard Rosa, F. J. Hernandez-Adrián, Holly Ackerman, Barry Gaspar, and Achille Mbembe. Michaeline Crichlow has been a particularly sustained and creative collaborator in enterprises including working groups, the "Sea is History" project, and our "States of Freedom: Freedom of States" event with Pat Northover, Matthew Smith, and others at the University of the West Indies-Mona. Many thanks for the philosophical inspiration of my Romance Studies chair Roberto Dainotto and to my French colleagues for supporting this phase of "continental drift" of my work from France to the Caribbean, while recognizing that nineteenth-century France remains prominent on my intellectual cartography. Mellon Visiting Professor and Haiti Lab affiliated faculty member Jean Casimir has been important in this project and will be even more so in the next one. To the colleagues who have helped me make Duke a place where one can speak and work in *Kreyòl*, Jacques Pierre and Gaspard Louis, profound thanks for your transformative projects, as well as to creolists Marc Prou and Ben Hebblethwaite. Even my humanities dean at Duke, Srinivas Aravamudan, has been a Caribbeanist inspiration for me, and from the inception of this project.

Daniel Desormeaux, Nick Nesbitt, Doris Kadish, and Chris Bongie consistently challenge my thinking with their remarkable work, and the social genesis of our projects is a true pleasure, as is also the case with Chris Miller, Charles Forsdick, Doris Garraway, Alec Hargreave, David Murphy, Dominic Thomas, and Michel Degraff. Marina van Zuylen has stubbornly refused to enter the Haitian Studies fold—so far—but knows that I write for her... Diana Robin has nurtured our intellectual connection across the Renaissance Italy/Haitian revolutionary divide with the strategic intelligence of true friendship.

At the University of Wisconsin-Madison, Tejumola Olaniyan introduced me to the field of African diaspora studies. My French department colleagues, including Aliko Songolo and Bill Berg, were steady mentors and insightful interlocutors. Warwick Anderson and Rick Keller indirectly contributed to the genesis of this project in their encouragement of my work on pathology and healing in colonial Saint-Domingue. Rob Nixon introduced me to the key concept of mediated literature, and Susanne Wofford helped me to explore the resonance of Haiti-related research in the larger humanities community. Intensive and sustained discussions on cosmopolitanism with Vinay Dharwadker, Rebecca Walkowitz, Susan Friedman, and Venkat Mani prompted me to interrogate the generic parameters of Afro-diasporic expression in the era of slavery through the models of cosmopolitanism and world literature.

Graduate students have been highly valued voices in the research and pedagogical dialogues underpinning this work; Julia Gaffield, Mitch Fraas, Reginald Patterson, Laura Wagner, Christy Mobley, Aude Dieudé, and Lesley Curtis have all contributed to the development of Haitian Studies at Duke, sometimes in poignant moments like Laura Wagner's co-teaching of "Haitian Creole for the Recovery" after her return from earthquake-stricken Haiti, or Julia Gaffield's discovery of the only currently known Haitian government-issued printed copy of the Haitian Declaration of Independence. Duke undergraduate Andrew Walker and Madison undergraduate Andrew Miller have done excellent Haiti-related research for me. Subha Xavier, Mary Claypool, Olivia Donaldson, Gretchen O'Dell, and Linda Brindeau are just some of the Madison graduate students whose lively investigations of the colonial and the postcolonial continues to inspire me. Laura Wagner demonstrated the impassioned expertise that underlies all her Haiti-related endeavors in reading and providing editorial suggestions for several chapters in this book, even as she has reached out to her own readership with memorable prose.

My mentor Barbara E. Johnson did not live to see the fruition of this project she had so meaningfully encouraged; my instinct to uncover the traces of the literary production of Haitian Revolutionary leaders is a testimony to Barbara's consistent engagement with the politics of literature.

I am grateful to Edouard Duval-Carrié for providing permission to use an image of his painting "Toussaint Planant" for the cover of this book, as well as for his current brilliant collaborations in the Haiti Lab.

Many thanks to Anthony Cond, Alison Welsby, and Helen Tookey at Liverpool University Press for their patient stewardship of this project.

A shorter version of Chapter 1 previously appeared in Doris Garraway's edited volume *Tree of Liberty: Cultural Legacies of the Haitian Revolution in the Atlantic Worlds* (Charlottesville, VA: University of Virginia Press, 2008), and is reprinted with permission of the University of Virginia Press. Elements of Chapter 2 were published in the *International Journal of Francophone Studies* 1:3, and are reprinted with the journal's permission. Many thanks to the *Journal of Haitian Studies* for granting permission for the publication of a revised and further developed version of my 2009, 15:1–2 article. Parts of Chapter 7 were published in the *Yale Journal of Criticism* 17:1 in 2004. Related French essays on early Creole poetry were published in *Langue et identité narrative dans les littératures de l'ailleurs*, ed. Marie-Christine Hazaël-Massieux and Michel Bertrand (Aix-en-Provence: Presses Universitaires de Provence, 2005), and *Relire l'histoire et la littérature haïtiennes*, ed. Christiane Ndiaye (Port-au-Prince: Presses nationales d'Haïti, 2007).

I sincerely thank the Center for Latin American and Caribbean Studies and the Duke University Center for International Studies at Duke, and Graduate School of Arts and Sciences, the Center for European Studies, the Institute for Research in the Humanities at the University of Wisconsin-Madison, and the Camargo Foundation for supporting my my research.

My deepest thanks go to my husband, Jim Jenson, and our sons Emery and Cole, as well as to my father-in-law Bill Jenson, and my parents, Mary and Ken Carpenter.

This book is dedicated to my sister Grace as she rediscovers her own voice.

Introduction
Race and Voice in the Archives:
Mediated Testimony and Interracial
Commerce in Saint-Domingue

The fundamental purpose of this book is to introduce a literary tradition that sprang directly from the Haitian Revolution, by Haitians. Not literature from afterwards, like Haitian writer Jean Casimir's Creole and French treatise on the Revolution, *Pa Bliye 1804*; not literature from elsewhere, like Alejo Carpentier's wonderful historical fiction *The Kingdom of this World*; not literature on the symbolic resonance of the Haitian Revolution or "the idea of 1804" in Nick Nesbitt's philosophical coinage; but the first Haitians speaking publicly and potently for their culture in the revolutionary era, and becoming authorial voices whose words left a profound mark on the Western world.

Despite the wealth of materials representing early Haitian voices, scholars have proven reticent in treating them as literary sources, or even as reliable political sources. The naturalization of the slave narrative as the genre most associated with blacks' self-expression in the era of Caribbean and American slavery privileged an autobiographical mandate. Early texts by blacks devoted to state-building in a racialized world, which was the fundamental motivation for the public texts of Toussaint Louverture and Jean-Jacques Dessalines, or to poetic representation of the social and sexual interrelations that marked the complex interracial space of colonial culture, which is the major preoccupation of popular Creole poetry, have proven more challenging to recognize and categorize appropriately. This heteroclite corpus[1] of political texts and correspondence, political memoirs, and early Creole poems challenges readers to think outside the box of the dominant genre of early Afro-diasporic literature in the Anglophone world: the slave narrative. The literature of the Haitian Revolution and independence puts the focus not on slavery per se, but on the means through which individuals and communities revolutionized the discursive sphere as well as the political sphere of Atlantic modernity.

The Black Atlantic in French and Creole (*Kreyòl*)

"We have at our disposal not a single written testimony on the reality of slavery coming from a slave,"[2] declared Louis Sala-Molins in 1987 concerning the literary legacies of the French slave-holding colonies. This assessment has remained largely unchallenged, despite the convergence of many previously marginalized threads of literary culture in recent historicist research such as Christopher L. Miller's *The French Atlantic Triangle: Literature and Culture of the Slave Trade* (2008), with its sophisticated consideration of factors that narrow "the gap between the discourse of the Anglo-American Atlantic, influenced by slave narratives, and that of the French Atlantic, without those texts as such."[3] Overall, however, literary reconstructions of African diasporan literature from French New World colonialism are organized around the conventional caveat articulated by Catriona Cunningham in "Literarily Tracing One's Roots" in 2005, that "As there was no written documentation by slaves, the only evidence is that of European missionaries and colonizers."[4] This alleged silence of the slave in the French/Francophone print traditions contrasts with the existence of a considerable body (more than 6,000 texts) of slave and ex-slave narratives in the Anglophone arena (the United States, England, the British Caribbean, and Canada), dating from the mid-eighteenth century through the 1930s, when the Federal Writers' Project collected and transcribed oral testimony by a final generation of ex-slaves.[5] Henry Louis Gates rightly asserts that "No group of slaves anywhere, at any other period in history, has left such a large repository of testimony about becoming the legal property of another human being."[6]

The slave narrative has so strongly impressed readers as the voice of the socially voiceless that long after the era of slavery, the genre of the "neo-slave narrative"—fictional recreations of slave narratives—has thrived not only in the Anglophone but the French/Francophone literary traditions. The slave narrative often has set the very codes, according to Dwight McBride, through which readers are prepared to "understand the experience of slavery."[7]

The perception of the absence of written testimony coming from French-owned slaves or former slaves has made the "francophone" or later postcolonial French-language corpus of literature the only viable area of literary study for readers of Caribbean literature. It is important to resituate late colonial and early postcolonial letters from Haiti as a bona fide area of literary study and teaching. The early Haitian corpus I study here also virtually necessitates engagement with Haitian history and language, which is arguably advantageous not only for the expansion of commitments in research and education, but for the ability of an international community to meet Haiti and its development struggles on its own cultural terms.

The slave narrative, when taken as the gold standard of literary testimony from the socioracial substrata of Western colonialism, obscures the existence of genres other than the slave narrative that *were* produced, through complex and mediated processes by French colonial slaves, former slaves, and their descendants in the early postcolonial period. The privileging of a single form of literary testimony, in one language, disrupts our view of a longer continuum of multilingual New World African diasporan expression and discourages comparative study of the African diaspora across language traditions.

My attempt to destabilize theories and methodologies that have privileged the slave narrative at the expense of less unified elements of the early African diasporan literary field parallels newer work in African-American and black Atlantic research. As Francis Smith Foster notes in *Love and Marriage in Early African America*, "Even before Phyllis Wheatley's book of poems appeared in 1773, African Americans were writing and publishing sermons and minutes of meetings, poems, essays, and autobiographies. At least by 1817 [...] we had black editors and publishers, printers and marketing agents, journalists and correspondents [...]."[8] Robert Reid-Pharr has critiqued the "Big Bang" contextualization of the slave narrative,[9] as I discuss in Chapter 7. Paradigms of world literature are drawing attention to diverse patterns of diasporan literary and linguistic history, such as Wai Chee Dimock's idea of American literature "across deep time."[10]

The French and Creole African diasporan texts I study here date from the era of the Haitian Revolution (1791–1803) and the Dessalines era of Haitian independence (1804–1806), in which Haitians forged the precarious sovereignty of the black nation. If in the Anglophone context, the slave narrative is generally marked by testimony about "becoming the legal property of another human being," as Gates says—about capture and captivity, or birth and youth in slavery—the French colonial and early postcolonial tradition by slaves and former slaves offers particularly detailed accounts of *un-becoming* the legal property of another human being—and, unfortunately, *becoming* the national equivalent of "brigands" on the international scene... sovereign "brigands." On a level of subjective national and individual identity, revolutionary and independence documents show the forging of a fully free consciousness, resulting in confident international overtures, on the part of the Haitians. Early openness on the part of the U.S. to deal with Haiti as a bona fide independent economic partner morphed over the course of the Dessalines era into U.S. adherence to an embargo whose terms had been set above all by the former French colonial power on Hispaniola. Even more damningly, the legitimacy of Haiti's independence from France was put into question in an array of political and legal contexts.

Both sides of this process of un-becoming slaves and becoming sovereign "brigands" unfolded during the Caribbean Age of Revolution. French-owned slaves theoretically gained freedom and citizenship for at least a period of eight years (from the French abolition of slavery in 1794 to the beginning of a localized Napoleonic reimposition of slavery in Guadeloupe, Santo Domingo, and other locales in 1802). In Haiti, official emancipation preceded the French abolition decree by one year, occurring under French Commissioner Sonthonax in 1793, although unofficial emancipation had been gained by force in the insurgency beginning in 1791. Against major odds, re-enslavement in Haiti was successfully and permanently fought off; 2004 marked the 200th anniversary of the former colony's independent nationhood. But we have failed to appreciate just how close re-enslavement actually was for independent Haiti—as close, I show in Chapter 2, as a rogue French general in Santo Domingo who refused to leave the island and managed to convince the Western powers of a continuous French sovereignty on Hispaniola from 1802–1809.

The texts I address here from revolutionary and independent Haiti tell the story of un-becoming a slave in contexts ranging from libertine interracial sexual and social transactions to international maritime law. They challenge us to develop readings of early African diasporan textual culture in the framework of independence and postcolonial transition, rather than the presumed posterity of slavery that is the backdrop for much of the early Afro-American tradition. They also show the narrative structures born of defensive awareness of hegemonic incursions, from Toussaint Louverture's recreated dramatic dialogues between himself and his political rivals, to Dessalines's rhetorical construction of colonial identity around the contagion of conquest and guilty mastery.

Haitian revolutionary letters are marked by a patent refusal by the former slaves of Saint-Domingue to remain personally framed by the contingency of enslavement—no matter how historically omnipresent the political and economic structures of slavery proved to be. Dessalines did not comment on his own autobiographical experience of slavery, but was quick to try to make the French feel the bite of its stigma, commenting in the Haitian Declaration of independence, "Esclaves! ... laissons aux Français cette épithète qualificative: ils ont vaincu pour cesser d'être libres"[11] ("Slaves! ...Let us leave that qualifying epithet to the French themselves: they have conquered to the point of ceasing to be free"). The French for Dessalines were not just masters of slaves—they themselves were slaves to their slavery practices, enslaved by enslaving, conquered by their repeated conquests.

Toussaint Louverture only very rarely referred to his earlier status as a slave, in a couple of references from the final period of his life. In a proclamation to a military assembly in the period following the invasion of Napoleon's forces, which is preserved in the appendix to Joseph Saint-Rémy's 1853 edition of the

Mémoires du général Toussaint Louverture, Toussaint[12] made a rare reference to the Haitian majority's experience of slave life as the foundation for a bond of trust between him and his countrymen.[13] (I discuss this reference at length in Chapter 1.) He also wrote in his memoirs, as part of his repeated owning and unowning of the humiliations imposed by Napoleon, "J'ai été esclave, j'ose l'avouer; mais je n'ai jamais essuyé même des reproches de la part de mes maîtres" ("I have been a slave, and I dare to admit it; but I never once endured so much as a reproach from my masters" [*Mémoires,* 90]). These scant and resistant references to personal enslavement make it challenging to read Haitian revolutionary leaders' texts as autobiographical and therefore as literary in the terms of the slave narrative. But they give a literary character to the historical world of challenges to slavery, and a personal profile to the overwhelming odds and disappointments that came with those challenges.

"Scribal Politics"

From within the print cultures of modernity, Haitian revolutionary leaders' lack of formal schooling or alphabetization has also made it counter-intuitive to contextualize them as authors. Yet a quick mental survey of the world history of political cultures within and outside of alphabetic literacy will confirm that lack of formal schooling in the art of writing cannot inherently disqualify Haitian revolutionary leaders as political thinkers and authorial voices. In the era of the Haitian Revolution and independence, military and political texts were typically collaboratively produced between leaders and secretaries, with processes including dictation, discussion, and editing and refinement of the product. This was true in the rest of the Euro-American sphere also. Yet George Washington is not considered a tag-along in texts transcribed and published by secretaries. Even now, in a time in which authorial voice is strongly associated with individual genius, solitary writing, and specifically authorial access to print culture, it would be inaccurate and narrow to equate the capacity to speak and influence in the political and civic sphere with alphabetization. In the context of societies with strong socioeconomic divides such as Haiti, it is particularly relevant to consider the varieties of technological and lettristic partnering and alibis in democratic communication.

The mediated literature of the Haitian Revolution is a phenomenon related to what Chris Bongie, in *Friends and Enemies: The Scribal Politics of Post/colonial Literature,* describes as "the fact that the birth of the post-colonial state (like that of any state) is inseparable from the emergence of an intellectual elite charged with *mediating* the state's power."[14] These mediators—"scribes, clerks, intellectuals, authors,"[15] such as the Baron de Vastey in the literary edifice of King Henry Christophe, are, for Bongie, the other side, the dependent twin, the "frère ennemi" (the friend and enemy) of the power of the state. These often forgotten scribes allow Bongie to articulate a literary life of postcolonialism that falls between the cracks of the Euro-American modern ideal of the autonomous literary author—a status inaccessible to the marginalized literary producers of the early postcolonial state—and the "nostalgic culturalism"[16] that is a hallmark of contemporary literary recreations of early postcoloniality. My own focus on mediation is somewhat different, in that the documents produced by the first leaders of the blacks in Haiti exemplify, in themselves, both political power and the most tenuous but determined approaches to the magical sphere of literary and mediatic persuasion. Toussaint himself, as I will explain below, must be seen as a "scribe" as well as a politician, and Dessalines, I will argue, was too deeply involved in the invention of scribal processes to be assigned securely to the "power" side of what Bongie calls "the scribal relation to power."

In effect, the phenomena I describe in this book represent a historical stage just before the emergence of the scribal politics assessed by Bongie beginning in the Christophe era—after the death of Dessalines. The literary corpus I analyze here is marked by its tenuous, eruptive nature, its forging of entirely new pathways to inscription and influence. It is legitimately, in this sense, very different from the two centuries of literature that would follow it in Haiti. One could argue that the subsequent formalization of the scribal politics outlined by Bongie, in conjunction with the solidification of class associations around various dimensions of literary voice and experience in Haiti, would lead to some conventionalism and self-censorship in the nineteenth-century Haitian tradition, some "bovarysm,"[17] along with the flowering of a greatly expanded field of Haitian literary participants. There is a radicalism to the literature of the Haitian Revolution and Dessalines eras that is difficult to trace again prior to the twentieth century in Haiti.

Where texts produced by formally unschooled Haitian political leaders have long been neglected as literary texts through a sense that they were somehow unauthored, popular poetry in the black cultural arena of the Caribbean has long been relegated to the literarily invisible category of "folklore," even when individual documents have been published or preserved in non-folkloric collections and speak to different literary legacies and audiences. In the field of popular poetry, there is an inverse analogy to the phenomenon in which political leaders' texts were later ascribed to their secretaries. Colonial and exiled collectors, transcribers and editors of popular Creole literary material from mixed race or slave communities often appropriated it as their own product, and have been enduringly associated as authors rather than editors of contemporary oral literature. Furthermore, the crumbling of a colonial culture that prompted the collection and transcription of popular poetry was followed by the attempt within Haitian letters to promote a poetry that would translate fully to the tonalities and generic identities of metropolitan poetry, rather than presenting a radical contrast of subject matter and language.

The literary tradition studied here fits into several identity niches, including the black Atlantic or the New World African diaspora. It harkens back to the "New World" synonymity of the term "American" at the time, which could designate a person born in the Americas of any background. It also presents the problem of conceptualizing such liminal categories as the Franco African-American, or the Afro-Creole, or the Afro-French Caribbean. In 1798 the black general Moyse wrote to "Citoyen Bonaparte" ("Citizen Bonaparte") to express his hopes for the united destinies of the French and "vos frères d'Amérique" ("your American brothers"),[18] and this sense of an American common ground was pervasive in the materials analyzed in this book. Although the political texts of this tradition are written in French—and also abundantly published in English translation in the United States—a portion of the literary texts I examine here are composed in the African-French hybrid of Haitian Creole. A couple of the literary texts I refer to here are literally from the United States (nineteenth-century New Orleans) although they are direct descendants of Haitian popular traditions. French studies are enriched by integration of the early creolized literatures originating within French colonialism and decolonization. Likewise, American studies benefit from recognition of the linguistic and creative diversity of voices from the French-identified "Americas," a project brilliantly launched with regard to texts of diverse languages by Mark Shell and Werner Sollors in the *Multilingual Anthology of American Literature: A Reader* (2000), but currently less broadly traced among the larger "American" African diaspora.

Comparative rather than nation-based or even language-based study of early print and manuscript culture throughout the slave-holding environments to which populations of the African diaspora were scattered has an inherent historical logic. To be a slave was to be excluded from citizenship in the "nation" with its infrastructure of rights and obligations. The common denominator of the slave narrative genre is thus the status of its represented subjects as slaves or former slaves rather than as inhabitants of, say, nineteenth-century South Carolina or Jamaica. The Middle Passage yielded an impressively large extra-national collectivity.

But a comparative approach is also harmonious with the observation that representational modes in diverse "American" slave-holding environments were formed as much by local identity and practices as by earlier African continental traditions, common factors of adaptation, and syncretic cultural transmission processes. Hip-hop scholarship has begun to question the utility of what Imani Perry calls a "romantic Afro-Atlanticism" which "appears without conflict in the academic world" but "is deeply conflicted in the actual interaction between peoples of African descent in the 'New World.'"[19] Perry's objection is rooted in the use of a diasporan methodology for a twentieth- and twenty-first-century musical genre, but even in the slave-holding era it is essential to take into account the degree to which local identification with and resistance to the colonial or slave-holding power molded African diasporan literature wherever it occurred. This is why Napoleon Bonaparte is a preeminent cultural icon in nineteenth-century Afro-Francophone New Orleans literature, but not in African-American traditions in neighboring states, even though Louisiana was by then also a part of the United States. In the Caribbean, the French Revolution provided a crucial discursive model and infrastructure for print culture mediation, whereas English abolitionism was arguably a more influential ideological paradigm in the United States.

Linguistic variation, not only between national languages but even under the umbrella of a single language such as English, clearly also germinates and encodes major differences of cultural personality. Ultimately, one of the epistemological advantages of "romantic Afro-Atlanticism" is the potential to demystify the globalized and sometimes transhistorical idea of the "slave," while simultaneously remaining alert to widespread postcolonial and African legacies. One such extra-regional phenomenon observed in my research is the occurrence of "dissing" and "signifying" speech strategies in Haitian revolutionary-era African diasporan documents—forms of challenge to dominant discourses also found throughout African American literature and popular verbal arts.

Politics and Sex

This book interweaves research on the libertine sphere in the French colony of Saint-Domingue with research on the culture and politics of the Haitian Revolution; as such, it follows in the footsteps of a venerable predecessor, Colin Dayan's *Haiti, History, and the Gods* (1998), which brought the fields of sex and politics into a unified field of inquiry. My focus is not on the historical role of sex in revolutionary and independence politics (for example, the role of interracial relationships in the lives of political and military leaders). It is worth noting, however, that the chronicles of the times suggest there would be no shortage of relevant material in that area, as in Pamphile de Lacroix's account of the French army's discovery of a locked box containing love letters and locks of hair "of all colors"[20] among the personal effects of the deported Toussaint Louverture; or Leclerc's cryptic comment, "On a arrêté aujourd'hui une des maîtresses de Toussaint venue ici pour m'assassiner"[21] ("Today they arrested one of Toussaint's mistresses, who had come to kill me"); or the potentially remarkable importance of

French Commissioner Sonthonax's open liaison with a woman of color, Marie Eugénie Bléigeat; or numerous other examples of interracial unions in the top ranks of leadership in Saint-Domingue/Haiti. Instead, this book is inspired by the convergence of money and the stakes of personal sovereignty or autonomy in slavery, international diplomatic or economic status, and the colonial libertine economy. The late colonial period was characterized by a structural antagonism between colonial subjugation of non-whites and colonists' fetishistic sexual valorization of non-whites as debased and yet fascinating others; non-whites represented the lowest of the low, to whom, in a libertine context, colonists were willing to give all. How did this irony find its way both into revolutionary challenges to white supremacy and to discursive challenges to acceptable fields of representation of the self and the state? As Dayan wrote of sexual values and transactions between different elements of the hyper-racialized colonial society in Saint-Domingue, when sexual intrigue and despotism were inextricably merged, courtesans and procurers sometimes attained a certain paradoxical and dialectical mastery: "In a bind of covert mutuality, where masters became slaves and slaves, masters—the reversible world Hegel would later describe—the proprietor becomes possessed by his possession."[22] Where Doris Garraway, in *The Libertine Colony*,[23] so convincingly theorizes the relationship of sexuality and desire to economies of dominion and constructions of race in the Caribbean, I chart literarily the sexual and political synergies of what Dayan called the "reversible world" of both the master–slave dialectic and the Haitian Revolution. Although my chapters on political texts and their histories are in the first part of this book, and chapters on the Creole poetry of the libertine encounter are assessed the second part, each distinct literary corpus challenges, in its own way, white Euro-American literary hegemony by voices from Saint-Domingue's reversible worlds.

In the first part of this book, "Authorizing the Political Sphere," I analyze political documents issued by former slaves who were leaders of the Haitian Revolution. These political texts, including correspondence, manifestoes, and proclamations by the ex-slave leaders, are nearly indecipherable outside of their historical context, and my readings in Chapters 1 through 5 are decidedly historicist. I contend, however, that the words of Toussaint Louverture and Jean-Jacques Dessalines are literary in the degree to which they harnessed poetics to persuade large audiences, represent the stakes of freedom and domination, and engage in political construction of themselves and their constituencies.

These political—and simultaneously literary—texts support Laurent Dubois's contention that key parts of what is considered to be French revolutionary ideology developed primarily through Caribbean revindications, interrogations, and contestations of the Rights of Man and other legacies of the Enlightenment. "Central aspects of the universalism presented by imperial powers of the nineteenth and twentieth centuries (as well as in the world order of the twenty-first) as products of Europe's intellectual heritage," Dubois asserts, "in fact originated in the colonial Caribbean"[24] in the course of arguments and battles, and indeed war, over how French rights could be applied to the colonies:

> The enslaved revolutionaries challenged the racialized colonial system of the day, deploying the language of republican rights and the promise of individual liberty against a social order based on the denial of their humanity. In winning back the natural rights the Enlightenment claimed as the birthright to all people, however, the formerly enslaved laid bare a profound tension within the ideology of rights they had made their own.[25]

History and literature mingle in this section because the vocation of the literary scholar to understand and appreciate the significance of narrative or poetic representations becomes hopelessly—and meaningfully—entangled with the forces that allowed, or repressed, those representations.

Part One opens with a chapter devoted to the problem of news: the Haitian Revolution as public relations, as innovated by Toussaint Louverture. I explore details of how Toussaint entered the mediatic arena, what we can surmise of the French reception of Haitian correspondence and proclamations, and the "politics" of a decolonization discourse articulated in French, which Dayan equates with "the language of the masters"[26] even when manipulated by black and mixed-race insurgents. Toussaint expertly deployed an Enlightenment and sentimental rhetoric that veiled his challenge to the workings of hemispheric notions of race in transatlantic print culture even as he brought questions of universal human rights back to his own subjectivity, his own lived history, and implicitly, his own body, in a subtly radical challenge to the exclusive and excluding alibi of European universalism.

There was nothing subtle about the radicalism of Jean-Jacques Dessalines's discursive death match with European obliviousness to its self-selected paradigm of the human. Dessalines is in many ways the star of this book, as three chapters are devoted to the literary legacies of this hero of Haitian cultural patrimony. Chapter 2, "Before Malcolm X, Dessalines: Postcoloniality in a Colonial World," analyzes the precocious "Black Atlantic" or "postcolonial" forms of rhetoric employed by Dessalines and his secretaries. Even while appreciating the literary dynamism of Dessalines's anticolonial interventions, the chapter outlines forces that were threatening the Haitians' independence far more concretely, and enduringly, than we have realized. Chapter 3, "Dessalines's America," documents Dessalines's determined outreach to an American media sphere that he saw as the appropriate public for the self-representations of free men. His choice of the U.S. journalism market challenged the racial parameters underlying the act of declaring independence. It also helped to raise U.S. support for "neutral" commercial relations between the U.S. and Haiti, which were arguably Dessalines's strategic foundation for the creation and maintenance of economic and political sovereignty. That economic relationship, initially thriving, was gradually choked off due to the combined problems of the ongoing French presence on the island of Hispaniola, and the scandal around Jeffersonian support for the decolonizing mission of General Francisco Miranda in partnership with the major figures in U.S. neutral commerce with Haiti. Chapter 4, "Between the Lines: Dessalines's Anticolonial Imperialism in Venezuela and Trinidad," interprets texts that did not make it into print: mysterious subtexts of Dessalines's actual or rumored attempts to spread Haitian revolutionary emancipation to Santo Domingo, Trinidad, and Venezuela. Chapter 5 concludes this section with a reading of narratives of the kidnappings that haunted Haitian revolutionary leaders and their families, not just in the Louverture family, where not only Toussaint but his wife and children were seized against their will and deported, but also in the family of Henry Christophe. Christophe's eldest son, Ferdinand, who had been sent for his education to France under the guardianship of Christophe's sister-in-law, was forcibly removed to a Parisian almshouse after the independence. Ferdinand subsequently died, allegedly of abuse, as did his aunt, who had been interned at La Salpêtrière. A virtually unknown text in the papers of Moreau de Saint-Méry presents this entire appalling episode in the voice of a female former slave, now a part of Paris's small black community, who had witnessed some of the events in question and did her best to piece together the larger sequence and its relationship to Napoleonic grudges. I read this startling text and other narratives of Haitian revolutionary kidnappings as a paradigm for Haitian engagement with manuscript and print culture itself—an engagement in which threats to speakers' basic autonomy and security, mapped over forced voyages between metropolitan and colonial spaces, were repeatedly inscribed.

The second part of the book, "Authorizing the Libertine Sphere," moves from the political to the sexual domain of a colonial culture in the process of disaggregation and reconstitution in postcolonial form. These chapters assemble evidence of a thriving, intertextual, but generally verbal poetic culture dating from the colonial period yet collected and in some cases published from the very inception of the Haitian nation. In literary material composed or transcribed or collected—the distinction is not always clear—in the second half of the eighteenth century and into the first decade of the independence, courtesans, dandies, and procurers vaunt their social power and strategic intelligence.

Chapter 6 explores the influence of an idea of "traumatic indigeneity" on forms of literary "collecting" by exiled colonists that led to the unusual preservation or publication of popular lyrical material, particularly from the courtesan milieu of the "libertine colony." Popular texts describing the courtesan's negotiations of racial and economic hierarchy became "collectible" primarily from the vantage point of early nineteenth-century "postcolonial" consciousness and nostalgia. The destabilizing effects of the Haitian Revolution caused colonists to recognize the singularity of libertine interracial commerce, and thus to record a literature normally considered incompatible with the elite registers of print culture. The songs themselves are also radical to the extent that they represent courtesans' strategic ambitions to gain autonomy through exploitation of the very racial and gender hierarchy in which they themselves were victimized and exploited. This corpus on what one might call the politics of sex indicates that the liminal status of courtesans in colonial society—as in many other societies, such as nineteenth-century France—generated challenges to numerous discourses of morality and race. Conversely, they represent perhaps the most costly submission in colonial society, that of women and girls, and by extension of their relatives, to the sexual predations of the dominant class. They represent, ultimately, colonial economic and social mobility in the African diaspora as inseparable from division and alienation.

Chapter 7 introduces the first Creole poetry anthology and reassesses the theoretical paradigm of the colonized "mimic man" in relation to colonists' appropriations of Creole literature and the centrality of an oblique male figure, the "Candio," as a rival and generator of female desire. In chapter 8 I analyze the gender politics of woman as commodity against the background of slave-holding societies, using unpublished poems from courtesan culture, linked to the female figure of the *cocotte*, as my primary texts.

Eye Witnessing

The existence of this provocative literary record from a revolutionary window of time is best documented with one's own eyes, which is to say by viewing handwritten manuscripts in the archives, through which one can associate "hands" with voices and voices with the various forms of mediation that led to their preservation in textual form. For that reason, in this introduction I propose to guide the reader through a textual and photographic exhibit of neglected or unknown African diasporan documents of the Haitian revolutionary era. My use of (an admittedly limited corpus of) photographic figures also signals the almost journalistic interest of many of the texts in question—not solely in their life as printed messages, but in their historical object life, fit for writing up and illustration as "news." Some of these texts impacted upon the dramatic unfolding of political history, and some also functioned as a part of the journalistic record at the time. Above all, the small documentary dimension of this book is meant to aggressively counter the decades of insistence that there was no textual culture by French-owned slaves. Even the critical works most useful in identifying the skills and creativity of slaves, such as Jean Fouchard's *Les Marrons du syllabaire* or Patrick Chamoiseau and Raphaël Confiant's *Lettres créoles*, have thematized symbolic or potential "maroon" (escaped slave) print participation, and non-print forms of literary art ranging from rock inscriptions to folklore. By contrast, in keeping with my own emphasis on textual artifacts, the remainder of this introduction will be structured around anecdotes from the archives. Having worked with the manuscripts into which a certain ghostly condition of personhood seems to be compressed and preserved in small material traces like the physical signature, the reader in the archives mutely responds, I was there, and I saw.

The Black General's Will to (Literary) Power

The Archives nationales in Paris house remarkable collections of correspondence and other documents issued by the former slave leader Toussaint Louverture in particular, but also by other black generals, including Jean-Jacques Dessalines and Toussaint's adoptive nephew Moyse. The first time I realized that I was holding in my hands a personally handwritten (see figure 1) plea to Napoleon from the imprisoned Toussaint, a lump rose in my throat; every loop of ink on the fragile paper seemed like a physical remnant of the general's needs and determination. In the same sheaf of documents I had already read in a letter to Napoleon Bonaparte from his aide-de-camp Caffarelli, dated 13 Prairial year 11, that this document had been found in Toussaint Louverture's jail cell at the Fort de Joux at the time of his death, not among his belongings, but on his corpse, hidden under his headscarf (figure 2). Caffarelli's note read: "J'ai l'honneur de vous adresser des papiers qu'on a trouvés sur Toussaint Louverture après sa mort dans les plis d'un mouchoir qui couvrait la tête" ("I have the honor of sending you the papers we found on Toussaint Louverture after his death in the folds of a handkerchief that covered his head").[27] Toussaint had hidden this and a handful of other documents because he had been forbidden to write, some months earlier, by order of Napoleon,[28] who chafed at being the addressee of the doomed slave leader's impassioned self-defense and critique of his deportation by the French. Toussaint was determined to remain armed with an inscribed rhetoric of protest even to his death, like a literary second skin.

Toussaint's secret preservation of a few texts on his person may also have

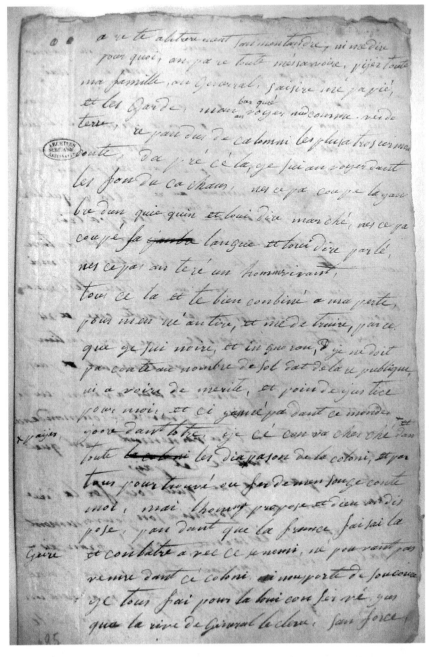

Figure 1. Published with permission of the Archives nationales AF IV 1213.

This photo shows part of a loose leaf page of Toussaint's handwritten memoir, in a selection of documents addressed to Napoleon Bonaparte.

Figure 2. Published with permission of the Archives nationales AF IV 1213.

Note from Aide-de-camp Caffarelli to Napoleon Bonaparte, documenting the materials found in Toussaint Louverture's headscarf after his death.

been a proactive attempt at legal self-representation. He may have been informed in the early fall of 1802 of plans to put him on trial. This plan had been shelved when General Leclerc noted on September 26 to the General-in-Chief of the Colonial Ministry that putting Toussaint Louverture on trial would only energize his supporters:

> Je ne manque pas de pièces pour lui faire son procès, si on veut avoir recours à ce qui s'est fait avant l'amnistie que je lui ai accordée; depuis je n'en ai aucune. Dans la situation actuelle des choses, sa mise en jugement et son exécution ne feraient qu'aigrir les esprits des noirs.[29]

> (I do not lack documents to put him on trial, if we want to have recourse to what transpired before the amnesty I granted him; after that period, I have nothing. In the current climate, his sentencing and execution would only embitter the blacks.)

The possibility of a legal defense, and the challenge—and allure—of representing himself to Napoleonic authority and to posterity, permeate the Toussaint papers in the french National Archives. In the memoirs, Toussaint in fact repeatedly argued for his right to a trial. Where Leclerc roamed free, Toussaint complained, "Je suis au fond d'un cachot sans pouvoir me justifier" ("I am in the depths of a dungeon, unable to justify myself" [*Mémoires*, 99]). The French government was alleged to be just: "Ne dois-je pas participer à sa justice?" ("Shouldn't I participate in its justice?" [99]). He went so far as to demand a trial, with full consideration of literary evidence: "Je demande que le général Leclerc et moi, nous comparaissions ensemble devant un tribunal, et que le gouvernement ordonne que l'on m'apporte toutes les pièces de ma correspondance" ("I demand this: that General Leclerc and I should appear together before a tribunal, and that the government should order all items of my correspondence to be presented as evidence" [100]).

Prior to analysis of the content of archival documents like the extensive yet partial handwritten version of the memoirs by Toussaint, however, how can Toussaint's actual authorship, the imprints of his intentionality and investment in self-representation, be verified? Questions of handwriting, transcription, translation, and dissemination are necessary to even the most basic reading of (former) slaves' texts as authored documents. As it happens, matters pertaining to the textual authenticity of Toussaint's writing are parabolic of the stakes of the denial of a textual tradition by French-owned slaves.

Toussaint's handwriting in the documents found in his headscarf, and in a couple of handwritten letters analyzed in Chapter 1, or in the handwritten but partial copy of the memoirs, is distinctly similar to his signature on the voluminous correspondence otherwise transcribed by secretaries. His degree of manual control in these texts varies from one document to another, notably as his health dwindled in the final months of his life. But his idiosyncratic rendition of French—his personal reconstruction in writing of the sophisticated military and political discourses in which he had been immersed verbally—constitutes a unique and unmistakable signature. The language of Toussaint's handwritten texts amounted to the personal idiom of an extraordinarily intelligent individual who had had a crash encounter with literacy, featuring invented spellings, approximate punctuation, and strange slippages in the determination of meaning. Here is an example of a passage from the documents found in his headscarf, in the form of a letter to Napoleon that was also an excerpt from the memoirs:

A re te abitrerement san montandre, ni me dire pour quoi, an pa re toute mésavaire, piÿer toute ma famille, an general, saisire mé pa pié, et les garde, man bar qué, man voyer nu comme ver de ter, re pan dre de calomni les plusa tros cer mon conte, da pré cé la, je sui an voyer dant les fon du ce ca chau, nes ce pa coupe la janbre dun quie quin et loui dire marché, nes ce pa coupé la langue et loui dire parlé, nes ce pas an teré un homme vivant?[30]

The equivalent of this handwritten passage, presumably gleaned from the texts dictated to secretaries, was edited by Saint-Rémy as follows:

On m'a envoyé en France nu comme un ver; on a saisi mes propriétés et mes papiers; on a répandu les calomnies les plus atroces sur mon compte. N'est-ce pas couper les jambes à quelqu'un et lui ordonner de marcher? N'est-ce pas lui couper la langue et lui dire de parler? N'est-ce pas enterrer un homme tout vivant? (*Mémoires*, 86)

In the single English translation, published by John Relly Beard in 1863, the passage is indistinguishable from the educated and reserved prose one might have expected of a political memoir of the time, with the image "naked as an earthworm" simply left out. In fact, the translation makes this prison memoir by a former slave so polished that readers might plausibly have guessed that it was "fake":

They have sent me to France destitute of everything; they have seized my property and my papers, and have spread atrocious calumnies concerning me. Is it not like cutting off a man's legs and telling him to walk? Is it not like cutting out a man's tongue and telling him to talk? Is it not burying a man alive?[31]

But a rendering of the text into an English idiom as personally fashioned as the original French might read like this:

To a rest arbitrerely, without hearringme, or telling me why, tak ing all myethings, pilajing mye whole family, en general, seezing mye pay pers, and keep them, em barkingme, spred ding the mos atro shish lys abowt me, a kord ing after that, sendingme naked as en erthwerm to the deps of this dun jon, isn this like cuhting off the legge of a some one and tellingim walk, isent this like cuhting out the tongue and tellingim talk, isent this bur ee ing a man alive?

Effacement of the traces of Toussaint's linguistic navigation of the all-important world of textual self-representation and media persuasion has contributed to the fate Toussaint wanted to avoid at all costs: interpretations of his texts as apocryphal and therefore unworthy of attention, as occurred after the first publication of excerpts of the memoirs in the French journal *La Presse* in 1843. Toussaint's memoirs to date have only been published in edited form, not in the signature idiom discussed above. Until a groundbreaking 2005 article by Haitian scholar Daniel Desormeaux,[32] the memoir had received almost no attention in the otherwise superb new research generated by historians in the final decades of the twentieth century.

Toussaint either handwrote, edited with handwritten notations, or oversaw and signed with a handwritten addendum several copies of his memoirs; the cumulative effect of these different versions is one of overwhelming authentication and concern for preservation. The process and personnel involved in the transcription of the different copies of the memoir is, unfortunately, difficult to account for in detail. Correspondence, held in the French National Archives, documenting the seizure of Toussaint's papers from his jail cell as ordered by Napoleon indicates that the imprisoned general had already generated "mémoires écrites" ("written memoirs") in the plural by October of 1802, five months before his death. Division General Ménard records the fact that he had sent these materials to the Ministry of War on 6 Frimaire year 11 (November 27, 1802):

> Par mon rapport du 20 brumaire des n.442 je vous ai annoncé que j'avais ordonné au comdt. [commandant] du fort de joux de saisir les papiers et mémoires écrites qu'avait voulu conserver Toussaint Louverture; j'ai l'honneur de vous les adresser cy joints au nombre de 9 cahiers, y compris quelques lettres et feuilles separées, il ne reste plus actuellement à Toussaint que ses vêtements usuels et le reçu de quadruples que lui a donné le comdt. d'armes. [...]
> Je vous salue avec respect,
> Ménard[33]

(By my report of the 20 Brumaire (November 11) in the number 442 series, I announced to you that I had ordered the Commander of the Fort de Joux to seize the written papers and memoirs that Toussaint Louverture

wanted to keep; I have the honor of sending them to you here, numbering
9 notebooks and some letters and individual papers. Toussaint now has
in his possession nothing more than his daily clothing and the quadruple
receipts given him by the Commander. [...]

I salute you respectfully,
Ménard)

Ironically, the bibliophile Napoleon, despite his determination to strip
Toussaint of every sheet of paper, nevertheless preserved the seized material
as part of the French patrimony. Yet the papers of Toussaint in the National
Archives do not appear to add up to Ménard's startling number of the "9
notebooks" taken from Toussaint, which may mean that not all the papers
were preserved.

The copies at the National Archives in the AF IV 1213 file include
1) the "Précis d'un mémoire de Toussaint Louverture," which is a terse
summary of the memoirs' content, written by another party; 2) a full copy
written by Toussaint in small, cramped handwriting absolutely filling the
page, apparently in response to a shortage of writing material; 3) another
copy written by a secretary (distinct from the author of the summary),
with corrections handwritten by Toussaint; 4) an additional copy, by the
same secretarial hand, and apparently representing a finalized draft, and
concluding with a handwritten and signed plea by Toussaint to Napoleon;
5) lastly, loose-leaf pages representing excerpts or approximate copies of
excerpts and letters to Napoleon. Daniel Desormeaux's forthcoming critical
edition of the memoirs of Toussaint Louverture will shed invaluable light on
the circumstantial context and content of each of these documents.

In the copy handwritten by Toussaint, the idiosyncrasies of Toussaint's
French are similar to those found in the loose-leaf documents, but not as
pronounced, attesting to Toussaint's intense effort to master his handwriting
and language in this memoir, and no doubt also to the deterioration in his
health by the time he recreated, from memory, the excerpts in the loose-
leaf documents found on his person. From these documents it is clear that
although Toussaint worked with a secretary, he wrote the primary version
personally, and remained deeply invested in the details of each version,
closing the finalized draft again with his own handwriting.

A great deal of Toussaint's early prison time must have been devoted to the
creation of this *oeuvre*, which represents a remarkably writerly achievement—
a concentrated, multiply revised autobiographical narrative produced in a
few short weeks. In addition to the three copies (plus the summary and
loose-leaf pages) in the National Archives, another copy was housed at
the colonial archives. This colonial archives (Archives d'Outre-mer) copy
is the one transcribed by Paul Roussier in the appendix to the *Lettres du
général Leclerc* (fn. 1, 39). Although Roussier did not provide a call number

for the version he published, and I have not personally seen this copy at the Archives d'Outre-mer in Aix, Roussier provided a photo of the last page of the copy he used. It is definitely transcribed by a *different* secretarial hand, and again includes a handwritten postscriptum paragraph by Toussaint, with only slight variations from the postscriptum in the National Archives copy (figure 3). The seal on the colonial archives copy is illegible in the Roussier photo, but slightly different from the seal in the National Archives copy.

The handwritten addenda on the two distinct secretarial final drafts of the memoirs feature a discourse of wounding and healing that had also appeared in an earlier handwritten letter by Toussaint, which I analyze in Chapter 1. The captive Toussaint describes Napoleon, ironically enough, as the doctor capable of healing the wounds of Toussaint's rupture with France:

> Premier consul per de toute les militer, juge in tegre, de fan seur de linosance, prononcé dont sur mon sor, més plai et tre profound, porte les remede saluter, pour lan péché de ne jan mai ou ouvrir, voussete med cien, je conte antier ment sur votre justice, et votre blance,
> Salut et respec[34]

> ("First Consul, father of all military men, just judge, defender of innocence, pronounce, then, on my destiny, my wound is very deep, please bring the salutary remedy, to prevent it from ever reopening, you are a doctor, I count entirely on your justice, and your balance,
> Greetings and respect" [signed with the initial "L" and the 3 suspension points that Toussaint uses as an abbreviated signature])

The manuscript is stamped with an oval seal bearing the words "EMPIRE FRANCAIS DIRECTION GENERALE DES ARCHIVES." In the version used by Roussier, the same passage reads:

> Premire consul,
> Pere de toute les militer, Defan seur des innosant, juge integre, prononcé dons sure un homme quie plus mal heure que coup pable, gairice mes plai illé tré pro fond, vous seul pouvet portes les remede sa lu ter, et lan pé ché de ne jamai ouver, vous sete mede cien, ma position et més service merite toute votre a tantion, et je conte an tier ment sure votre jus tice, et votre balance,
> Salut et respec,
> Toussaint Louv...

The colonial archives text transcribed and photographed by Roussier may possibly be one of the missing "cahiers" described by Ménard. In addition, Saint-Rémy had noted that he had seen a copy in the possession of General Desfourneaux (*Mémoires*, 18). It is almost certain then that there were five

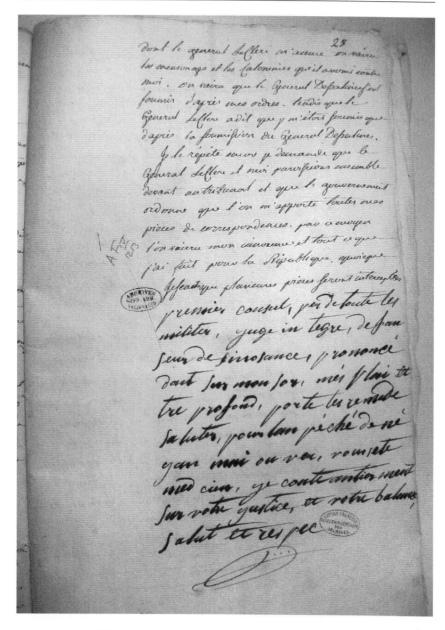

Figure 3. Published with permission of the Archives nationales AF IV 1213.

Handwritten postscriptum to Napoleon Bonaparte at the end of one of the copies of Toussaint Louverture's memoirs.

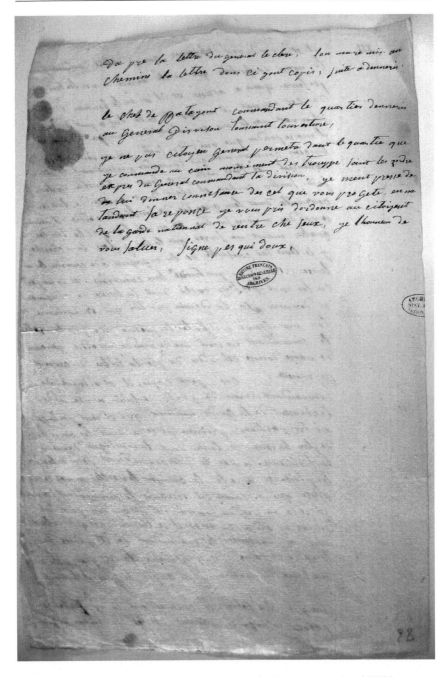

Figure 4. Published with permission of the Archives nationales AF IV 1213.

Handwritten reconstitution of a letter from Pesquidoux.

copies, which makes it possible that there were even more, amounting virtually to an attempt to self-publish the memoir without the aid of a printing press.

The complex paper trail for Toussaint's memoir attests to the black general's profound will to literary power. Multiple copies undoubtedly signal his well-grounded fears that his captors would destroy or otherwise silence his testimony. One extraordinary detail of the handwritten fragments attests to this concern with particular pathos. Toussaint had personally transcribed, probably from memory, a piece of correspondence from someone else, Commander Pesquidoux, that had been in the papers seized from Toussaint by the French, and which he hoped would exonerate him (see figure 4). Toussaint had signed this correspondent's name, rendered as "pes qui doux," in his own hand. (The actual letter from Pesquidoux is published in Roussier,[35] and the relative parity between the content of the real and the recreated letter attests to the acuity of Toussaint's determined acts of memory.) Toussaint's final writings illustrate the politics of literacy as summarized by Robert Stepto with regard to the African American tradition: "Authorial control is a necessary, self-protecting aggression [...]."[36]

In the face of such evidence, to deny that Toussaint's memoir is truly a former slave's narrative of the conditions of his betrayal by one of the most (in)famous figures of Western imperialist history is to turn a deaf ear to the black general's desperate attempts to authenticate and preserve his own speech act and defend his historical legacy.

A (Former) Slave's Narrative, Yet Not a Slave Narrative

Why do we not count even Toussaint's painstakingly authenticated memoir as, to return to the terms of Sala-Molins's mournful survey, "a single written testimony on the reality of slavery coming from a slave"? After all, like Toussaint, the narrative subjects of the vast majority of slave narratives were also ex-slaves, as Frances Smith Foster explains: "Written after the physical escape had been accomplished and the narrators were manumitted or fugitive slaves, these narratives were retrospective endeavors which helped the narrators define, even create, their identities as they attempted to relate the patterns and implications of their slavery experiences."[37]

The cosmopolitan and transnational nature of the slave narrative is frequently cited as characteristic of the texts of the black Atlantic, but the differences between Toussaint's memoir and the model of the slave narrative serve as a reminder of its generic specificity—a specificity partly rooted in the culture of Anglophone abolitionism. In the slave narrative genre, an individual's trajectory, represented in a literary discourse characteristic of the print culture and language of imperialistic states, frames an implicit or explicit condemnation of the abuses of Western slave-holding culture. The slave narrative was profoundly conditioned by the ideological desires and production capacities of abolitionists; abolitionism as a movement and a discourse mediated its development and its reception.

By contrast with abolitionism in Anglophone environments, French abolitionism helped not so much to produce narratives in a certain genre as to produce texts of revolutionary dialogue with (former) slaves—political correspondence, manifestoes, treatises, and constitutions--in the context of the interconnections of the French and Haitian Revolutions and the demands of Caribbean non-whites that they be accepted as interlocutors. The former slaves' "black Jacobin" identity was influenced by abolitionist transmission of revolutionary documents to the Caribbean arena. In this limited sense, narratives of "un-becoming" a slave, like narratives of becoming a slave, also bear abolitionist fingerprints, especially when addressed to the French public. But abolitionists were only one element in the dissemination of revolutionary texts and ideology, and so they should not be credited (as they were blamed at the time) for an overwhelming role in shaping "black Jacobin" consciousness. As Dubois has suggested, there are only conceptual obstacles to viewing the slaves or former slaves as the most proactive and effective group of abolitionists of all.[38]

In the Anglophone environment, abolitionism did not necessarily limit the literary or the testimonial potential of the genre, but it did shape it. For McBride, abolitionist discourse privileges the slave as "the real" in the Western fetishization of "true discourse": "the slave represents a state of nature. [...] The slave is the material—the real, raw material—of abolitionist discourse. The slave is the referent, the point, the very body around which abolitionist discourse coheres and 'makes sense.'"[39] At the same time, the slave using the narrative structure of the genre is invested in a discursive contract with readers and producers; McBride notes that "The 'reader' is not only constructed *by* the witness, but the imagined reader becomes completely discursive *for* the witness."[40] In effect, to the degree that the slave serves symbolically as access to the real—the traumatic real—the relationships between narrative subjects and readers become more and more predictably governed by discursive conventions. The slave is at once an "impossible witness" and a co-generator of what Foster calls "rigidly patterned, didactic works."[41]

This raises important questions about "qualification" for the witnessing of slavery. The conventions of the slave narrative genre clearly suggest that after an individual has established an identity as a free person, his or her narrative still stands as direct testimony of enslavement. But would an individual born into slavery with one enslaved parent, an individual emancipated in adolescence and relatively thoroughly integrated into white society, necessarily still represent slavery in his or her narrative? If so, the memoir of General Dumas, the father of Alexandre Dumas père, to which Desormeaux has also drawn attention, would also constitute a slave narrative. Or a child born free, but raised by two former slaves? This would make the memoir by Toussaint's son Isaac Louverture a testimonial from slavery. At what individual or generational remove from actual enslavement do we cease to consider a non-white individual in a colonial or slave-holding culture to be a potential source of testimony from slavery? These questions are meant not to expand the category of "slaves," but to show the overdetermination of slavery as a defining category of identity and generic form in Afro-diasporic literature.

Toussaint's memoir is as direct a testimonial from a former slave as most slave narratives, and it is an important text of black Atlantic political literature and a necessary point of comparison with the writings of Frederick Douglass, among others. Toussaint's memoir did not describe his life as a slave, but rather his embattled attempts to share power with, or wrestle power from, metropolitan authorities after the abolition of slavery in the colony. At the time of his imprisonment, this was the crux, the identity-forming episode, of his slavery experiences in a broader sense—experiences that had previously spanned life as a relatively privileged slave, life as a freed slave and (formally, at least) a slave owner, and life as a leader in an anti-slavery revolution. His "slavehood" was a complex affair, internally as well as externally reflective of the reversible worlds of Saint-Domingue and its dialectical performances of dominion and subjugation. Although at the end of his life his kidnapping and imprisonment by the French uncannily paralleled the experience of enslavement, he protested against it as someone for whom such treatment was unthinkable.

The politics of the mediated trajectories of "coming to writing" by the socially voiceless—or by anyone—are interpreted very differently from one era to another. Early scholarly observations of abolitionist influence tended, sometimes with more than a *soupçon* of racism, to discredit slaves' voices as "inauthentic," or even as derivative echoes of editors' voices.[42] More recent scholarship, influenced by ideas of the universality of mediation in all print culture, has promoted the paradigm of collaborative (auto)biography[43] as a means of recognizing—without romanticizing or marginalizing—mediated expression by those not empowered to speak publicly.

Most of the texts I will examine in this book were, like slave narratives, heavily mediated, but often through strikingly different mechanisms of mediation. In American slave narratives, someone other than the subject of the narration, generally someone far more educationally and socially privileged than the (former) slave, provided mediating services that might have included any or all of the following: transcription, editing, publishing, or even a compositional role in creating paradigms of individualized moral subjectivity, linear historicity, and other structures that typically underpin Western narrative but may not have been central to most slaves' representational consciousness. British Caribbean slave narratives were even more consistently and fully mediated in the passage to print culture, since, according to Nicole Aljoe, they were virtually all dictated and most were also translated:

> They are all dictated texts; there is an emphasis on orality—slaves spoke in Creole and therefore texts needed translation for British readers; [...]. Furthermore, most of the narratives relied on first-person narration and purported to be "by" the slave or free black narrator, and were primarily designed to provide readers with authentic and authoritative evidence about the details of the slave system in the West Indies.[44]

In the context of Haitian political writings, the mediation comes from a different angle of power relations: Haitian leaders almost universally employed secretaries in their political writings, just like their French military counterparts. In the initial slave insurgency, the earliest secretaries for the blacks were white prisoners (the eighteenth-century counterpart of "embedded journalists") and French-educated Haitians of mixed race. There may have been white secretaries on occasion from the ranks of sympathetic colonists, and almost certainly later on from the French military. In the early independence, there can be no question that mixed-race Haitians formed the primary pool of secretarial labor. In that period, some secretaries (previously anonymous as a general rule) began to reveal their names on important documents by political leaders; one finds among them the names of famous nineteenth-century Haitian writers, such as Juste Chanlatte.

The role of secretaries, and the apparently perfect mastery of continental French discursive conventions found in Haitian revolutionary political documents, has led some historians to downplay the interest of the black generals' texts. Dayan sees a profound alienation in their "ventriloquy" of French revolutionary discourse: "We should not underestimate the horror of this ventriloquy: the implications of a liberation that cannot be glorified except in the language of the former master."[45] This paradigm of ventriloquy is on the one hand highly expressive of the linguistic and cultural transference necessary to the former slaves' communication with the French, and it also points to the quality of pastiche of French revolutionary texts that is sometimes present in Haitian revolutionary texts. But on the other hand, it overlooks the fascinating dynamics of the former slaves' authored speech acts. These dynamics can be seen in the ease with which Toussaint's "authentic" speech was given enough superficial editing to look "fake" in his memoir. They can also be explored through the diasporan leaders' own stated awareness of the influence of French political rhetoric: their meta-discourse on the politics of colonial representation.

In Dessalines's independence declaration, composed with the assistance of the mixed-race secretary Boisrond-Tonnerre and others but strongly influenced by the overarching ideas and speech poetics of the unschooled general, the narrator condemns "our indulgent credulity, conquered not by the French armies, but by the piteous eloquence of their agents."[46] (This theme presents an interesting transnational parallel to the "discourse of distrust" in the African American tradition as described by Stepto.)[47] In other documents, Dessalines showed a similar preoccupation with the effects of French writings on the colonized. In a post-independence proclamation issued to the inhabitants of neighboring Santo Domingo (the Dominican Republic), which he hoped to govern, Dessalines first warned against "seduction" by the writings of French officers who were attempting to gain a foothold there.[48] Dessalines, like Toussaint, was also keenly aware of the potency of his own political image, although unlike Toussaint, he relished the horror he inspired in proponents of colonialism. "Remember," the narrator exclaims in the independence declaration, "[...] that my name is held in horror by all those who want slavery, and that despots and tyrants pronounce it only when cursing the day I was born."

The interest of Dessalines's political thought, discussed in Chapters 2, 3, and 4, in no way disqualifies his secretary Boisrond-Tonnerre as a black Atlantic author of very significant merit. Before his assassination in 1806, the youthful Boisrond wrote a memoir that serves also as a history of the Haitian Revolution. Like Toussaint's memoir, this text constitutes an urgent reclamation of narrative political power and identity. Boisrond, like Dessalines, was a radical voice. The fact that the voices of general and secretary are forever interwoven in revolutionary correspondence does not lessen their importance.

The case of Boisrond-Tonnerre raises another question of a mismatch between French and Anglophone categorizations of Afro-diasporic authors. Boisrond fit in the category of the *gens de couleur*, a category often used to separate out mixed-race subjects in Haiti, where pigmentocracy was entrenched. Variations on color associated with degrees of African and Euro-American ancestry were not nearly as routinely used to describe non-white writers in Anglophone slave-holding environments, where "one drop" ideologies and epistemologies of race made blackness an all-encompassing category for individuals with African ancestry. In the United States, Haitian-descended writer W. E. B. Du Bois is rarely categorized as a mixed-race writer rather than a black writer, as he likely would have been in the Haitian context. Although the scholarly retention of the practice of differentiating mixed-race and non-mixed-race subjects in the Haitian milieu is attentive to important historical discursive and class factors, it has the effect of obscuring a hemispheric rather than national African diasporan collectivity. Dessalines, in article 14 of the 1805 Haitian constitution, dismissed the convention of verbal classifications of racial admixture by legally designating all Haitian citizens as "blacks" (even whites): "the Haytians shall henceforth be known only by the generic appellation of *blacks*."[49] In this book devoted to African diasporan literary practices in revolutionary-era Haiti, I follow the American practice of generally referring to non-white members of the African diaspora as "black," except in reference to specific historical discourses of their racial status.

The political documents of the black leaders have always been important resources for historians of the Haitian Revolution. Toussaint Louverture and his fellow black generals were anything but subalterns at the height of their military careers, and they have been lavishly studied. And yet their political and autobiographical documents until recently have not been treated as writings per se, as though there were no story to be told specifically as a product of the Haitian leaders' own historical voices. Nesbitt's *Jean-Bertrand Aristide Presents Toussaint Louverture and the Haitian Revolution* (2008), and Desormeaux's forthcoming work on the memoirs of Toussaint Louverture, help to fill the gap surrounding the voluminous political texts of Toussaint Louverture, but there is no anthology of the documents issued by Dessalines. Carolyn Fick, in her account of the role of the masses in the Haitian Revolution, takes the much-needed step of subordinating the story of Haitian revolutionary leaders to that of their compatriots, but passes over the degree to which the leaders' entry into print culture documents the mysteries of their own sudden rise "from below."[50] Historically, the clear reluctance of Haitian historians to draw attention to the lack of schooling in the technology of writing on the part of Haitian revolutionary leaders has been a significant factor in their neglect as political voices, even if, from a contemporary perspective, their inventive adaptations to a new world of letters is more likely to be received as a source of wonderment.

The debate on "subaltern" speech is both helpful and mismatched in the exploration of slaves' engagement with print culture. A class-based Marxian paradigm inspired by Antonio Gramsci's work on the "subaltern classes," it highlights precisely what is occluded from many studies of slave testimonials: the effects of class in slaves' and ex-slaves' lives and access to textual or print culture. In the slave narrative genre, the abolitionist stamp is nowhere more obvious than in the framing of black individuals' experiences in slave-holding societies as fundamentally a question of enslavement or emancipation. Working against slavery, abolitionism tactically and understandably privileged identity based on enslavement as a locus of ethical resistance and paradoxical voice. Whereas in the Haitian tradition, racially encoded class—and the relationship of classes to hegemonic colonial power—arguably created the dominant identity structure within which slave status was a substructure.

Based on the Haitian literary record, it is fair to conjecture that there is no natural or inevitable impulse of persons who have experienced enslavement to narrate their life story around that fact. Among Haitian revolutionary political leaders, only one, Dessalines, referred frequently to colonial enslavement as a determining violence, and those references are a part of a larger pattern of black Atlantic philosophical radicalism on his part, in which he was as likely to borrow "indigenous" (native American or Caribbean Indian) identifications, such as the motif of the "Armée Inca" (see figure 5) as to remain specifically focused on slavery.

This is not to say that the difference between slavery and mastery is not very often, even most often, what is at stake, whether it is referred to in those terms or not, in black Haitian revolutionary-era texts. Toussaint's epistolary struggle with Napoleon is a paradigmatic example of this tension. But narrative subjects in the Haitian revolutionary era did not write to a reader identified with that discursive code. Napoleon, obviously, was not an abolitionist. Enslavement was arguably subordinated in Haitian former slaves' autobiographical consciousness to their manumitted adaptations and identities, in which desires for class mobility frequently permeated subjectivity. (By contrast, white revolutionaries—and their descendants—in France never tired of describing themselves as slaves, from the lyrics of the "Marseillaise" to the idealist novel.[51])

This orientation away from enslavement as an overarching category of traumatic identity problematizes literary uses of slavery interpreted as "social death," a construct first elaborated by Claude Meillassoux but further developed and interrogated in Orlando Patterson's *Slavery and Social Death*. As Patterson notes, "The slave is violently uprooted from his milieu" and he is then "incorporated as the permanent enemy on the inside."[52] In Saint-Domingue, social death took on particularly life-giving characteristics in the revolutionary era, as slaves infused their "enemy on the inside" status into military and political self-representation. If slavery involved social death, a successful slave insurrection, and eventually national independence for the former slave colony, involved reanimation—a reanimation to which the literature of the Haitian Revolution bears witness.

"Social death" is a resonant metaphor for enslavement, but as with the conventions of the slave narrative, it can create an obstacle to conceptualization and representation of the historical dynamism and diversity of slaves' social engagement. It risks making the slave into a mystical category of (non)being, and frames the search for slaves' textual self-representations as paradoxical.

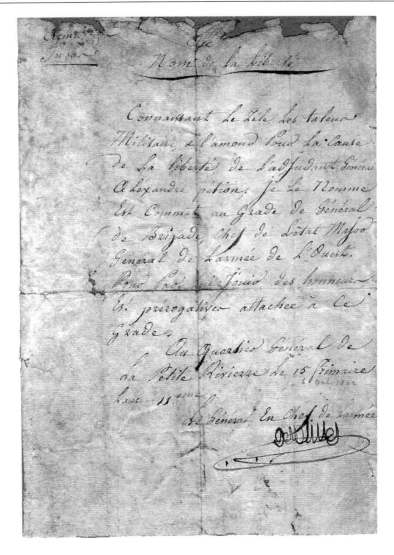

Figure 5. Published with permission of the Bibliothèque haïtienne des pères du Saint-Esprit (BHPSE) at the Collège Saint Martial in Port-au-Prince, Haiti.

Hand-signed document by Dessalines with the notation "Armée Inca" ("Inca Army") in the top left corner, dated 15 frimaire Year 11 (December 6, 1802).

None of this changes the fact that the majority of slaves, in all Western colonial slave cultures, were "impossible witnesses," those whose stories we will never hear, as opposed to the minority, almost always relatively privileged, like Toussaint, who did manage to bear witness. This is the chiasmus behind Gayatri Spivak's negative answer to the question "Can the Subaltern Speak?" In John Beverley's concise summary, "If the subaltern could speak—that is, speak in a way that really *mattered* to us—then it wouldn't be subaltern."[53] When the subaltern or the socially "dead" slave does, in Spivak's words, come "to offer an object of seduction to the representing intellectual,"[54] his or her social death has become a life-giving form of symbolic capital, despite its simultaneous status as stigma. The "socially dead" person is henceforth prepared, even if in the most marginal way, to enter the world of commerce in cultural capital, including the pursuit of such basic forms of "social mobility" as safety or the protection of personal freedom, through textual or print culture.

And yet, in the case of Haitian revolutionary speakers, awareness of the near impossibility of subaltern speech did enter the formal record. Writing in prison, by hand, Toussaint would note, "Le gouvernement français est trop fort, trop puissant, pour que le général Leclerc le compare à moi, qui suis son subalterne" ("The French government is too strong, too powerful, for general Leclerc to plausibly compare it to me, his subaltern" [*Mémoires*, 100]). The notion of "Kidnapped Narratives" that I present here addresses the liminal category of texts by empowered speakers in contexts of communicative suppression, including not only the deposed leader in his dungeon, but Dessalines proclaiming sovereignty in a slave-holding international domain; or texts by unempowered speakers that were only marginally preserved or disseminated (like lyrics from popular culture). Ultimately, *Beyond the Slave Narrative* charts early Haitian literary history in terms of the seductions of representation within political and poetic contexts of mediated authorship—authorship by a cast of "unauthorized" characters including anticolonial revolutionaries, builders of a new black state, and courtesans negotiating social mobility.

Strange Bedfellows

The pairing of courtesans with generals may seem incongruous in a study of African diasporan print culture from the Haitian revolutionary era. But conquest was arguably central to the ambitions, skills, and identity of both groups, in different ways. The testimony of courtesans and generals reflects their strategic response to a paradox that affected both groups. On the one hand, late colonial Saint-Domingue was distinguished by the worst conditions for slaves in Western colonialism; and on the other hand, it was distinguished by the variety and number of opportunities for slaves to move into (relatively) elite positions, from the female slave as *ménagère* or manager of a plantation household, to the male slave as *commandeur* or overseer, to the *gens de couleur* who were often educated in France. At the beginning of the Haitian insurgency, there were almost as many free *mulâtres* and blacks in Haiti as there were whites. Over the course of the Haitian Revolution, the French army in Saint-Domingue was extraordinarily hybrid, with frequent examples of black military leaders commanding units with extensive white staffing. Like Haitian political leaders, the black or mixed-race women who served as mistresses in the late colonial or revolutionary period had unusual access to the world of whites, to which we largely owe our ability to "hear" their speech, as lyrics were collected and in some cases published. An underlying premise of this book is that the social hybridity to which the songs of the courtesans bear witness also informed the discursive unfolding of the Haitian Revolution. Strange bedfellows, by the terms of the draconian racial hierarchy of colonial Saint-Domingue, in the separate domains of both sex and politics yielded a hitherto unnoted variety of representational subjects and discourses. The courtesans' songs are particularly difficult of access, in that gender and class identity, in addition to racial hierarchy and linguistic marginalization, contributed to their almost complete suppression as objects of textual and print culture.

Which brings me to an anecdote from the colonial archives in Aix-en-Provence. Leafing through the heavy, dusty binders of a colonial ethnographer's unpublished research on Saint-Domingue and its 1804 metamorphosis, I came across a Creole poem, scrawled in an unknown hand, on a page bearing traces of a mathematical sum in the margin (see figure 6). This incompletely erased calculation poignantly symbolized the subject matter of the poem, in which an established courtesan scolds a newcomer to the trade for taking a lover for sentimental gratification rather than money:

> It's not enough, Zabette, my dear,
> To take a *Dombo* [lover] in the spirit of friendship.
> Only a stupid girl does it that way
> And she makes us pity her.
> How do you expect to gain high standing
> If you don't make money?
> They will say Zabette is a fool,
> She doesn't know how to make whites pay.

The handwriting on the manuscript was difficult to decipher, and one Creole word in the final stanza, perhaps "digo," which seemed also to appear in a term resembling "digoteriz," was mystifying. I photographed the text,

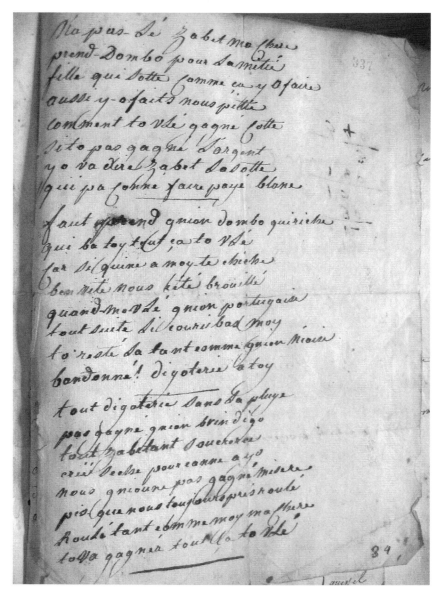

Figure 6. Published with permission of the Archives d'Outre-mer
in Aix-en-Provence, France. F3, vol. 141 *bis*, 337.

Handwritten copy of "Zabette" poem, in a hand not seen elsewhere in the *Notes
Historiques* of Moreau de Saint-Méry, with a partially erased mathematical
calculation in the margin.

scrutinizing the handwriting and language of the text from time to time over the succeeding months. One day, after looking at woodcuts of agricultural practices in Saint-Domingue, it came to me: "digo" was a shortened version of the term "indigo," the plant frequently cultivated on Saint-Domingue for the production of blue dye in indigo workshops or "indigoteries." "Digoteriz" would thus be "indigoterice," a female indigo worker. The recalcitrant young courtesan in the poem, "Zabette," apparently is fresh from a previous life on an indigo plantation, and presumably thus also from slavery; hence her lack of know-how. The narrator chides: "You indigo worker, you!" To persuade Zabette to mediate love with money, the narrator develops a metaphorical parallel between the water necessary to the indigo planter's product and the high prices necessary to the flourishing reputation of the courtesan. The courtesan's economic status is, she concludes, more resilient than that of the colonist ("sabitant" or "habitant"). The courtesan will never have to endure the drought that afflicts the thirsty indigo industry as long as she remains "ready to roll":

> An indigo farm without rain
> Will not make a drop of indigo.
> Colonists without wells
> Cry that it is dry for their sugarcane.
> [But] we are not going to live in [such] misery
> Because we're always ready to roll;
> Roll like me, my dear;
> You will have everything you want.

Beyond the reference to working on an indigo plantation, the race of the narrator and her interlocutor is not specified, but whites are clearly contextualized as "others" to be exploited for their privileges: nothing could be more ridiculous, we are reminded, than a courtesan who "doesn't know how to make whites pay."

When I encountered this manuscript, which I will refer to from here on in as "Zabette," I reflected on those who had handled it before me. This text, and other similar literary artifacts of Saint-Domingue's famously libertine society, was first collected by the white lawyer Moreau de Saint-Méry in his voluminous *Notes historiques* ("Historical Notes") housed in the Archives d'Outre-mer. Moreau was born in Martinique in 1750 and died in Paris in 1819, but he lived and worked in Saint-Domingue for long enough to write a richly detailed and authoritative ethnographic description of the French colony, the *Description topographique, physique, civile, politique et historique de la partie française de l'île de Saint-Domingue*, published in 1797. The *Notes historiques* consist not only of information used in or left over from the *Description*, but of texts collected and never published. There are texts about any and all aspects of colonial life, from pages of newspapers with ads about runaway slaves, to an anonymous memoir about the events of the first nights of the 1791 slave insurrection, to notes on fashions worn in the court of Haitian King Henry Christophe.

The *Notes* were sometimes written or transcribed from other texts by Moreau himself, and sometimes by unidentified secretaries who were individually responsible for long sections of the transcription. Other sections, like that in which the poem cited above is found, are more eclectic, grouping texts written by various hands on various kinds of stationery. This diversity of the textual artifacts points to their origins in the popular culture of the colony. The *Notes* are often undated, but there are some dated texts on colonial issues from as early as the first part of the eighteenth century, collected after the fact by Moreau, while the latest texts I came across were from 1816. The bulk of the materials in the *Notes* document the late colonial period in Saint-Domingue, extending through the Haitian Revolution, and well into the independence period. As such, they represent not only a complement to the colonial material published in the *Description*, but also a fragmentary and overlooked body of work on the historic era in which slaves from the African diaspora for the first time overturned a colonial regime and established an independent nation.

In 1909 the historian Pierre de Vaissière first published parts of three related poems from Moreau's *Notes* in his description of the lives led by the women of mixed race, or *mulâtresses*, of Saint-Domingue. Vaissière briefly hypothesized that such texts were performed by black women or women of color ("color" in the Haitian colonial context denotes mixed race) who were also described in the poems. He constructed this hypothesis by associating the Creole poems with the unpublished entry written by Moreau personally in the *Notes* to describe the figure of the *cocotte*, the young mixed-race or black companion to a white mistress. ("Cocotte" translates in continental French usage in a less specialized sense as a "honey" or "darling," sometimes applied to women of "easy virtue": "tarts" or courtesans.)

Moreau had recounted in his *Notes* that the *cocottes* lived in conditions of extraordinary intimacy with their mistresses, often sharing the same bedroom and eating casual meals together. Yet a simultaneous tendency to antipathy or "éloignement" pervaded their social relations. The most explosive part of Moreau's "Cocotte" explains that element of antipathy, and perhaps also the name "cocotte." The white women often shared with the *cocottes* not only their leisure time, but their men: "The Creoles end up depending on this entourage of women of color—some of whom are also the mistresses of their husbands, their brothers, or their sons—for all their entertainment."

The entertainment provided by the *cocottes* featured, according to Moreau, the songs that they "lisped in their sweet and languid Creole." These songs represented, as in "Zabette," aspects of the same interracial sexual ties that bound white women and women of African descent together in the midst of an often violently enforced socioracial hierarchy.

Although Vaissière forged the connection between Moreau's note on the *cocotte* and the poetic manuscripts in the *Notes*, he did not provide any further commentary on the *cocotte*'s role as poet and entertainer—a sort of troubadour negotiating a lyrical pathway through the ethical minefield of sexual and proprietary relationships. And in fact Vaissière distorted rather than clarified the interest of the Creole poems, by asserting that these "innumerable songs almost all celebrate love in a tender and sentimental mode."[55]

This synopsis is certainly not descriptive of the poem cited above. If anything, "Zabette" constitutes a challenge to sentimental modes in love and poetry through its revelation of transactions and values normally repressed not only in the domain of the lyric but also in colonial ideology. "Zabette" focuses on feminine "professional" or class solidarity, and frames the tension between people of color and whites as a competitive one, in which subordinate women triumph by learning to raise their commodity price on the sexual market. The originality of a late eighteenth-century poem expressing black or mixed-race women's awareness and mastery of the social and financial stakes of their own sexual circulation in colonial society is very striking. There is also a melancholic irony in its account of the construction of independence through a refusal of affective or marital bonds, compounded by the insinuation that to give of oneself is to become a throwaway—Zabette is "abandoned." This alienated humanity is belied in the poem by the proposal of having "everything you want."

The extent to which Vaissière not only overlooked the singularity of these poems but also frankly misunderstood their language and content can be gauged by the poetic stanza he chose to illustrate his assertion concerning the sentimental mode of the poetry in question. Since I will also analyze this poem, the full title of which was given by Moreau as "Réponse de Lisette" ("Lisette Answers Back"), at length in Chapter 8, I will simply present here, with a brief commentary, my literal translation of the verses quoted by Vaissière:

> If you meet Zabelle [when you go to town],
> You will make sweet eyes at her.
> Since you find her so beautiful,
> Well! Go ahead and take her.
> She has the build of a bean-pole,
> And the face of a sparrow.

Far from being a tender and sentimental description of "the encounter with the beloved"[56] as Vaissière claims, this is a poem of rivalry in which the female narrator, Lisette (the heroine of another poem) insults the new object of her lover's attentions, Zabelle. This poem innovates as a song of feminine challenge based not only insult but also on the narrator's assertion of her own superior seductive charms, including her more rounded "bounda" or *derrière*.

This song is an example of a poetic genre that would survive through the contemporary era in Haiti. In 1958 Gilbert Gratiant composed a Creole poem, founded on popular oral traditions, in which a black woman and a "femme-koulie" (a woman of combined African and Indian ancestry) insult one another and sing their own praises.[57]

Prior to its transcription, translation, and analysis here, "Zabette" and a number of other texts like it have languished in the archives for over two hundred years, although a small anthology of similar texts was published by a colonist exiled in the United States in 1804 (see Chapter 7). At the beginning of the twenty-first century, how are we to read this anonymous late eighteenth-century colonial poem or song in Creole in which a non-white female narrator defends the symbolic and real economies of interracial sexual transactions?

Since songs like "Zabette" were traced in their own time to black or mixed-race women who, in at least some cases, served whites in colonial Saint-Domingue, they would seem to represent not only early African diasporan literary expression, but also literary expression by slaves or former slaves. In this case, surely they would also, like Toussaint's memoirs, constitute an example of Sala-Molins's hypothetical category of "written testimony on the reality of slavery coming from a slave" in French colonial culture.

Yet such a categorization, however necessary, is fraught with difficulty. For one thing, as I will discuss in subsequent chapters, in the very rare cases in which early Creole literary texts were attributed by contemporaries to specific individuals, those designated individuals were white. This problematizes the hypothesis of direct testimony in the larger corpus generally attributed to the *cocottes* by Moreau. It in no way disproves this hypothesis, however, as there is strong and sometimes incontrovertible evidence that transcription was confused with authorship, and that some attributions were a form of appropriation of popular material from non-white classes by whites. We have no documentation that these women ever wrote down these songs, but we also lack documentation that they did not. There were women of color in Saint-Domingue who were educated in convents, and there were actresses of color, another sign that there were literate women of color. Even if one insists on categorizing the courtesans' songs as oral literature, their transcription and their association with specific elements of the black population far predates the larger ethnographic movement toward the collecting of oral literature from slave culture. First published in the Haitian revolutionary era, the courtesans' songs are in a unique category, and yet they are a chronological counterpart to the textual record of the black generals.

Like the political writings in Part One, these poems challenge conventional expectations concerning the nature of the "testimony" issuing from slavery. In "Zabette," independence results from successful negotiation of the conditions of interracial libertinage. This unfamiliar formula for slave testimony is startlingly plausible upon further consideration of the libertine economics of slave culture.

Unlike the slave narrative in which the combination of representations of sensationalistic violence and high moral tone created an effect of what Robin Winks has called "pious pornography,"[58] these texts are unrepentant. Whereas the plight of the "tragic mulatta" in the literature of the slave-holding United States shows the alienation and prohibitions associated with social mobility, in this Haitian literature of the late colonial era, we see the not-so-tragic *mulâtresse* as a decision maker, carefully contextualized within the astonishing socioracial complexity of libertine society. These texts also help us to identify, however, the points of traumatic tension for women in libertine culture: choices based on financial rather than emotional considerations, betrayal of other women in a household through men's relationships "on the side," and the unspoken banal tragedies of sexual violence and the sundering of black couples and families.

Independence, in effect, no matter how elusive or costly, is represented in lyrics from Saint-Domingue's courtesan culture as well as in proclamations by revolutionary generals or Haiti's first national leader. The literary history that emerges from these texts is fundamentally representative of Haiti's trajectory from colony to sovereign black nation.

This book is not conceived as an exhaustive survey by any means. I do not study the proclamations of the French commissioners of Saint-Domingue, despite the fact that some were issued in Creole as well as French, making them important parts of Haiti's transcultural Creole heritage. Nor do I explore early religious texts in Creole. Saint-Domingue's thriving theatrical life unfortunately has been preserved in too few cases, although I do briefly invoke one Creole opera that thematizes courtesan culture extensively. As a general rule, in the chapters that follow, I address selected Haitian texts that are, from my perspective, particularly illustrative of the stakes and the framing of black textual culture in slave-holding eras.

From the example of Toussaint Louverture, it is clear that (former) slaves were sometimes nothing less than desperate to leave written testimony of the reality they had experienced. In the process, we find a new "French" corpus of writings from slavery and anticolonial revolution, revealing the French and Creole dimensions of the black Atlantic. The subjective tracings of the process of un-becoming slaves, and the historical categorizations of the first state of black freedom as a paradox of sovereign "brigandry," provide visceral access to a national literary tradition forged in uniquely challenging circumstances; circumstances that haunt the trajectory of Haiti to this day.

Notes

1. What kinds of numbers are involved in this textual corpus? There are several hundred examples of the political texts and correspondence. The corpus of political memoirs from this period in Haiti features examples by Toussaint Louverture, Louis-Félix Boisrond-Tonnerre, and (later) by Isaac Louverture. In the area of Creole poems, there are only a couple dozen such texts, but their representation of different subject positions in the colonial milieu makes each rare example important.

2. Louis Sala-Molins, *Le Code noir, ou, Le calvaire de Canaan* (Paris: Presses Universitaires de France, 1987), 209n.

3. Christopher L. Miller, *The French Atlantic Triangle: Literature and Culture of the Slave Trade* (Durham, NC: Duke University Press, 2008), 33.

4. Catriona Cunningham, "Literarily Tracing One's Roots: A Re-Construction of Antillean History," in *Uncertain Relations: Some Configurations of the 'Third Space' in Francophone Writings of the Americas and Europe*, ed. Rachel Killick (Oxford: Peter Lang, 2005), 130.

5. See the invaluable documentation and collection of electronic texts provided on the "North American Slave Narratives" website at: http://docsouth.unc.edu/neh/index.html

6. Henry Louis Gates, Jr., ed., *The Classic Slave Narratives* (New York: Penguin Books, 1987), ix.

7. Dwight McBride, *Impossible Witnesses: Truth, Abolitionism, and Slave Testimony* (New York: New York University Press, 2001), 3.

8. Francis Smith Foster, ed., *Love and Marriage in Early African America* (Boston, MA: Northeastern University Press, 2008), xv.

9. Robert Reid-Pharr, "The Slave Narrative and Early Black American Literature," in *The Cambridge Companion to the African American Slave Narrative*, ed. Audrey Fisch (Cambridge: Cambridge University Press, 2007), 137–49.

10. Wai Chee Dimock, *Through Other Continents: American Literature Across Deep Time* (Princeton: NJ: Princeton University Press, 2006).

11. Declaration of Independence, Archives nationales, AF III 210.

12. Since the name "Toussaint" was a lifelong, given name, whereas "Louverture" was added later, I follow the dominant convention of referring to this leader by his first name in most cases.

13. "La Conduite que j'ai tenue à Saint-Domingue est connue de tous mes concitoyens; ils sont convaincus de mon amour pour la liberté, parce que la majeure partie d'entre eux, comme moi était esclave [...]" ("My conduct in Saint-Domingue is known

to all my fellow citizens; they are convinced of my love of freedom, because the majority of them like me were slaves"): Toussaint Louverture, Proclamation to the generals and commanders of the army "under my orders," dated March 1, 1802, in the appendix to Toussaint Louverture, *Mémoires du général Toussaint-Louverture*, ed. Joseph Saint-Rémy (Paris: Pagnerre, 1853), 116. I discuss this passage at length in Chapter 1. Although there is no indication of an archival location or publication source, there is considerable reason to believe that it is authentic. First of all, the period after Leclerc's seizure of power in Saint-Domingue in the spring of 1802 is a period of full "black-out" of Toussaint's proclamations and correspondence in the international media, and no doubt in the colony's own news organs. Secondly, the proclamation very precisely follows the rhetorical mold of recreation of remembered, imagined, or documented dialogue that Toussaint had inaugurated in his successful attempt to discredit the French Commissioner Sonthonax. This unusual model of self-defense through dramatic recreation of the other's ostensibly self-incriminating statements is particular to Toussaint's rhetorical politics. Without access to an actual court of law, he creates the fiction of a successful legal dialogue to persuade others of the righteousness of his position. Further evidence for the document's authenticity lies in Toussaint's documentation in the memoirs of Leclerc's attempt to persuade the former slaves that Toussaint meant to effectively re-enslave them, which put the onus on Toussaint to establish a common bond of inherent resistance to a shared past of enslavement: "N'a-t-il pas cherché à soulever les cultivateurs, en leur persuadant que je les traitais comme des esclaves et qu'il venait pour rompre leurs fers?" ("Didn't he try to instigate revolt among the cultivators, by persuading them that I was treating them as slaves and that he was there to break their chains?" [*Mémoires*, 59]).

14. Chris Bongie, *Friends and Enemies: The Scribal Politics of Post/colonial Literature* (Liverpool: Liverpool University Press, 2008), 32.

15. Bongie, *Friends and Enemies*, 32.

16. Bongie, *Friends and Enemies*, 34.

17. See Deborah Jenson on the history of the idea of Haitian bovarysm in "Bovarysm and Exoticism," in *Columbia History of Twentieth Century French Thought*, ed. Lawrence Kritzman (New York: Columbia University Press, 2006), 127–30.

18. Letter from General Moyse to Napoleon Bonaparte with signature by Moyse, dated "Messidor? [sic] l'an huit," Archives nationales, AF IV 1213, 31.

19. Imani Perry, *Prophets of the Hood: Politics and Poetics in Hip Hop* (Durham, NC: Duke University Press, 2004), 17.

20. Joseph François Pamphile de Lacroix, *Mémoires pour servir à l'histoire de la révolution de Saint-Domingue* (Paris: Pillet aîné, 1819), 2:105.

21. Paul Roussier, ed., *Lettres du Général Leclerc, Commandant en chef de l'armée de Saint-Domingue en 1802, publiées avec une introduction par Paul Roussier* (Paris: Société de l'histoire des colonies françaises, 1937), 191.

22. [Colin] Joan Dayan, *Haiti, History, and the Gods* (Berkeley, CA: University of California Press, 1998), 197.

23. See Doris Garraway, *The Libertine Colony: Creolization in the Early French Caribbean* (Durham, NC: Duke University Press, 2005).

24. Laurent Dubois, *A Colony of Citizens: Revolution and Slave Emancipation in the French Caribbean, 1787–1804* (Chapel Hill, NC, and London: University of North Carolina Press, 2004), 4.

25. Dubois, *A Colony of Citizens*, 3.

26. Dayan, *Haiti, History, and the Gods*, 4.

27. Archives nationales, AF IV 1213, 22.

28. Alfred Nemours, *Histoire de la captivité et de la mort de Toussaint Louverture* (Paris: Berger-Lavrault, 1929), 242.

29. Letter from General Leclerc to the General-in-Chief of the Colonial Ministry, dated September 26, 1802, in Roussier, ed., *Lettres du général Leclerc*, 242.

30. Archives nationales, AF IV 1213, 25. All translations from Creole (*Kreyòl*), French, and from Toussaint Louverture's idiosyncratic French in this book are mine unless indicated otherwise.

31. John R. Beard, *Toussaint Louverture: A Biography and Autobiography* (Boston: James Redpath, 1863), 321.

32. Daniel Desormeaux, "The First of the (Black) Memorialists: Toussaint Louverture," *Yale French Studies* 107 (2005), "The Haiti Issue," ed. Deborah Jenson, 131–45.

33. Ménard's letter to the Ministry of War is found in the Archives nationales, AF 1213, and is numbered 458.

34. Toussaint Louverture, handwritten postscriptum to his memoirs, Archives nationales, AF IV 1213, 28.

35. Roussier, ed., *Lettres du général Leclerc*, 336.

36. Robert B. Stepto, *Behind the Veil: A Study of Afro-American Narrative* (Urbana, IL: University of Illinois Press, 1991), xi.

37. Frances Smith Foster, *Witnessing Slavery: The Development of the Ante-Bellum Slave Narratives* (Madison, WI: University of Wisconsin Press, 1979), 3.

38. Laurent Dubois, "An Enslaved Enlightenment: Rethinking the Intellectual History of the French Atlantic," *Social History* 31:1 (February 2006), 1–14.

39. McBride, *Impossible Witnesses*, 6.

40. McBride, *Impossible Witnesses*, 2.

41. Foster, *Witnessing Slavery*, xxx.

42. See Frances Smith Foster's summary of this critical trend in *Witnessing Slavery*, xvii–xviii.

43. The same question of editorial influence and (auto)biographical collaboration preoccupies a number of fields, including Native American Studies; see Susan Forsyth, "Writing Other Lives: Native American (Post)coloniality and Collaborative (Auto)biography," in *Comparing Postcolonial Literatures: Dislocations*, ed. Ashok Berry and Patricia Murray (New York: St. Martin's Press, 2000), 144–58.

44. Nicole N. Aljoe, "Caribbean Slave Narratives: Creole in Form and Genre," *Arthurium: A Caribbean Studies Journal* 2:1 (spring 2004), 6.

45. Dayan, *Haiti, History, and the Gods*, 4.

46. Declaration of Independence, January 1, 1804, Archives nationales, AF III 210.

47. Stepto, *From Behind the Veil*, 198.

48. Jean-Jacques Dessalines, "Proclamation ou Sommation Faite au Général qui commandait à Santo-Domingo, Au Cap, 8 février 1804, Jean-Jacques Dessalines, Gouverneur-Général aux habitants de la partie Espagnole," Archives d'Outre-mer, F3, vol. 141, 550.

49. "Constitution of Hayti," published in the *Aurora General Advertiser*, July 17, 1805.

50. Fick proposes in effect that there were many dimensions of leadership in the Revolution, rooted largely in elite hierarchies among slaves and emancipated slaves on plantations. Her argument will be crucial to my analysis of power dynamics

in courtesans' songs, which reflect parallel hierarchies in the intimate spaces of plantations and cities. See Carolyn Fick, *The Making of Haiti: The Saint-Domingue Revolution from Below* (Knoxville, TN: The University of Tennessee Press, 1990).

51. The use of a discourse of slavery to define revolutionary identity has been widely noted by scholars, including Srinivas Aravamudan, who points that Jean-Paul Marat's *Les Chaînes de l'esclavage* "is remarkable for the ease with which it uses the word *esclavage* [slavery] to discuss metropolitan politics—while being completely oblivious to the colonial referent of the word": *Tropicopolitans: Colonialism and Agency, 1688–1804* (Durham, NC: Duke University Press, 1999), 306. I discuss the obsessive use of slavery as an analogy for the condition of white women in George Sand's *Indiana*: Deborah Jenson, *Trauma and Its Representations: The Social Life of Mimesis in Post-Revolutionary France* (Baltimore, MD: Johns Hopkins University Press, 2001), 183–209.

52. Orlando Patterson, *Slavery and Social Death: A Comparative Study* (Cambridge, MA: Harvard University Press, 1982), 38–9.

53. John Beverley, *Subalternity and Representation: Arguments in Cultural Theory* (Durham, NC: Duke University Press, 1999) 1.

54. Gayatri Spivak, "Can the Subaltern Speak?" in *Marxism and the Interpretation of Culture*, ed. Cary Nelson and Lawrence Grossberg (Urbana and Chicago: University of Illinois Press, 1988), 285.

55. Pierre de Vaissière, *Saint-Domingue (1629–1789): La Société et la vie créoles sous l'ancien régime* (Paris: Perrins et Cie, 1909), 315.

56. Vaissière, *Saint-Domingue*, 315.

57. Gilbert Gratiant, "L'Echappée-coulie," cited in Patrick Chamoiseau and Raphaël Confiant, *Lettres créoles: tracées antillaises et continentales de la littérature, 1655–1975* (Paris: Hatier, 1991), 45–6.

58. Cited in Foster, *Witnessing Slavery*, 20.

PART I
Authorizing the Political Sphere

1

Toussaint Louverture, "Spin Doctor"? Launching the Haitian Revolution in the Media Sphere

Il promettait de jeter le voile de l'oubli sur les événements qui ont eu lieu à Saint-Domingue

(It threatened to drape a veil of amnesia over the events that had transpired in Saint-Domingue)

Toussaint Louverture, letter to Napoleon Bonaparte from on board the *Hero* en route to captivity in France

Media and Philosophical Mediation between the Worlds of Masters and Slaves

Hegel's dialectic of master and slave was deeply informed, according to Susan Buck-Morss in "Hegel and Haiti," by the philosopher's reading of news stories about the upheavals in Saint-Domingue during his time in Jena. To make this case, Buck-Morss examined the unusually extensive media coverage of Saint-Domingue in *Minerva*, a newspaper important to Hegel's world outlook, which published between 1804 and 1805 "a continuing series, totaling more than a hundred pages, including source documents, news summaries, and eyewitness accounts."[1] With the hindsight provided by Buck-Morss's research, it seems inevitable that Hegel's profoundly influential paradigm would have emerged in dialogue with the representation of the slave revolution in Saint-Domingue. Buck-Morss's compelling analysis of the diffusion and reception of information about Haiti in the German media raises fascinating questions about the intellectual reception of the Haitian Revolution in other countries, especially France. Yet the significance of the reception of news of the Revolution cannot be properly understood without considering the more fundamental question of how news was produced within and exported from Saint-Domingue during the Revolution, and what roles the ex-slaves played in disseminating their political demands and interpretations of events. If, as Buck-Morss argues, "the Haitian Revolution was the crucible, the trial by fire for the ideals of the French Enlightenment," and "Every European who was a part of the bourgeois reading public knew it,"[2] then the Haitian Revolution begs to be explored as a media phenomenon, not only for its philosophical influence, but for the political significance of the mediatic *prise de la parole* by former slaves.

Buck-Morss sidestepped the French media's interest in the Haitian Revolution with the observation that "there was censorship in the French press after 1803."[3] Napoleon Bonaparte's increasingly tight control of the French media in the year leading up to the inauguration of the French Empire did indeed limit representation of Saint-Domingue as it approached independence in 1804, but there was widespread mediatic representation of the Haitian Revolution in France prior to 1803. And even after 1803, despite the undeniable sudden straitjacketing of the news in France (including the cessation of direct communication between Haitian revolutionary leaders and the French media), newspapers such as the *Journal des débats* continued to reprint major Haitian stories that ran elsewhere in the world. It was in the New York *Commercial Advertiser* on June 4, 1804, that Dessalines's manifesto of April 28, composed with the assistance of secretary Juste Chanlatte, was first published, with its visceral language of colonial slavery as cannibalism: "Oui, nous avons rendu à ces vrais cannibales guerre pour guerre, crimes pour crimes, outrages pour outrages. Oui, j'ai sauvé mon pays, j'ai vengé l'Amérique" ("We have paid back the real cannibals in full, war for war, crime for crime, outrage for outrage. I have saved my country; indeed, I have avenged America").[4]

The Haitian revolutionary leaders' careful launching of their political strategies, philosophical justification, and self-representation in international media amounted to an epochal eruption of black Atlantic consciousness into the print cultural environment of Euro-American readers. The dissemination of their documents in the media opened an often unsettling philosophical mediation between the worlds of masters and slaves. It is not surprising to find that the French publication of Dessalines's manifesto in the *Journal des débats* on August 7 had unsettled a leading political theorist in France, Benjamin Constant. In his journal, Constant interrupted his reflections on the hypocrisy of morality (he was working on his *opus* on religion) to ponder his own discomfort with the "savage" style of Dessalines: "Proclamation de Dessalines. Il y a quelque chose de sauvage dans ce style nègre, qui saisit d'une particulière terreur nous autres, accoutumés aux formes et à l'hypocrisie de l'état social. Que d'horreurs dans les deux sens!"[5] ("I just read Dessalines's proclamation. There is something savage in this negro style that grips those of us who are accustomed to the forms and hypocrisy of the social world with a particular kind of terror. What horror lies in both extremes!") The hypocrisy that Constant was busy critiquing in the "social world" translates for him into a lack, a frightening absence, in Dessaline's manifesto, productively destabilizing Constant's role as a social critic.

Before Independence: Correspondence

This chapter is devoted to the figure who first pioneered the Afro-diasporic media and literary dimension of the Haitian Revolution: Toussaint Louverture. Where his successor Dessalines is today the popular hero of Haitian political consciousness, additionally associated with the warrior-like *lwa* Ogoun in vodou culture, it was Toussaint who forged a dialogue of tenuous peer relationship with metropolitan and colonial leadership, and out of it an enduring foothold for critique and mobility. Where Dessalines was the bold voice of the blacks' *independence*, Toussaint was the first hero of the black's *correspondence*. Correspondence was a foundation for independence through Toussaint's tortuous acquisition of the status of legitimate interlocutor—and in this status we find the only sense in which the apocryphal notion that Toussaint had claimed to be the "black Napoleon" holds true, which is to say in the sense of a fundamental parity of communicative claims, and audience, and ultimately, of philosophically justified revolutionary leadership.

Toussaint Louverture, whether through personal inclination or purely strategic navigation of discursive identities, drew heavily on Enlightenment and sentimentalist tones and values that contrast dramatically with the starkly exalted radical claims made by Dessalines. As such, Toussaint created a persona deeply sympathetic to paradigms of the personal genius of universal history.[6] Without his communicative diplomacy in literary form, it is not clear that the Haitian Revolution would have "translated" from paradigms of class and race upheaval to a paradigm of black historical/national genesis, as it did in literary commemorations of Toussaint's legacies by writers throughout the nineteenth century, ranging from William Wordsworth ("To Toussaint L'Ouverture," 1802) to Alphonse de Lamartine (*Toussaint Louverture*, 1850), to Wendell Phillips ("Toussaint L'Ouverture, A Lecture," 1861). And yet his communicative diplomacy consistently was marked as much by offense as defense, as in his development of an extraordinary genre of recreated dramatic monologue between himself and his colonial opponents, showing them in the worst possible light.

For all his greater palatability to literary and scholarly communities, Toussaint was in the end as responsible for what Nick Nesbitt called "The

Idea of 1804"[7] as those who were, unlike Toussaint, still free and alive to see and craft the formal independence of Haiti. In this chapter I trace Toussaint's legacies primarily in texts in the *Ancien moniteur* and the *Gazette de France* between 1797 and 1802 (considered in relation to handwritten letters by Toussaint). It was under Toussaint, after all, that Thomas Jefferson would perceive that the blacks had organized "a sovereignty de facto."[8]

Spinning Slave Insurrection

As we see in contemporary political campaigns, media coverage doesn't just happen, nor is it a neutral forum. "Spin" is a discourse that essentially limits the range of possible descriptions through the repetition of carefully chosen parameters in order to prime public consciousness to receive a political message. In contrast to propaganda, used to instill and implement doctrine, any programmatic content "spin" contains is subordinate to "hype," to popularization of a discourse. "Spin" is often a strategy deployed to counter negative popular perception or media campaigns. Since the insurrection in Haiti had initially brought disastrous press coverage in France,[9] it was important for Haitian revolutionary leaders to gain some control of their public representation if they were going to work successfully with the French government.

Toussaint was particularly gifted in this area. According to one 1796 account, he was literally (re)named for his ability to open conciliatory dialogue: the revolutionary activist and chronicler Jean-Philippe Garran wrote, "On prétend que ce nom de *Bréda* étoit celui de l'habitation où il avait était esclave, et qu'il reçut celui de *l'Ouverture* de la facilité qu'il mettoit à toutes les ouvertures de conciliation"[10] ("People say that the name *Bréda* was that of the plantation where Toussaint had been a slave, and that he got the name *the Opening* from his facility in creating conciliatory openings").

This "ouverture" or opening also, of course, stimulated alarm in the French domain; Toussaint was later associated with the "black Spartacus" figure alluded to by Guillaume-Thomas Raynal. As Srinivas Aravamudan notes, "If Toussaint never really read the black Spartacus passage, Haitian historiography would have needed to invent an equivalent incident," because of its ability to "both confirm and undermine established truths," and represent "a world turned upside down."[11] Raynal had theorized precisely such an upending of worlds of slavery when he hypothesized that with the advent of a black Spartacus, "Then the Black Slave Code [*Code noir*] will disappear, and the 'White Slave Code' will indeed be terrible if the victor merely follows the laws of revenge!"[12] Toussaint's alleged identification with the Raynal trope was positively featured in a 1799 story in the *Ancien Moniteur*, written based on information provided by an anonymous "citizen just back from Saint-Domingue." The article recounted that Toussaint's intellectual faculties had been shaped through his contact with freed blacks, and that

> Il ne pouvait concevoir par quelle fatalité l'esclavage se trouvait si près de la liberté, et comment une différence dans l'épiderme avait mis une si énorme distance d'un homme à un autre. Ses idées s'aggrandirent en entendant plusieurs fois citer des passages de Raynal. Il parvient à se procurer son ouvrage. [...] Il avait souvent les yeux sur cette page où Raynal paraît annoncer le libérateur qui devait arracher à ses fers une grande portion de l'espèce humaine.[13]

> (He could not fathom the contingency through which slavery existed side by side with liberty, or how a difference of the epidermis had left such a gulf between one man and another. His ideas developed further when he heard people quoting from Raynal. He managed to acquire a copy of the book. [...] He often returned to the page where Raynal seems to be predicting the liberator who would break the chains of a large portion of the human species.)

The time period of Toussaint's handwritten letters, and of his texts in the *Ancien moniteur* and *Gazette de France,* involved a particular need for damage control, as it is the era of Toussaint's difficulties with agents sent by the Directory and the Consulate. (The handwritten texts in effect show the damage, and the dictated media texts the damage control.) The agents sent by France had to walk the fine line of working with local leaders while also trying to moderate or undermine their political power, because of the obvious potential for this power to blossom into independence from the metropole. Toussaint's communications with the French public give a positive spin to his political and military triumphs over French agents including Léger Félicité Sonthonax (definitively expelled from Saint-Domingue in August 1797), Gabriel Marie Théodore Joseph d'Hédouville (expelled in October 1798), and Philippe-Rose Roume (imprisoned in Saint-Domingue in November 1800). I will argue that Toussaint counter-balanced the subversive aspects of his pursuit of political autonomy in a colony teetering on the edge of postcoloniality by "spinning" the Haitian Revolution for an Enlightenment audience.

Self-representation in the world media by former slaves opens questions of access and knowledge. Experience as a consumer of the media would seem to be a prerequisite for being able to "spin" a revolution, and it would also seem plausible that revolutionary leaders who had been slaves, including Toussaint Louverture, Jean-Jacques Dessalines, and Henry Christophe, unlike such French-educated men of mixed race as Vincent

Ogé and Julien Raimond, had no firsthand acquaintance with the French media. But the latter assumption rests on a presumed impermeability of the boundaries between the worlds of black and white, alphabetized and analphabetized, uninformed and informed that the Haitian Revolution contradicts from its earliest moments. Jean Fouchard has made a case that there were literate slaves in Saint-Domingue, who had gained their skills either through earlier Islamization in Africa or through education by clergy, sympathetic members of white households, or other educated slaves.[14] On a related axis, Catherine Reinhardt has argued that just as the "givers" and "recipients" of freedom in emancipatory conflicts cannot be decisively identified, discourses of freedom in the Haitian revolutionary era are marked by disjunctive and interstitial forms of representation involving a kaleidoscopic array of participants.[15]

Contemporaneous observers also wrestled with the issue of the discursive mechanisms for Haitian revolutionary events. The legislator Charles Tarbé speculated on the causes and mechanisms of the "révolte des nègres" in his report to the National Assembly of February 29, 1792: "Mais à quelle cause attribuer cette insurrection combinée de 50 mille nègres, au même jour, au même moment?"[16] ("How can we explain this insurrection by fifty thousand negroes, on the same day, at the same moment?") It was triggered and structured not just by "ce besoin impérieux d'être libre, qui est inné" ("this imperious and innate need to be free"), he suggests, but also by local "fêtes... célébrées en l'honneur de la liberté" ("festivals... celebrated in honor of liberty"), combined with "le grand nombre d'écrits" ("the abundance of writings") about the French Revolution that had been circulating for two years in the colony.

This assertion of the combined influence of revolutionary festivals and media in Saint-Domingue on revolutionary consciousness among slaves is startling. Certainly in France, as Mona Ozouf and others have shown, revolutionary festivals were choreographed to provide publicly accessible allegories of revolutionary values, bolstering the elite print culture version of the Revolution with a larger public spectacle. Colonial revolutionary festivals of whatever scale would have broadened the colonial audience for print messages beyond the demographics of literacy in Saint-Domingue into the "readable spaces" of public life.[17] Tarbé's contentions deserve more historical exploration than I can provide here. There were revolutionary festivals in Saint-Domingue later in the 1790s, such as the celebration of the anniversary of the French abolition of slavery around a large tree, "l'Arbre de la Liberté."[18] It is also well known that in Saint-Domingue, as in France, colonists adopted symbolic costumes to indicate their political allegiances (not only the *pompons rouges* and *pompons blancs* but also, for members of the "assemblée générale," a scarf of black crepe to serve as "un signe distinctif

[...] qui rappelleroit à tous la douleur dont son coeur étoit pénétré" ("a distinctive sign [...] to remind everyone of the Assembly members' heartfelt pain"), and for the competing "assemblée du Nord," a scarf with red in addition to black, "l'image du sang dont son territoire étoit arosé" ("the image of the blood saturating their territory").[19]

The widespread distribution of French revolutionary propaganda in the colony was noted by numerous observers besides Tarbé. A 1792 report on *L'état actuel de la marine et des colonies* by J. A. Le Brasseur notes that in the months leading up to the August 1791 slave revolt, "On vit encore arriver dans la Colonie la lettre d'un Evêque Constitutionnel [the abbé Grégoire] dont le but était de soulever tous les esclaves, pour conquérir leur liberté, et beaucoup d'autres brochures incendiaires qui n'annonçaient que trop ce que les Habitans avaient si fort à craindre"[20] ("There arrived in the Colony a letter by a Constitutional Bishop [the abbé Grégoire], the goal of which was to incite the slaves to rebel, to conquer their liberty. With it came many other incendiary brochures that announced only too clearly what the *habitants* [colonial property owners] had to fear"). The gesture by Napoleon and Leclerc in 1802 of issuing Creole translations of some of their proclamations, despite the fact that anyone who could read would be a speaker of French even if he or she was a speaker of Creole as well, reflects French awareness that the content of print texts was reaching non-reader audiences. Both Laurent Dubois and Nick Nesbitt have been struck by the resonance of the discovery of pamphlets of the "Declaration of the Rights of Man" in the pocket of an executed Haitian revolutionary insurgent.[21]

Haitian revolutionary discourse arguably emerged in intimate dialogue with revolutionary documents from France. There are intriguing parallels between the symbolic discursive act that accompanied the beginning of the slave insurrection, the "Serment du Bois Caiman" ("Oath of the Cayman Woods"),[22] and the "Serment du Jeu de paume" in France. Grégoire's June 1791 "Lettre aux Citoyens de couleur et négres libres de Saint-Domingue" ("Letter to Citizens of Color and Free Negroes of Saint-Domingue") dramatically (but wrongly, since in fact it was only white deputies who represented the colonies at that time) asserted that deputies of color from the colonies had taken an oath at the Jeu de Paume to continue their work until a revolutionary constitution was finished, but were expelled from the Assembly in May of 1791 because of their race. This expulsion represented "un abandon des principes et une brèche à la religion du serment"[23] ("an abandonment of principles and a breach of the religion of the oath") on the part of the French, Grégoire argued. Grégoire returned to the terminology of sacred oaths repeatedly in the letter, as in his exhortation for the slaves to "jurer avec nous de vivre et de mourir sous nos loix. Un jour, le soleil n'éclairera parmi vous que des hommes libres [...]"[24] ("swear with us to live and die by our laws. One day, the sun will illuminate among you free men only […]").

Colonists were convinced that this text had been highly influential in the slave milieu. The colonist Joseph-Pierre Du Morier wrote, "Il y a bien peu de Nègres qui sachent lire; mais c'est par eux qu'ont été lus, dans des assemblées nocturnes, les écrits qui ont soulevé les ateliers de la plaine du Cap"[25] ("There are very few Negroes who know how to read; but it is by those few that the texts that stirred rebellion in the workshops of the plains of the Cap were read in the nocturnal assemblies"). Dubois concurs that many participants in assemblies leading up to the revolt were effectively delegates, "privileged slaves" such as drivers and *commandeurs* or workshop overseers.[26] These delegates were not only capable of mobilizing large numbers of subordinates, they were at times familiar with the revolutionary debates raging in colonists' social gatherings.[27] Although it has been well established that the ceremony of the Bois Caïman contains elements similar to some found in West African blood pacts,[28] assessment of the reception of French revolutionary media suggests that the "Oath's" influences may have well been more syncretic. One overlooked detail which again suggests the importance of revolutionary models on the slave insurgency is an anonymous memoir by the procurer of the Clément plantation, "Révolution de St. Domingue." This firsthand witness claims that Boukman made a plantation manager from whom he took a cache of weapons on the night of August 22 sign a "déclaration."[29]

Sometimes the dissemination of French revolutionary media among non-white or mixed-race populations of Saint-Domingue was even more direct than letters and articles destined indirectly to a public of slaves: Toussaint himself reportedly subscribed to the French newspapers. In an interview with an anonymous "citizen newly returned from Saint-Domingue" that was published in January 1799 in the *Moniteur*, we learn that "Pour se mettre au cours des événements, il [Toussaint] s'adressa à un Européen philanthrope à qui il remit les fonds nécessaires pour un abonnement aux journaux français"[30] ("In order to keep abreast of current events, he [Toussaint] contacted a European philanthropist to whom he sent the necessary funds for a subscription to the French newspapers"). In addition to his journalistic subscriptions, Toussaint had been coached by a mixed-race political mentor prior to his own definitive engagement with the cause of the slaves: "A cette époque, un homme de couleur, connu par la zèle qu'il a mis a défendre la cause de ses frères, faisait concevoir à Toussaint le projet d'être aussi défenseur des siens" ("At that time a man of color, known for his zeal in defending the cause of his brothers, helped Toussaint likewise to conceptualize the project of being a champion of his own").

Certainly a "Toussaint" figures in the French media very early on, as a signatory of a lucid and compelling address to the National Assembly dated December 6, 1791, only three-and-a-half months after the beginning of the slave revolt. Tarbé's *Rapport* to the National Assembly presents this document, which closed with the notation "Signé Jean François, *général*, Biassou, *maréchal-de-camp*; Desprez, Mauzeau, Toussaint, et Aubert, *commissaires ad hoc*. Au Camp général de la Grande-Rivière, le 6 décembre 1791."[31] Although there was more than one "Toussaint" active in this historical context, there are several reasons to believe that the Toussaint in question was the one who would become the *ouverture* or opening between demographic factions in the revolutionary conflict. I will contextualize the operations of political dialogue in the Camp de la Grande-Rivière before returning to the question of Toussaint's role in this document.

General François Kerverseau was one of the contemporary observers (Garran was another) who claimed that Toussaint had initially served as the *secretary* of Georges Biassou in the revolutionary camp of the Grande-Rivière. In this main insurgent camp, where the imprisoned local colonial official and future chronicler M. Gros was serving as the secretary of Jean-François, Biassou and Jean-François had become the primary leaders after the decapitation of Boukman in mid-November. Like most other colonial historians, Kerverseau was hardly a sympathetic observer, and yet his descriptions allow, as Dubois puts it, insurgent voices to "bleed through" the hegemony of colonial discourse. Kerverseau viewed Toussaint as a "puppet master," pulling the strings of negotiations from behind the "curtain" of his meager role as secretary:

Toussaint, façonné par un long esclavage au manège de la flatterie et de la dissimulation, sut masquer ses sentimens et dérober sa marche, et n'en fut qu'un instrument plus terrible *dans les mains des désorganisateurs*. Ce fut lui qui présida à l'assemblée où il fit proclamer chefs de l'insurrection Jean-François, Biassou et quelques autres, que leur taille, leur force et d'autres avantages corporels semblaient désigner pour le commandement. Pour lui, faible et chétif, et connu de ses camarades par le nom de *Fatras Bâton*, il se trouvait trop honoré de la place de secrétaire de Biassou. C'est de ce poste obscur où il se plaça lui-même, que, caché derrière le rideau, il dirigeait tous les fils de l'intrigue […] Il savait lire et écrire, et c'était le seul.[32]

(Toussaint, influenced by his long enslavement and the veritable education it had provided in the areas of flattery and dissimulation, knew how to mask his feelings and conceal his intentions, and was thus an even more terrible *instrument in the hands of the disorganizers*. He was the one who presided over the assembly at which Jean-François, Biassou, and others were chosen as leaders, because their size, strength, and other physical advantages seemed to suit them to a military command role. As for himself, puny and sickly, known to his comrades as *Skinny Stick*, he said he was only too honored by the position of secretary to Biassou. It was from this obscure post to which he had relegated himself that, hidden behind a curtain, he served as puppet master for the whole plot [...] He knew how to read and write, and he was the only one who did.)

Kerverseau fails to contextualize Toussaint's puppet mastery in relation to the many people of color and white prisoners in the camps who did know how to read and write, such as the hostage secretary Gros. At best, Toussaint may have been the only one *among the blacks* in this particular camp who knew how to read and write. But since the blacks were at this point the main force of the insurgency, his position to translate from the inside may indeed have given Toussaint unusual communicative power. Gros himself would claim that "Sans le nègre Toussaint à Bréda [...] la conférence se serait terminée sans succès"[33] ("Without the negro Toussaint at Bréda [...] the conference would have ended in a stalemate"). If Toussaint as "commissaire ad hoc" was effectively a master of discourse, a spin doctor, in the meetings of the insurgents with the civil commissioners, this would have given him a significant additional layer of training in the language of colonial and revolutionary politics.

Tarbé contextualizes the address as a response to two important points of legislation passed by the National Assembly in September, news of which had only reached the camp of the slaves via the *commissaires civils* who had arrived from France in the final days of November. The insurgent camps were deeply disappointed by the news that, although the king would continue to control the "exterior regime" of colonial policies, notably in the area of trade, "laws concerning the state of unfree persons and the political status of men of color and free blacks"[34] would be passed within the colonies. On the positive side, the National Assembly had passed an amnesty for those involved in "acts of revolution" both in France and in the colonies. The insurgent document responds to these two points in detail.

With regards to the amnesty, the representatives of the slave camp state that although in the previous months they had been "enveloppés" ("caught up") in the "grands malheurs" ("great misfortunes") afflicting the colony, they now wished to "coopérer à l'avenir" ("cooperate in the future"). As concerned the thorny problem of local control of race-based policies, the insurgents proposed that the king's recent acceptance of key revolutionary documents should have jurisdiction in the colonies as well. The document praises the French Revolution's formalized ideals concerning race (the decree had after all proclaimed that "Tout homme, de quelque couleur qu'il soit, jouit en France de tous les droits de citoyen"[35] ("All men in France, of whatever color, hold full rights of citizenship"), and expresses the slaves' anticipation that these ideals would be applied to the colonies in the near future. It notes that the king's acceptance of the Constitution was officially "pour la mère-patrie, qui exige un régime absolument distinct de celui des Colonies"[36] ("for the mother country, which necessitates a regime that is absolutely distinct from that of the Colonies"). Yet in the spirit of the king's "paternal solicitude" if not yet in the letter of the law, the spirit of his "sentiments de clémence et de bonté, qui ne sont pas des lois, mais des affections du coeur" ("feelings of clemency and goodness, which are not laws but heartfelt affection"), the speakers in the address believe that the spirit of the Constitution "doit franchir les mers" ("must cross the sea"). They go on to suggest to the Assembly that "il seroit même intéressant que vous déclariez [...] que votre intention est de vous occuper du sort des esclaves" ("it would even be useful for you to declare [...] that it is your intention to attend to the fate of the slaves") and to make this declaration known promptly to the slaves' "leaders."[37]

The problem with representations of Toussaint as not only a signatory but also an important contributor to this early printed Haitian revolutionary treaty is that his level of comfort with the technology of writing has always been controversial. His status as a hero of the Haitian revolutionary patrimony no doubt has served as an obstacle to assessment of his linguistic capacities (and furthermore to the establishment of a reliable corpus of the texts he generated), since from the standpoint of a certain Haitian Francophilic nationalism, semi-literate writings by Toussaint could be seen as a stain on the honor of his legacy. From other standpoints, the political coming to writing of a former slave is a remarkable phenomenon, the complexities of which should be unveiled. To what degree did Toussaint really have command of spoken and written French?

Documents issued by Toussaint range from those not only transcribed but also signed by secretaries, to those transcribed by secretaries but signed by Toussaint personally, to occasional letters written entirely in his own hand. I know of several examples of the latter kind, along with a handful of letters and letter-like documents that overlap with Toussaint's memoirs, written during his captivity in France in 1802. Given the abundance of Toussaint's dictated communications and his apparent ease in composing the two 1798 and the 1802 documents, it seems likely that other handwritten texts are either scattered in diverse archives, lost or destroyed, or in the hands of private collectors. Even the two handwritten letters I will examine here are not widely known; Colin Dayan frames Toussaint's literacy as hearsay ("it is claimed that Toussaint Louverture knew how to read and write").[38]

The handwritten letters answer the question of Toussaint's particular French abilities in direct self-expression (although not the separate question of his French abilities in the dialogic process of dictating and editing the formulations of secretaries, which I will address later). However, because of their non-public nature, they are not entirely typical of Toussaint's public relations statements. After the address line of the first letter in question, Toussaint writes "nallant et venant" ("while coming and going"), which presumably meant that he was on the road (where perhaps he lacked a secretary), although the sensitive nature of the correspondence itself might also have justified not using a secretary.

This letter is an epistle of invective dated simply from year six of the Revolution, on Toussaint's official stationery, addressed to the "general and agent of the Directory in Saint-Domingue," who, although unnamed, is most likely Hédouville. The unusual quality of the language in the letter is only rarely inspired by Creole structures. The most strikingly "foreign" quality of Toussaint's writing, which is not at a first glance comprehensible to a Francophone reader, in fact derives from nothing more "foreign" than his phonetic orthography, relatively arbitrary punctuation, and unconventional syllabic separations of words. Read aloud, the texts sound close to conventional French. Toussaint had in effect learned enough French, and enough writing, to create his own linguistic system for transcribing the complex political and military discourses of his environment.

The letter, marked by a strong reliance on repeated figures of speech, expresses righteous outrage and personalized conflict. As noted above, Hédouville was one of several agents sent by France with whom Toussaint entered into conflict over issues of political influence and jurisdiction. The Directory, briefly under the power of the former colonist Viennot de Vaublanc, had essentially sent Hédouville to limit Toussaint's power. Not only Hédouville but his subordinates, whom Toussaint mentions in the letter, were openly careless in their dealings with Toussaint despite his preeminence in the colony.

Dubois summarizes the dynamics of Toussaint's resentment: "He [Toussaint] had reason to be angry with the French Government, which had sent a man with no colonial experience, surrounded by a racist entourage, to give him orders."[39] In the letter, Toussaint depicts the Citizen Agent as an enemy of the republic and of men, but this general man, ambitious and concerned for his own interests, yet honorable, also seems to represent Toussaint himself. According to Toussaint, the Citizen Agent is a master of "passing" in the sense of making a thing pass for its opposite, and this pattern of misrepresentation causes Toussaint pain. Here is a transcription and a translation of Figure 7 (in the translation of which I have tried to avoid both the historical trend of editing Toussaint's utterances beyond recognition, and such literalism that the meaning remains obscure):

> Enmi de la chose publique, Enmi de lordre et la tranquilité, de homme
> pour leur in te ré par ticulier, de homme, an biseiux. veut fer pa cé lé mal

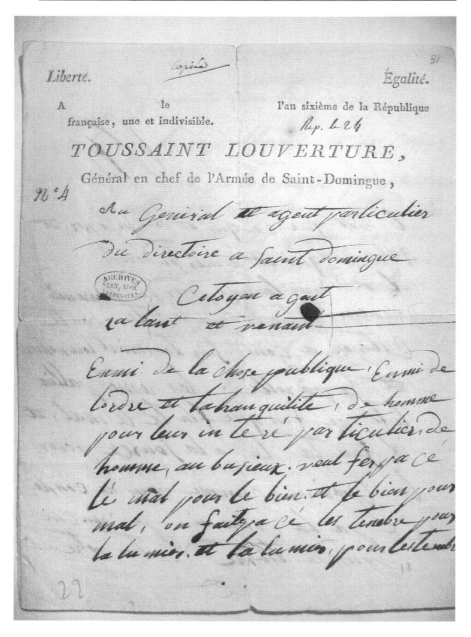

Figure 7. Published with permission of the Archives nationales in Paris, France: AF III 209.

Handwritten letter from Toussaint Louverture to Hédouville.

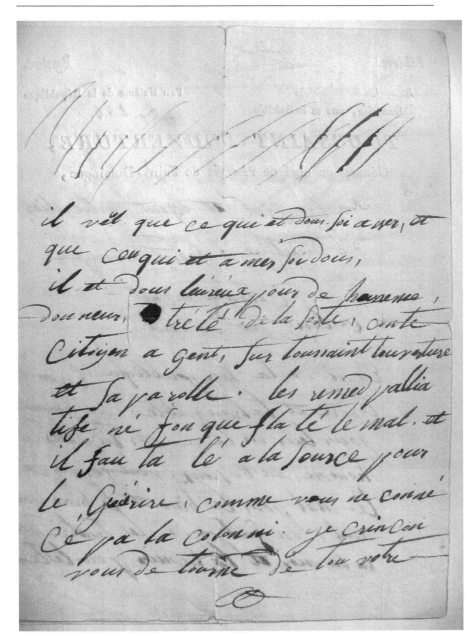

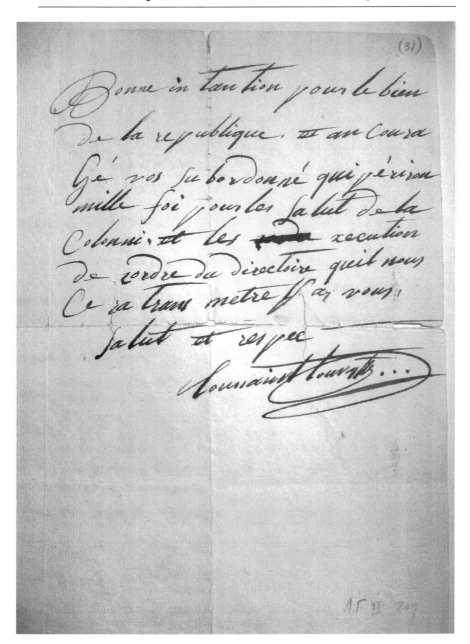

pour le bien, et le bien pour le mal, on faite, pa cé les tenebre pour la lu mier, et la lu mier, pour les tenebre. Il veut que ce qui et dous soi amer, et que ceu qui et a mer soi dous, il et dous leureux pour de homme don neur, trété de la sorte, conte Citoyen a gent, sur Toussaint louverture et sa pa rolle.[40]

(The enemy of the public thing [the republic], enemy of order and tranquility, of men for their particular interest, of ambitious men, wants to make evil pass for good, and good pass for evil, in fact he passes darkness pass for light, and light for darkness; he wants what is sweet to be bitter, and what is bitter to be sweet. It is painful for men of honor to be treated in this way, on the part of the Citizen Agent, on Toussaint louverture and his word.)

Toussaint's metaphor of political pain and his use of a quasi-medical spiritual discourse is characteristic of a broad array of his communications. Through figures of pain and healing, he conveys a vivid psychological and physical political subject, even though here he is not just the pained subject, but also the doctor threatening to excise the pathology at its source:

Les remed pallia tife né fon que fla té le mal. et il fau la lé a la source, pour le guérire, comme vous ne conné ce pa la colonni. je crin con vous de tourne de tou votre Bonne in tan tion pour le bien de la republique, et an coura gé vos subordonné qui périron mille foi pour les salut de la colonni, et les xecution de zordre du directoire quil nou ce ra trans metre par vous,

     Salut et respec,
     Toussaint Louverture

(Palliative remedies only flatter the pathology, and one must get to the source to heal it. As you do not know the colony, I fear that you are being diverted from all your good intentions with regards to the well-being of the republic, and are encouraging your subordinates who will perish a thousand times for the colony and the execution of the orders of the Directory that will be transmitted to us by you,

     Salutations and respect,
     Toussaint Louverture)

The second handwritten letter (see Figure 8) dates from this same period and conflict. It is addressed to Toussaint's fellow military leader Dessalines. This letter has a telegraphic military urgency: it makes no attempt to persuade or dramatize. It is surprising that in a personal letter to a close associate on military matters, Toussaint chose to communicate in his non-standard French—presumably at the risk of being misunderstood— rather than in Creole. Since his instructions were followed and the

Haitian generals prevailed, however, we can assume that Dessalines was in fact familiar with Toussaint's particular discourse and had no trouble understanding it.

In the letter, written in October of 1798, Toussaint addresses Dessalines as "Commandant an chef de la vile de Saint mar et de pandance" ("Commander in chief of the city of Saint Marc and its dependencies"), a reference to their triumph over the British in Saint Marc earlier in 1798. The elimination of the French/British conflict brought tensions between the French and the local army to a head. The letter concerns Toussaint's adoptive nephew, the general Moyse, who was in charge of Fort-Liberté in the vicinity of Le Cap. Hédouville believed that Moyse was rallying the blacks to rebel against the conditions of their agricultural labor, and in October Hédouville removed Moyse from his post at the fort and replaced him with a local black official. Moyse called on Toussaint, who in turn summoned Dessalines and Christophe, and the French were quickly routed. On October 23, only five months after his arrival, Hédouville and his associates were forcibly re-embarked for France. (Interestingly, in the letter Toussaint seems intent on preventing the French from embarking, but this may have been a preliminary strategy to first seize their papers and garner intelligence prior to their expulsion.)

> Je voussa vé parlé pour le for liberté a van theiye, et bien il est au pour voire de la troupe Blanche par le zordre de Hedouville pour li pere la force de france, le general Moyse ce trou vé an de hore san pou voire y rantre de peché vous a pre pa ré douze san homme pour mar ché conte le cap pour le sa rete, avant quil san barque.[41]

> (I had spoken to you concerning the Fort Liberty the day before yesterday. Well, it is in the power of the white troops, on the orders of Hédouville to liberate the French forces. General Moyse found himself outside [the fort] without being able to get in. Hurry up and prepare twelve hundred men to march against Le Cap to stop them, before they embark.)

The second page of the letter refers indirectly to the fact that many black soldiers had been sent home after the defeat of the British, and would now need to be remobilized. It also orders Dessalines to treat the new leadership of the fort in terms that eerily foreshadow Toussaint's later handwritten complaints about his own kidnapping to France in 1802.[42]

> Au ci tau re su ma letre prene vo pré cotion a re te le commandement de la place fete le metre an suite san pouvoire par le avec qui ce soi prendre tou ce papier quel conque et fer me sa me son fer metre cet fami de hore, fete pase les ce lé par le conmiser de pourvoire Executif prandre tou le

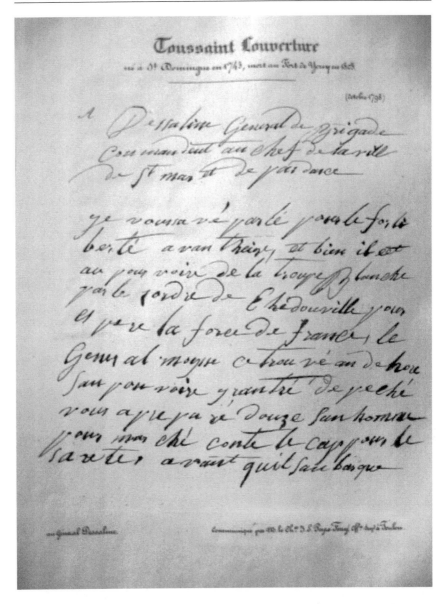

Figure 8. Published with permission of Houghton Library. Autograph File, T. Houghton Library, Harvard College Library.

Handwritten letter from Toussaint Louverture to Dessalines.

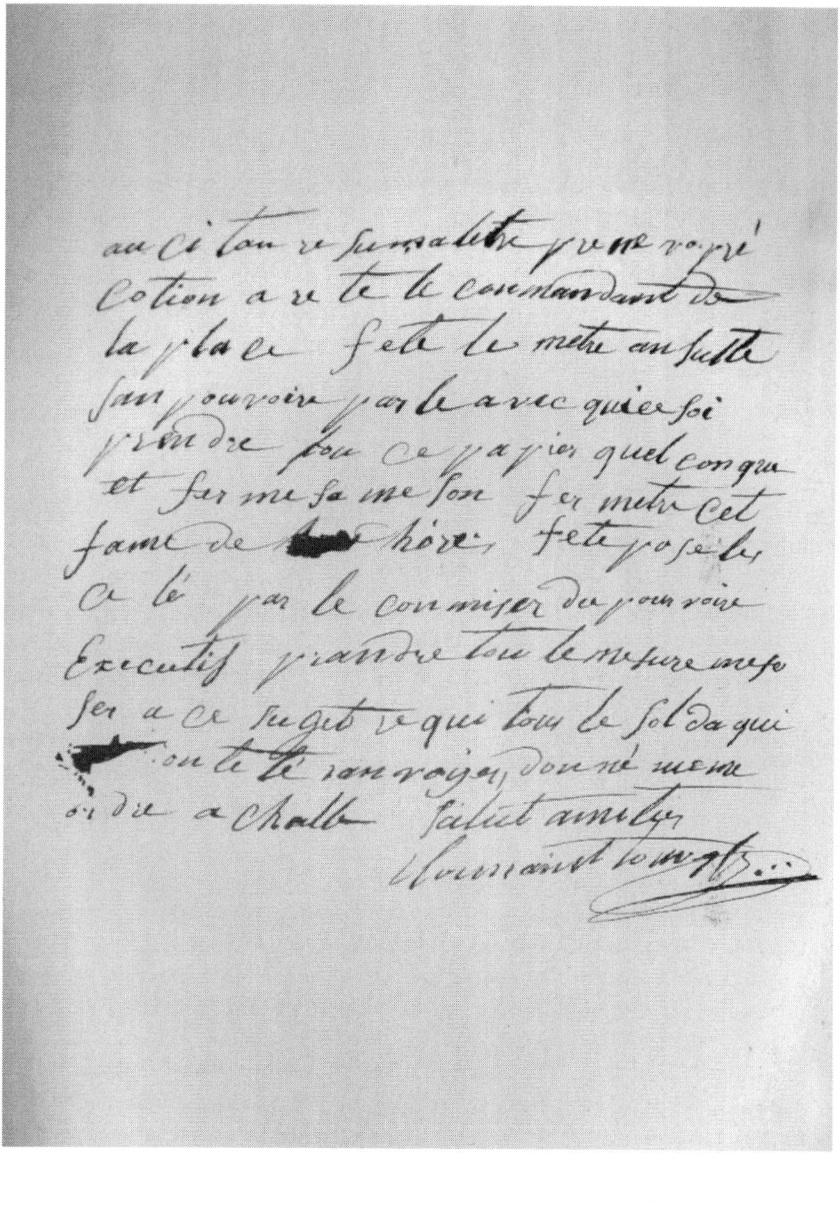

mesure nese ser a ce suget requi tous le solda qui on te te ranvoyer, donné meme ordre a Chalb[43]

> Salut amities
>
> Toussaint Louverture

(Immediately upon receiving my letter take your precautions, arrest the leadership of the place, have him then put without being able to talk to anyone at all, take all his papers of whatever kind, and close his house, have this family put out. Send the sealed documents to the Commissioner of Executive Powers, take all the necessary measures on this point, summon all the soldiers who were sent away, give these same orders to Chalb.

> Salutations, friendship,
>
> Toussaint Louverture)

The closing, "amitiés" ("friendship"), is a unique departure from Toussaint's usual formalities, and gives a glimpse of the register of personal relationships among the black revolutionary leadership.

When Toussaint dictated his letters to secretaries, he apparently gained considerable expressive benefits from the processes of dialogue and revision that were involved, but these processes were very much a product of his communicative prowess. The most satisfying account of the mechanisms of Toussaint's transcribed correspondence is in M. E. Descourtilz's 1809 *Voyages d'un naturaliste*, which describes the revolutionary leader's genius in dictating and editing messages via his secretaries. Descourtilz, who had been taken prisoner by the Haitian army, recounts the scene of writing:

> Je lui vis en peu de mots exposer verbalement le sommaire de ses adresses, retorquer les phrases mal conçues, mal saisies; faire face à plusieurs secrétaires qui alternativement présentaient leur rédaction; en faire retrancher les périodes sans effets; transposer les membres pour les mieux placer ; enfin se rendre digne du génie naturel annoncé par Rainal.[44]

> (I saw him in few words verbally lay out the summary of his addresses, rework the poorly conceived, poorly executed sentences; confront several secretaries presenting their work by turns; redo the ineffective sections; transpose parts to place them to better effect; making himself worthy, all in all, of the natural genius foretold by Raynal.)

Descourtilz's description of Toussaint's redactive talents is especially interesting because it documents a composite writing process based on Toussaint's mastery not only of dictation, but also of the transcription and production of texts by numerous secretaries.

Language Politics: French vs. Creole

Descourtilz also claims that Toussaint was committed to the use of French rather than Creole: "Je fus un jour très mal écouté pour avoir voulu lui parler le patois du pays, car il ne s'en servait que pour haranguer les ateliers ou ses soldats"[45] ("I was very poorly received one day when I tried to speak the patois of the country with him, because he only used it to harangue the workshops or his soldiers"). This contrasts with Dessalines's ideas of the politics of language, a contrast that reflects the individual dynamism of linguistic and rhetorical strategies among Haitian revolutionary leaders. Descourtilz recounts that Dessalines foreswore the use of French after Napoleon's armies had landed in 1802, in a conscious appropriation of the local discourse and a rejection of colonial semiotics:

> Dessalines, commençant à se prononcer ouvertement contre l'armée expéditionnaire, évitoit, détestoit jusqu'à leur idiome; c'est pourquoi il reprit très-sévèrement le fils d'un propriétaire des Gonaïves, qui, créole de Saint-Domingue, s'avisa de lui parler en français: *Tiembé langue à vous*, lui dit-il en le toisant avec dédain, *pourquoi chercher tienn' les autr'?*[46]

> (Dessalines, when he began openly to articulate his opposition to the expeditionary army, avoided and detested their very idiom; this is why he chided very severely the son of a landowner from Gonaives, who, even though he was a Creole from Saint-Domingue, took it into his head to speak French: *You have a language of your own*, he said with a scathing look, *why seek to have others instead?*)

When one considers, however, that Toussaint's French was what Haitians call a *français marron* ("maroon French"), the distinction between the two leader's politics of language is less absolute.

Henry Christophe, who became the first king of Haiti in 1811, appeared to be content to communicate in the colonial languages of French or English. He also, however, is known to have commented on the political valences of speech. At the beginning of the French debarkation in 1802, Christophe's verbal response to Leclerc's emissary was reported in the French press in the following blunt terms: "Vous parlez comme un colon, comme un propriétaire, je n'ai point de confiance en vous"[47] ("You speak like a colonist, an owner, I don't have the slightest confidence in you"). The formal document of his refusal to accommodate Napoleon's army is characterized by a more restrained irony: "J'ai l'honneur de vous faire savoir que je ne pouvais vous livrer les forts et la place confiés à mon commandement [...]"[48] ("I am honored to inform you that I am unable to surrender to you the forts and the territory that have been entrusted to my leadership [...]").

Toussaint's "writing" method on a certain level parallels that of Napoleon, who was also known for his skill in issuing statements through secretaries, yet it also points to a singularity of media representations in the Haitian revolutionary context. In both their production and their reception, Haitian media representations are partly verbal and partly "print," partly individual and partly collective. Written texts in the Haitian revolutionary context, from the address from the Camp de la Grande Rivière to Napoleon's Creole proclamations to Toussaint's letters, bridge gaps of language, literacy, nation, and social status.

Correspondence as Journalism

These obliquely generated letters, proclamations, and addresses *were* the stuff of media reporting in that era. Rather than a journalist's byline, articles on international matters were often preceded by cryptic notations such as "Le gouvernement a reçu officiellement, sur la situation des Colonies, des nouvelles intéressantes" ("The government has officially received interesting news concerning the situation in the colonies"). An individual, like Toussaint writing to the Directory, or a group, such as the Camp de la Grande Rivière writing to the *Assemblée*, would issue statements, and these statements were, at the will of the government and the media, disseminated as news. This chain of media communication is so indeterminate in terms of author, audience, and writing technology that it resembles Freud's description of the unconscious as a "mystic writing pad," except that here the "unconscious" is the diffuse, conflictual space between revolutionary slaves, revolutionary masters, and the secretaries that connected them.

The journalistic element of political correspondence in this time period reveals its unusual communicative power: letters and proclamations published in the press had the power to mold public opinion. They should, as such, be categorized in the company of political writings normally seen as more "public" and "permanent" by the print audiences of modernity, notably political essays or political letters in anthologized form.

Yet the mediation bridging Toussaint's speech acts and the polished French texts that represent him to us of course leaves open the possibility that his secretaries were responsible for some of the content as well as the form of his formal communications. This is precisely the claim made by Jules Michelet's young wife, Athenaïs Mialaret, whose father allegedly had served as Toussaint's secretary during the Revolution. She asserted in her autobiographical preface to Michelet's combined naturalist and biographical meditation *L'Oiseau* that during the Revolution her father had helped to articulate Toussaint's thought. As yet no basis has been found either to prove or disprove her contention, but it indicates the vulnerability of Toussaint's verbal legacy to appropriation. It furthermore suggests that Romantic writers may have seen Toussaint as a Romantic character written by history, speaking lines that they would like to have articulated for him.

> [Mon père] se trouva dans la grande crise du règne de Toussaint Louverture. Cet homme extraordinaire, qui avait été esclave jusqu'à cinquante ans, qui sentait et devinait tout, ne savait point écrire, formuler sa pensée. Il était bien plus propre aux grands actes qu'aux paroles. Il lui fallait une main, une plume, et davantage: un coeur jeune et hardi qui donnât au héros le langage héroïque, les mots de la situation. Toussaint, à l'âge qu'il avait, trouva-t-il seul ce noble appel: *le premier des noirs aux premiers des blancs?* Je voudrais en douter. S'il le trouva, du moins, ce fut mon père qui l'écrivit.[49]

> ([My father] found himself in the great crisis of Toussaint Louverture's reign. This extraordinary man, who had been a slave until the age of fifty, who felt and divined everything, did not know how to write or formulate his thoughts. His was the domain of great acts rather than words. He needed a hand, a pen, and more: a young and bold heart to provide the heroic language for the hero, the words for the situation. At his age, did Toussaint come up with the noble formula *The first of the blacks to the first of the whites* on his own? I would doubt it. Or at least if he did come up with it, it was my father who wrote it.)

Yet even in speech acts divided between speaker and writer, Toussaint had a very distinctive style that counters the suggestion that there were colonial "puppet masters" (to return to Kerverseau's trope) speaking for Toussaint. Even the ambiguities and ironies of his statements and alliances recur sufficiently throughout the years of his generation of texts to be encodable as "authentic." The singularity of his voice calls into question strict associations of authorship with the individual print genesis of texts, since he is arguably very much the author of his dictated writings.

Bridging Decolonization with Sympathy

In the years between the defeat of the Spanish in Santo Domingo in 1795 and the beginning of the Napoleonic military expedition of 1802, Toussaint engaged very actively in representing his cause. He consistently invested his official communications with a simultaneously emotional and philosophical tone. Toussaint did not target colonialism itself as a racist structure, but he navigated around the racism inherent to the metropolitan tolerance of colonialism and slavery by establishing a field of sympathy, in a subjective appeal to psychological and spiritual equality that bolstered his political moves.

In Napoleon's launching of the expedition to reclaim authority in Saint-Domingue, we can read his implicit concerns that Toussaint was creating the constitutional and political infrastructure for a de facto decolonization. Toussaint's attempt to forge a discourse of sympathy with French media audiences was a kind of rhetorical Trojan horse, with a paradoxically decolonizing effect. In the letter Napoleon sent to Toussaint care of his invading general Leclerc, one can discern an ironic allusion to just this potentially subversive use of sincerity; Napoleon in effect challenges Toussaint to respond to the French army arriving on his shores with soulful appreciation: "C'est dans ces circonstances que nous nous plaisons à espérer que vous allez nous prouver, et à la France entière, la sincérité des sentiments que vous avez constamment exprimés dans les différentes lettres que vous nous avez écrites"[50] ("We now look forward to having you prove to us, and to all of France, the sincerity of sentiment that you have so constantly expressed in the different letters you have written to us").

Toussaint's correspondence abounds with examples of the sincere sentiment to which Napoleon sardonically alluded. On 1 Germinal year 4 (March 21, 1796), Toussaint sent a report to the plenipotentiary minister of the French Republic in Philadelphia, Citizen Adet, which was published in the *Moniteur*. Toussaint evokes a horrible plot in Cap Français, in the description of which it becomes clear that French sovereignty, the National Convention, liberty and equality, the white European race, and the freedom of the former slaves are all simultaneously threatened:

> [...] la souveraineté est outragée [...] le coup le plus funeste est porté aux principes de la Convention nationale, à la liberté et à l'égalité; et si le projet des factieux eût eu le plein succès qu'ils en attendaient, s'en était fait de la race blanche européenne dans cette partie de la République; l'extinction entière était combinée par les méchants, et l'esclavage allait succéder à la liberté [...][51]

> ([...] sovereignty was gravely violated [...] the most dire blow was struck against the principles of the National Convention, liberty, and equality; and if the plotters' plan had had the success they fully expected, it would have been all over for the white race in this part of the Republic; the evildoers had set their sights on complete extinction, and slavery was going to follow liberty [...])

Toussaint was eager to reassure the French that they could count on him. An issue of the *Moniteur* from January 1797 notes that the government had received "Une première lettre du général Toussaint Louverture... [qui] annonce que la France peut compter sur l'armée de Saint-Domingue qu'il commande" ("A first letter from general Toussaint Louverture... [which] announces that

France can count on the army of Saint-Domingue under his command"
[111]). In the letter itself, Toussaint praises the French for their benevolent
emancipatory acts and implies that the slaves who have been glorified as
men rather than objects will behave only to the credit of France: "Jamais la
France ne se repentira d'avoir rendu libres des hommes qui se glorifient d'un
titre qui les honore, et qui fait leur bonheur" ("France will never repent of
having freed the men who justifiably revel in a title that honors them and
constitutes all their happiness" [112]). Toussaint clearly knew how to flatter
his audience; freedom in Saint-Domingue is presented as an abolitionist
gift, rather than a self-emancipation wrenched from tyranny. In a second
letter, Toussaint claims that the courage born of the slaves' new liberty will
inevitably overcome the English enemies of France: "Nous ne tarderons pas à
faire sentir aux Anglais ce que peut le courage né de la liberté" ("We will not
delay in making the English feel the brunt of a courage born of liberty"). The
French emancipation of the slaves is presented as an affective investment that
will be rewarded with fidelity, just as the slaves' freedom is such an edifying,
transformational experience that all their actions will be cast in the image of its
glory. As is evident in the above quotes, Toussaint's speech style is emotional,
welding, as he noted in an address to the people of Saint-Domingue,
"les principes et les sentiments"[52] ("principles and feelings").

In January of 1798, the *Moniteur* published a long letter from Toussaint
in which he forcefully rebuts an injurious report by the former colonist
Vaublanc on the trustworthiness of the black army:

> Rendez auprès du Directoire combien est grande l'affliction que m'a causée
> le rapport de Vaublanc, relativement aux noirs; [...] quelle injustice! quelle
> fausseté! [...] quel coup de foudre pour un coeur sensible comme le mien,
> qui aime ses frères et met tout en usage pour les rendre dignes des bienfaits
> que la France leur a accordés par son immuable decret! (134)

> (Convey to the Directory the great affliction that Vaublanc's report
> concerning the blacks has caused me; [...] what injustice! What falsity! [...]
> What a thunderbolt for a sensitive heart like mine, for one who loves his
> brothers and does everything possible to make them worthy of the benefits
> that France has granted them through her immutable decree!)

Toussaint is careful to include all of France as the addressee of his message:
"Déclarez de ma part à la France entière, que si elle se montra protectrice
de l'humanité souffrante et abandonée, elle n'aura jamais lieu de se repentir
de ses bienfaits" ("Declare to all of France on my behalf that if she will
show herself to be the protector of suffering and abandoned humanity, she
will never have reason to repent of her good deeds"). Although he uses
metaphors of fraternity to refer to the blacks, his tone casts the French

nation and its representatives almost as a parent-savior, and the inhabitants of Haiti as children. The slaves were "suffering humanity," now "restored to themselves." Toussaint makes himself the personal guarantor of the blacks' future virtuous behavior: "Dites-leur que je me rends leur caution" ("Tell them that I will be their guarantee"). Toussaint's "spin" on the Haitian Revolution is ideologically oblique. It foreshadows what Françoise Vergès calls the "colonial family romance" created through French Republican colonial rhetoric,[53] and yet Toussaint is not only participating in the construction of this discourse, he is also using it to camouflage his own political autonomy in relation to the agents sent by France.

In effect, whereas Lamartine would be criticized for his 1850 play *Toussaint Louverture* for seeming to put a Lamartinian discourse into the mouths of the former slaves,[54] Toussaint himself spoke like Lamartine *avant la lettre*. (Following the troping of Toussaint as the "Napoléon noir," perhaps we should actually call him the Lamartine noir; or perhaps we should call Lamartine the "Toussaint blanc.") Toussaint arguably figures in the ranks of the French or Francophone pre-Romantics, including Bernardin de Saint-Pierre and Rousseau, who graft subjectivity and *citoyenneté* together. This Enlightenment discourse provided pre-conditioning for pre-Romantic conceptions of the political self.

The Sonthonax Drama: Toussaint as Political Dramaturge

French readers were apparently attracted to this passionate and sensitive voice appealing to their sense of justice, compassion, or fidelity. Toussaint's letters in the press were quoted at length or in their entirety as news stories. Sonthonax's own access to the press after his final, forced return to France provides a telling contrast.

Madison Smartt Bell's *Toussaint Louverture: A Biography* provides the most detailed account to date of the veiled war of words and will between the Haitian general and the French commissioner who had first abolished slavery in Saint-Domingue in 1793, and who at certain points apparently considered the option of independence for the colony. Toussaint's relationship with Sonthonax—at times intimate and at times bitterly tense—was structured around upheavals including Sonthonax's first return to France, where he was tried and vindicated by the National Convention in October of 1795; Sonthonax's return to Saint-Domingue in May of 1796; and Toussaint's final confrontations with Sonthonax in early August of 1797, followed by a disgraced Sonthonax's departure to France on August 24.

Toussaint, perhaps fearing a major backlash in France after his expulsion of Sonthonax, devised an ingenious literary format for the communication of his accusations against the French commissioner, as he explained in the text itself, which was his first document to be widely disseminated in the U.S. media. I am using the English translation through which the piece was presented to U.S. audiences:

> To present this conversation to my fellow citizens with more precision and order, and that nothing may be omitted that was said, I have chosen the form of dialogue. For the questions which were put to me were deeply engraven in my memory; I hope, by pursuing this method, to forget nothing and to render in this manner my government and fellow citizens witnesses of this conference.[55]

Bell notes that "On September 4, 1796, he sent a version of his dialogue with Sonthonax (so incriminating to the latter) as a report to the minister of marine in France."[56] The dialogue was also published as a pamphlet at Roux's press in Saint-Domingue that same fall.[57] Its publication in the U.S. in early October, with a probable turnaround time of at least four weeks, likewise suggests that Toussaint pursued publication in the beginning of September, only two weeks after Sonthonax's departure.

As Bell comments, "This *pièce de theater* may very well be a work of fiction but it served as Toussaint's justification for pressing Sonthonax to leave the colony."[58] As we can see, however, from Toussaint's introduction to the dialogue as published in the *Philadelphia Gazette*, Toussaint's literary plan was even more complex than simply to further engrave the discussion in his memory by transcribing it, or to dramatize the two political leaders' conversations in dialogue form. He meant to make the French government and his fellow citizens into virtual *witnesses* of the interactions he wanted them to judge. No drama without audience: the readers of this text were invited into the theater in the round of history, animated by dangerous and emotionally compelling machinations.

One cannot help but think of Saint-Domingue's unusually robust theatrical culture when one reads this piece. Toussaint seems experienced both in explaining the mechanisms of the drama—he insists that he is reproducing "the same expressions, the same words, and the chain in which the questions and answers were given"—and in infusing it with all the pathos of Judas's transgressions, and the apostles' witnessing, in the gospels. Imagine a curtain rising on famous actors—Toussaint and Sonthonax were famous actors, after all, on the political stage—locked in the unfolding of a tragic conflict:

> The commissioner Sonthonax—Do you repose confidence in me; do you love me?
> General Toussaint—Yes, Commissioner, I do repose confidence in you; I love and respect you.

S. If you love me; if you love yourself and your brethren, there is a very simple mode of securing your well-being.
T. What mode?
S. To declare ourselves independent of France. What do you think of it? That is my project.
T. (Surprised and embarrassed)—This is very bold. But give me some time to think before I answer you.
S. 'Tis good, 'tis good; I am sure that you will find it good. I know your principles; I know how much attached you are to liberty (we were sitting; he said, come a little nearer; I do not hear you well, draw a little nearer.)

Come a little nearer, indeed! And yet this is no maudlin vaudeville. The two leaders discuss whether there is or is not reason to suspect the French of revoking the freedom of the blacks; whether their rights are constitutionally protected; and many other issues that would prove in the remainder of Toussaint's life to be not only historically justified concerns, but the decisive future dramas of his career. But here, Sonthonax threatens to usurp these dramas with his own dominance—specifically, his self-appropriation of the liberty of the blacks. We feel, as soon as he says it, how unforgivable it is, retrospectively, for a white abolitionist to have legally abolished the slavery that the slaves were in the process of historically abolishing:

S. It is I am the founder of your liberty; I am the only supporter of the blacks; it is I have defended them against the colonists; you should rely on me. Had it not been for me, the liberty would not have been proclaimed; I am your true and only friend; you should believe me.

Sonthonax, with these lines, clearly revokes the ground on which Dessalines could later proclaim in the Declaration of Independence, "We dared to be free when we were not free, by ourselves and for ourselves."

Toussaint responds to Sonthonax's warning that "the colonists will overcome you" with an answer that functions almost like a brief poetic monologue, literally heightening the senses of his readers by invoking the senses repeatedly:

T. I would rather see than hear; but these are only suppositions you are framing. In spite of the colonists, the republic has decreed liberty; and then she is not frightened by noise. Don't you remember what I asked you on your arrival, when you asked me, why did I not come to you at the time I began to combat for my liberty. I answered you then, that I had not confidence in you, because I knew you not.

Seeing, hearing, not being frightened by noise, remembering... And in this evocation of heightened sensory vigilance, the threatened Toussaint stakes out his own ground; the French Republic had declared liberty, not Sonthonax; and Toussaint was fighting for his freedom before Sonthonax even arrived. Judas is again obliquely and distantly evoked; not only is Sonthonax proving to be a betrayer, but Toussaint, with "I knew you not," vaguely recalls, but inverts, Peter's denial; what is being denied here is the blacks' immediate relationship to both freedom and violence. It is not a surprise when some moments later, Toussaint has to remind Sonthonax that he is white, after Sonthonax suggests the inevitable necessity of killing white colonists.

The drama was undeniably effective, to the extent that in real life Sonthonax found himself unable to play his own role as agent/actor. The press records are startling in their documentation of the deaf ear the French turned to their returning anti-hero. In February of 1798, the register of the "Conseil des cinq cents" in the "corps législative" notes in the *Moniteur* that when Sonthonax requested the chance to defend himself verbally against Toussaint's accusations, his plea was turned down. Only after two members grudgingly pointed out that "Sonthonax étant représentant du peuple, le conseil ne peut lui refuser de se disculper des imputations graves qui lui ont été faites" (146) ("Sonthonax being a representative of the people, the Council cannot very well refuse him the opportunity to defend himself against the grave claims that have been made") was he allowed to proceed. This triumph over his apparently hostile audience gained him little media attention, however, as the remainder of the article reads, in its entirety: "Sonthonax obtient la parole: il entre dans tous les détails relatifs à sa mission" ("Sonthonax has the floor; he enters into all the details relative to his mission"). End of story.

Final Chapters

In April of 1799, the *Moniteur* printed a letter from Toussaint in which he referred to his difficulties with the agents sent by France with metaphors of stormy horizons and clear dawns: "Enfin, après les orages qui ont obscurci notre horizon politique dans les derniers jours [...] l'aurore a relui pour le peuple de Saint-Domingue" (638) ("At last, after the storms that have darkened our political horizon in recent days [...] light has dawned again for the people of Saint-Domingue"). He says that once he has ensured the happiness of the inhabitants of the colony and the triumph of France, he will be able to die happy, "et mon dernier soupir sera une expression de reconnaissance pour la République, comme mes derniers regards se tourneront vers elle" ("And my last breath will be an expression of gratitude for the Republic, just as my last look will be to her").

Toussaint "spun" the Haitian Revolution with great rhetorical and strategic power, counterbalancing and at times overwhelming the narratives of French leaders stationed in Saint-Domingue, such as Sonthonax. This capacity for self-representation on the part of "suffering humanity" was in itself a revolutionary discovery for the bourgeois European reading public. What remains to be integrated into our cultural understanding is how, in the midst of our cult of the *droits d'auteur*, of originality in print culture, a distinctive and revolutionary voice can make itself heard in a hybrid, collaborative, even collaborationist, medium as "news." Media statements produced by authors framed by their linguistic difference and partial literacy were received by readers who in turn were only partially literate in reading problems of human equality. Toussaint's engagement in trans-Atlantic political dialogue would decisively exceed the limitations placed on non-whites' self-representation under the colonial systems of slavery and racialist social hierarchy, creating a discursive "opening" parallel to the historical "opening" of Haitian independence.

At the same time, it is important to "hear" the moments when the record goes silent, and to grapple with the problem of the history that transpired in that vacuum. After the arrival of the French forces under the leadership of Napoleon's brother-in-law Leclerc in the first week of February 1802,[59] there are few direct representations of Toussaint's words or experiences. We know that on May 6 of 1802, Leclerc wrote to Napoleon that he had received a letter from Toussaint "dans laquelle je voyais un désir bien prononcé de se rendre" ("in which I read a very pronounced desire to surrender").[60] On May 7, he reported to the First Consul that all the rebel leaders had surrendered,[61] and that he was folding the colonial troops into his own forces.

But in the U.S. press, the rare article about Toussaint, relying exclusively on reports from colonial residents, reported that throughout May Toussaint was continuing to fight. A testimonial from Cap Français on May 23 expressed the conviction that "if there should not arrive from France, some reinforcements in a very little time, we shall find ourselves in a great deal of touble, and not unlikely that Toussaint will still be Governor of St. Domingo, which is the fear of every citizen."[62] Whichever account was true, the fact that Toussaint was not represented in Saint-Domingue or international newspapers during this last spring gives the impression of some kind of profound retreat from public life. But of course, the colonial printing apparatus was unlikely, with the avatar of the First Consul's power and wishes on the scene, to continue publishing Toussaint's texts, whether he was continuing to produce them or not.

An unlikely place for a rare exception to this rule of non-representation for Toussaint that spring is the appendix of Joseph Saint-Rémy's version of Toussaint's memoirs. It contains a very lengthy proclamation by Toussaint, divided into a series of articles, with the closing instructions that it should be sent to all the generals and commanders of the army "sous mes ordres"[63] ("under my orders"), who would take the necessary measures to have it distributed in the "armée ennemi" (enemy army), "afin de sauver, s'il est possible, une infinité d'innocents" ("in order to save, if possible, an infinity of innocents" [*Mémoires*, 119]). It is dated March 1, 1802, from Petite-Rivière, with Henry Christophe certifying that it was a true copy. Those instructions alone strongly vouch for the authenticity of the proclamation. Toussaint, still signing with the title "Governor of Saint-Domingue," was racking his brains for possible means of continuing to distribute his propaganda, and had come up with the mechanism of person-to-person infiltration of the "French" army's hopelessly hybrid spaces, structures, and affiliations. Several passages of the proclamation are very precisely attempts to bring the local troops, of whatever color, back under his own command, and to reach out philosophically to the new French forces. The proclamation is structured like the dramatic dialogue with Sonthonax, in an alternation between Toussaint and Leclerc, with Toussaint refuting refutation and critiquing sections of proclamations and letters by General Leclerc. Each numbered article represents a text by Leclerc, followed by Toussaint's riposte, in a proclamation, counter-proclamation format. Leclerc's texts are clearly framed not as fictive or subjectively reconstructed texts, but as official statements.

The document has all the hallmarks of Toussaint's defensive/offensive dialectical political imagination. It reads like a trial, a drama, the last word in an endgame of simultaneously colonial and anticolonial collaboration. The passages Toussaint cites from Leclerc are in many cases statements with which Toussaint would also later engage in his memoirs written at the Fort de Joux, such as the decree through which Toussaint and Christophe were made "hors la loi" (outlaws), and this layering of Toussaint's response to remembered injustices further demonstrates the text's authenticity. On the level of rhetoric, it features some of the familiar odd drawing out of tropes into reversals that are not fully reversals, but performative extensions of emphasis, as in the mirror image I analyze below which functions almost as a metaphor of false consciousness, but not quite.

Somewhat more frank in tone than Toussaint's texts to metropolitan leaders, the proclamation features a profound reading of liberty as something that cannot be reduced to mere sentiment. Toussaint, in this unique text, embraced his former enslavement as a bond of common identity with his fellow countrymen, even those who were "free people of color":

> La conduite que j'ai tenue à Saint-Domingue est connue de tous mes concitoyens; ils sont convaincus de mon amour pour la liberté, parce que la majeure partie d'entre eux, comme moi était esclave, et que le petit

nombre de ceux qu'on appelait libres était encore, comme le reste, sous le joug accablant du despotisme le plus absolu. (*Mémoires*, 116)

(My conduct is well known to all my countrymen; they are convinced of my love of freedom, because the majority of them like me were slaves, and the small number of those who were called "free men" still labored, like everyone else, under the crushing yoke of the most absolute despotism.)

Freedom is also at the core of what Toussaint viewed as an unforgivable misstep by Leclerc. Leclerc had announced, "J'ai promis la liberté à tous les habitants de la colonie, je saurai leur en faire jouir" ("I have promised freedom to all the inhabitants of the colony, and I will be able to give them its enjoyment" [116]). This comment from a real historical proclamation, published in the *Moniteur* on 2 Germinal year 10 (March 23, 1802), incensed Toussaint in the same way that Sonthonax's claims to have singlehandedly emancipated the blacks had incensed him.

This proclamation from Toussaint's hunted last spring as a leader may not be a slave narrative, but it gives readers piercing insights into what freedom meant for him, and for the revolutionary community he led through both words and action. Freedom for Toussaint, despite a lifetime of negotiations, was non-negotiable:

On ne peut pas donner à une personne ce dont elle a déjà la jouissance; le général Leclerc ne peut donc donner aux habitants de la colonie une liberté qu'ils avaient déjà reçue de Dieu, qui leur avait été ravie par l'injustice de leurs tyrans, et qu'ils ont dû reconquérir et conserver au prix de leur sang; [...] la futilité de cette promesse démasque aux yeux les intentions perfides du général Leclerc, aussi clairement que s'il se présentait devant un miroir où il verrait et ferait voir sa figure, puisqu'il est dans l'impossibilité de tenir la promesse qu'il a faite. (117)

(You cannot give a person that with which he or she is already endowed; General Leclerc thus cannot give the colony's inhabitants a freedom they had already received from God, and which had been ravished from them through the injustice of their tyrants, compelling them to win it back and preserve at the price of their own blood; [...] the futility of this promise unmasks General Leclerc's perfidious intentions before our eyes, as clearly as if he were standing in front of a mirror in which he saw his reflection and reflected it to others too, because he cannot possibly keep the promise he has made.)

Notes

1. Susan Buck-Morss, "Hegel and Haiti," *Critical Inquiry* 26:4 (summer 2000), 838.
2. Buck-Morss, "Hegel and Haiti," 837.
3. Buck-Morss, "Hegel and Haiti," 839.
4. *Journal des débats et loix [sic] du pouvoir legislative et des actes du gouvernement*, August 7, 1804. All translations are mine unless otherwise noted.
5. Benjamin Constant, *Journaux intimes*, ed. A. Roulin and C. Roth (Paris: Gallimard, 1952), 123.
6. On the paradigm of universal history, see Susan Buck-Morss, *Hegel, Haiti, and Universal History* (Pittsburgh, PA: University of Pittsburgh Press, 2009), and F. Nick Nesbitt, *Universal Emancipation: The Haitian Revolution and the Radical Enlightenment* (Charlottesville, VA: University of Virginia Press, 2008).
7. See F. Nick Nesbitt, "The Idea of 1804," *Yale French Studies* 107 (2005), "The Haiti Issue," ed. Deborah Jenson, 6–39.
8. "The most promising portion of them is the island of St. Domingo, where the blacks are established into a sovereignty de facto, and have organized themselves under regular laws and government." Thomas Jefferson, letter to James Monroe, November 24, 1801. Cited in Archibald Alexander, *A History of Colonization on the Western Coast of Africa* (Philadelphia: William S. Martien, 1846), 67.
9. The impact of this devastating coverage is represented by author Claire de Duras in her black heroine Ourika's dashed hopes for a renewed social identity in the wake of popular perceptions of atrocities by the blacks in Saint-Domingue. See Claire de Duras, *Ourika* (New York: MLA, 1994), 20.
10. J.-Ph. Garran, *Rapport sur les troubles de Saint-Domingue*, 2 vols. (Paris: Imprimerie nationale, 1797–99), 2:313.
11. Srinivas Aravamudan, *Tropicopolitans: Colonialism and Agency, 1688–1804* (Durham, NC: Duke University Press, 1999), 303.
12. Cited in Aravamudan, *Tropicopolitans*, 302.
13. Article on Toussaint Louverture, anonymous, 1799, A. Ray, *Réimpression de l'ancien Moniteur: seule histoire authentique et inaltérée*, vol. 29 (Paris: H. Plon, 1863), 585 *bis*.
14. See Jean Fouchard, *Les Marrons du syllabaire: Quelques aspects du problème de l'instruction et de l'éducation des esclaves et affranchis de Saint-Domingue* (Port-au-Prince: Henri Deschamps, 1988).
15. Catherine Reinhardt, "French Caribbean Slaves Forge Their Own Ideal of Liberty in 1789," in *Slavery in the Caribbean Francophone World*, ed. Doris Kadish (Athens, GA: University of Georgia Press, 2000).
16. Charles Tarbé, "Rapport sur les troubles de Saint-Domingue, fait à l'Assemblée nationale, par Charles Tarbé, depute de la Seine-Inférieur, au nom du comité colonial, le 29 février 1792" (Paris: Imprimerie nationale, 1792), 25.
17. See Roger Chartier, *Lectures et lecteurs dans la France d'Ancien régime* (Paris: Seuil, 1987).
18. Agent Roume, "Discours," 16 Pluviôse year 7 (Port-Républicain: Gauchet, 1798), 1.
19. Garran, *Rapport sur les troubles de Saint-Domingue*, 2:228–9.

20. J. A. Le Brasseur, *De l'etat actuel de la marine et des colonies* (Paris: L. P. Couret, 1792), 31.

21. See Laurent Dubois, *Avengers of the New World: The Story of the Haitian Revolution* (Cambridge, MA: Harvard University Press, 2004), 105, and Nesbitt, "The Idea of 1804," 29.

22. See David Geggus for an assessment of current historical research on the Oath, *Haitian Revolutionary Studies* (Bloomington, IN: Indiana University Press, 2002), 81–92.

23. The text I consulted for Grégoire's letter is a colonial denunciation of it, providing a colonist's vituperative gloss and the original text in side-by-side columns. Anonymous, *Dénonciation de M. l'Abbé Grégoire et de sa LETTRE du 8 Juin 1791, adressé aux Citoyens de couleur et nègres libres de Saint-Domingue, et des autres Isles Françaises de l'Amérique, etc.* (Paris: Au Bureau de la feuille du jour, 1791), 18–19.

24. Anonymous, *Dénonciation de M. l'Abbé Grégoire*, 24.

25. Joseph-Pierre Du Morier, *Sur les Troubles des colonies* (Paris: Didot Jeune, 1791), 37.

26. Dubois, *Avengers of the New World*, 97.

27. See H. Pauleus-Sannon's classic *Histoire de Toussaint Louverture*, 3 vols. (Port-au-Prince: A.A. Héraux, 1920–1933).

28. See Robin Law, "La Cérémonie du Bois Caïman et le 'pacte de sang' dahoméen," in *L'Insurrection des esclaves de Saint-Domingue (22–23 août 1791)*, ed. Laënnec Hurbon (Paris: Karthala, 2000), 131–47.

29. Anonymous manuscript, "Révolution de St. Domingue, Contenant tout ce qui s'est passé dans la colonie française depuis le commencement de la revolution jusques au depart de l'auteur pour France," October 1792, contained in the *Notes historiques de Moreau de Saint-Méry*, Archives d'Outre-mer, F3, vol. 141, 203: "Le 22 aout à onze heures du soir, le nègre Bougman cocher de l'habitation Clément dont j'étais procureur, à la tête de quelques nègres venus du Limbé et d'autres du quartier de l'Acul va sur l'habitation… s'empare des armes du citoyen Tutheil, charpentier et gérant de cette habitation et après s'être contenté de lui faire signer une Déclaration à sa guise, il l'emmène avec lui." There is unfortunately no further mention of this mysterious declaration brought by Boukman on the opening night of the slave insurgency.

30. *Réimpression de l'Ancien moniteur, seule histoire authentique et inaltérée de la révolution française depuis la réunion des Etats-généraux jusqu'au Consulat* (Paris: Plon, 1854), Nivose year 7 [January 1799], 585 *bis*.

31. Tarbé, "Rapport sur les troubles de Saint-Domingue," 11.

32. Kerverseau's statement is cited in Beaubrun Ardouin, *Etudes sur l'histoire d'Haïti* (Port-au-Prince: François Dalencour, 1958), 1:51.

33. Cited in Pierre Pluchon, *Toussaint Louverture* (Paris: Fayard, 1999), 73.

34. Dubois, *Avengers of the New World*, 125.

35. *Loi portant que tout homme est libre en France, et que, quelleque soit sa couleur, il y jouit de tous les droits de Citoyen, s'il a les qualités préscrites par la Constitution, donnée à Paris, le 16 Octobre 1791*, based on the "Décret de l'Assemblée nationale, du 28 septembre 1791" (Paris: De l'imprimerie royale, 1791), 2.

36. Tarbé, "Rapport sur les troubles de Saint-Domingue," 7.

37. Tarbé, "Rapport sur les troubles de Saint-Domingue," 10.

38. [Colin] Joan Dayan, *Haiti, History, and the Gods* (Berkeley, CA: University of California Press, 1995), 4.

39. Dubois, *Avengers of the New World*, 219.

40. Toussaint Louverture, letter to the "general and agent of the Directory in Saint-Domingue," year 6, Archives nationales, AF III 209, 31.

41. Pierre Dominique Louverture to General Dessaline [*sic*] [in facsimile], 1 Oct. [*sic*: should read "Oct."] 1798. Autograph File, T. Houghton Library, Harvard College Library.

42. See the discussion of Toussaint's handwritten 1802 texts in the introduction.

43. "Chalb" should be read as "Charles B," the Haitian general Charles Belair, often referred to as a nephew of Toussaint.

44. M.-E. Descourtilz, *Voyages d'un naturaliste à Saint-Domingue*, 3 vols. (Paris: Dufart, 1809), 3:245–6.

45. Descourtilz, *Voyages d'un naturaliste à Saint-Domingue*, 3:251.

46. Descourtilz, *Voyages d'un naturaliste à Saint-Domingue*, 3:281.

47. *Gazette de France* n.1587, vendredi 3 floréal, an X de la République, 854.

48. Cited in Ardouin, *Etudes sur l'histoire d'Haïti*, 5:7.

49. Jules Michelet, *L'Oiseau* (Paris: Hachette, 1857), xx.

50. Letter from the First Consul to Toussaint Louverture, 27 Brumaire year 10, Appendix IV, Paul Roussier, ed., *Lettres du Général Leclerc, Commandant en chef de l'armée de Saint-Domingue en 1802, publiées avec une introduction par Paul Roussier* (Paris: Société de l'histoire des colonies françaises et Librairie Ernest Leroux, 1937), 307–9.

51. *Réimpression de l'Ancien moniteur: Directoire exécutif*, vol. 28 (Paris: Plon, 1863), 365–6.

52. Toussaint Louverture, letter to the inhabitants of Saint-Domingue concerning the execution of Moyse, 5 Frimaire year 10, reprinted in the *Nouvelles officielles du Journal du soir, Courrier de la République française*, feuille de 30 pluviose an X, n. 717, no pagination.

53. See Françoise Vergès, *Monsters and Revolutionaries, Colonial Family Romance and Métissage* (Durham, NC: Duke University Press, 1999).

54. Léon-François Hoffmann cites the anonymous critique of the play in the *Bibliothèque universelle de Genève*: "L'auteur paraît ne pas s'être le moins du monde inquiété de la couleur de ses personnages, il l'a complètement abandonnée au teinturier du théâtre. Ses personnages, en effet, ont beau avoir la peau noire, ils parlent tous le langage de *Jocelyn* et des *Méditations*." Hoffmann, "Introduction," *Toussaint Louverture* (Exeter: University of Exeter Press, 1998), xix.

55. *Philadelphia Gazette*, October 7, 1797

56. Madison Smartt Bell, *Toussaint Louverture: A Biography* (New York: Random House, 2008), 153.

57. *Extrait du rapport adressé au Directoire exécutif par le citoyen Toussaint Loverture, général en chef des forces de la République Française à Saint-Domingue. Première conférence entre le commissaire Sonthonax et le général Toussaint Louverture, relative au dessein du premier de déclarer la colonie de Saint-Domingue indépendante de la France, et d'égorger tous les Européens* (Cap français: Imprimerie P. Roux, 1797).

58. Bell, *Toussaint Louverture*, 151.

59. The French forces arrived first on the coast of the formerly Spanish part of the island, which was nominally French at that time. Although in his letters to Napoleon Leclerc seems to document the arrival of the French in Cap Français in early February of 1802, he sent a letter to the French Minister of the Marine

attesting that the French forces arrived at Cap Français on January 29. This account, published in Paris on March 13, was translated for the *Evening Post* on May 11, 1802.

60. Roussier, ed., *Lettres du Général Leclerc*, 141.

61. Roussier, ed., *Lettres du Général Leclerc*, 145.

62. *American Citizen*, June 18, 1802.

63. Toussaint Louverture, *Mémoires du général Toussaint-Louverture*, ed. Joseph Saint-Rémy (Paris: Pagnerre, 1853), 116.

2

Before Malcolm X, Dessalines:
Postcoloniality in a Colonial World

Nous avons osé être libres sans l'être, par nous-mêmes et pour nous-mêmes

(We dared to be free when we were not free, by ourselves and for ourselves)

Jean-Jacques Dessalines, Haitian Declaration
of Independence, January, 1804

… que les puissances n'accordent jamais aux peuples qui, comme nous, sont les artisans de leur propre liberté

(… which powers never concede to people like us who are the authors of their own liberty)

Jean-Jacques Dessalines, acceptance of his
nomination as emperor, August, 1804

Struggles against colonialism and slavery are not inevitably, but rather circumstantially, aligned, even within the same hemispheric region and historical period. Haiti's literature, from the 1804 independence onward, was postcolonial: it remained infused with anticolonial fervor and was sometimes oriented toward future regional decolonizations. In the U.S., the Afro-diasporic population focused its political imagination on emancipation from slavery. The slave narrative, despite its dominant themes of human subjugation in a racialized context, is difficult to situate with regard to colonial or postcolonial dynamics. Although William Ashcroft, Gareth Griffiths, and Helen Tiffin proposed in 1989 that the independence of the United States from Britain constituted an example of eighteenth-century postcolonialism,[1] independence from Britain certainly did not entail a historical rupture with racial hierarchies and contingent practices of enslavement as they had developed in this New World space. Through the mechanisms of U.S. journalistic media, however, Jean-Jacques Dessalines's independence proclamations, which were in many ways manifestoes of postcolonial freedom, circulated in the same environments in which the slave narrative was being produced.

Haitian independence documents are a literary form *par excellence* of early nineteenth-century postcolonial thought, whereas the slave narrative stands as a bulwark of evidence against enslavement practices. One could argue that a fundamentally individual or humanist ethos of emancipation marks the narrative subjectivity of the slave narrative, while a specifically political, military, and economic engagement with revolutionary statehood and its domestic and international infrastructure and identity marks Haitian independence documents. Yet any *systematic* attempt to distinguish them based on content would be artificial. Even if the slave narrative illuminates the subjugation of the individual, where the Haitian independence documents highlight the group's need for collective autonomy, Haitian collective identi-fications are often symbolized in individual terms, and individual discourses of independence overlap with political constructs. Furthermore, the slave narrative is, of course, an international or black Atlantic genre, resounding from locations grounded in different political realities. The words of Robert Wedderburn in England in 1820 reflect a refusal of moderation and a valori-zation of independence that echoes that of Dessalines, but the independence is personal in Wedderburn's case: "I have committed my defense to paper; and I have endeavoured to be as moderate as the nature of the case and my own independence will permit [...]"[2] Dessalines, in turn, aimed in the Haitian Declaration of Independence to "consolider [votre liberté] par des lois qui assurent votre libre individualité"[3] ("consolidate [your freedom] through laws that guarantee your free individuality").

In the New World, colonialism and slavery *usually* went hand in hand, even if in the specific cases of Haiti and the U.S. they were separate. Reading Dessalines's postcolonial thought in the era of the slave narrative involves sobering reminders that the greater world of economic and political power that was historically (and contingently) aligned with Euro-American Caucasian ethnicity would almost irresistibly force back together the separate fields of black postcolonial and black slave identities. In effect, in this chapter and the next two, as I present Dessalines's documents as an overlooked dialogic foundation in a longer chain of radical African diasporan thinkers, I am compelled from the start to acknowledge that we have not traditionally aligned Dessalines with Frederick Douglass, Aimé Césaire, Frantz Fanon, Malcolm X, and many others only partly because of failures to account for his authorial role and creativity. The other side of this story is that a world of colonial interests succeeded, ultimately, in reducing his identity to that of a renegade slave, that paradox of a sovereign "brigand," and a litmus test for the ongoing viability of dominion over slaves in the New World.

Postcolonial History in Theory and Postcolonial Theory in History

How legitimately can we refer to Dessalines as an early nineteenth-century postcolonial voice, given the long-term associations of the postcolonial with historical events, critiques, and identity politics of the mid- to late twentieth century? Since the eclipse of a certain form of late twentieth-century postcolonial theory in which, as Frederick Cooper summarizes, there was at times a "double occlusion" resulting from "turning the centuries of European colonization overseas into a critique of the Enlightenment, democracy, or modernity,"[4] there have been numerous reconsiderations of the relationship of postcolonialism to history. For Cooper, such reconsiderations have the potential to reveal both "the specificity of colonial situations" and "the importance of struggles in colonies, in metropoles, and between the two."[5] For Ella Shohat, who queried "When, exactly, does the 'postcolonial' begin?"[6] in 1992, exploration of these temporal parameters highlights not only the forgotten continuity of postcolonial and Third World studies, it also prompts further productive questions of the politics of any single historical framework: "Which region is privileged in such a beginning? What are the relationships between these diverse beginnings?"[7]

The insufficiently theorized beginnings of the postcolonial may conceal insights, Shohat suggests, into why the notion of the postcolonial "does not lend itself to geopolitical critique"[8] in the context of contemporary conflicts such as the Gulf War and the Iraq War. In this chapter, I will be engaging not so much with how to theorize postcolonial history, as with how to situate postcolonial theory in history—how to expand the domain of postcolonial theory and its twentieth-century black Atlantic canon to include earlier "theorists" from an earlier "beginning" of the postcolonial. Dessalines, I will propose, left textual traces of anticolonial philosophy not just in early nineteenth-century post-revolutionary practice, *but in theory.* These "theoretical" antecedents help to articulate the politics of the postcolonial, and they also expand the conventional chronological and linguistic boundaries of black Atlantic radicalism.

Paul Gilroy's paradigm of the black Atlantic was inspired by the failure of nationalist paradigms when "confronted by the intercultural and transnational formation" of black participation in "abstract modernity."[9] Curiously, however, the construct of the black Atlantic remains documented predominantly with Anglophone materials, particularly with regard to pre-twentieth-century modernity. Since languages tend to function as extensions of national(ist) paradigms, this creates an implicit national and imperial frame for an explicitly transnational concept. "England and Englishness" are deconstructed by black history in Gilroy's research, but *English*—in the Caribbean, the United States, Africa, and Britain—remains uncontested as the language in which New World/Western black history is represented. From Crispus Attucks to Olaudah Equiano, Denmark Vesey to William Cuffay, Wedderburn to Frederick Douglass, Marcus Garvey to Claude McKay, and Teddy Riley to Funki Dreds, the black Atlantic is Anglophone, even when the English in question is a second language. The travels or exile of Martin Delaney, W. E. B. DuBois, Nella Larsen, Richard Wright, and Quincy Jones in Liberia, Haiti, Denmark, Paris, and Sweden also reach us in English form. Gilroy's work frequently refers to black Atlantic writings *about* the Haitian Revolution, but not *from* the Haitian Revolution. This monolingual casting of the transnational research net excludes most direct representations of the Haitian Revolution, which was by any measure a major black Atlantic contribution to abstract modernity.

Without taking into account Haitian revolutionary "theorizations" of an early nineteenth-century "beginning" of the postcolonial, it is difficult to fully consider the Enlightenment as an ideological dynamic both illuminated and refashioned by slaves or former slaves and their political battles in the revolutionary Caribbean. Since postcolonial theory originally emerged partly as a contestation of Enlightenment humanism, reinterpreted as a paradoxical conceptual foundation for imperialist modernity, it is especially congruent to integrate voices from a late eighteenth- and early nineteenth-century interrogation of the politics of universalism fueled by rejection of colonialism and slavery.

The universalism of the French revolutionary "Rights of Man"—with "Man" representing an exclusively delimited category—was openly challenged in the Haitian Revolution, and in 1804 French colonial power in Saint-Domingue was overthrown not by colonists, as in the American Revolution, or by the colonized, as in Algeria, but by the slaves of colonists.

Yet as we saw in Chapter 1, the most celebrated Haitian revolutionary leader, Toussaint Louverture, viewed the colony as indissociable from the Republic. Toussaint appeared to see the interests of the former slaves as compatible with metropolitan revolution; or at least, this is true of the political values that he reflected back to the French. Evidence to temper this non-independence model includes Toussaint's practical inability to tolerate the colonial authorities sent to revolutionary Saint-Domingue, from the abolitionist Léger-Félicité Sonthonax to the racist comte d'Hédouville, and also his tacit encouragement of Anglophone powers in their conviction that he was simply waiting for the right moment to declare independence from France. Nevertheless, in his own writings, Toussaint had not fundamentally targeted the colony as an unacceptable political and economic organization the way that he had targeted slavery as an unacceptable practice. Toussaint's fellow general Henry Christophe, despite moments of strong articulation of anticolonial consciousness and distrust of the metropole, became known under his own later rule for his longstanding competitive emulation—or parody—of the French monarchy, replete with dukes and duchesses of Limonade and Marmalade, so he seems less likely to serve as a catalyst for a general epistemological challenge to colonialism. Mixed-race Alexandre Pétion, who ruled in the south while Christophe ruled in the north, initially had participated in the Napoleonic military expedition *against* the blacks, and only defected from the colonial army after the kidnapping of Toussaint, so he is a similarly unlikely source of general anticolonial ideology. Michel-Rolph Trouillot, in *Silencing the Past*, draws our attention to the importance of maroon and *bossale* leaders of pre-independence insurrections, who may have been more radical in their challenges to colonialism than the well-known Haitian generals and leaders affiliated with the French military—but they left virtually no textual traces.[10] Maroon anticolonialism in effect proves, if not the axiom that the subaltern cannot "speak," at least the axiom that the true outsider cannot speak in enduring textual traces, since access to print culture necessitated access to center-oriented institutions.

Unlike these other Haitian revolutionary leaders, Dessalines, throughout his rule from 1804 to his assassination in 1806, explicitly contextualized himself as radically anticolonial and pro-independence. Historian Carolyn Fick notes the significance of the one snippet of an alleged 1802 Creole (*Kreyòl*) speech by Dessalines to his soldiers that we currently know of, as transcribed by a French prisoner, the naturalist M.-E. Descourtilz.[11] (Descourtilz had also recorded, as I pointed out in Chapter 1, that Dessalines championed the anticolonial politics of using Creole rather than French.) Descourtilz quotes Dessalines as saying, in the third person, to an assembly of his countrymen, "Dessalines va rend' vou z'autr libres"[12] ("It is Dessalines who will make you all free"). Descourtilz interpreted the speech as a claiming of independence: "Alors je vous rendrai indépendans" ("Then I will make you independent"). Independence, was, in fact, probably what was at stake in Dessalines's speech; after all, slavery had been abolished in Saint-Domingue since 1793, so Dessalines did not need to promise emancipation from slavery.

Dessalines unambiguously promoted himself as a singular proponent of anticolonial ideology and black independence. In his famous "I have avenged America" manifesto of April 28, 1804, he described himself as more faithful than Toussaint had been to the quest to overthrow colonial tyranny:

Peu semblable à celui qui m'a précédé, à l'ex-général Toussaint Louverture, j'ai été fidèle à la promesse que je vous ai faite en prenant les armes contre la tyrannie; et tant qu'un reste de souffle m'animera, je le tiendrai, ce serment. Jamais aucun colon ni Européen ne mettra le pied sur ce territoire à titre de maître ou de propriétaire.[13]

(A little unlike him who has preceded me, the ex-general Toussaint Louverture, I have been faithful to the promise which I made to you when I took up arms against tyranny, and whilst the last spark of life remains in me I shall keep my oath. *Never again shall a colonist or a European set his foot upon this territory with the title of master or proprietor.*)[14]

Dessalines went on to contextualize this anticolonial axiom, this rejection not just of slavery but of any colonial or European mastery and ownership, as "the fundamental basis of our constitution." In the Haitian Declaration of Independence or "Acte d'indépendance," Dessalines cautioned that it was not enough to have expelled the factions "qui se jouaient tour à tour du fantômme [*sic*] de liberté que la France exposait à vos yeux, il faut par un dernier acte d'autorité nationale, assurer à jamais l'empire de la liberté [...]"[15] ("that endlessly replayed France's shadow puppet show of liberty, we must in a last act of national authority forever guarantee the ascendance [or empire] of liberty"). The ghostly liberty of the French Revolution would be replaced by liberty's anticolonial empire[16] in Haiti—and elsewhere, as I will discuss in Chapter 4.

The Ex-Slave Leader as Political Author

The same questions that haunted descriptions of Toussaint Louverture's authorial role, as addressed in the introduction, must be considered with even more care in the case of the unschooled General Dessalines. In Dessalines's case, lack of alphabetization can be viewed not just as the absence of a skill, but also as a degree of distance from the Foucauldian "disciplining" of the imagination by the normative claims and mimetic conditioning of any culture's educational system. Those normative claims and mimetic conditioning have been described through metaphors like Fanon's "white masks"—and Dessalines is one of the notably unmasked voices of the Afro-diasporic tradition. But what about the frequently cited caveat that Dessalines's transcribed proclamations, notably the Haitian Declaration of Independence, were actually written by his secretary Louis Félix Boisrond-Tonnerre?

Denials of Dessalines's possible authorial role were long made outside of Haiti in the name of racism rather than scholarship. The French *Journal des débats et lois du pouvoir législatif: et des actes du gouvernement* hastened to state "the obvious" about Dessalines's proclamations, which is to say that surely they were authored by renegade whites: "Il est également inutile de faire observer que la proclamation qu'on vient de lire n'est l'ouvrage ni de Dessalines, qui ne sait pas signer son nom,[17] ni d'aucun individu de sa couleur"[18] ("Nor is there any need to state the obvious, which is to say that the above proclamation is not the work of Dessalines, who is unable to sign his own name, nor of any other individual of his color"). Some day, the paper asserted, the blacks would be only too happy to acknowledge that their "atrocious counsel" should be attributed in fact to "apostate whites, who came from Europe to turn these ferocious animals against their own kind." Far from being a statesman with an *oeuvre*, Dessalines in this account is a ferocious animal and, at the same time, a puppet.

In Haitian historiography, nationalist pride has inadvertently fueled a parallel lack of attention to Dessalines's textual legacy, through unquestioning acceptance of distinguished nineteenth-century Haitian historian Thomas Madiou's rousing account of Boisrond-Tonnerre's scripting of the Declaration of Independence. David Geggus summarizes the story that has been transmitted from history to history through the centuries:

> Louis Boisrond-Tonnerre, who wrote the declaration of independence, was passionately anti-European but, Paris-educated, of mixed racial descent, and several generations removed from slavery, he had little personal connection to Africa. Dessalines entrusted him with writing the independence proclamation on December 31st after rejecting as too staid an earlier attempt by another French-educated mulatto, Charéron. Boisrond supposedly declared, "To draw up the act of independence we need the skin of a white man for parchment, his skull for an inkwell, his blood for ink, and a bayonet for a pen." He sat up all night to work on the document.[19]

This independence scene is often embellished with details such as the multiple bottles of rum drained by Boisrond through the night as the ink flowed.[20] The next morning, according to Madiou, the General-in-Chief Dessalines, "couvert d'habits dorés, tenant entre ses doigts enrichis de pierreries l'acte de l'indépendance que venaient de signer au palais du gouvernement nos plus illustres guerriers, monta sur l'autel de la patrie"[21] ("draped in gold cloth, holding between fingers weighted with precious stones the Declaration of Independence that our most illustrious warriors had just signed in the presidential palace, mounted the altar of the fatherland"), where he presided over Boisrond's reading of his (Boisrond's) text. The nation, in this account, was signed, sealed, and delivered in the course of one night and day, authored by the scribe.

Where did Madiou come up with these details? Madiou casts Dessalines's role in the independence ceremony as imperial in style, when Dessalines at this point was clearly presenting himself as a humble military leader, a general-in-chief fresh from the battlefields. This should further alert us to the propagandistic import, rather than the historical rigor, of Madiou's dramatic recreation.

No major account of the independence era prior to Madiou's history mentioned an authorial role for Boisrond, and it is not clear where Madiou might have found a contemporary account with privileged (eyewitness) information. Boisrond-Tonnerre himself, after all, in his memoirs of the revolutionary era, which were first published in Haiti in 1804,[22] makes no mention of the independence proclamation and a heroic role for himself in its composition. His memoirs feature in the original appendix only an odd selection of correspondence from Pauline Bonaparte (the wife of General Leclerc and sister of Napoleon) and her relatives. In 1805, Marcus Rainsford made the following summary of the independence: "[Dessalines] appointed the first day of the year for a solemn pledge of hatred to the French government, and an abjuration of all ideas of conquest and aggrandizement."[23] Certainly Rainsford does not associate the Declaration with Boisrond-Tonnerre; he twice alludes to another of Dessalines's secretaries, B. Aimé, but Boisrond-Tonnerre is not mentioned at all. Louis Dubroca, in the 1806 version of his defamatory biography of Dessalines, mentions a "Declaration of treachery" by Dessalines, Christophe, and Clerveaux, which undoubtedly refers to the November 1803 proclamation by those three generals, and a proclamation of Dessalines as Governor-General for life dating from May of 1804; but there is no allusion to Boisrond-Tonnerre.[24]

Later, Drouin de Bercy, whose 1814 work was steeped in the issue of whether France should recognize the independence of Haiti, referred very specifically to a January 1, 1804, independence document, but again without mention of Boisrond.[25] The Haitian historian Baron de Vastey, in the 1819 *Essai sur les causes de la révolution et des guerres civiles d'Hayti*, cites a convocation of military leaders "on the 1st of January, 1804," with the purpose of taking "into consideration such measures as would be most conducive to the happiness, the liberty and the independence, of the people,"[26] but Boisrond-Tonnerre is not identified. Neither Pamphile de Lacroix[27] nor Placide Justin and James Barskett mention a special role by Boisrond.[28]

There appears thus to be no evidence for Boisrond-Tonnerre's alleged authorship of the Haitian Declaration of Independence other than Madiou's compelling description of a scene of imperial grandeur in which we can ill-imagine the anachronistically jewel-encrusted Dessalines fussing over figures of speech.

The erroneous attribution of an authorial rather than a secretarial role to Boisrond-Tonnerre should also partly be laid at the doorstep of subsequent historians who took Madiou's account and distilled it to a simplified and more certain form. The larger scope of details even in Madiou's own account contradict any framing of Dessalines as external to the process of the production of the document. In his discussion of the pre-Independence Day process, Madiou evokes a collective act of composition in which Dessalines's editorial comments were authoritative. He states that Dessalines had set the date of January 1 for the proclamation, and put all of his secretaries, including but not limited to Jean-Jacques Charéron, to work on its composition. After several days, the secretarial team was still laboring. On December 31, Dessalines read this draft, which was heavily influenced by the American Declaration of Independence, and conveyed his disagreement with numerous elements of its style and content. Dessalines then, according to Madiou, charged Boisrond with the task of representing his (Dessalines's) feelings to the public.[29] It is plausible that Dessalines had instructed Boisrond as to the precise nature of those feelings.

Quite apart from Madiou's views of the authorial genesis of the Declaration of Independence, there is abundant *literary* evidence that Dessalines, not Boisrond, was the crucial conceptual voice of the document in the narrative proclamations (the extended prose writings in the first person) from late 1803 through the final months of 1804. These texts were the cornerstone of the symbolic architecture produced by Dessalines to create a Haitian political identity and agency that would resonate on the world stage; it was meant to duel in importance with Euro-American self-fashioning. And as I will show below, his conceptual fingerprints were all over them.

Dessalines as Political "Author"

Dessalines's documents are marked by a singular rhetorical and poetic ferocity, and a sustained incredulous protest against the hypocrisy of colonial racism. We do not need to rely on any single text to make this case; we can point to the recurrence of specific tropes in different parts of Dessalines's textual corpus—his *oeuvre*—transcribed by different secretaries.

Consider, for example, Dessalines's reiterated critiques of the "epithets" used to marginalize the Haitians. The Declaration of Independence turns the "qualifying epithet" of "slaves" back on the French, as previously noted: "Esclaves!… laissons aux Français cette épithète qualificative: ils ont vaincu pour cesser d'être libres"[30] ("Slaves!… Let us leave that qualifying epithet to the French themselves: they have conquered to the point of ceasing to be free"). In his journal of the period of the surrender and evacuation of the French, on December 2, 1803, he had critiqued the labeling of the Haitians as "brigands," alluding to "l'affreuse épithète de brigands"[31] ("the appalling epithet of brigands").

From the November 29 proclamation by Dessalines, Christophe, and Clerveaux, with its metaphor of the bloody tatters of the veil of prejudice, to the ardent rejection in the Declaration of Independence of the imprints of a cruel French colonial culture all over the laws, customs, and cities of Haiti, to the famous evocation of the irritated genie/genius of Haiti rising from the seas in the April 28 "I have avenged America" proclamation, Dessalines's late 1803 and early 1804 texts share recurrent types of symbolism, tone, structures of address, and strategies for persuasion and self-justification. In place of Toussaint's defensive and arguably pre-Romantic rhetorical identification, Dessalines's voice calls into question the politics of European cultural models, and militates for free access to a New World public sphere.

If Dessalines were not the primary authorial voice directing an admittedly complex redactive process, one would expect that the proclamations by different named secretaries[32] would differ sharply from one secretary to another. If Boisrond were the true Haitian *génie* ("genius") behind the devouring onslaught of ideas and images in the Haitian Declaration of Independence this stylistic mark would, logically, be absent in texts by two other secretaries named in multiple Dessalines texts: B. Aimé and Juste Chanlatte. But there is a fluid, sustained, and critical structure of metaphor in the major Dessalinian texts, regardless of secretarial signature. Dessalines generally was attentive to established political tropes, but rather than reiterating them, he recast them so that they were simultaneously appropriated and critiqued.

The Tree of Slavery and Prejudice

For example, in the "I have avenged America" proclamation,[33] Dessalines redeploys the classical "tree of liberty" metaphor to striking effect. The revolutionary French had made the "tree of liberty" a centerpiece of popular celebrations of the Revolution. In Saint-Domingue, the "tree of liberty" had also been celebrated by the French commissioners and by Toussaint.[34] When Toussaint was seized and deported by the French, he proclaimed, "In overthrowing me, they have uprooted in Saint-Domingue only the trunk of the tree of the liberty of the blacks; it will grow back because its roots are deep and numerous."[35] The tree of liberty in Toussaint's Gonaïves statement had been transformed to the tree of liberty *of the blacks*. But for Dessalines, liberty in the mouths of the French was a euphemism for the veiled fetishes of slavery and prejudice, and so the tree of liberty became "l'arbre antique de l'esclavage et des préjugés" ("the ancient tree of slavery and prejudice"). Likewise, the French, renowned throughout the Western world as champions of the rights of man, were for Dessalines "les implacables ennemis des droits de l'homme" ("the implacable enemies of the rights of man"). He claimed to have given the signal through which the justice of God had worked through the slaves to bring down "the axe" upon this blighted tree.

But it is the further development of this metaphor that is truly striking. Dessalines imagines that the "infernal politics of the Europeans" had surrounded the tree with a triple layer of bronze armor, making it all but invulnerable. Once the Haitians have felled the armored tree of slavery and prejudice, they place its triple bronze protection against their hearts like a coat of arms, or a magical amulet. The contact of the bronze against their hearts makes them as cruel as their enemies (ruled perhaps by "la loi d'airain," "iron law"), and their vengeance becomes like an overflowing torrent—precisely the "lavalas" metaphor used in the identity of Aristide's political party—uprooting and carrying away everything that opposes it:

> J'ai levé mon bras, trop longtemps retenu, sur leurs têtes coupables. A ce signal, qu'un Dieu juste a provoqué, vos mains, saintement armées, ont porté la hache sur l'arbre antique de l'esclavage et des préjugés. En vain le temps, et surtout la politique infernale des Européens, l'avaient environné d'un triple airain; vous avez dépouillé son armure, vous l'avez placée sur votre coeur, pour devenir (comme vos ennemis naturels), cruels, impitoyables. Tel qu'un torrent débordé qui gronde, arrache, entraîne, votre fougue vengeresse a tout emporté dans son cours impétueux.[36]

> (I raised my arm, too long restrained, over their guilty heads. At this signal, unleashed by a just God, your hands, sacredly armed, brought down the axe on the ancient tree of slavery and prejudice. In vain had time, and above all the infernal politics of Europeans, layered it with a triple armor of bronze; you stripped it of its armor, you placed it over your heart, to become [like your natural enemies], cruel and merciless. Like an overflowing torrent that roars, uproots, and pulls, your vengeful fire carries away everything in its impetuous course.)

Similarly, in the November 1803 proclamation of independence, signed by the secretary B. Aimé, Dessalines approaches the problem of slavery and liberty not in tragic and sentimental terms like those of Toussaint, but with vivid and shocking symbolism meant to continually reintroduce the trauma of slavery from the perspective of an exuberant promise or threat that it would never again be tolerated. "Nous jurons de ne les jamais céder à aucune puissance, quelle qu'elle soit sur la terre; le voile effroyable du préjugé est déchiré en pièces; et il l'est à jamais. Malheur à quiconque oseroit tenter d'en rajuster les sanglans lambeaux!"[37] ("We swear never to yield them to any power on earth. The appalling veil of prejudice is torn to pieces, and will stay sundered forever. Woe to whoever would dare to piece back together its bloody rags!") This long metaphor infuses a strange corporeality into the abstraction of the idea of prejudice: either the veil of prejudice has concealed wounded bodies, becoming bloodied in the process, or it has its own fantastical body, so that when it is torn apart by those who had suffered under it, it bleeds. Whether its sanguinary appearance is due to its aggressive nature or to the vengeance through which it has been dismantled is not clear. In either case, prejudice, an abstract psychological construct, is inseparable for Dessalines from the visceral evidence of violence. To use this violence in a new rhetoric that would serve in the crafting of new laws is the clear goal of this former slave as political speaker.

Conversely to this stylistic similarity of the independence texts generated by Dessalines, we can note that separate writings authored by Boisrond and also by Chanlatte in their own names are distinctly stylistically different from Dessalines's proclamations. The important memoirs of Boisrond-Tonnerre are in some ways prosaic and disorganized in their recounting of Haitian revolutionary history when compared with the impassioned documents generated by Dessalines. Even where Boisrond speaks in dramatic and unforgiving terms, we do not find the highly condensed and fluid symbolism that characterizes Dessalines's texts. Here is an example: "Le moment des crimes est arrivé; lecteur impartial, vous allez juger quels furent les bourreaux et quelles furent les victimes"[38] ("The moment of the crimes was upon us. Impartial reader, you will be the judge of whom among us played the role of executioner and victim"). In the concluding passages of the memoirs, Boisrond comes closer to the streaming metaphorical rhetoric of the proclamations than anywhere else, but each succeeding image is separate, not organically connected: the abyss can be measured by the eye; the Haitians hold liberty in their hearts; they hold the keys to that liberty in their hands.

> Haïtiens, que le courage d'un héros a relevés de l'anathème du préjugé, en lisant ces mémoires, vous mesurez de l'oeil l'abîme d'où il [Dessalines] vous a retirés! Et vous, esclaves de tous les pays, vous apprendrez par ce grand homme, que l'homme porte naturellement dans son coeur la liberté, et qu'il en tient les clés dans ses mains.[39]

> (Haitians, freed of the anathema of prejudice by a hero's courage, in reading these memoirs, your eye will measure the abyss from which he [Dessalines] rescued you! And you, slaves of all countries, you will learn from this great man, that every man carries liberty in his heart, and that he holds the key to it in his hands.)

Juste Chanlatte in some of his later writings, notably the 1824 *Histoire de la Catastrophe de Saint-Domingue*, did occasionally demonstrate significant overlap with the rhetoric of Dessalines. However, this overlap sometimes appears to show the influence of Dessalines's proclamations on him rather than vice versa. Consider the following passage, which is virtually a pastiche of the metaphor (discussed above) of the veil of prejudice from the first proclamation of independence, which was not signed by Chanlatte but by the secretary B. Aimé: "Quelle plaie horrible de l'humanité que nous venons de découvrir! Ah! Puisque nous avons eu le courage de soulever ce voile, hâtons-nous d'en déchirer les lambeaux dégoûtans![40] Et puissant-ils ne jamais reparaître sur la surface du globe!"[41] ("What a horrible wound we discover in humanity! Oh! Because we had the courage to lift this veil, let us hurry to shred the rest of its disgusting tatters! And let them never again appear on the surface of the globe!")

Dessalines's secretaries were not necessarily poised to challenge European logic in the same ways as this former slave whose body was reputedly covered with the scars of punishment. At this time in Haitian history, the role of secretary most often indicated that the individual in question had received an education in France. (We can see from the case of Toussaint's oblique secretarial role in the very early stages of the Haitian Revolution that this was not invariably true, however.) Geggus notes that "Chanlatte was raised in Paris and spent the period 1798–1803 in the United States. Boisrond was educated in Paris and lived there approximately 1792–1800, when he was aged 16–24."[42] Unfortunately, I have never yet found identifying information concerning the mysterious "B. Aimé" (occasionally rendered simply as "Aime" without the accent mark, or as "Amie"). His name resembles an abbreviation of "bien-aimé" ("beloved"), which may signal that it was a pseudonym, or it could possibly be a sign of a less privileged racial/cultural background, since former slaves did not necessarily have a conventional division of Western familial patronym and first name, and were sometimes known by descriptive nicknames.

It is clear that Dessalines's secretaries (with the exception of the secretarial voice in one decree, which I will discuss below) were well schooled in the conventions of political discourse of the time, and especially in French (and American) revolutionary discourse. This is the mimetic identification with France on the part of the Haitian elite that led Colin Dayan to comment of Haitian political texts in general:

> What strikes a reader of the various French proclamations during and after the revolution is the astonishing homogeneity of what was said, no matter who speaks or for what purpose. Debates in the revolutionary assemblies in Paris, the words of Georges-Jacques Danton and Robespierre especially, once printed in newspapers in Saint-Domingue, were recycled as formulas or favored shibboleths by those who took on the burden of politics and the prerogative of French in the new republic.[43]

Charles Moran likewise believed that he had found a concrete example of the mimetic influence of French revolutionary rhetorical conventions in the following lines from the "I have avenged America" speech: "What do I care what judgment contemporary and future races will pronounce against me? I have done my duty." These lines showed, he argued, "practically the identical language used by Danton on a somewhat similar occasion [...] 'Que m'importe le jugement de la posterité sur cette mesure que commande la politique pourvu que je sauve mon pays?'"[44]

Dessalines's proclamations are undeniably mediated texts, produced in conjunction with educated advisors and secretaries who had mastery of the technology of writing and were familiar with a stock of distinguished political tropes, and yet they are marked by an internal, innovative integrity as a corpus. Although they borrow from the "lights" of Western revolutionary thought, Dessalines's proclamations manifest an ongoing effort to replace Western cultural hermeneutics with those from his own environment and history as a slave in Saint-Domingue.

Poetics/Politics of Violence

As noted in Chapter 1, Dessalines's insurgent and vengeful rhetoric transfixed European and American readers. This horror was especially visceral when contemporaneous news stories confirmed what was obliquely proposed or defended in the proclamations: actual massacres of the island's small groups of remaining whites. Dessalines's ideology concerning violence resembled in principle Malcolm X's objective of "complete freedom, justice, and equality *by any means necessary*," but in the Age of Revolution, the "necessary means" were inscribed on the register of action rather than principle.

Long before the statement of Malcolm X that "Nobody can give you freedom. Nobody can give you equality or justice or anything. If you're a man, you take it," Dessalines had provided a terrible historical example and an inspiring theoretical formulation of the same idea in the Haitian Declaration of Independence: "Nous avons osé être libres sans l'être, par nous-mêmes et pour nous-mêmes" ("We dared to be free back when we were not free, for ourselves and by ourselves"). The issue of Dessalines's historical violence does not fall within the scope of this book's ambitions, although it haunts them. Unlike Frantz Fanon, who dedicated his life to healing yet claimed that "Violence is a cleansing force. It frees the native from his inferiority complex and from his despair and inaction; it makes him fearless and restores his self-respect,"[45] Dessalines was a self-styled "warrior," immersed in a high-stakes antislavery war against not only France, but other colonial powers in the Caribbean region.

World judgments of Dessalines's actions show willy-nilly something he insisted upon in political writings: the different accounting applied to (former) slaves' lives and those of (former) masters. Dessalines is the first Haitian to draw attention to the large-scale mortality of the blacks at the hands of the whites, as in this chilling reminder in the Declaration:

Citoyens indigènes, hommes, femmes, filles et enfants, portez vos regards sur toutes les parties de cette île; cherchez-y, vous, vos épouses, vous vos maris, vous vos frères, vous vos soeurs; que dis-je? Cherchez-y vos enfants, vos enfants à la mamelle! Que sont-ils devenus?... Je frémis de le dire... la proie de ces vautours.[46]

(Indigenous citizens, men, women, girls and boys, cast your eyes around this island in every direction; search in every corner, you, look for your wives, you, for your husbands, you, for your brothers, you, your sisters; no, worse! Look for your children, your babes at the breast! What has become of them?... I shudder to say it... They were the prey of those vultures.)

In the limited but appalling massacres of the remaining small populations of whites in the spring of 1804 the war had ended, but for Dessalines, the French represented an active threat. "Il existe des français dans notre île, et vous vous croyez libres et independents" ("There are still Frenchmen who remain on our island, and yet you believe yourselves to be free and independent").[47]

Dessalines tried to publicize the scale of Haitian losses that had occurred not in military battles but in massacres by drowning, suffocating, hanging, and other forms of assassination from the era of the French military invasion led by Leclerc through the departure of the French troops under Rochambeau. In a proclamation called "Extract from the Secret Deliberations of the Government of Hayti, *LIBERTY! INDEPENDENCE, OR DEATH!, THE GOVERNOUR GENERAL*," which was published in early May in the U.S., and therefore coincided in its composition with the April 1804 massacres of whites in Haiti, Dessalines numbers wanton executions of blacks from 1802–1803 at 60,000. This number was no doubt exaggerated; Alexander von Humboldt had estimated the Haitian population at 375,000 in 1802 under Toussaint (diminished from approximately 530,000 in 1780), with a further drop to 348,000 by the time of the departure of the French in late 1803;[48] this gives a decrease of 27,000, which presumably would have included evacuations by whites. Dessalines insists, beyond numerical accounts, on a deeply traumatic era of racial violence.

[...] considering that there still remains in the Island of Hayti, individuals who have contributed either by their guilty writings or by their sanguinary accusations to the drowning, suffocating, assassinating, hanging and shooting of more than 60,000 of our brethren under the inhuman government of Le Clerc and Rochambeau.[49]

For Dessalines, the ties of ancestral fidelity were the foundation for a new society. Thus if the new Haitians failed to avenge these victims of the Middle Passage and of Napoleon Bonaparte's troops, the very bones of their forefathers would expel them from shared tombs: "Descendrez-vous dans la tombe sans les avoir vengés? Non, leurs ossements repousseraient les vôtres" ("Will you be granted entry to shared tombs if you have not avenged them? No, their very bones will expel yours").[50]

Dessalines foreshadows what Cornell West described as Malcolm X's willingness to "accent the hypocrisy" of society, a willingness that made Malcolm "the prophet of black rage—then and now."[51] In the complex historical and textual record that gives us access to the person of Dessalines, we find a prophet of black rage, not only in the "then" of Malcolm's time and now, but long before then: and we are still struggling to decode the prophecy.

No matter how well justified in his texts, Dessalines's historical record does hint at legacies, so far nearly intractable in a wide array of postcolonies, of traumatic repetition of the violence and low estimation of the value of human life that were hallmarks of colonialism. Robert Fatton notes that a genealogy of Haitian leaders from the independence to the present day "have claimed that their own person embodied the popular will."[52] This "authoritarian habitus" in Haiti is a colonial legacy, as Fatton sees it: "The legacies of the repressive despotism of colonialism, and the violence of the revolutionary struggle for emancipation have decisively shaped the Haitian authoritarian habitus. Colonial society was conflict-ridden; [...] Haiti was bound to inherit the wounds of racial and class enmity."[53] Dessalines himself reminded his countrymen in his acceptance of his imperial nomination that he was governing in the most difficult of historical transitions: "Mais n'oubliez pas que c'est dans les temps les plus orageux que vous me confiez le gouvernement du vaisseau de l'Etat"[54] ("Do not forget that you are conferring upon me the government of the vessel of state at the stormiest of times").

Smashing Idols

In the first half of 1804 especially, Dessalines showed great confidence— probably excessive confidence—in the capacity of his printed words to justify his regime, quell the predatory opposition of Western metropoles, and establish autonomous cultural and political boundaries. His texts were meant, I will argue, to have a quasi-magical[55] effect: an anticolonial poetics in the service of the representation of former slaves' experience and subjective claims, leading to or protecting the establishment of their subversive dominance over colonial authority. In my reading, this ambition of Dessalines through his proclamations differs sharply from the ambitions of Toussaint Louverture: Toussaint arguably felt that if he could translate his and the blacks' experiences and claims into terms comprehensible to metropolitan cultures, those cultures would have a meeting of minds with the Haitians, leading to mutually sympathetic and persuasive dialogue. But Dessalines, of course, had observed Toussaint move from collaboration to deportation, from surrender to death in a cold cell.

Dessalines frequently returned to projections of power determined not by the state but by the glory of the warrior, through which he contested Western political values, identities, and institutions, ranging from Abrahamic religious monotheism to abstract rationalism. There are frequent references to "idols" and "relics" in proclamations he issued through both Boisrond-Tonnerre and Juste Chanlatte. On first glance, in these references Dessalines appears to be adopting the Western critique of religious or magical materialism, but using it against the West itself. On closer examination, it becomes plausible that he is critiquing the power of Western idols without renouncing other magical practices and powers. Or he may be doing both.

First, through an assimilation of French revolutionary anticlerical discourse in which religion is equated with pagan beliefs and unjust practices, Dessalines condemns slavery as a concrete "idol" of a larger sacralized field of Western prejudices and hierarchical values through which the French were actively attempting to subjugate the Haitians. And then he vaunts the power of the Haitians' own alignment with supernatural forces. Thus in his acceptance of his imperial nomination (which I will discuss at length below), he contends the blacks had been enslaved as a "sacrifice" to the French "idol" of prejudice. For Dessalines, the Haitians had smashed the French idol of prejudice through their own autonomous agency, which was, he implies, the only way abolition could actually overthrow the Western beliefs of which the institution of slavery was a projection:

[Les] hommes qui prédilectent leur indépendance au préjudice de cette considération que les puissances n'accordent jamais aux peuples qui, comme nous, sont les artisans de leur propre liberté, [...] n'ont pas eu besoin de mendier des secours étrangers pour briser l'idole à laquelle nous sacrifions. Cette idole, comme Saturne, dévorait ses enfants, et nous l'avons foulée aux pieds.[56]

([The] men who founded our independence to the prejudice of that consideration which powers never concede to people who like us are the authors of their own liberty [...] have no occasion to beg for foreign assistance to break the idol to which we were sacrificed. That idol, like Saturn, devoured its children, and we have trampled it under our feet.)

This passage, like so many others that Dessalines published in 1804, quite precisely foreshadows the terms of Hegel's assertion that freedom from bondage could not come in the form of a gift. In Germany, as Susan Buck-Morss noted, Hegel had access to several major texts produced by Dessalines in *Minerva*.[57] Consider the echoic relationship between the famous line in the *Philosophy of Right*, "Even if I am born a slave, [...] still I am free in the moment I will it"[58] and Dessalines's assertion in the Declaration of Independence that Haiti was "fier d'avoir recouvré [*sic*] sa liberté, et jaloux de la maintenir; effrayons tous ceux qui oserait tenter de nous la ravir encore"[59] ("proud to have recovered their freedom, jealous to maintain it, and determined to overcome anyone who would try to ravish it from them again"). Consider, as well, this statement from Dessalines's military field journal, the "Journal de campagne," which was also published in *Minerva*:[60]

Et si des hommes qui veulent être libres parce qu'ils le peuvent, sont encore connus en France sous l'affreuse épithète de brigands, qu'elle renvoie, s'il lui est possible, pour les combattre, le petit nombre de soldats français que notre climat et notre humanité ont épargnés.[61]

(And if we, as men who desire to be free because we can be free, are still known in France by the appalling epithet of "brigands," let France send back to fight us, if she can, the meager numbers of French soldiers who were spared by our climate and our humanity.)

Just as we can read Dessalines as a forerunner to Malcolm X and Frantz Fanon, we should perhaps consider the proto-Hegelian resonance of his proclamations as the proto-Dessalinean resonance of the Hegelian master–slave dialectic.

As the amplitude of this latent dialogic relationality between Haitian leaders' texts and other forms of radical thought is revealed, it prompts the question of *why* acknowledgment of a historical referent in the Hegelian master–slave paradigm has been so crucial in drawing the attention of literary and theoretical scholars to the Haitian Revolution, and its media imprint, in the first place. Did we have to have Hegel to have Haiti in a certain philosophical sense? When Dessalines, in the Declaration of Independence, proclaimed that France, for all its military engagements with other nations, "n'a jamais vaincu celles qui ont voulu être libres" ("never conquered those who wanted to be free"),[62] was it somehow through its prefiguration of a future Hegelian response that it eventually became manifest to theorists of a black Atlantic modernity? What other currents of philosophy should we recognize as imbricated with the mediatic literature of the Haitian Revolution, and in what complex directionality of circulation and influence?

Colonial Magic in Santo Domingo

A critique of French magical projections of colonial power appears in Dessalines's proclamation (first dated in the U.S. media as May 8, 1804, but backdated on a manuscript copy in the *Notes historiques* to February 8, 1804),[63] composed with Chanlatte, to the inhabitants of Santo Domingo (the current Dominican Republic). Dessalines was determined to overthrow French control of Santo Domingo, and in his proclamation he mocked the Dominicans' delusions with regards to the powers of the Europeans:

> Vous sauvera-t-il ce ministre imaginaire lorsque le fer et la flamme à la main je vous poursuivrai jusque dans vos derniers retranchemens ? Eh ! Sans doute ses pensées, ses grimaces, ses reliques ne pourront m'arrêter dans ma course. Vous préservera-t-il de ma juste colère ?

> (Will that fanatical priest save you when with fire and sword I have pursued you to your furthest entrenchments? Ah! Without doubt, his prayers, his grimaces, his relics, will fail to halt my course. Will he protect you from my righteous anger?)

Who was this fanatical priest aligned with the French colonization of Santo Domingo? Emilio Cordero Michel suggests it was José Vásques, who had served as a royalist agent in the army of Jean-François until 1795, encouraging the assassination of "des enfants, des femmes et des hommes innocents qu'il tenait pour *athées, régicides et juifs*"[64] ("women, children, and innocent men he viewed as *atheists, regicides, and Jews*"). Santo Domingo during the French Revolution had served as an asylum for *prêtres réfractaires*, priests who refused to take a revolutionary oath of compliance to a civil constitution. In this period of the *Era de Francia en Santo Domingo*,[65] Vásques, along with Father Vives, cultivated the hostility of the Dominicans against the Haitians whom he qualified as "heretics and cannibals."[66] However, the fanatical priest to whom Dessalines referred was more likely the French bishop Mauviel, initially a friend of the Abbé Grégoire and a designated intermediary with the Haitians, who had then joined the Leclerc forces and helped General Kerverseau to retake Santo Domingo from Haitian command in 1802. Auguste Matinée, in his digest of the lengthy writings of Mauviel, claims that Dessalines "honora Mauviel d'une sortie violente dans une de ses proclamations. Il le traita de *prêtre fanatique*"[67] ("honored Mauviel with a virulent tirade in one of his proclamations. He called him *fanatical priest*"). Mauviel was known for inspiring the French forces and their Spanish allies under General Ferrand with his "pastoral" sermons. But either identification shows Dessalines's targeting of anti-revolutionary uses of Christian discourse: when the Haitian army invaded Santo Domingo in

June of 1804, Father Vásques, who was known to have severely provoked the Haitian leader, was slain at the altar of his church in St. Yago.

This literal identity of the priest figure in the proclamation does not make him less of a metaphysical icon for the contrast between Dessalines's beliefs and those of the Europeans, however. Dessalines noted that he had come to count the citizens of Santo Domingo among his "children," but warned them that if they aligned themselves with the relics and projected power of the French, his vengeance would be as drastic and effective as that of nature's offended boundaries:

> Qu'ils apprennent donc que je suis prêt, que la foudre va tomber sur leurs têtes : qu'ils sachent que mes soldats impatiens n'attendent qu'un signal pour aller réconquérir les limites que la nature et les éléments nous ont assignées. Encore quelques instans et j'écrase les débris des français sous le poids de ma puissance.[68]

> (Let them learn that I am ready; that the thunderbolt will strike them down. Let them know that my soldiers impatiently await the signal to go and reconquer the boundaries that nature and the elements have assigned us. Just a few minutes more and I will have crushed the debris of the French under the weight of my power.)

Even after his defeat in Santo Domingo (for reasons that I will discuss in Chapter 4), Dessalines continued to explain his motives in terms of the desire to destroy the supreme idol of a religiously inflected colonialism. The "Adresse de l'Empereur au peuple, à son retour du siège de Santo Domingo" ("Address of the Emperor to the People Upon His Return from the Siege of Santo Domingo"), dated April 12, 1805, stated that, incensed by a January proclamation by Louis Ferrand, he had resolved to invade Santo Domingo "et d'y effacer jusqu'aux derniers vestiges de l'idôle suprême" ("to destroy the last traces of the supreme idol").[69]

Animating Nature

Dessalines arguably aspired to the legacy of Makandal, the slave who was executed in 1757 for his attempt to organize an anticolonial revolution by mass poisoning, as much as to that of Toussaint Louverture. In the "I have avenged America" proclamation, we see that for Dessalines, poison was on a continuum with the yellow fever that had decimated the French troops (killing even their leader, Leclerc), and the fires with which the Haitians had thwarted Napoleon's attempted repossession of cities that had come under the control of the ex-slaves. Poison, disease, and conflagration were all manifestations of the supernaturally offended spirit of the slaves, animating the natural realm in sympathetic cataclysm. He warned the world that the sea itself would rise up against hostile naval incursions:

> Qu'elle vienne cette puissance assez folle pour m'attaquer! Déjà, à son approche, le génie irrité d'Hayti, sortant du sein des mers, apparaît, son front menaçant soulève les flots, excite les tempêtes; sa main puissante brise ou disperse les vaisseaux; à sa voix redoutable, les lois de la nature obéissent; les maladies, la peste, la faim dévorante, l'incendie, le poison volent à sa suite… Mais pourquoi compter sur le secours du climat et des éléments? Ai-je donc oublié que je commande à des âmes peu communes, nourries dans l'adversité, dont l'audace s'irrite des obstacles, s'accroît par les dangers?[70]

> (Let that nation come that may be mad and daring enough to attack me. Already at its approach, the irritated genius of Hayti, rising out of the bosom of the ocean, appears; his menacing aspect throws the waves into commotion, excites tempests, and with his mighty hand disperses ships, or dashes them to pieces; the laws of nature obey his formidable voice; diseases, plague, famine, conflagration, poison, are his constant attendants. But why calculate on the assistance of the climate and of the elements? Have I forgotten that I command a people of no common call, brought up in adversity, inspired to even greater audacity by obstacles and danger?)

Dessalines's environmental poetics of invincible revolution was quite elaborate. Even if the colonists should penetrate the seaside cities, he warns, in a reference to the successful guerilla tactics of the former slaves and maroons, "woe to those who approach too near the mountains!" Jean Fouchard's formulation of the "maroons of liberty" is consistent with Dessalines's identification of postcolonial Haiti with the military sanctuary of the mountains.

The Haitian Revolution is, of course, believed to have begun with the ceremony and the Oath of the Caiman Woods, which Haitian historian Hérard Dumesle provided in Creole (*Kreyòl*) form in 1824, and several passages from Dessalines's declarations echo phrases from the oath. The Creole version was transcribed as follows:

> Bondié qui fait soleil, qui clairé nous en haut,
> Qui soulévé la mer, qui fait grondé l'orage,
> Bon dié la, zot tandé? caché dans youn nuage,
> Et la li gadé nous, li vouai tout ça blancs faits!
> Bon dié blancs mandé crime, et part nous vlé bienfets
> mais dié lá qui si bon, ordonnin nous vengeance;
> Li va conduit bras nous, li ba nous assistance,
> Jetté portrait dié blancs qui soif dlo dans gié nous,
> Couté la liberté li palé coeurs nous toùs.[71]

Here is a literal translation from the Creole:

> God who makes the sun that illuminates us from on high,
> Who embroils the seas, who makes the storm growl,
> God is there, do you hear?, hidden in a cloud,
> And there he watches us, he sees everything the whites are doing!
> The God of the whites orders crime, and wants no benefits for us,
> But that other God, who is so good, orders us to take vengeance;
> He will guide our arms, he will give us assistance;
> Cast down the portrait of the god of the whites, who thirsts for tears in
>   our eyes;
> Listen to liberty, it speaks in all of our hearts.

Dessalines's figure of the irritated genius of Haiti in the "I have avenged America" proclamation resembles the environmental eruptions of God in the oath, who sends growling thunder from his righteously vengeful vantage point in the clouds.[72] In Dessalines's November 1803 independence proclamation, the phrase "Le Dieu qui nous protège, le Dieu des hommes libres" parallels the distinct emanations of God in the oath, where the initial figure of "Bon dié" splits into the God of the whites and the God who sees and is present for the blacks. That God will guide the slaves' arms; similarly, in Dessalines's first independence proclamation, the God of free men, who protects the blacks, orders them to raise their victorious arms. In a stunning line at the end of the "I have avenged America" proclamation, Dessalines explains that he has extended his mercy only to whites who had taken an oath to live with the former slaves in the woods: "une poignée de blancs, recommandables par la religion qu'ils ont toujours professée, qui, d'ailleurs, ont prêté serment de vivre avec nous dans les bois, a eprouvé ma clémence. J'ordonne que le glaive les respecte [...]"[73] ("A handful of whites, commendable by the religion they have always professed, and who have besides taken the oath to live with us in the woods,[74] have experienced my clemency. I order that the sword respect them [...]"). In effect, Dessalines is promising to spare the whites who have taken an oath of the woods. Although we cannot know precisely what he meant by this idea of living with the blacks in the woods,[75] or how it correlated to the "religion" that this tiny handful of whites had always professed, it is at least an odd coincidence with the language of the "Serment du bois Caïman."

Nature symbolism is especially prominent in the "I have avenged America" proclamation, as in the reference to the "lois de la nature" already cited, but it also appears throughout the other texts. In the proclamation to the inhabitants of Santo Domingo, as previously mentioned, he outlined his determination to reconquer "les limites que la nature et les éléments nous ont assignés" ("the boundaries that nature and the elements have assigned us"). (Although "la loi naturelle" was an omnipresent Enlightenment trope, it is used very differently in Dessalines's proclamations, to describe an almost military union between the blacks and a protective, animated environment.) In the Declaration of Independence, Dessalines lauds "notre climat vengeur" ("our vengeful climate"), and asks when the Haitians will grow weary of breathing in the same air as that breathed by the French: "Quand nous lasserons-nous de respirer le même air qu'eux?"

The African Emperor in the Postcolonial New World

The "empire of liberty" cited in the Declaration of Independence soon became a political institution in Haiti: the first Haitian empire. We learn from Dessalines's acceptance of his nomination as emperor, ostensibly dated either January 25 or February 15, 1804, that he viewed himself as a warrior, and would remain identified as a general even in his new, more prestigious, role as emperor. This proclamation, signed by Dessalines, Governor-General, and by the Adjutant-General Boisrond-Tonnerre, was widely published in English translation in the United States, although not until October and November of 1804, almost six months after the apparent date of the original proclamation:

> I am a soldier! War has ever been my portion, and as long as the cruelty, the barbarity, and the avarice of our enemies bring them to our shores, I will justify your choice; and combatting at your head, I shall prove that the title of your General will ever be honorable to me.[76]

What did this confusing metamorphosis of Dessalines from soldier to emperor indicate concerning the meaning and chronology of empire in postcolonial Haiti?

The First Consul Napoleon Bonaparte's imperial nomination had occurred during a special session of the French Tribunat on May 1, 1804, and news of it would have arrived in Haiti by early June. During this fateful session of the Tribunat, Citizen Curée had introduced a motion "1) que le Gouvernement de la République soit confié à un Empereur; [et] 2) que l'Empire soit héréditaire dans la famille de Napoléon Bonaparte, actuellement Premier Consul" ("1) that the Government of the Republic be assigned to an Emperor; 2) that the Empire be hereditary in the family of Napoleon Bonaparte, currently First Consul").[77]

Taken at face value, the January 25 or February 15 dates listed in different versions of the text of Dessalines's imperial nomination and acceptance would thus seem to indicate that his own nomination as emperor preceded that of Napoleon. But the almost binaristic contrast of style and content between the two immediately raises the question of which nomination and acceptance actually responded to and critiqued the terms of the other. Although Curée's motion, and the rapturous accord of all members of the Tribunat but the beleaguered Lazare Carnot, was delivered in heroic terms ("Charlemagne avait gouverné la France en homme qui était supérieur de beaucoup à son siècle" ["Charlemagne had governed France precisely in his capacity as a man superior to his own era"]),[78] the final French confirmation was dry, pompous, and legalistic. It stressed that the "imperial dignity" would be hereditary, passing on from male to male by primogeniture among Napoleon's children or those of his brothers. It stipulated details ranging from the role of the senate under the empire to the residences of the emperor and the salary percentages of a hypothetical future "minor emperor" and regent.[79]

By contrast, Dessalines's acceptance speech is dramatic and personal ("I am a soldier!"). Not only is it focused on his warrior status, it has a strong communitarian tone. Dessalines speaks in the acceptance of never allowing his sword to "sleep" in order to pass on his own valor to the national family of warriors:

> The supreme rank to which you elevate me tells me that I am become the father of my fellow citizens, of whom I was the defender; but the father of a family of warriors never suffers the sword to sleep if he wishes to transmit his valor to his descendants, to inure them to battles.[80]

Although the power of his sword can be magically transmitted, and will guarantee the safety of his soldiers, Dessalines specifically renounces heredity ("ancestry") in the transmission of imperial power:

> I renounce, yes, I formally renounce, the unjust custom of transmitting my power to my family. I shall never respect ancestry, but when the talents requisite for a good governor are united in the subject. Frequently the head which is fired by the burning ardor of youth, contributes more effectually to the happiness of his country than the cool experience of age, which temporizes at the moment when temerity alone should govern.

This non-dynastic transmission of power reflects Dessalines's belief that authority is earned through prowess and the inspired military exhibition of paternal concern for the national family.[81] For Dessalines, authority is also compensated in full by this national military/spiritual bond. In the Declaration of Independence he noted that he had never sought any material gains from his leadership role, but considered himself paid in full by the Haitians' hard-earned freedom: "Je ne suis riche que de ta liberté" ("I am rich only in your liberty").

In the acceptance document, Dessalines's distrust of the moderating influence of age is a sign of his belief in the necessity of not just one revolution, but revolutions in the plural: "If the sober passions make common men, half measures will arrest the rapid march of revolutions." Revolution was an ongoing process, and leaders were necessarily revolutionaries. There were no partial revolutions for Dessalines, in theory or in practice.

It is not just in the acceptance speech that Dessalines seems intent on differentiating Haitian political structures from French structures. The document of the nomination of Dessalines by the assembled generals contains wary reflections that might best be categorized within the identity politics of postcolonial consciousness. On the one hand, the signatories choose to confer upon their chief "an august and sacred title, which will concentrate in him the forces of the state, [and] will be imposing abroad [...]" The title of emperor is strategically necessary to counter or compete with the ever-more imposing edifice of French state power: *to be imposing abroad*. The first article of the Haitian Constitution of May 1805 would echo this essential need: "Le peuple habitant l'île ci-devant appelée Saint-Domingue, convient ici de se former en état libre, souverain et indépendant de toute autre puissance de l'univers, sous le nom de l'empire d'Haïti"[82] ("The people inhabiting the island formerly known as Saint-Domingue here agrees to form a free state, sovereign and independent from all other powers in the universe, under the name of the Empire of Haiti").

The generals had also reflected deeply on the contaminated political origins of Dessalines's original independence-era titles, "General-in-Chief of the Indigenous Army," and "Governor-General for Life." They noted, "the title of Governor-General, [...] supposes a secondary power depending upon a foreign authority, whose yoke we have shaken off forever." General-in-Chief of the Indigenous Army was a title straight out of the French colonial era in Saint-Domingue, and Toussaint had adopted the title of Governor-General for Life only to be toppled and deported by the French: both titles, they implied, connoted secondary standing and dependence on French colonial authority.

Was the empire of Jean-Jacques actually to some extent an anti-empire, an updated strategy to counter French colonial, and now imperial, power? It was. Madiou confirms that Dessalines's nomination and acceptance had been backdated to January 25 or February 15 of 1804, but they had actually been composed in August,[83] giving the Haitians time to ponder their institutions in relation to evolving international trends. This is why the nomination and acceptance did not appear in American newspapers until early October (and in the Haitian *Gazette Politique et commerciale* in November). Dessalines asserted that his imperial enterprise would "impress upon the nations least friendly to liberty, not the opinion that we are a herd of revolted slaves, but that we are men who have founded our independence [...]." The sense of redress in the structure of the Haitian Empire of a monumental historical subjugation, the curse of Ham, remained palpable in the Constitution in 1805, where Dessalines and his co-signatories articulated their principles "En face de la nature entière, dont nous avons été si injustement et depuis si longtemps considérés comme les enfants réprouvés"[84] ("In the face of all of nature, whose punished children we have been so unfairly and so continuously considered to be").

The Haitians' manipulation of dates, in which they attempted to compete with French power by appearing to pre-empt empire, does not reduce the interest of the Haitian imperial identification; on the contrary, it shows Dessalines's conscious differentiation of his own practices and beliefs from those of the European metropole he had defeated. Haitian emperors have been belittled as mimic emperors, but Dessalines was also a critic emperor, just as his empire was also an anti-empire.

The mimetic tensions of Dessalines's empire eerily foreshadow the mid-nineteenth-century denigrations of the second French empire of Louis-Napoleon III and the second Haitian empire of Soulouque I as speciously mimetic, a phenomenon Colin Dayan acutely analyzed: "Rereading events in France through the quizzing glass of Haiti is to clarify the reciprocal dependencies, the uncanny resemblances that no ideology of difference can remove. Who are the *true* cannibals? Who is 'aping' whom?"[85] Spenser St. John, Dayan notes, concluded from the doubling of Haitian and French second empires that "All black chiefs have a hankering after the forms as well as the substance of despotic power."[86] Homi Bhabha would see this form of repetition instead as a sign of how state identity is denaturalized outside of the appropriations of empire: "The figure of mimicry is locatable within what Anderson describes as 'the inner compatibility of empire and nation.' It problematizes the signs of racial and cultural priority, so that the 'national' is no longer naturalizable."[87] Dessalines was bent on smashing the idols of French colonial power, but partly through an attempt to make Haitians literally the "authors of their own liberty" by rescripting the forms of empire.

Dessalines's proclamations illustrate Steven Slemon's conception of postcolonialism as a poetics, a contestatory relationship of writing to the power that undersigns cultural identity. But Manichean difference did not, for Dessalines, collapse back into a transnational psychic displacement analogous to processes of translation or effects of doubling and irony. Dessalines was deeply engaged in a translational project of making former slaves' cultural references and boundaries readable, but it was done to conquer and supplant the power of the masters. He may have been a mimic emperor, but never a mimic man.

"The Island of St. Domingo Is a Dependence of France"

Dessalines's struggles to articulate his authority and radical contestations at the same time were grounded in the realities of his time, when, to a degree we tend to overlook, the French remained an ongoing threat. When Dessalines said, in the Declaration of Independence, "There are still Frenchmen on our island," or "cast your eyes around this island in every direction," one cannot help but notice that he is speaking in island-wide terms, not in terms of west versus east, or this and that side of a boundary. The adoption of the term "Hayti" as the name of the country, referring back to an indigenous name for the island at the time of the arrival of Columbus, further suggests that the Haitians imagined the overthrow of French colonial rule in terms of an island of freedom, rather than a free section of an island. When Dessalines, in the Declaration of Independence, urged that the Haitians imitate the example of people who had preferred to be "exterminés que rayés au nombre des peuples libres" ("exterminated rather than struck from the ranks of free peoples"),[88] he appears to be referring most directly to the Tainos who had governed the whole island before Columbus. Did he see "Hayti" as the equivalent of today's Hispaniola, and what was the state of colonial identity and threats from the other side of the border?

Unfortunately for today's readers, accustomed to a convenient differentiation of Haiti, on the western side of the island, from the Dominican Republic on the eastern side, and of both these nations from the island of Hispaniola as a whole, linguistic usages from the revolutionary and independence eras make it difficult to follow the geopolitical distinctions in texts of the time. The name for the French colony in the west and the Spanish colony in the east were translations for each other: Saint-Domingue and Santo Domingo. A Spanish speaker discussing the region we know as Haiti would then have called it Santo Domingo, just as French speakers called the area we know as the Dominican Republic Saint-Domingue. For English speakers, the French side of the island was called St. Domingue—or the spelling variants San Domingue, St. Domingo, or San Domingo—and the Spanish side likewise. In references to the island as a whole, the term "Hispaniola" was only occasionally featured in texts of that time; the "island of St. Domingo" was sometimes employed to clarify the distinction of the part versus the whole. And Santo Domingo of course was also the name of the capital city of the colony of Santo Domingo. This slippage of regional signifiers, combined with the remarkable mutability of nations' colonial control—a veritable game of musical chairs in which a metropole's ascendance might amount to a few ships in a harbor, or to its use of privateers to seize ships in a harbor—has contributed to the erasure of a key element of Haitian postcolonial identity, and a similarly key element of threat to that postcolonial identity. It is all too easy to lose sight of the fact that when the French were defeated, they did not leave Hispaniola entirely—a ragtag contingent moved from Saint Domingue to Santo Domingo, from which outpost they exerted a confounding influence that would have a major impact on the eventual economic marginalization of Haiti.

What is known "Era de Francia" in Spanish-speaking Santo Domingo had its origins in an earlier moment of the Haitian Revolution. In 1793, Toussaint Louverture, along with significant numbers of the black insurgents, had joined ranks with the Spanish army to fight against the French. As Madison Smartt Bell explains, "Spain was at war with France, and the colonists of Spanish Santo Domingo had adopted the rebel slaves of the French colony as auxiliaries to their own military."[89] After the realignment of Toussaint Louverture with the French Republic in 1794 following the official abolition of slavery by France, Toussaint and his black "French" forces turned against the Spanish forces and won; they were largely responsible for bringing this Spanish territory under French control. Under the complex terms of the treaties of Bâle, Spain then ceded Santo Domingo to France in 1795—for which, at the time, the French were deeply grateful to Toussaint.

The actual French colonial infrastructure in 1795 was minimal, however. Don. J. Garcia remained in power in Santo Domingo for all intents and purposes. Shockingly, as Steeve Coupeau notes, from 1795 to 1801 not only was slavery practiced in Santo Domingo, but there was an active slave trade, with recurrent kidnappings of former slaves from Saint-Domingue (Haiti) into re-enslavement in Santo Domingo.[90]

Toussaint found the kidnappings of black citizens increasingly intolerable, and no doubt also had his eye on an island-wide extension of his sphere of governance. After initial incursions in 1800, he invaded Santo Domingo in 1801, and succeeded in publicly abolishing slavery there in late January.[91] From that time on, all of Hispaniola was under Toussaint's rule. He put his brother-in-law Paul L'Ouverture in charge of Santo Domingo, and General Clerveaux in charge of St. Yago. The 1801 constitution that Napoleon found so worrisome made Toussaint Governor-General of "Saint-Domingue" in the broadly encompassing sense of Hispaniola, and made the "indigenous" inhabitants, as the French called the non-whites in Santo Domingo, free.

When General Leclerc arrived with the Napoleonic expedition in Saint-Domingue in the early spring of 1802, he first invaded ports in Santo Domingo, and then went on to Le Cap. In a letter to the Minister of the Marine in France, Leclerc reported that from Le Cap, he had immediately dispatched General Kerverseau (also sometimes called Picherou-Kerverseau) "with a large squadron to St. Domingo,"[92] to bring the entire island of Hispaniola under actual French rule. By the end of February, Kerverseau had re-established French rule, defeating Toussaint's avatars among the Spanish:

the *Era de Francia* had begun. And soon, those who remained vulnerable to enslavement among the ranks of the "indigenous Spaniards"—meaning, again, the non-white residents—were re-enslaved once again. According to Eugenio Matibag, Kerverseau had again re-established slavery in Santo Domingo in July of 1802.[93] At some point in this period of the Leclerc era, General Ferrand followed Kerverseau with other French troops to Monte Cristi in Santo Domingo.

But of course Leclerc died of yellow fever in Saint-Domingue in November of 1802. Between October and early December of 1803, the French had been routed. When the nation of Haiti was born, what happened to the French in Santo Domingo? The plan was for them to evacuate; but Dessalines had in fact overlooked mention of this apparently insignificant concern in his arrangements with Rochambeau. And Ferrand turned out to be psychologically wedded to the continuation of French rule on the island to an extraordinary degree. Historian Frank Moya Pons states that Ferrand refused to evacuate Santo Domingo or surrender to the British: "On January 1, 1804, the same day as the proclamation declaring the independence of Haiti, Ferrand executed a coup d'état, deposed Kerverseau, and declared his command over the remaining French troops on the island."[94] Ferrand would ultimately choose to put a bullet in his brain in 1808 rather than to accept the final defeat of the French on Hispaniola.[95] On some level a rogue remnant of Napoleonic government, Ferrand would nevertheless confuse the Euro-American sphere with his locally issued, legalistic decrees and *arêtes* against neutral commerce with Haiti, making it just plausible that the French were still at war with Haiti, and that there were legal considerations, overlapping with fears of aiding the transition of former slaves to international sovereign partners, to prevent the establishment of new diplomatic and trade ties.

The record of precisely how Ferrand managed to put Dessalines's postcolonial sovereignty into question is murky, and historians have largely shied away from the question of why Dessalines wrote *two* major proclamations of threat to Santo Domingo, the one on May 8, 1804, and the other, "Adresse de l'Empereur au peuple, à son retour du siège de Santo-Domingo,"[96] on April 12, 1805. But U.S. legal documents of lawsuits on maritime seizure of "prize" vessels in the waters around Hispaniola, combined with journalistic publication of eyewitness reports on Haitian/French military skirmishes, help to fill in the blanks of this obscure but eventually critical contestation of Haitian sovereignty. I will only address the 1804 military interactions between the Haitians and the French here, as the 1805 siege will be discussed in Chapter 4.

Dessalines's May 8 proclamation "aux habitants de la partie espagnole" ("to the inhabitants of the Spanish part") was, as previously noted, an immediate precursor to an invasion of Santo Domingo. This attack involved the defeat of the Haitians at Cibao by the French. It ended with the defeat of the Haitians in June at St. Yago. The *Morning Chronicle* on September 4, 1804, reported a "Capt. Depraid's" account of the events:

> On the 3rd June the brigands of St. Domingo made an attack on St. Jago. The Spaniards, who were in number 7000 men, sent to St. Domingo for a French officer to command them. Gen. Deveaux was sent by gen. Ferrand for that purpose. The brigands were defeated and driven back with considerable loss.

According to the Philadelphia *Aurora General Advertiser* of August 29, Dessalines's losses in the battle at St. Yago had numbered "one thousand men killed and many more wounded." Dessalines had then "cruelly ordered several whites and mulattoes to be massacred."

Why is there no clear record of this spring 1804 loss on the part of the Haitians to the former colonial master in the historical record? Madiou mentions it briefly, not as a venture of Dessalines's, but as a skirmish among Haitian and French officers.[97] But Dessalines's forceful May 8 proclamation to the inhabitants of the Spanish part strongly suggests that he was in fact preparing to (re)claim this territory that had gone back and forth between the French and the blacks since the early 1790s. American newspapers did view the May 8 proclamation to the inhabitants of the Spanish side of the island as referring to a concrete plan to attack. The *Philadelphia Evening Post* on June 5 claimed that "On 14th May, Dessalines left the Cape by way of Port-de-Paix and Gonaives, for the purpose of enforcing the terms of the following proclamation, which he had caused to be issued in that part of the island of St. Domingo inhabited by the Spaniards."

Mauviel's writings confirmed that the defeat of Dessalines's forces in Santo Domingo in the late spring of 1804 did not have to do with the valor or resistance of the local Spaniards or of Ferrand's forces, however: Dessalines was taken by surprise by a French squadron under the command of Admiral Missiessy.[98]

Dessalines himself may have avoided committing the details of the unhappy venture to paper. After all, as I will discuss in Chapter 4, when Dessalines did discuss his failed invasion of Santo Domingo in 1805, the news definitely heartened the defenders of slavery. In the U.S. Senate in January of 1806, Senator Jackson would comment damningly that he had seen a published letter by General Ferrand stating that the Haitians had been defeated by the French in Santo Domingo, and that the independence of Haiti was a fiction:

> As to the total separation of the self-created Emperor and nation of Hayti, and its independence of the parent country, and under which gentlemen

declared our rights of trade founded on the laws of nations—the late attack on that General by the Emperor proved it did not exist [...][99]

It was after these unhappy reminders for the Haitians of ongoing French contestation of Haitian sovereignty that the world began to notice the ongoing presence of the French. U.S. journalistic accounts saw it as a very surprising turn of events for the French. The Philadelphia *Aurora General Advertiser* noted on August 29, 1804,

> By several late arrivals from France, we have been informed that the government having conceived that all was lost at St. Domingo, after the evacuation of the Cape, have experienced an extreme satisfaction on receiving the unexpected account of gen. Ferrand's possessing the whole of the ci-devant ["formerly"] Spanish part of St. Domingo, with the remains of the French army.

Ferrand's aide-de-camp Castet had at this point arrived in Baltimore to negotiate better conditions from the French chargé d'affaires, Pichon. If Ferrand had for a moment been operating virtually unknown to the French government, he was quickly claimed and supported by the French metropolitan administration—although only just enough to keep his operation alive for several years of production of legal challenges to the international parties who would attempt neutral commerce with the Haitians.

Given the importance of the prospect of unfettered U.S. trade with Haiti, Ferrand's use of privateers quite naturally aroused great indignation on the part of American merchants. In the spring of 1804 they did not hesitate to publicize these threats to American trade in the waters around Haiti. The *Philadelphia Evening Post* (April 18, 1804) presented news "of a most alarming nature", to wit: "About fifteen French privateers are constantly bringing in every American vessel bound to St. Domingo, or which is suspected of trading with the Haytians." The captain of the *Mars*—a ship that would later figure prominently in the legal cases about prize vessels from 1804—reported that "about forty of these vessels were at St. Jago when the Mars sailed." It is no doubt in relation to these stories of harassment of U.S. trade that the issue of sovereignty on the "ci-devant" Spanish side of Hispaniola began to come up.

The history of what to us looks like piracy but which read at the time as a complex legal dance of jurisdiction is best gleaned from U.S. court cases, which cited and reproduced Ferrand's documents. One case, involving the brig the *Happy Couple*, was tried in the British Court of Vice-Admiralty in Halifax, Nova Scotia, in the same time-frame as the events in question, and appears to have strongly influenced Dessalines; I will discuss that case in Chapter 3. But the most revealing documentation of Ferrand's French regime in Santo Domingo came in later cases, of which Dessalines of course would not have been aware, but which he arguably saw coming, as the major threat to Haitian sovereignty in his lifetime.

We learn in the lengthy 1808 Supreme Court appeal of a South Carolina circuit court case, Rose vs. Himely, that on February 23 of 1804, Ferrand, via French privateers, had seized the American vessel *Sarah*, commanded by Captain Rose. This was a banal and uninteresting event in the turbulent waters of the era, where "hostile takeovers" of floating commercial ventures were the rule rather than the exception. But on March 1, "Captain General Ferrand" had issued an *arête* from a French government tribunal in Santo Domingo, declaring that any vessels landing near "coast occupied by the revolters," would be "arrested by the vessels of the state."[100] Ferrand's *arête* made no distinction between Haiti and Santo Domingo on the island. As the Supreme Court summarized, Ferrand was "declaring the port of Santo Domingo to be the only free port in that island."[101] Was this legal? The court was divided, but noted that Ferrand had cited a legal precedent for his own *arête*: "General Leclerc had formerly issued a similar *arête*" on October 9, 1802. The court found the question of the legality of Leclerc's *arête* just as complicated as Ferrand's.

In another, similar case that came before the Pennsylvania Supreme Court in 1810, Cheriot vs. Foussat, the court quoted at length from a document produced by a special commission in Santo Domingo in July of 1804 to explore the seizure as lawful prize of the aforementioned American vessel *Mars*, seized sailing from Jeremie on February 3, 1804. This case documents that Ferrand was already seizing "neutral" vessels trading with Haiti from the very beginnings of independence, "In the name of the French government," and "presided by general Ferrand, captain general and commander in chief of the island of St. Domingo."[102] Once again, the document represents an existing French governmental sphere not just of the former Spanish colony, but of the island as a whole, based on the 1802 Leclerc legal *arêtes* on Santo Domingo as well as Saint-Domingue.

Dessalines was well aware of the critical nature of the challenges posed by the outpost of the French under the command of Ferrand. Having conquered the French, he was cruelly aware of their ongoing presence just on the other side of the border of the new black nation; and having conquered the French, he was then defeated by the French—on their territory, not his—six months later. But this defeat, barely mentioned in historiography, and there only in the most confused terms, was nothing compared to the legal challenges by the French to American commerce with Haiti. Was "the prohibition, by France, of all trade with the revolted blacks of Santo Domingo [...] an exercise of a municipal, not a belligerent right"?[103] How might the law of nations be applied to questions of slaves and sovereignty resulting from their insurrections anyhow? Slaves, considered as property of people rather than people per se, as the court reflected, were in an oblique relationship to the law of nations:

> The law of nations knows no such description of people as slaves, and it is not, in fact, every description of slaves who are destitute of rights of property; even within the bounds of the United States, widely different are the opinions entertained, and laws existing, on this subject.[104]

The court appeared sensible of the numerous paradoxes of a defeated French colonial power exerting its legal might against its former slaves, now free and arguably sovereign, and particularly of the ways that such positions could create injustices for American citizens. But the attempt to redress the injustices of the French claims was, in effect, beyond the scope of U.S. courts, as one Justice reflected: "It is not in our courts that redress is to be sought for the errors or injustices of foreign adjudications."[105] If France was on the island, and considered herself at war with Haiti, who was the U.S. to say that, legally, this was not the case? "France has not yet relinquished the contest, and until she does, I think that all ports of the island are still ports of France."[106] How can we read Dessalines's violence in quite the same way when we have read this legal opinion about the aftermath of the Haitian Revolution:

> This is civil war of the most odious kind; slaves against their masters. It is said, indeed, that they were free. But the same power which had declared them free, had since declared them to be slaves. But whether they are to be considered as free rebels, or as revolted slaves, we had no right to trade with them.[107]

Not only Dessalines's poetics and politics of violence, but Haiti's developmental trajectory quite generally must be considered in light of this virtually unknown yet successful strategic maneuvering of France to assert itself as Hispaniola's sovereign ruler—a sovereignty exerted with the single goal of marginalizing, not governing, Haiti. Slaves, as political nonentities, undecipherable with regard to the law of nations, were vulnerable to an almost entirely discursive argument—the decrees issued by Ferrand which only made their way to courts because of prize cases—against their emancipated sovereignty.

Thus in the 1811 legal case Clark vs. the United States, the earlier cases based on the Ferrand documents were used as precedent to conclude something that was almost entirely paradoxical by then, given that the French had been nowhere on the island since 1809: "The island of St. Domingo is a dependence of France."[108] This statement, nonsensical on a political/historical level, was nevertheless reiterated in the 1816 case Gelston and Schenck vs. Hoyt, where it was argued that "Courts cannot recognize the independence of revolted colonies."[109] The inability of a court to see past the last colonial claim to a decolonized black nation was argued in part on a precedent established in Rose vs. Himely. In Gelston vs. Hoyt they determined that the Chief Justice's "dictum" on Hayti in Rose vs. Himely should in fact be treated as an "opinion" of the Supreme Court. "Courts of justice must consider the ancient state of things as remaining unaltered, and the sovereign power of France over that colony as still subsisting."[110] This decision, which in effect determined that consent and recognition of independence must be given by the former colonizer before the "revolted colony" could be recognized as independent, even if the former colonizer had long since evacuated the premises, was also based on a legal case in England that similarly moved from questions of prize vessels to problems of the ongoing French sovereignty on the island of St. Domingo.

There was a similar case in England: a March 1808 case on "prize causes" brought before the Lords Commissioners of Appeals. The court in Gelston vs. Hoyt understood the Lords Commissioners as having "decided that St. Domingo was still, in point of law, under the dominion of France."[111]

Regardless of how one might read the independence of Haiti with regard to the law of nations, the law *courts* of nations were able to move from proclamations issued by the tattered establishment of a lone French general in Santo Domingo to confirmation of the French sovereignty of Hispaniola. Postcolonial stances by Dessalines—and postcolonial aggressions by Dessalines—require contextualization against not only the assertion that Hispaniola was still French, but that it was impossible to recognize a revolted colony's legal claims for independence without the preexisting permission of the defeated colonial power.

X-ing Out the Slave Narrative

Long after he had actually earned his new Arabic name, Malcolm X remained best known by the "X" conferred generically on Nation of Islam members to replace their "slave names"[112] until they had earned an Arabic one. This is no doubt because the "X" expressed something unique to his ideology and activism. This "prophet of Black rage" often indirectly suggested that outside of some future pan-African reinvention—from scratch—of society, African Americans could have no genuine hope. The "X" of his transitional status resonated with this oblique oxymoron of nihilistic rebirth. In 1962 he wrote, "There is no justice for us black people. There is no future for us nor our children in 'civilized' America."[113] Without overtly advocating the violence that had infused both the poetics and the tactics of Dessalines, Malcolm X taught hatred of the white blood that circulated in his own body, which he viewed as a legacy of rape, just as Dessalines chafed at breathing air that had been breathed by white masters.

When Dessalines claimed to have "avenged America," he was, in part, claiming a new start in radical fidelity to the historically oppressed peoples of post-Columbian America. In the Declaration of Independence he promised a stable government to the "indigenous people" of the country. Malcolm X and Dessalines, separated by language, nation, and almost two centuries, were nevertheless part of a black Atlantic tradition whose leaders have, all too often, had to imagine rather than read their dialogue.

Dessalines, in conjunction with his secretaries, left one of the earliest known *oeuvres* of radical black Atlantic political theory, in which he contested every trace of French colonial slaveholding culture—and, indirectly, showed exactly what black independence movements were up against. For Dessalines, despite his eighteenth-century birth, a genre like the slave narrative, born at the crossroads of slaves' trauma and the abolitionist politics of Christian redemption, could not have expressed his ferocious determination never to submit to Europeans or their psychological and cultural traditions. These unique documents, French-language challenges to "Frenchness," provide us with a pre-twentieth century and non-Anglophone model of the "beginning" of the postcolonial—marked with an "X" for its precocious prophecy of black rage.

Notes

1. Bill Ashcroft, Gareth Criffiths, and Helen Tiffin, *The Empire Writes Back: Theory and Practice in Post-Colonial Literatures* (New York: Routledge, 1989), 2.
2. Robert Wedderburn, "Extracts from Wedderburn's Speech in His Own Defence," in *Black Writers in Britain: 1760–1890*, ed. Paul Edwards and David Dabydeen (Edinburgh: Edinburgh University Press, 1995), 146.
3. Le Baron Linstant de Pradine, *Recueil général des lois et des actes du gouvernement d'Haïti* (Paris: A. Durand, Pédone-Lauriel, 1886), 1:4.
4. Frederick Cooper, "Postcolonial Studies and the Study of History," in *Postcolonial Studies and Beyond*, ed. Ania Loomba, Suvir Kaul, Matti Bunzl, Antoinette Burton, and Jed Esty (Durham, NC: Duke University Press, 2005), 403.
5. Cooper, "Postcolonial Studies," 401.
6. Ella Shohat, *Taboo Memories, Diasporic Voices* (Durham, NC: Duke University Press, 2006), 238. The essay "Notes on the 'Postcolonial'" was initially published in *Social Text* 31–32 (spring 1992), 99–113.
7. Shohat, *Taboo Memories*, 238.
8. Shohat, *Taboo Memories*, 233.
9. Paul Gilroy, *The Black Atlantic: Modernity and Double Consciousness* (Cambridge, MA: Harvard University Press, 1999), 1.

10. Michel-Rolphe Trouillot, "The Three Faces of Sans Souci," *Silencing the Past* (Boston: Beacon Press, 1995), 31–69.

11. Carolyn E. Fick, *The Making of Haiti: The Saint-Domingue Revolution from Below* (Knoxville, TN: The University of Tennessee Press, 1990), 212. Fick joins with C. L. R. James in asserting that Dessalines saw the stakes of independence with such acuity "because he, as opposed to Toussaint, could see no further" (233).

12. M.-E. Descourtilz, *Voyages d'un naturaliste*, 3 vols. (Paris: Dufart, 1809), 3:359–60.

13. "Proclamation relative au massacre des français," *Recueil général des lois et des actes du gouvernement d'Haïti*, 1:24.

14. *New York Commercial Advertiser*, June 4, 1804.

15. Jean-Jacques Dessalines, Declaration of Independence, January 1, 1804, Archives nationales, AF III 210. The Archives nationales manuscript of the declaration differs in small ways from the conventionally cited version in Thomas Madiou, *Histoire d'Haïti* (Port-au-Prince: J. Courtois, 1849), 3:115–18.

16. Although "empire" in this context most directly translates as "victory" or "ascendence," the other meaning of "empire" remains salient.

17. As we know, Dessalines was able to sign his name; examples of his signature are photographed in Timoléon C. Brutus, *L'Homme d'airain: Etude monographique sur Jean-Jacques Dessalines, Fondateur de la nation haïtienne* (Port-au-Prince: Imp. N. A. Théodore, 1947) and Gaétan Mentor, *Dessalines: L'Esclave devenu empereur* (Pétionville, Haiti: Gaétan Mentor, 2003). There are many examples of hand-signed manuscripts by Dessalines in the Caribbean, the United States, and Europe; the Boston Public Library has a particularly extensive series of autographed letters by Dessalines.

18. Editorial comment following the reprinting of a part of the Haitian Declaration of Independence, translated from a March 8 publication in New York, in *Journal des débats et lois du pouvoir législative: et des actes du gouvernement*, May 6, 1804.

19. David Patrick Geggus, *Haitian Revolutionary Studies* (Bloomington, IN: Indiana University Press, 2002), 208.

20. See Charles Moran, *Black Triumvirate: A Study of Louverture, Dessalines, Christophe— The Men Who Made Haiti* (New York: Exposition Press, 1957), 117.

21. Madiou, *Histoire d'Haïti*, 3:115.

22. Louis Boisrond-Tonnerre, *Mémoires pour servir à l'histoire d'Hayti* (A Dessalines: De l'imprimerie centrale du gouvernement, 1804; Port-au-Prince, Haiti: Editions des Antilles, 1991). I have not been able to consult the original edition.

23. Rainsford would have had access to the May 1805 imperial constitution, which consecrated January 1 to national independence festivals throughout Haiti, and his comment seems particularly geared to that historical information. Marcus Rainsford, *An Historical Account of the Black Empire of Hayti, Comprehending a View of the Principal Transactions in the Revolution of Saint Domingo* (London, Albion Press, 1805), 348.

24. Louis Dubroca, *Vida de J. J. Dessalines, gefe [sic] de los negros de Santo Domingo* (Mexico: Zúñiga y Ontiveras, 1806), 47, 68.

25. Drouin de Bercy, *De Saint-Domingue, de ses guerres, de ses révolutions, de ses ressources* (Paris: Hocquet, Barba, Eymery, et Lenormant, 1814), 24.

26. Pompey-Valentin, Baron de Vastey, *An Essay on the Causes of the Revolution and the Civil Wars of Hayti, being a sequel to the political remarks upon certain French publications and journals concerning Hayti*, trans. W.H. M.B. (Exeter: Printed at

the Western Luminary Office, For the Translator, For Private Circulation, 1823), 42–3. The reference for the French original is Baron de Vastey, *Essai sur les causes de la révolution et des guerres civiles d'Hayti, faisant suite aux réflexions politiques sur quelques ouvrages et journaux français, concernant Hayti* (Sans-Souci, Hayti: De l'Imprimerie royale, 1819), 42–3. Vastey's work is particularly significant because he documents the tremendous energies that went into debates during the reign of Henry Christophe around whether/how Haiti's independence from France should be formalized. Although scholars today assume that Haiti was understood internally to be independent as of 1804, Vastey's work demonstrates that a certain "invention of tradition" was still necessary to the consolidation of Haiti's postcolonial identity. Documents from the Christophe years may ultimately reveal the provenance of the particular vision of the Haitian Declaration of Independence that we find in Madiou.

27. François Joseph Pamphile de Lacroix, *Mémoires pour servir à l'histoire de la révolution de Saint-Domingue* (Paris: Pillet aîné, 1819), 2:254.

28. Placide Justin and James Barskett, *Histoire politique et statistique de l'île d'Hayti* (Paris: Brière, Libraire, 1826), 411.

29. Madiou, *Histoire d'Haïti*, 3:144–5.

30. Declaration of Independence, Archives nationales, AF III 210.

31. The "Journal de campagne" by Dessalines (and Boyer) is in the *Notes historiques de Moreau de Moreau de Saint-Méry*, Archives d'Outre-mer, F3, vol. 141, 497–508. This quote is from the last page, 508.

32. Who were the other secretaries of Dessalines, besides the three whose names certify the authenticity of his most prominent proclamations, viz. Boisrond-Tonnerre, Chanlatte, and Aimé? Timoléon Brutus describes them as a diverse and competitive group: "Les secrétaires dont il s'inspirait avec confiance ne s'entendaient pas sur un même sujet. Le bouillonant Boisrond-Tonnerre, quioque moins experimenté que Juste Chanlatte à qui l'on prêtait beaucoup plus de bon sens et aussi une science plus froide, flattait si habilement le chef, que sa voix l'emportait presque toujours sur le raisonnement pondéré des autres. Bazelais, Charéron, Dupuy, Diaquoi, Carbonne, Roux parmi les conseillers privés de Dessalines, restaient des secrétaires modérés." *L'Homme d'Airain*, 1:353.

33. The earliest version of this text that I have located in the U.S. media dates from June 4 in the *New York Commercial Advertiser*. In France, the *Journal des Débats* published what it called "l'extrait d'une proclamation qui fut publiée par Dessalines, le 28 avril dernier," on August 7, 1804. The *Journal* did not specify the source of the original French publication, and the extract given is derived from an American newspaper, documented only with the following reference: "*Nouvelles étrangères, Etats-Unis d'Amérique*, New Yorck [sic] 18 juin." The French version is somewhat abbreviated in comparison with American versions.

34. See Agent Roume, "Discours," 16 Pluviôse year 7 (February 4, 1799) (Port-Républicain: Gauchet et Co., 1799), 1.

35. Cited in Pamphile de Lacroix: "He addressed these memorable words to the division chief Savary, commander of the vessel: 'In overthrowing me, they have only knocked over in Saint-Domingue the trunk of the tree of the liberty of the blacks; it will grow back by the roots, for they are deep and numerous.'" *Mémoires*, 2:203.

36. *New York Commercial Advertiser*, June 4, 1804.

37. Proclamation of November 29, 1803, signed by "Dessalines, Christophe, Clerveaux" and the secretary B. Aimé, published in the *Journal des débats* of February 21, 1804. This text had been published in early January in the United States. The French copy, with many other news stories about Saint-Domingue and Jamaica, was apparently translated from articles in English papers published in early February, although a couple of the news items have their source in New York.

38. Boisrond-Tonnerre, *Mémoires*, 69.

39. Boisrond-Tonnerre, *Mémoires*, 119.

40. "Dégoutans" ("dégoutant") is one of many archaic spellings found in these texts from the early nineteenth century journalistic sphere. I have noted "sic" only by the most jarring of these spellings. Many of the translation choices made in nineteenth-century newspapers may also seem awkward to contemporary readers.

41. J. Bouvet de Cressé [and Juste Chanlatte], *Histoire de la Catastrophe de Saint-Domingue* (Paris: Librairie de Peytieux, 1824), 5.

42. Geggus, *Haitian Revolutionary Studies*, 301, fn. 71.

43. [Colin] Joan Dayan, *Haiti, History, and the Gods* (Berkeley, CA: University of California Press, 1995), 5.

44. Moran, *Black Triumvirate*, 118.

45. Frantz Fanon, *The Wretched of the Earth* (New York: Grove Press, 2004), 51.

46. *Recueil général des lois et des actes du gouvernement d'Haïti*, 1:3.

47. *Recueil général des lois et des actes du gouvernement d'Haïti*, 1:3

48. James Franklin, *The Present State of Hayti (Saint Domingo)* (London: J. Murray, 1828), 173.

49. *Repertory* (Massachusetts), May 8, 1804.

50. *Recueil général des lois et des actes du gouvernement d'Haïti*, 1:3.

51. Cornell West, "Malcolm X and Black Rage," in *Malcolm X in Our Own Image*, ed. Joe Wood (New York: St. Martin's Press, 1992), 48.

52. Robert Fatton, "The Haitian Authoritarian Habitus and the Contradictory Legacy of 1804," *The Journal of Haitian Studies* 10:1 (spring 2004), 22.

53. Fatton, "Authoritarian Habitus," 26.

54. "Proclamation du Gouverneur général qui accepte le titre d'empereur," *Recueil général des lois et des actes du gouvernement d'Haïti*, 1:14.

55. Throughout this chapter I uneasily employ the word "magic" because I feel that Dessalines believed in the capacity of projections of identity and beliefs to empower or subdue social forces. His textual legacies indicate his belief in a supernaturally justified overthrow of colonialism and vengeance of a double field of African ancestors and extinct indigenous populations.

56. *Recueil général des lois et des actes du gouvernement d'Haïti*, 1:13.

57. See *Minerva*, edited by Johann Wilhelm von Archenholz (Hamburg: Hoffmann, 1805), 276–93.

58. Cited in Susan Buck-Morss, *Hegel, Haiti, and Universal History* (Pittsburgh, PA: University of Pittsburgh Press, 2009), 61.

59. *Recueil général des lois et des actes du gouvernement d'Haïti*, 1:3.

60. The "Journal de campagne" was published in *Minerva* in the second half of 1804, under the title "Zur neuesten Geschichte von St. Domingo. Actenstücke zur Geschichte der Revolution in St. Domingo," 506–20.

61. "Journal de campagne," Archives d'Outre-mer, F3, vol. 141, 508.

62. *Recueil général des lois et des actes du gouvernement d'Haïti*, 1:3.

63. The manuscript closes "Au quartier-général du Cap le 8 février 1804, l'an 1er de l'Indépendance," and is labeled "Proclamation ou Sommation Faite au Général qui commandait à Santo-Domingo, Au Cap, 8 février 1804, Jean-Jacques Dessalines, Gouverneur-Général, aux habitants de la partie Espagnole," Archives d'Outre-mer, F3, vol. 141, 550.

64. Emilio Cordero Michel, "Dessalines en Saint-Domingue espagnol," in *Saint-Domingue espagnol et la revolution nègre d'Haïti*, ed. Alain Yacou (Paris: Karthala, 2007), 421.

65. Michel, "Dessalines en Saint-Domingue espagnol," 413.

66. Michel, "Dessalines en Saint-Domingue espagnol," 419.

67. Auguste Matinée, *Anecdotes de la révolution de Saint-Domingue racontées par Guillaume Mauviel*, in *Notices, Mémoires et documents publiés par la Société d'agriculture, d'archéologie et d'histoire naturelle*, vols. 6–8 (Saint-Lô: Imprimerie d'Elie Fils, 1885), 276.

68. "Proclamation [… de] Jean-Jacques Dessalines, Gouverneur-Général, aux habitants de la partie Espagnole," Archives d'Outre-mer, F3, vol. 141, 550.

69. *Recueil général des lois et des actes du gouvernement d'Haïti*, 1:36.

70. *Recueil général des lois et des actes du gouvernement d'Haïti*, 1:24.

71. The transcription of Creole, and especially of accent marks, is very irregular. Hérard Dumesle, *Voyage dans le nord d'Hayti, ou révélations des lieux et des monumens* (Aux Cayes, Haiti: De l'imprimerie du Gouvernement, 1824), 90.

72. Although to our ears, the image of the "growling storm" may seem like a poetic enhancement unlikely to have been featured in the discourse of slaves, Descourtilz specifically noted the use of this image in his record of his revolutionary-era sojourn in Saint-Domingue: "Les nègres appellent le tonnerre *mari-barou*. De là, *mari-barou li après cogné*, veut dire, le tonnerre gronde" ("The negroes call the thunder *mari-barou*. Thus, *mari-barou li après cogné* means the thunder is growling"). *Voyages*, 2:352, fn.1.

73. *Recueil général des lois et des actes du gouvernement d'Haïti*, 1:24.

74. The 1989 Deschamps edition of Madiou alters this phrase, perhaps correcting for incongruity, to "vivre avec nous dans les lois" rather than "les bois." However, the original edition of Madiou's transcription of the proclamation had "vivre avec nous dans les bois" ("to live with us in the woods"), as do all 1804 French versions or translations to English in the U.S. media.

75. Did Dessalines simply mean what Descourtilz had quoted him as saying, "Blanc qui savé manger calalou, li pour nous" ("The white person who knows how to eat callaloo is the one for us")? Descourtilz, *Voyages*, 3:281.

76. *New York Commercial Advertiser*, October 10, 1804.

77. Imperial nomination of Napoleon Bonaparte, *Moniteur universel*, May 1, 1804 (11 floréal, an 12 de la République).

78. *Moniteur universel*, 11 Floréal year 12.

79. The report of the "Organic Senatus Consultum" of Floreal, year 12, stated in Article 1 that "The government of the republic shall be entrusted to an emperor, who assumes the title of emperor of the French." *The Daily Advertiser*, July 26, 1804.

80. *New York Commercial Advertiser*, October 10, 1804.

81. It also, of course, follows the model of the non-hereditary transmission of power in Toussaint's 1801 constitution, but Dessalines gives this "American" practice an individualized and military ethos.

82. Article 1 in the "Discours préliminaire" of the Haitian Constitution, in *Recueil général des lois et des actes du gouvernement d'Haïti*, 1:48.

83. Madiou, *Histoire d'Haïti*, 3:170. The first trace of an actual Haitian announcement of empire dates from July 15, according to a news item that began to circulate in the American media in mid to late August. The *Enquirer* in Richmond, Virginia, published this "Extract of a letter from Aux Cayes, to a gentleman in Baltimore, dated July 15," on August 22, 1804: "This will serve to inform you, that the English admiral, who has communication with the Negroes of this Island, has put it into the head of Gen. Dessalines, to cause himself to be proclaimed 'Emperor of Hayti;' and he is to be crowned in a few days at Port-au-Prince." That vague but possibly authentic reference to a Haitian Empire in mid-July had been preceded, however, by rumors of a Haitian governmental mirroring of the new French Empire, rumors that were generated in the spirit of satire rather than actual news. For the mordant wits of the time, nothing made Napoleon Bonaparte more comical than the idea of a black Napoleon. The *New York Daily Advertiser* on July 26 cited a June 8 article from the *Cork Chronicle* in Ireland, describing the events in Paris as "The Imperial Pantomime," replete with proliferation of titles and dignities: "A marshal of the empire [is to be called] *'monsieur le maréchal,'* and when addressed colloquially or in writing, *'monseigneur.'*" The parody of the French imperial self-fashioning was only heightened by the prospect of a tropicalization of Napoleonism: "While all this gorgeous mummery is going forward at Paris, Dessalines, the sworn foe of the French race, is also founding a new government in *St. Domingo*, and in spirit and principle congenial with that of his defeated rival the emperor of the French." What the article is referring to, however, is not really a declaration of Haitian empire, but the third part of the "Acte d'indépendance," in which Dessalines, who is identified in the first two parts as "Général en chef," is proclaimed "Gouverneur général à vie d'Haïti" (*New York Commercial Advertiser*, March 24), with the right to name his successor. Despite the attempt to satirize Napoleon through the parallel with Dessalines, the *Cork Chronicle* was also intent on differentiating the profoundly humane Haitian justification for autonomous self-reinvention from what they saw as the formalistic frivolity of Napoleonic self-reinvention:

> There is this difference however between the gallant barbarian of Hayti and the new emperor; that the former found his country groaning under the most tremendous and sanguinary yoke in the world, from which he redeemed her, while the later had no such deliverance to effect, and overthrew only a domestic tyranny of the day, to establish one of perpetuity; that Dessalines was invited by his brethren in arms to hold the rude sway over a community of soldiers, while Bonaparte unelected and self-imposed, first seized upon power by force, continued it by fraud, and confirmed it by crimes.

84. *Recueil général des lois et des actes du gouvernement d'Haïti*, 1:48.

85. Dayan, *Haiti, History, and the Gods*, 13.

86. Dayan, *Haiti, History, and the Gods*, 10.

87. Homi K. Bhabha, *The Location of Culture* (New York: Routledge, 1994), 125.

88. *Recueil général des lois et des actes du gouvernement d'Haïti*, 1:4.

89. Madison Smartt Bell, *Toussaint Louverture: A Biography* (New York: Random House, 2008), 19.

90. Steeve Coupeau, *The History of Haiti* (Westport, CN: Greenwood Press, 2008), 29.

91. See Arthur L. Stinchcombe, *Sugar Island Slavery in the Age of Enlightenment* (Princteon, NJ: Princeton University Press, 1995), 205.

92. *Evening Post*, May 11, 1802.

93. Eugenio Matibag, *Haitian-Dominican Counterpoint: Nation, State, and Race on Hispaniola* (New York: Palgrave, 2002), 84.

94. Frank Moya Pons, *The Dominican Republic: A National History* (Princeton, NJ: Markus Weiner Publishers, 1998), 109. Unfortunately Moya Pons does not cite documentation for his assertion of this stunning symmetry between the declaring of independence from French colonialism in Haiti and of French rule in Santo Domingo.

95. American newspapers reported that when a large Spanish force from Puerto Rico landed, Ferrand "marched out at the head of a very fine corps, [...] [but] the major part of them, who were Spaniards, and who were exasperated by the outrages committed by the French against their country, deserted his ranks [...] Enraged to see himself thus abandoned by his only hope, Gen. Ferrand terminated his existence by blowing out his brains with a pistol." *Carthage Gazette,* January 30, 1809.

96. *Recueil général des lois et des actes du gouvernement d'Haïti*, 1:36–8.

97. Madiou, *Histoire d'Haïti*, 3:156.

98. Matinée, *Anecdotes de la révolution de Saint-Domingue*, 283.

99. *Abridgement of the Debates of Congress, From 1789 to 1856*, ed. Thomas Hart Benton (New York, D. Appleton, 1857–1861), 351.

100. *United States Supreme Court Reports*, vols. 5–8 (Rochester, NY: Lawyers Cooperative Pub. Co., 1901), 618–19.

101. *United States Supreme Court Reports*, 704.

102. *Reports of Cases Adjudged in the Supreme Court of Pennsylvania*, vol. 3 (T. & J. W. Johnson, & Co., 1889–1890), 225.

103. *United States Supreme Court Reports*, 608.

104. *United States Supreme Court Reports*, 704.

105. *United States Supreme Court Reports*, 707.

106. *United States Supreme Court Reports*, 707.

107. *United States Supreme Court Reports*, 615.

108. Clark vs. the United States was heard in the Circuit Court of Pennsylvania in October 1811. *Reports of Cases Determined in the Circuit Court of the United States*, vol. 3 (Philadelphia, PA: J. & J. W. Johnson, Law Booksellers, 1853), 101–7.

109. Edwin Burritt Smith and Ernest Hitchcock, eds., *Reports of Cases Adjudged and Determined in the Supreme Court of Judicature and Court for the Trial of Impeachments and Correction of Errors of the State of New York*, Book 5 (Newark, NJ: The Lawyers' Cooperative Publishing Company, 1883), 734.

110. Smith and Hitchcock, eds., *Reports of Cases Adjudged and Determined in the Supreme Court*, 745.

111. Smith and Hitchcock, eds., *Reports of Cases Adjudged and Determined in the Supreme Court*, 745.

112. As biographer Kofi Natumbu explains, "All Africans brought to the Americas were initially given the last name of the slaveholder who 'owned' them." *Critical Lives: The Life and Work of Malcolm X* (Indianapolis, IN: Alpha Books, 2002), 140.

113. Natumbu, *Critical Lives*, 255.

3

Dessalines's America

The news of the entry into the colony of two blacks from Saint-Domingue bearing the proclamations of Dessalines turned out to be only an unfounded rumor. But the decree I had the honor of mentioning to you [...] really was printed, in both French and English, in the newspapers of the United States.

Bertolio, May 3, 1804[1]

The Government of the Island of *Hayti* (St. Domingo) has directed the publication of the following arête in the papers of the United States.

Columbian Centinel (Massachusetts), May 5, 1804

1. Declaring Independence

The moving public spectacle of the inauguration of the first black president of the United States in January of 2009 prompted many Haitians and friends of Haiti to think back to the ascension of the first black leader in a New World nation, Jean-Jacques Dessalines, in January of 1804. The coming to power of Dessalines coincided with the celebration of the new nation's independence through a formal declaration of independence. Thomas Jefferson described the U.S. Declaration of Independence as "an instrument pregnant with [...] the fate of the world,"[2] and it was in Haiti, as David Armitage has noted, that the declaration of independence as a genre began its trajectory from a single nation's document to a "global history" of "imitations and analogues."[3]

Haiti's own Declaration of Independence or "Acte d'indépendance" is hardly fully described as an "imitation" or "analogue," however; it is entirely different from the U.S. Declaration of Independence, and stands as one of the most remarkable monuments of black Atlantic textual history. Furthermore, it was only one of a series of major independence documents released by the Haitian government in the independence era. This chapter argues that the Haitian independence documents also stand as a remarkable monument of *American* literary history, because Dessalines had, precisely, targeted America as a larger media sphere for his new sovereign speech acts. Americans across the cities and small towns of the eastern seaboard were a rapt audience— whether fascinated or horrified—for the literary self-construction of the new black nation's independence in 1804 and 1805.

This little-noticed phenomenon of Dessalines's strategic penetration of an American journalistic "republic of letters" also demonstrates that he had set his sights on a "market of letters": economic dealings with Americans that were underwritten partly by the legitimating quality of the international profile of Haitian government infrastructure and ideology, no matter how controversial its identity. The independence documents in the new nation implicitly articulated terms of parity with the U.S. as a fellow former colony. Dessalines's production of a poetics of the Haitian independence represents the forging of an intense and intentional media dialogue between Haiti and the United States as neighboring republics in hemispheric history.

Not only did Dessalines view America as the most effective media sphere to replace the relationship Toussaint had established with the French metropolitan republic of letters, he also saw himself, on a certain level, as American. "I have avenged America," he famously noted in his proclamation of April 28, 1804. As Ashli White notes in *Encountering Revolution*, "American" identity in the early nineteenth century was hardly constrained to the boundaries of the United States:

> Today "America" is a shorthand appellation for the United States (at least in North American circles), but in the eighteenth century [...] Saint-Domingue and the United States were both at times referred to as "America," and native born inhabitants from both domains were sometimes called "American."[4]

The United States was the most emblematic space of the political construction of what this wider-ranging Americanness *meant* (even if other parts of the Americas were more emblematic of its indigenous resistance to colonization). Dessalines's sense of his affiliations with the American environment appeared to be both ideological and economically pragmatic. He arguably saw the U.S. and Haiti as two countries of free men, despite

American slavery—which he directly critiqued—because of their self-emancipation from colonial rule.

This was a point that a writer identified only as "An Injured Man of Color" made in an essay of protest published in the *Commercial Advertiser* on May 25, 1804, against the routine use of the term "brigands" to identify the Haitians. "Why apply the title of brigands and robbers to the people of that Island?" he queried. Didn't the term implicitly tarnish the reputations of the American merchants who so happily traded with the "brigands," ostensibly trafficking in stolen goods gotten from the alleged robbers? "It is very strange, that masters of vessels, who go to that Island, and hold commercial intercourse with robbers, [...] publish to the world their own disgrace." But beyond this clever projection of the taint of brigandage back onto the name-callers rather than the insulted, the article called on American traders to recognize the Haitians fully as fellow anticolonial revolutionaries:

> When you fought for your independence, when you resisted the arm of Britain [...] were you not elated with your success? [...] Did your souls spurn at the man who dared to call you rebels and traitors? Is not the cause for which the Haytians fought the same in principle with yours?

Dessalines was no doubt also positively influenced by the fact that the U.S. had presented itself as the more neutral party in its extensive commerce with Saint-Domingue throughout the Haitian Revolution. Over the course of the Haitian Revolution, the Haitians had actively fought off the incursions of both the English and the Spanish, whereas there was no history of an attempted U.S. conquest of the French colony.

Even before Haitian independence, Dessalines had written to President Jefferson on June 23, 1803, that once the "executioners" of the blacks were expelled, Saint-Domingue would offer a tremendous economic opportunity for the U.S.:

> The people of the St. Domingue have thrown off the yoke of tyranny and sworn the expulsion of their executioners [...] Trade with the United States, Mr. President [...] presents an opportunity for the mariners of your nation. [...] I will assure, with all the authority that has been confided in me, that United States ships will be safe and able to profit from our exchanges.[5]

As Gordon S. Brown notes, Jefferson and Madison, after confessing the existence of this letter to the French agent in the U.S., Louis André Pichon, had agreed not to answer Dessalines.[6]

This history likely informed Dessalines's active pursuit of U.S. publication of his government's early documents. Haitian independence documents were as a rule printed significantly later in Europe than in the U.S., often with notes that the texts had come via New York or other American cities. The German philosopher Hegel and his contemporaries, for example, mainly encountered the major documents of the Haitian independence in the newspaper *Minerva* (as discussed in Chapter 1) in the spring of 1805.

After the defeat of the French, the U.S. stood to become Haiti's primary trading partner, and the economic intimacies that arose from this circumstance are the major underpinning of the unexpected and brief openness of the U.S. to Haitian international identity politics. Dessalines wrote a letter to an American merchant that was translated and published in the Philadelphia *Aurora General Advertiser* on September 4, 1804, in which he said "The people of your country, who wish to come to this island for the purpose of opening a store, or merely to sell their cargoes, shall always find safety and protection." (This surprisingly overt claim of Americans' rights in Haiti was articulated in contrast to Dessalines's complaint in the letter about U.S. pursuit of entirely unregulated exports from the island: "I forbid a foreigner entering our ports [...] purchasing produce directly from the hands of individuals, to the detriment of the administration, or the merchant already established").

Given the failure of the U.S. to recognize Haiti's independence until 1862 under Lincoln, it might seem logical to assume that there was a united front of revulsion at the emergence of a black nation. But the journalistic record shows that, initially, this was not the case. The entrenched opposition of American abolitionist and pro-slavery groups was triangulated by maritime merchants, whose relationship to race politics proved economically contingent and pragmatic. The field of Americans looking with interest to the economic vacuum left by the French in Saint-Domingue was also broadened by resentment of Napoleon Bonaparte and a desire to operate with full autonomy in the New World geographic area. An editorial in the Maine *Kennebec Gazette* on May 23, 1804, dismissed Jefferson's desire not to offend the French over Haiti with the following caustic critique: "There is more hope that St. Domingo will preserve its independence than that we shall ever *retrieve* ours."

Federalists, according to White, were often aligned with pro-Haitian trade positions through their resistance to Napoleonic projections of dominion, whereas Democratic Republicans were often aligned with anti-Haitian trade positions articulated around respect for the law of nations and preservation of American slavery interests.[7] Democratic Republicans tended to view Haitian independence as a Pandora's box with regard to American slavery. But responses to Haitian independence often emerged in the form of debate and in specific, highly variable reactions to Dessalines's proclamations. Even one of the newspapers most associated with Democratic Republican positions, the Philadelphia *Aurora General Advertiser*, initially acknowledged Haiti's right to declare independence. Indeed, the paper described the right to declare independence as "unquestionably inherent" in the black republic:

> We have read part of the address of the black general Dessalines, on the declaration of the independence of St. Domingo. On this subject we presume there are few who entertain dissimilar sentiments: the right to proclaim independence was unquestionably inherent in the people of that island, and there is not a doubt but that the colonial system, pursued since the assumption of the supreme authority of France by Bonaparte, provoked the severance at an earlier period than it would otherwise have taken place.[8]

The editorial went on to state firmly, "The United States are necessarily much interested in St. Domingo."

In the early Haitian independence era, the U.S., no matter how firmly aligned on levels of cultural and ethnic identification with the European metropoles, flirted with the notion of a New World ("American") commercial sphere in which, by dint of geography and the common structural value of anticolonial "freedom," it would be the dominant player.

This window of New World or "American" identification did not stay open for long. Congressional momentum gathered over the course of 1805 for meaningful (rather than symbolic) legal limits on U.S. trade with Haiti, and by late February of 1806, a law was passed in Congress prohibiting it. But throughout 1805 and 1806, these commercial controls were highly debated at every pass, and the effects of the prohibition were gradual. February of 1806 did not represent an actual beginning of a true embargo. Tim Matthewson notes that official trade statistics, while not thoroughly reliable, nevertheless show a dramatic trend downward from $6.7 million in U.S. exports in 1806, "to $5.8 million in 1807 and to $1.5 million in 1808."[9] Such statistics suggest that the embargo did not begin to have teeth in terms of compliance for at least a year after its February 1806 establishment, but had radically reined in U.S. trade relationships with Haiti over the course of 1807 and above all in 1808. In effect, most of the 1804–1806 Dessalines era was a time of robust U.S. trade relationships with Haiti, mediated by dynamic cultural encounter in the journalistic field.

In this chapter I present Dessalines's conquest of access to a U.S. journalistic sphere for which news of the Haitian independence—still considered subversive information in many environments—became part of the profile of current events. I then explore the gradual but undeniable foreclosure of an initial U.S. openness to Haiti, not in terms of American ideological camps and what Matthewson no doubt rightly describes as the eventual "Triumph of Racism,"[10] but in terms of journalistic and political

debates involving Haiti. I examine journalistic responses to the 1805 continuation of General Ferrand's strategies for French sovereignty on Hispaniola
(already foregrounded in terms of the events of 1804 in Chapter 2), and to the
problem of international "neutrality" in relation to a nation of former slaves.
These debates, while certainly not exclusive in influencing the determination
of anti-Haitian politics in the U.S., allow us to trace Haiti/U.S. international relations in an interactive sense, as a dialogue in which Haiti was
active in representing itself. Among the various historical narratives one
could develop to tell the story of this era, the one I present here is narrated
by, with, or against Dessalines; it is the story of what Dessalines meant for
America, and what America meant for Dessalines.

Read All About It: Anticolonial Victory

The first independence proclamation issued by Dessalines was not the Haitian
Declaration of Independence itself, but a shorter text from November 29, 1803,
co-signed by Dessalines's fellow generals Henry Christophe and Philippe
Clerveaux. This document, which states unequivocally, "L'indépendence
de Saint-Domingue est proclamée" ("We declare the independence of
Saint-Domingue"), clearly predates the renaming of the French colony
of Saint-Domingue as "Hayti." The November 29, 1803, date marks the
immediate aftermath of the November 18 defeat of the French at Vertières,
the final period of Dessalines's negotiations of the French surrender with
General Rochambeau, and, most importantly, the date of the evacuation
of the French army from Cap Français. The symbolic departure of the
French as masters of the colony was accompanied, as historian Thomas
Madiou notes, by the first major public celebration of Haiti's independence
in the streets of Le Cap, complete with "hymnes de liberté"[11] ("anthems of
freedom"). This first independence proclamation would take the American
journalistic sphere by storm, resulting in the odd coincidence by which U.S.
readers were deluged with news of an independence proclamation for the
new black republic during exactly the same window of time in which the
formal Haitian Declaration of Independence was being produced: January of
1804. There is an eerie quality to the simultaneity of independence in Haiti
and in U.S. media coverage, a "real time" convergence of representation and
reality.

How had the proclamation gotten to U.S. editors? We see Dessalines's
outreach to U.S. journalists in the tantalizing trace of a note from his secretary
in the proclamation, the mysteriously named B. Aimé, to Philadelphia
newspaperman Samuel Relf. Aimé asked Relf, in the name of the free men
of Saint-Domingue and the unbiased nature of all republics, to publish the
proclamation he was sending.

Monsieur Relf,

Vous êtes invité, au nom des hommes libres de St. Domingue, et au nom de l'impartialité qui doit caracteriser tout bon républicain, d'insérer dans votre prochain numéro la proclamation incluse. Vous obligerez infiniment

Votre très humble

B. Aimé

Secrétaire

(Mr. Relf,

You are invited, in the name of the freemen of St. Domingo, and, above all, of the impartiality which ought to be the stamp of a good republican to insert in your next number, the enclosed proclamation.

You will infinitely oblige your most humble and obedient servant,

B. Aimé)[12]

Relf (1776–1823) was the publisher of the *Philadelphia Gazette and Daily Advertiser*, an evening newspaper in Philadelphia, but the proclamation first appeared, with the note published as a preface to the proclamation, in a daytime paper, *Poulson's Daily Advertiser*, on January 5, 1804. It then appeared, without the note from Aimé, in the *Aurora General Advertiser* on January 5, and in the *Gazette and Daily Advertiser* on the evening of January 6. Since Aimé's poignant note was often published with the proclamation, it arguably constitutes a part of this first independence text.

There is currently no known original or authenticated contemporary duplicate of this first proclamation of independence from the French. That absence of an original,[13] combined with the fact that it was formally issued from "Fort Dauphin" when Dessalines was known to have been at Le Cap on November 29, led Madiou to categorize the text as apocryphal.[14] I have argued in Chapter 2 that the proclamation nevertheless bears all the hallmarks of Dessalines's literary style. The lack of original or contemporary duplicate copies could well have resulted from the widespread distribution of the text to U.S. newspapers, which almost universally failed to maintain archives of correspondence. The mismatch between the date and Dessalines's whereabouts that day should not be used as a decisive marker, because early Haitian independence documents were sometimes backdated in the early independence to consolidate their symbolic impact. The placement of the text in U.S. newspapers by Dessalines's own secretary is surely evidence of its authenticity. Aimé definitely was the signatory to other texts, sometimes simply of duplicates collected by Moreau de St. Méry, such as a handwritten copy of the "I have avenged America" proclamation,[15] so we know that he was a real associate of Dessalines. (I will also discuss further on subsequent communications of his on behalf of Dessalines in the U.S. media.)

This November 29 proclamation was clearly received as a proclamation of independence by U.S. newspapers. The *New York Daily Advertiser* of January 7, 1804, preceded the document with the note, "The following proclamation of independence of the island of St. Domingo has been published by the three principal military chiefs." The *Trenton Federalist* (New Jersey) of January 9, 1804, noted "The Island of St. Domingo has been declared independent by the Negro Chiefs [...]." Several newspapers, including the *Middlebury Mercury* (Vermont) on January 18, included under the headline of the document the line "In the name of the black people and men of color in St. Domingo."

This first proclamation of independence was also fairly conciliatory in nature. Dessalines summons up the span of more than a decade in which the blacks had spilled their own blood to fight the longstanding errors of the French, but he notes also that the blacks have allies outside of their own ranks: "Nous savons qu'il est parmi vous des hommes qui ont abjuré leur anciennes erreurs, renoncé à leur folles prétentions et reconnu la justice de la cause pour laquelle nous versons notre sang depuis douze années" ("We know that there are among you men who have renounced their longstanding errors, their insane claims, and recognized the justice of the cause for which we have been spilling our blood for twelve years"). This first proclamation reached out in fraternity: "Nous traiterons en frères ceux qui nous aiment" ("We will treat those who love us like brothers").

At this point of the independence, for Dessalines, the god who protected the blacks—and who so resembles both of the distinctly separate gods of the Oath of the Caiman Woods—was guiding not their vengeance, but their clemency: "Le Dieu qui nou protège, le Dieu des hommes libres nous ordonne de leur tendre nos bras victorieux" ("The God who protects us, the God of free men, orders us to open our victorious arms"). Here the god of the freed slaves is guiding their arms, just as in the Oath of the Caiman Woods ("li va conduit bras nous"). This structure may have resonated with readers who had seen Toussaint Louverture use a rhetoric similar to that in the Oath of the Caiman Woods much earlier, in a 1797 proclamation published in the U.S.:

> The God of nature, he who governs the universe, will not forsake us whilst we are employed in the defense of a cause which is become his own, hence we only endeavor to restore men to the liberty which he gave them, and which other men would have deprived them of without offending and contravening his immutable will. We are but the instruments of his mighty power, and the executors of his just vengeance. He employs Frenchmen to break the chains under the weight of which people of both hemispheres groan.[16]

The editorial comment prefacing Toussaint's remarks had noted how unlike normal military discourse they were:

> Toussaint Louverture, has addressed the military in warm language, urging them by every motive of liberty, patriotism, and even humanity [...] His address, on this occasion, dated the 21st of May, concludes thus, which it must be confessed is not much in the modern style of military men--.

Toussaint may have used a particular language of natural and divine revindication for the anti-slavery cause specifically when addressing the mixed racial ranks of the French army (all "French" by the terms of the time) in Saint-Domingue; his persuasive style in speaking to his soldiers seems rooted in the oral religious/political tradition of which the Oath of the Caiman Woods is one manifestation. If this style was rare in Toussaint's rhetoric, however, it was the norm for Dessalines, and required that American readers immerse themselves in a relatively untranslated version of Haitian discourse.

The November 29 document sped through the American journalistic public sphere like wildfire, appearing in most towns or cities with newspapers on the eastern seaboard and into the south:

January 5	*Poulson's Daily Advertiser*	Philadelphia, PA
January 6	*Evening Post*	New York, NY
	Gazette of the United States	Philadelphia, PA
January 7	*American Citizen*	New York, NY
	Daily Advertiser	New York, NY
January 9	*Trenton Federalist*	Trenton, NJ
	Centinel of Freedom	Newark, NJ
January 10	*Connecticut Herald*	New Haven, CT
	Federal Republican	Elizabethtown, NJ
January 12	*National Intelligencer and Washington Advertiser*	Washington D.C.
January 13	*Newburyport Herald*	Newburyport, MA
January 14	*Mirror of the Times, & General Advertiser*	Wilmington, DL
	New England Repertory	Newburyport, MA
	Newport Mercury	Newport, RI
	Providence Gazette	Providence, RI
	Virginia Argus	Richmond, VA
January 16	*Reporter*	Brattleboro, VT
	Salem Register	Salem, MA
January 17	*Republican Spy*	Boston, MA
	Farmers' Cabinet	Amherst, MA
	Oracle Post	Portsmouth, NH

January 18	*Charleston Courier*	Charleston, SC
	Courier	Norwich, CT
	Middlebury Mercury	Middlebury, VT
January 19	*United States Chronicle*	Providence, RI
	Windham Herald	Windham, CT
January 20	*Eastern Argus*	Portland, ME
January 21	*Sun*	Dover, NH
January 24	*Bee*	Hudson, NY
	Columbian Minerva	Dedham, MA
	Spooner's Vermont Journal	Windsor, VT
January 25	*Hampshire Gazette*	Northampton, MA
January 30	*Sun*	Pittsfield, MA
February 3	*Farmer's Gazette*	Sparta, Georgia
February 7	*Green Mountain Patriot*	Peacham, VT
February 11	*Political Observatory*	Walpole, NH
February 22	*Tennessee Gazette and Mero-District Advertiser*	Nashville, TN

From this pattern of dissemination, it is clear that the Haitian independence—or, in the words of a racist article on the political personalities of Haiti, the *"New Black Republic* of St. Domingo" (*Otsego Herald*, March 29, 1804)—was a topic of very widespread public interest.

We see the political credibility applied to the new black republic, and the sense of parallel lives of democracy, even in a debate on the importation of slaves in Congress in February of 1804, where a motion was entertained to tax purchases of slaves. Mr. Bard gave St. Domingo as the exemplification of the ability of slaves to learn—even to learn the art of war—to avenge themselves, and to assert the rights of man:

> [They are] capable of becoming proficients in the art of war. To be convinced of this we have only to look at St. Domingo. There the negroes felt their wrongs, and have avenged them; they learned the rights of man, and asserted them; they have wrested the power from their oppressors, and have become masters of the island.[17]

Declaring Black Sovereignty, Introducing Hayti

The actual Haitian Declaration of Independence or "Acte d'indépendance" arrived in the U.S., in partial form, in early March. The only known Haitian government-issued copy of the Declaration of Independence was recently uncovered by Duke University doctoral student Julia Gaffield in the British National Archives. The most detailed information about this document, as Gaffield found, came from British diplomatic notes and correspondence.

In early January of 1804, the British Agent Edward Corbet, who had negotiated with Toussaint Louverture earlier in the decade, was sent by Governor Nugent of Jamaica to re-initiate negotiations with General-in-Chief Dessalines. Captain Perkins brought the *Tartare*, with Corbet aboard, to Port-au-Prince on January 15, after previous adventures in the port of Jérémie.[18] Madiou reprints part of Dessalines's January 19 response to Nugent, in which he thanked Nugent for the return of 34 Haitian prisoners, captured by the British as "French" prisoners during the British–French hostilities of the Haitian Revolution.[19] The diary of Lady Nugent, wife of Governor Nugent, recounts that Corbet returned from Haiti on the evening of January 24, and that he met with her husband concerning Dessalines's response on January 25.[20] Corbet's own January 25 notes outline his presentation to Nugent of a Haitian Declaration of Independence that was, sometime between his arrival on January 15 and his departure after January 19, hot off the presses in Haiti:

> I now beg leave to lay before your Excellency their declaration of Independence. This piece, wherever it may have been composed, was not published until after my arrival at Port-au-Prince, for the Copy I now have the honor of presenting to you had not been an hour from the press.[21]

We can therefore firmly associate the Haitian government printing of the Declaration of Independence with the third week in January of 1804. Unfortunately, no authenticated original handwritten copy is currently known to exist, although a number of non-signed, handwritten duplicates can be found in various archives, including the Archives nationales in Paris,[22] the Archives d'Outre mer in Aix, and the Jamaican archives.

The process of production revealed in Corbet's correspondence provides important confirmation of several things: 1) that the Declaration had definitively been printed by the *imprimerie du gouvernement* as a lengthy three-part text sometime in the third week of January of 1804; 2) that Corbet did not know the actual date or process of composition of the Haitian Declaration of Independence; and 3) that there was an active printing infrastructure in Haiti from the inception of the independence period. This last point is particularly revealing because there appear to have been no functioning newspapers in Haiti in the early months of 1804. Although the *Gazette du Cap* would ultimately replace the earlier *Gazette de St. Domingue*, the first newspaper in independent Haiti, the *Gazette politique et commerciale d'Hayti* was first published in November of 1804.[23] However, the Bibliothèque des Pères du Saint Esprit at the Collège St. Martial in Port-au-Prince also includes printed government documents—some of them hand-signed by Dessalines—from as early as March of 1804. But with the Declaration of

Independence, we know that the Haitian government was engaged in active self-representation at home as well as in its outreach to U.S. newspapers.

The Haitian Declaration of Independence is constituted of three sections. The first documents the assembly of the General-in-Chief of the "indigenous army" and his military leaders to form "un gouvernement stable" ("a stable government") for the "indigenous" inhabitants of the newly named republic of Hayti. Dessalines and his military leaders also swear an oath to live free of colonial rule and enslavement, or die. (This oath shows the "liberty or death" motif that was so influential in the American Revolution.) It lists 36 signatories from different sections of the Haitian army. It is in the lengthy second section, addressed not to an assembly of generals but to the people—"Citoyens!"—that Dessalines fully reveals his narrative voice. As the guardian of the idol of freedom to which his people have sacrificed themselves, Dessalines now enjoins them to join him in swearing to live free or die. In the third section, which is very short, the "generals in chief of the armies of the island of Hayti," proclaim Dessalines "Governor General for Life."

We may someday find indisputable proof that the three sections of the Declaration were in fact articulated and distributed on January 1 of 1804, as their dates would indicate; but in the current absence of that proof, it is worth noting that although the first and second parts of the Declaration are coherently related, the third part very plausibly could have been issued on a separate occasion. It is curious that Dessalines is referred to as "général en chef," in the first part, but "gouverneur général à vie" (the title Toussaint Louverture had given himself in 1801) in the third part. If the assembled generals had gone to the trouble in one meeting of approving the authority of Dessalines as General-in-Chief, would they then have moved on in the same meeting to nominate him as Governor-General for life, without revising the first document? It is also significant that the names of the military signatories are not the same in these first and last parts of the *Acte*. The first part is signed by six *généraux de division*—Christophe, Pétion, Clerveaux, Geffrard, Vernet, Gabart—and then by twelve *généraux de brigade*, five *adjudans-généraux*, two *chefs de brigade*, ten *officiers de l'armée*, and Boisrond-Tonnerre, making 36 signatures in all. By contrast, the third part of the *Acte* is signed by 17 officers in total, without the groupings by rank.

Although the version that Corbet brought to Nugent in the third week of January was the full tripartite text, the U.S. publication of the Declaration emerged piecemeal. The first U.S. publication that I have found is a translation of a long excerpt of the middle part in the *Evening Post* of New York, and dates from March 7. It was prefaced by this comment: "Extract from a Proclamation issued by Dessalines, General in Chief of the indegenous [*sic*] army at Saint Domingo, on or about the 16th of January last—." The editor of the *Evening Post* provided no further information, unfortunately, about the provenance of the text. Could this attribution be correct—was Dessalines's lengthy personal address to the citizens of Haiti first proclaimed during the period of Corbet's visit to Port-au-Prince?

The March 7 document in the *Evening Post* is the long prose statement by Dessalines that forms the second part of the *Acte*. Here is the *Evening Post* text with its vivid and challenging language, as the newspaper reading public of the East coast first received it:

The First Year of the Independence of the People of Hayti
Citizens Countrymen,
I have assembled on this solemn day those brave military men, who, on the eve of collecting the last breath of liberty, have lavished their blood to save it—Those Generals who have guided your efforts against tyranny, have not yet done enough for your happiness. The French name still hangs your country with mourning—every thing traces back the remembrance of the cruelties of that butchering people: —Our laws, our manners, our towns, all still wear the French image—what do I say! There exists Frenchmen [*sic*] in our Island, and you think yourselves free and independent of that Republic, which, it is true, has combated against all nations, but which has never vanquished those who would be free.

Ah! What victims of credulity and indulgence during fourteen years— Vanquished, not by French arms, but by the deceitful eloquence of the Proclamations of their agents. When shall we get tired of breathing the same air with them? What have we in common with a people who commit such cruelties? Compared to our patient moderation, their colour to ours, the extent of the seas which separate us, our avenging clime—all tell us sufficiently that they are not our brothers—that they never will become so—and that if they find refuge amongst us, they will still be the plotters of troubles and divisions.

Indegenous [*sic*] Citizens, Men, Women, Girls and Children—cast your eyes around every part of this Island—Seek you therein your wives, your husbands, your brothers, your sisters?—what do I say—seek you therein your children, your sucking babes? What is become of them?—the prey of French vultures! Instead of these endearing objects, the eye, dismayed, beholds their assassins, like tigers trickling yet with blood, whose presence reproaches your insensibility and guilty slowness in avenging them.

Remember that you have done nothing if you do not give nations a terrible but just example of that vengeance, which a people, proud of having recovered their liberty and jealous of maintaining it, ought to exercise. —Let us terrify all those who would dare ravish it from us—Let us begin with the French.

At the same time, on March 7, another version began to circulate widely. *The Daily Advertiser* of New York contextualized it as a fragment of a longer document provided by a survivor from Les Cayes: "By a gentleman Who Lately escaped, with other unfortunate sufferers from Aux Cayes, we are favoured with the following." This document was an entirely different translation, suggesting that it was in fact produced from a different copy of the text, rather than a reprint of the recent publication in the *Evening Post*. It also provides one half of a paragraph that is missing in the *Evening Post* version:

> Why do you delay to appease their manes.[24] Do you think your remains may repose in peace with those of your fathers, before you chase away tyranny? Your ashes in your tombs, without having avenged them? No, their bones would repulse yours with scorn.

The editor of the *Daily Advertiser* closed the long text with the reflection, "The above is evidently in a very imperfect and mutilated form; but to some of our readers, we believe, it will not be altogether uninteresting."

An additional reference to the Haitian Declaration of Independence appeared in *Poulson's Daily Advertiser* on March 10, identified as "News from Charleston" where it had apparently been issued on February 23: "A Proclamation of Dessalines, the Brigand Commander of St. Domingo, issued about the first of January, has been received at Kingston—in which he has declared that Island Independent, under the aboriginal name of *D'Hayte*." The timing, however, suggests that the news probably relates to Corbet's report in late January, since it would have taken only a short period of time for the mails to go from Haiti to Kingston, and an additional two-and-a-half or more weeks to arrive in Charleston, which points to late January transmission of the news. That brief news item was the first token that the French name, Saint-Domingue, would no longer "hang the country with mourning"—Haiti was born. At the same time, the identification of Dessalines as "Brigand Commander" implicitly cast Haiti as a Brigand Republic.

On March 24, the New York *Commercial Advertiser* published two more texts, correlating to the first and third parts of the Declaration of Independence, with this note: "The following article contains the sentiments and proceedings of General Dessalines, and his officers, respecting their future operations in the island of Hayti." This publication was followed by an individual's defense of the blacks against reports of violence against whites. That report, which was published in many newspapers, not only claimed that the final massacres by the French were mistakenly being blamed on the blacks, it evoked the violence the Haitians had suffered from dogs as ordered by Rochambeau. Overall, the testimonial was meant to assure Americans that the blacks were fair and welcoming trading partners. The independence was issuing in a new era of American trade:

The blacks have treated the whites who have not been in arms against them with hospitality and good faith; and have been punctual in their contracts. Many of the enormities reported, were committed by the mortified and chagrined French, and then laid to the charge of the blacks. [...] They [the blacks] have suffered so many cruelties from the two legged and four-footed bloodhounds, that they give them no quarter or mercy when they fall into their hands. Foreigners, particularly Americans, trading with them, are sure to meet with hospitality and fair dealing.

This same document was published in *Poulson's Daily Advertiser* on March 27 with a note attesting to receipt of "a complete copy of the discourse of General Dessalines, which preceded the Declaration of Independence of that Island." The editor of *Poulson's* spoke enthusiastically of the document's interest: "We shall take the earliest opportunity of giving it entire. The enthusiasm with which it was received may be collected from the account of the proceedings that followed its delivery and which we have deemed too interesting to withhold for a moment from our readers." (Unfortunately, no news appears to explain that reference to the "proceedings that followed its delivery.")

To my knowledge, no complete version of the Haitian Declaration of Independence ever appeared in the United States in 1804. Not only was the long middle part by Dessalines abridged, but the three separate parts of the *Acte* were not published together as one entity related to a single ceremony. Although the two major forms of the story of the Declaration of Independence—the long excerpt of the middle part as presented by the survivor from Aux Cayes, and the first and third parts together—were fairly widely published in the U.S., they were certainly less broadly disseminated, and in more fragmentary form, than the late November 1803 proclamation of independence. Was the document intended for internal consumption in Haiti rather than the eyes of the world? Or had the government expected Corbet and the British colonial government to promptly circulate it in the media, and then failed to rectify the distribution process after it turned out that they did not? Or is it possible that it was sent to the government of the U.S., rather than to newspapers, and that the government did not share it with the public? According to Tim Matthewson, Jefferson viewed direct communication with the government of Dessalines as risky, in relation both to the ever-watchful French and his Southern constituents.[25] The highly ambiguous sovereignty of Dessalines's Haiti in effect necessitated that the public sphere disseminate some of the communications that foreign governments refused to answer or acknowledge.

Dessalines's texts are characterized by an acute awareness of the psychological impact and manipulative potential of political proclamations; their power is a frequent subject of his own proclamations. In the "Declaration of

Independence," Dessalines condemns "notre crédulité et notre indulgence, vaincu non par les armées françaises, mais par la piteuse éloquence des proclamations de leurs agens" ("our gullibility and indulgence, vanquished not by the French armies, but by the piteous eloquence of their agents' proclamations"). He was likewise conscious of the potency of his own political image, and relished the horror he inspired in proponents of colonialism. In the Declaration of Independence, he urged, "Rappelle-toi [...] que mon nom est devenu en horreur à tous les peuples qui veulent l'esclavage, et que les despotes et les tyrans ne le prononceront qu'en maudissant le jour qui m'a vu naître" ("Remember [...] that my name is held in horror by all the people who wanted slavery, and that despots and tyrants pronounce it only while cursing the day I was born").

Despite the mysteries of its creation and dissemination, as portions of Haiti's Declaration of Independence circulated in the U.S. there was no question but that readers understood that it marked the firm sovereignty of the new nation. Many minds turned to the potential, and the lost potential, of a strong American relationship with Haiti. The *Commercial Advertiser* was one of a slew of papers to publish quotes from a document produced by a ministerial-level writer in England who waxed nostalgic about the now lost possibility of an American St. Domingo:

> If at any future time, it should be necessary that some Christian power should take possession of St. Domingo, we sincerely hope it will pass into the hands of the Americans. Situated as the United States are, possessing an immence length of coast, with little variation in their exportable commodities, to enable their rapidly increasing population to maintain a profitable intercourse with the rest of the world, some portion of the sugar trade is absolutely necessary. During her warfare with France, America might easily have secured St. Domingo [...] The possession of St. Domingo would have rendered the political and mercantile interest of Great Britain and America reciprocal and mutual.[26]

Another British editorial was published in *Poulson's American Daily Advertiser* (March 20, 1804) noting that the departure of the French "has completely established the sovereignty of the Blacks over the island of St. Domingo." In the face of this black sovereignty, the writer expressed sincere hopes that there would never again be a British attempt at "territorial acquisition" by either "conquest or treaty," but that future relations would be defined by "an intercourse purely commercial." How could this "intercourse purely commercial" not be the speciality of the U.S.?

"Printed, Published, and Posted Up"

Dessalines's manifest desire to defend himself to a national or international public through carefully coordinated interactions with American newspapers was next laid out in a decree with the date of January 14, 1804, that was published in numerous U.S. newspapers, in French and in English, in late March of 1804. This decree, offering to pay for the repatriation of black and mixed-race refugees from the Haitian Revolution in the U.S., contained the eloquent instructions that "this decree shall be printed, published, and posted up; and a copy thereof shall be immediately forwarded to the Congress of the United States." Or in French, "Veut et entend que le dit arrête soit imprimé, publié et affiché, et qu'un exemplaire en soit adressé directement au Congrès des Etats-Unis d'Amérique." Printed, published, and posted up, with copies to the center of the American political process: this was apparently the larger ambition, haphazardly implemented, of the government of Dessalines for his proclamations.

The January 14, 1804, decree on the repatriation of Haitians made it clear that the desirability of a close communicative relationship between the U.S. and Haiti did not outweigh Haitian empathy for blacks languishing in a country of slavery: "gémissant dans l'étendue des Etats Unis d'Amérique, retenus par défaut de moyens" ("suffering in the United States of America, for want of the means of returning"). The repatriation decree is also a notable text in the journalistic sphere because unlike the other proclamations issued from Haiti, the French versions do not correspond to the standards of educated French. The *United States Gazette* in Philadelphia on March 29 published a version that differed in several minute points from the version published in the *Evening Post* in New York on March 30. The *Gazette* version contains this line: "Il sera alloué aus le capitaines Américains, une some de quarante gourdes pour chaque individu qu'ils transporteront en ce pays." (The *Gazette* translated and corrected this sentence to read "There shall be allowed to the captains of American vessels, the sum of forty dollars for each individual they may restore to this country"). The *Evening Post* rendered the same line as "Il sera alloué aux dis capitaines Américains, une some de quarante gourdes pour unique individus qu'ils transporteront en ce pays." The discrepancies between the *Gazette* and *Evening Post* versions of the text perhaps can be attributed to editors' attempts to transcribe with authenticity a text that was difficult to read, either in terms of its handwriting or its intended meaning; or they may have received separate copies with slight variations. No secretary signed this document from Dessalines. Did the document reflect Dessalines's specific wording, in a French unique to his own understanding of the language? Or was it produced by a secretary who, like Dessalines, was manipulating a language in which he was not formally or fully educated? In either case, the text is a vestige of a moment in which Haitian leaders were seizing the power of print culture literally before their relationship to Western literacy was fully developed—*avant la lettre...*

"Inform the Nations of the World"

Another important glimpse into the inner workings of Dessalines's public relations apparatus came in the form of a February 29 *arête*. Again, the secretary B. Aimé contacted newspapers to distribute the document, and to characterize it. Although the letter was again written to a specific individual, Samuel Relf, it seems that other editors felt that they had received instructions to publish it also; the *Columbian Centinel* of Massachusetts would preface the *arête* with the comment, "The Government of the Island of *Hayti* (St. Domingo) has directed the publication of the following arête in the papers of the United States" (May 5, 1804). The actual letter from Aimé to Relf was first published in the *Philadelphia Gazette*, and then reprinted in other papers such as the *Chronicle Express* of New York on May 7, 1804 (quoted here). The note appealed to Relf's impartiality, and explained that the document was at first meant as a secret deliberation on the intended execution of those associated with purges by Leclerc and Rochambeau, but was being made public following defamatory reports of violence in Haiti. The document was meant to explain the executions as something very different from random massacres of whites:

> Mr. Relf,
> The government confiding in your impartiality, hopes that you will please to publish the enclosed Arrete. Although motives of a political nature required that this Arrete should at first be kept a secret, in order to insure its execution. It is at present the desire of the government to give it all possible publicity. —As evil disposed persons (of whom unfortunately there are too many) will not fail to charge us with causing an indiscriminate destruction of the whites, whether good or bad, who have remained in the island, it is right that the world should be undeceived by exposing the true motives which induced the government to a measure which has never affected and never will affect any but the guilty.
> I salute you respectfully,
> B. Aimé
> Gonaïves, April 1, 1804

The decree in question ordered the arrest of "any persons who are or shall be known to have taken an active part in the different massacres and assassinations ordered by LeClerc or Rochambeau." For Dessalines, this goal was entirely distinct from the "drowning, suffocating, assassinating, hanging and shooting" of large numbers of citizens in 1802 and 1803. He meant thus to show the world that Haiti behaved with neutrality toward whites as a general category, as distinct from the French:

> [to] inform the nations of the world, that although we grant an asylum and a protection to those who act candidly and friendly towards us, nothing shall ever turn our vengeance from those murderers, who have bathed themselves with pleasure in the blood of the innocent children of Hayti.

Aimé and Dessalines had misinterpreted, however, the degree to which Americans could be reassured by the notion of a carefully targeted rather than random execution of whites.

"I Have Avenged America"

The *Commercial Advertiser* of New York (also referred to as the *Mercantile Advertiser*) published two of Dessalines's most vengeful and inspired proclamations, the "I have avenged America" speech and the proclamation to the inhabitants of the Spanish part of the island, on a single day, June 4, 1804, taking up much of that issue of the paper. The editors' note that "The few Americans that were at the Cape, remained unhurt" paled next to their claims, via an American ship captain, that the two proclamations together framed the executions of 2,500 French men, women, and children (from Haiti and from Santo Domingo).

The April 28 proclamation, signed by Chanlatte, again shows significant rhetorical overlap with the Declaration of Independence signed by Boisrond; we see Dessalines's recurrent tropes piercing through the language of the two texts. Where Dessalines in the Declaration had asked how the Haitians could breathe the same air as the French, in the "I have avenged America" proclamation he said of the Haitian not willing to act against the French, "The air we breathe is not suited to his gross organs; it is the pure air of liberty, august and triumphant." Where in the Declaration he had presented the blacks as languishing in a torpor of subjugation to French colonialism, he imagines now that the re-enslaved populations of Guadeloupe and Martinique, slumbering in lethargy, would suddenly be ignited by the Haitian spark and explode into action:

> Perhaps a spark from the same fire which inflames us, will alight into your bosoms: perhaps at the sound of this commotion suddenly awakening from your lethargy, with arms in your hands, you will reclaim your sacred and imprescriptable rights.

The god of nature was ready to assist; it would "unchain on earth some mighty winds."

Dessalines was sufficiently proud of his role as avenger of the blacks to list his title in the 1805 Constitution of Haiti as "Jacques Dessalines, the avenger and deliverer of his fellow citizens." Vengeance and commercial neutrality were not incompatible. For Dessalines it did not seem incongruous to move from the chilling poetic challenges to European colonial mastery in the "I have avenged America" proclamation to this quite prosaic closing remark on the welcome that neutral commercial traders would find on the island: "I recommend anew, and order to all the generals of the department, etc., to grant succour, encouragement, and protection, to all neutral and friendly nations who may wish to establish commercial relations on this island." This closing functioned like a macabre wink at the Americans, the Danes, the Dutch, etc.—"Don't worry, this isn't about *you*."

In the May 8 proclamation issued to the inhabitants of neighboring Santo Domingo, Dessalines presciently warned against the "seductions" of the texts issued by Ferrand:

Déjà je m'applaudissais du succès de mes soins, qui ne tendaient qu'à prévenir l'effusion du sang; mais un prêtre fanatique n'avait pas encore soufflé dans votre âme la rage qui le domine ; mais l'insensé Ferrand n'avait pas encore distillé parmi vous les poisons du mensonge et de la calomnie. Des écrits enfantés par le désespoir et la faiblesse ont circulé aussi ; plusieurs d'entre vous, séduits par des insinuations perfides, briguaient l'amitié et la protection des français [...].[27]

(Already I congratulated myself on the success of my careful avoidance of bloodshed, when a fanatical minister kindled in your minds the rage that now fixates you; when the crazed Ferrand instilled in you the poisons of lies and slander. Writings originating in despair and weakness had also circulated; and some among you, seduced by perfidious insinuations, solicited the friendship and protection of the French [...])

The claim to French sovereignty on the island of Hispaniola was "slander," a poisonous brew, and yet they were already gaining converts to the French cause.

Only a few months later, the dialogic relationship—simultaneously mimetic and contestatory—between the Haitian and American declarations of independence would be interwoven with a new dialogic competition, as discussed in Chapter 2, between Dessalines' vision of independence and the founding of the French Empire of Napoleon Bonaparte. Was it a straightforward imitation? Not everyone thought so. The *Daily Advertiser* on November 16, 1804, would muse that it was a gesture of contempt: "In imitation or rather in contempt of Bonaparte, he has assumed the title of *Jacques le premier, Empereur d'Hayti*." Nevertheless, 1804 would end as a European/New World *"Imperial year,"* as noted in the *Gazette* (Portland, Maine) on December 3, 1804:

> Eighteen Hundred Four, will in future be distinguished as the *Imperial year*; having given birth to four new Emperors in the Old and New World; viz. *Napoleon* I, Emperor of France; *Francis* I, Emperor of Austria; *Jacques* I, Emperor of Hayti; and *Frederick* I, Emperor of Brandenburg [...]

This imperial turn of the new black republic was simply another attempt to compete with the discourses that were so effectively challenging the independence of Haiti. It was born, as Dessalines explained, of his zeal to protect the "enterprise" that was Haiti:

> à consolider notre entreprise, entreprise qui donnera de nous aux nations les moins amies de la liberté, non l'opinion d'un ramas d'esclaves, mais celles d'hommes qui prédilectent leur indépendance au préjudice de cette considération que les puissances n'accordent jamais aux peuples qui, comme nous, sont les artisans de leur propre liberté [...]

> (to consolidate our enterprise, an enterprise that will give the nations who are least friendly to freedom the image of us not as a passel of slaves, but as men who cherish their independence even in the knowledge that the major powers never grant it to people who, like us, are the artisans of their own liberty [...])[28]

Declaring empire was a more aggressive structure for declaring independence.

At least the more abolitionist of American papers remained inspired by the dark drama as well as the humanist illuminations of the proclamations coming from Haiti. They appeared fascinated by the role of the Haitian government in distributing documents. The *Balance and Columbian Repository* of Hudson, New York announced in their paper of October 16, 1804, that they had received official copies of Dessalines's imperial nomination documents "from the civil and military authorities":

> Our readers are already in possession of the fact that General Dessalines has been proclaimed emperor of Haiti. Since that circumstance is come to our knowledge, we have received from Cape Francois an official copy of the address from the civil and military authorities by which he was invited to accept imperial power; and his majesty's most gracious answer of acceptance.

The editors viewed these texts as inherently interesting because of the singularity of the slave emancipation and sovereign black history they documented: "every circumstance connected with so singular an event must be read with no little degree of interest." But when they spoke of their translation—of putting "these papers into an English dress," to "lay them before the public"—one cannot miss the fact that putting them in an English dress, however elegant, did not make them palatable to a slave-holding Anglophone world. The merchants trading in Haiti, however, were much less concerned about how the issues in question were "dressed."

2. Demanding Independence: Nations, Neutrality, and Race

Declaring independence, in all the documents cited in the first part of this chapter, did not have the impact the precedent of the American Declaration of Independence must have suggested: it did not make it so, did not make the black republic as independent as the nations it had chosen as its peers. Dessalines still had to demand recognition of Haiti's independence, to fight off colonial encroachments, and to struggle to make "neutrality" applicable to other nations' relationships with a black republic.

The "Injured Man of Color" who wrote an op-ed to the *Commercial Advertiser* (May 25, 1804) to protest the banal use of the metonym "the brigands" for "the Haitians" in media accounts was onto something important when he suggested that if the Haitians were indeed brigands and robbers, this surely reflected badly on the U.S. merchants who traded with Haiti also. The 1804 Santo Domingo events described in Chapter 2, in which the French general Ferrand (or, in Dessalines's words in the May 8 proclamation, the "insensé Ferrand" ["the madman Ferrand"]) began to seize U.S. prize vessels and to issue legal decrees justifying their confiscation, would quickly lead to the reframing of U.S. merchants as auxiliaries to the "brigands." Ferrand himself, in remarks made on October 11, 1805, claimed that "It is a matter of public notoriety that [...] many American vessels of this kind, are not only engaged in this execrable commerce but transport arms and ammunition from Dessalines' army from one port to another, and thus become the auxiliaries of the blacks revolted from France."[29] This was a charge that Napoleon Bonaparte had made personally to Jefferson in late July of 1804, according to the media:

> It is reported that Mr. Jefferson has been insulted in the most audacious manner, by Bonaparte in a letter of his own handwriting, in which he blames him [...] for permitting the American merchants to supply Dessalines, and the republick of Hayti with arms, ammunition, and provisions.[30]

The movement of goods in maritime space in this era was regulated by court cases, treaties, and interception of ships and confiscation of their cargoes, as influenced by a complex code of international relations referred to as the "law of nations." The law of nations was most often referenced in American legal cases or congressional proceedings with regard to the 1758 literary work by the Swiss philosopher Emmerich de Vattel, which in French was called *Droit des gens* (*Rights of People*), but in English has been conventionally translated as *The Law of Nations*. This Enlightenment treatise on natural law and its application to nations and sovereignty should arguably have been highly applicable to an oppressed people, as it was attentive to issues of a fundamental *human* sovereignty. It departed from the principle that "the obligations of the law of nature are no less binding on states [...] than on individuals."[31] But an inherent understanding of natural law as it applied to the human race—for example, the ability to comprehend the pain of others and therefore to establish societies motivated to avoid wounding experiences among the collective of individuals—was not enough, Vattel noted, to understand its translation to the law of nations.

The law of nature among nations was predicated since classical times on the principle that captivity and servitude "are contrary to the law of nature; since, by the law of nature, all men were originally born free."[32] But the law of nations was equally based on the near-universal conventions of "all kinds of contracts, those of buying and selling, of hire, partnership, trust, and an infinite number of others," some of which obviously involved the buying and selling of human individuals. This paradox of a humanist Enlightenment framework of international relations that failed to account for rights of people who happened to be slaves is evident in the somewhat strange relationship of the United States to Haiti. And yet the fact that the U.S. implicitly accepted the role of primary trading partner with Haiti in 1804 and 1805 suggests that we should be able to imagine the relationship of *neutrals* to *belligerents* within the scheme of natural law.

In brief, the law of nations prohibits commerce between belligerent states—states at war with each other, or in a close relationship to a nation at war—without prohibiting commerce between "neutrals" and a partner in another conflict. "Neutral nations," Vattel wrote, "are those who, in time of war, do not take any part in the contest, but remain common friends to both parties."[33] Conflict was described in terms of enmity in Vattel's work; the "hostis" or "public enemy," and the "inimicus" or "private enemy." Dessalines, not unlike Napoleon, fit into both categories for much of the colonial or slave-holding world, in that his proclamations brought the complexity of his personal psyche into the immediate arena of his public enemies. (James Stephen quipped that if Toussaint was both the Romulus and the Numa of Saint-Domingue, "Dessalines will be rather the Hostilius.")[34]

In the context of racial and master–slave relations, it would prove exceedingly difficult to discern who was belligerent and who was neutral, or what the "natural" alliance of former slaves and current "neutral" slaveholders might be. Unfortunately, Vattel had discussed slaves only in terms of classical realities: prisoners of war becoming slaves, or sovereign subjects being reduced to metaphorical slavery by tyrants refusing to permit their education.[35] Perhaps the one quote that Jefferson and his allies might have usefully applied to the Haiti issue was this: "Let him mistrust the selfish suggestions of that minister who represents to him as rebels all those citizens who do not stretch out their necks to the yoke of slavery—who refuse to crouch under the rod of arbitrary power."[36] Dessalines, the modern-day Hostilius, epitomized the refusal to crouch under the rod, but many metaphorical ministers represented Haiti's citizens to Jefferson as rebels.

In 1804, General Ferrand not only defeated the Haitians in Santo Domingo, but he established the foundational textual basis for a cascading series of political and legal conclusions that the free citizens of the new black republic were simply revolted colonized subjects of France. The first and most publicized of these legal conclusions was made in judging the case of the ironically named ship the *Happy Couple*. The vessel's captain, the Irish immigrant Thomas Storey, had sailed from New York at the time of the final defeat of the French in October of 1803 with a large cache of gunpowder and ammunition, to aid in the war against the French. Having been in Haiti throughout the early independence weeks, Captain Storey and the *Happy Couple* left St. Marc on February 22, 1804, but were captured by a British ship on March 8. The *Happy Couple* was eventually taken to Halifax for adjudication in the British Court of Vice-Admiralty there. Sentencing occurred a year later, on April 18, 1805, and was widely publicized in the U.S. It is important to remember that although the sentencing was done and publicized in 1805, Dessalines was almost certainly made aware of this interception, and that of the other American vessels captured after trade with Haiti, such as the *Sarah* (in Rose vs. Himely) in the spring of 1804, as well as of Ferrand's justifications of the confiscations.

Storey's affidavit specifically affirmed that he had brought the gunpowder to Saint-Domingue in October of 1803 "to prosecute the war against the French government,"[37] and one of the curious elements of this case is that it provides no clear bracketing of the chronology of the "war" against the French. Was it in November of 1803 only? Or was this American vessel still providing contraband of war in the spring of 1804? The court seemed to lean toward the idea of a continued war against the French—in effect, an ongoing rebellion against French colonial rule. The King's advocate, representing the captors of the *Happy Couple*, argued that admittedly, "a large portion of that island has thrown off the yoke of France,"[38] but suggested that this could be a temporary state of affairs. The judgment in the case affirmed that since gunpowder was a contraband article, its legality "must depend upon the national character of St. Domingo, under the present government."[39] Ironically enough, the court cited Toussaint's constitution of 1801—which had impelled Napoleon Bonaparte to invade Saint-Domingue over fears of its emerging independence—as a legal acknowledgment of French colonial sovereignty. The French subsequently, the court admitted, were defeated. "But might does not constitute right," the court observed; "and if France has a just title to the dominion of St. Domingo, no acts done by revolting negroes can divest it."[40] France, it noted, had never acknowledged the independence of Haiti, nor had Britain. The court presented it as a "datum" that St. Domingo, in the absence of any proof that it had "acquired another character,"[41] was "a French colony." This judgment, upheld on appeal in 1808, was published nearly in full in papers such as the *United States Gazette* (May 14, 1805).

In the spring of 1804 when the *Happy Couple* was confiscated, "America" for Dessalines still arguably represented a maritime, island, and continental space of "neutral" international relations, unchained to colonial hierarchies. Dessalines's earliest concerns about "neutrality" were simply that there might be French colonists lurking in neutral clothing. He explained in an April 1804 proclamation that he was perfectly in favor of the "négociants éphémeres" ("ephemeral merchants") who were truly unaffiliated with colonial governments. But he warned that America, Jamaica, and the Danish and Spanish islands should be wary of seafarers applying for naturalization, who were actually "French plotters or renegade blacks."[42]

By the summer of 1804, however, Dessalines had clearly perceived that the Haitians' relationship to American merchants was not going to be self-sustaining if the vessels of those merchants were continually intercepted and confiscated as lawful prizes by the French or other European powers. The threats of recolonization that Dessalines continually invoked in his proclamations were coming close to home.

The need for formal recognition of Haiti's independence was becoming urgent. It was reported in the U.S. media, following a French news story in the *Clef du Cabinet des Souverains*, that in the summer of 1804, just before the time of the decision to make Haiti an empire, Dessalines did in fact demand French recognition of the independence of Haiti:

> General Dessalines, the black Governor of Hayti, has sent dispatches to the First Consul stating that he has threatened the murder of all French inhabitants in the island of Hayti, if the government do not immediately acknowledge its independence, and promise a *yearly tribute* in arms, ammunition, artillery, etc.[43]

If this report was true, Dessalines's demand for Napoleon Bonaparte's recognition of Haiti's independence either disappeared into archives that have not yet been explored, or was discarded. The fact that there exists no collection of Dessalines's correspondence means that the absence of documentation for this journalistic claim does not immediately discredit it. Certainly French recognition would have been precisely what Dessalines needed to have Haiti's independence translate into international sovereignty rather than sovereign "brigandry."

Another contemporary news story, based on a report by none other than Captain Storey of the *Happy Couple*, made a related claim that also would have represented a strategic move on the chessboard of the law of nations: that Dessalines had declared war against Spain, and now threatened to confiscate Spanish vessels off Hispaniola.

> Capt. Storey, from Gonaives in addition to what was mentioned in our paper of Thursday, informs, that Dessalines had formally issued a proclamation of war against Spain, and in consequence the Haytians were employing their cruisers to intercept the Spanish vessels [...].[44]

Americans began to face the risk of being perceived as subversive by European metropoles, above all the French, for treating Haiti as a nation among nations. A remarkable editorial from the *Richmond Enquirer*, reprinted in the Maryland *American and Commercial Daily Advertiser* on February 26, 1805, noted that the constellation of American trade interests, black independence, and American independence challenged the existing conventions of political and legal logic:

> No subject has given rise to a more important debate during the present session of Congress or to more voluminous discussions in the public prints, than the trade of American merchants to this ill fated Island, none has probably suggested a greater variety of questions or been viewed in a greater variety of lights. [...] What was due to the government of France? What was due to the insurgents of St. Domingo? What was due to our own merchants?

Despite the prohibitions of American trade with Haiti by General Ferrand, the editorial recounted that not only did traffic with the "Brigands" continue unabated, but that in effect it served, for purposes of trade rather than ideology, to enable the continued independence of Haiti from the predations of the French government:

> that a part of this traffic even consisted in the introduction of arms and ammunition among them, without which they could not under certain circumstances have maintained their opposition to the mother country;

that partly to defend this trade, some of them even assumed to themselves the right of arming their vessels, and thus enabling them not only to resist the aggression of pirates but the search of lawfully commissioned cruisers of the French government [...]

The editorial acknowledged that despite the sovereign independence of Haiti, it was inarguably "at war with France." Perhaps then, the author reflected, France did have the right to demand that "neutral nations" restrict their trade with a country with which it was at war. And yet the editor felt that the restrictions imposed by France via Ferrand were more suitable to "a colony or a part of France" than to "an independent sovereignty." French control of a truly independent Haiti would be illegal. In the same pattern of Socratic questioning, he then examined the possibility that France was allowed, "by the same duty of self-preservation which binds individuals," when it realized that St. Domingo "was about to be torn from her sovereignty," to prohibit the American commerce, which "tended to defeat all her exertions for its recovery." What would one call this complex case within the law of nations? Perhaps the right of former colonists to try to recover dominion might be called "common law." But a footnote at the very end of the editorial recalled the earlier fierce opposition to George Washington's proclamation of "neutrality." The author thus suggested the legitimation of commercial neutrality through the historical connection to the American independence.

Neutral vessels had become a subject of increasing political contention between the U.S. and France in the spring of 1805. The *History of the United States of America during the Administrations of Thomas Jefferson and James Madison* by Henry Adams and Earl N. Harbert noted the trading quandary for the U.S. when France continued to maintain an official presence in Santo Domingo and wanted, but could not fully enforce, a general trade embargo with the free blacks of Haiti:

> There was hardly an armed vessel bearing the flag of France [that] pretended to maintain a blockade,—yet Napoleon claimed that the island belonged to him. General Ferrand still held points in the Spanish colony for France, and defeated an invasion attempted by Dessalines; nor did any government betray a disposition to recognize the black empire, or to establish relations with Dessalines or Christophe, or with a negro republic. On the other hand, the trade of Hayti, being profitable, was encouraged by every government in turn; but because it was, even more than other West Indian trade, unprotected by law, the vessels which carried it out were usually armed, and sailed in company.[45]

Neutral trade was encouraged by awareness that Haiti could become a powerful economic force in itself. A British editorial questioned the wisdom of coddling France by refraining from Haitian commerce, and pointed to the inherent equality of the empires of Haiti and of France:

> One of the complaints in the *Paris Moniteur* against *England* is, that any intercourse should be kept up with Dessalines; but surely he has as much right to be the Emperor of *Hayti* as BONAPARTE has to be Emperor of France. If the present negotiations should happen to end in Peace, we may reasonably expect, upon the same principle, that the *Haytian Gazette* will contain a complaint against us for carrying on any intercourse with BONAPARTE.[46]

In effect, from 1804 to 1806 traders were repeatedly asked to choose loyalty to the projects of European metropoles over the opportunities presented by a pirate-like domain of free trade with Haiti—whose citizens were identified in one editorial in the *Aurora* as "land pirates."[47] Neutral commerce with Haiti enriched American merchants but also effectively bolstered Dessalines's independent government. After several diplomatic wrangles with France, Senator Logan of Pennsylvania helped to pass a March 1805 bill prohibiting *armed* commerce with Haiti, although unarmed trade remained technically legal.

This and other ambiguous gestures of remorse toward France were fueled by uncomfortable reflections on the dependence of U.S. agriculture on slaves. As Adams and Harbert noted, "In truth, the Southern States dreaded the rebel negroes of Hayti more than they feared Napoleon."[48] The potential spread of black political and economic autonomy was implicit in the Philadelphia *Aurora*'s shift from its staunch editorial support in 1804 of Haiti's right to proclaim its independence. In March of 1805, the *Aurora* cautioned that just as Britain had not intended, by opposing France, to serve as an enabler of black political and economic autonomy in the New World, the U.S. should be careful not to sabotage its own domestic economic infrastructure by supporting the autonomy of former slaves:

> The idea that England approves of a black empire at Hayti is just as preposterous as to suppose that, when his next neighbour's house is in flames, a man could be mad enough to rejoice at it, and instead of reflecting that his own adjoining habitation was in the greatest danger, could throw oil on the flames.[49]

The *Aurora* even entertained the possibility that if the U.S. were to place its trade with Saint-Domingue above confraternity with France and England, those countries might attempt to foster insurrection among American slaves: "As well might England or France furnish our black population with the means of murdering our white people, as we undertake to defend and join St. Domingo against France."[50]

These debates made their way into the newly established Haitian media also, which in turn was distributed in the U.S., creating an intertextual and international field of debate on U.S.–Haiti neutral commerce. The Haitian *Gazette* had published editorials in which the mutual interest of an American commercial relationship with Haiti was seen as self-evident, and unthreatening to Haiti's independence: "The great interests which the American merchants find in the commerce of this country, guarantee to us their perseverance in continuing it. And whatever else Mr. Eppes and his partisans may say, the empire of Haiti is independent, and contains in itself the power of preserving this independence."[51] *Poulson's Daily Advertiser* noted that a Captain Boyer sailing from the Cape had provided a full file of the first issues of the postcolonial newspaper:

> Captain Boyer, of the schooner Harriot, from Cape François, yesterday obligingly handed us a regular file, from its commencement to the 22nd ult. of the *Gazette politique et commerciale d'Haiti*, printed "at the Cape, by P. Roux, printer to the Emperor." The editor states that the newspaper is published "under the auspices of his excellency the general of division *Vernet*, minister of finances." The motto is appropriate,
> L'injustice à la fin produit l'Indépendence [*sic*].
> VOLT.[52]

The New Hampshire *Farmer's Cabinet* likewise noted in April, "Among the articles from St. Domingo, we find, that a Gazette, Political and Commercial, is printed at the Cape, by P. Roux, printer to the Emperor of Hayti." The New York *Morning Chronicle* was another paper that reported having "received a file" [April 9, 1805] of all the issues of the Haitian *Gazette* to date, reinforcing the possibility that Haiti was pursuing a systematic strategy of self-representation in the U.S. In a strange feedback loop, U.S. newspapers thus were at times reporting on Haitian coverage of American positions regarding Haiti: the April 9 *Morning Chronicle* briefly referred to an article in the Haitian *Gazette* concerning "the sanction of congress to the trade with the empire of Haiti."

Many in the American arena agreed that Haitian sovereignty was not legally constrained by the nostalgic mastery and neocolonial aggressions of the French. An editorial by "Regulus" in the *Commercial Advertiser* outlined the methods and infrastructure of Haitian sovereignty:

> What, then, is the present political state of the dominion of Hayti? And what the history of that revolution, which brought them to their present state? To the first question my answer is, that they are independent of all nations upon earth; and being so, are entitled to all rights and privileges flowing from such independence. They have a sovereign of their own

election; they have civil and military establishments; they sustain foreign and domestic relations; and, to all intents and purposes, take rank with the nations of the world.[53]

Even as these debates on neutrality, sovereignty, and race were unfolding, General Ferrand, in Santo Domingo, was publicly contemplating mechanisms for the suppression of Haitian political influence in Santo Domingo in the most chilling terms.

Ferrand's War Against the Contagion of Haiti: The "Revolted Borderlands"

On January 6, 1805, Ferrand issued a stunning *arête*, not designated for international consumption, in which he proposed that the most effective way to suppress the rebellion of the blacks in the "colony of Santo Domingo" was to reduce the population.

> Toujours occupé des dispositions propres à anéantir la rebellion des noirs dans la colonie de Saint-Domingue, et considérant qu'une de celles les plus efficaces pour parvenir à ce but est d'en diminuer la population [...][54]

> (Always preoccupied by the means to crush the rebellion of the blacks in the colony of Saint-Domingue, and considering that one of the most effective means to achieve this goal is to reduce the population [...])

It was an extraordinary provocation, exemplifying the most genocidal logic of slavery. He instructed the "habitants" or property owners along the "frontière révolté" ("the revolted borderlands") of Santo Domingo to conduct raids on the black and colored population, seizing all children younger than fourteen, enslaving and relocating those children deemed subject to rehabilitation, and selling and deporting the children who were less redeemable. The fate of adults was simply not mentioned. But the children being reconditioned or deported were being rescued from the fate of a rebellion that would lead "inévitablement aux châtiments les plus terribles" ("inevitably to the most awful punishments"). It was, in effect, open season on Haitians and Haitian sympathizers in the borderlands, employing the population of the region in a devastating assault on itself. Class and racial divides alone would determine who would be kidnapped (or worse) or who would kidnap (or worse).

Article 1, after the generous observation that those employed in the suppression of the rebellion deserved to profit from their labors, "à se répandre sur le territoire occupé par les révoltés, à leur courre sus, et à faire prisoniers tous ceux des deux sexes qui ne passeront pas l'âge de quatorze ans" ("to fan into the territory occupied by the rebels, to run upon them, and to take prisoner anyone, of either sex, not older than fourteen years of age"). These prisoners would be the property of their captors. The remainder of the decree was primarily devoted to bureaucratic instructions on the registering and certification of all captives, and the single port (Santo Domingo) through which they could be sold and deported. Ferrand explained in the decree that the French officers would supervise this round-up and the protocols involved. He did explain that the hostilities should cease in the case of any rebel who demonstrated his or her submission to the emperor of the French and to General Ferrand, beyond any doubt of their good faith.

The decree, unlike the edicts issued by Ferrand concerning neutral trade, was not published widely—Ferrand ordered in the proclamation that 200 copies, in both French and Spanish, be posted throughout the departments of Ozama and Cibao. Dessalines felt compelled to reprint it in its entirety in the *Gazette politique et commerciale d'Haïti* to justify his invasion. He explained in his "Adresse de l'Empereur au peuple, à son retour du siège de Santo Domingo" ("Address from the Emperor to the People After His Return from the Siege of Santo Domingo") published on May 30, 1805, that after learning of Ferrand's decree, he had been persuaded of the urgency of destroying "the final vestiges of the European idol" in Santo Domingo—the idol of white supremacy and slavery.

Before "El Corte": The Round Up of Stolen Objects

These regions along the Haitian frontier would be the site of the genocidal 1937 event known in the Dominican Republic as "the cutting" (*el corte*, or in *Kreyòl*, the *kout kouto a*). Ferrand was not targeting the Spanish side of the border only. He specified that any blacks or persons of color seized from either the "colonie de Saint-Domingue" or "les colonies voisines" ("neighboring colonies") but not registered and certified, would be considered "des objets volés" ("stolen objects"), and duly confiscated as property. Ferrand had every intention, in other words, of extending a campaign for re-enslavement into Haitian territory.

As Emilio Cordero Michel points out, historians of the "Era de Francia" in Santo Domingo generally have not signaled awareness of this document by Ferrand, which certainly broached the fundamental problem, in Michel's words, of "la préservation du premier Etat créé par la race noire"[55] ("the preservation of the first nation created by the black race") in the Caribbean, as well as of the extreme vulnerability of black individuals and families anywhere in the borderlands. It aimed at a fatal division of those who would submit to colonial rule and those who were identified with the Haitian independence. It was the most incendiary possible challenge to Dessalines and the viability of black freedom and independence.

Dessalines invaded. In the attack, which took place in late March, he clearly targeted the French presence in Santo Domingo rather than the Spanish. As Michel summarizes, Dessalines sent ahead an emissary to convey that "il n'avait pas d'intentions hostiles contre les Dominicano-espagnols, qu'il allait vers la ville de Santo Domingo pour aider à expulser les français" ("he had no hostile intentions toward the Domicano-Spanish, he was heading for Santo Domingo to help to expel the French").[56] Dessalines's plan to protect the Haitian independence by protecting the sphere of its sovereignty was clearly readable to an international public: some of his own anticolonial correspondence with Ferrand—unfortunately not preserved in the *Recueil*—was disseminated in the U.S. media.

A May 15 news story in the *Spectator* published a summons from Dessalines to Ferrand (citing a "gentleman from St. Thomas" as the source for the text). The independent Haitian Empire, Dessalines explained, could not tolerate a continued French military presence on Hispaniola:

> Jean Jacques, the emperor of Hayti, to General Ferrand, commanding a division of the troops of the French Republic.
> As it is inconsistent with the laws and independence of the Empire, that any portion of the French army should be allowed to remain in the island, General Ferrand is summoned to surrender the city of St. Domingo in twenty four hours; if at the end of that time the city shall not be evacuated, it will be delivered to plunder, and all the inhabitants thereof be put to the sword.

Dessalines's forces conquered St. Jago (Santiago) without difficulty, but on their onward march, several obstacles arose. The willingness of the local non-whites—quite possibly a chastened and subjugated population—to join the Haitian forces proved uncertain. Michel asserts that substantial numbers of the slaves in Spanish Santo Domingo were also reluctant to join forces with their brothers on the western part of Hispaniola "de peur que les mesures de Dessalines les eussent attachés à la terre" ("for fear that Dessalines' policies would leave them chained to agricultural labor").[57] There may have been a propaganda campaign to this effect; articles reinforcing the fearful destiny of the laboring classes under Dessalines were published in the U.S. The *Pennsylvania Correspondant* on July 2 published an "Extract of a letter from a gentleman at St. Domingo, to his friend in this village, dated 'Pistel [Pestel], Island of Hayti, May 23rd, 1805,'" titled "Cruelty of Dessalines, Emperor of Hayti."

> One of his own favorite officers informed me, a few days since, that the emperor in riding thro' the country, came to a large coffee plantation, where there were one hundred negroes at work, collecting it; they complained,

saying that as they had to work in the heat of the sun, from morning to night, for a sustenance, it was very hard, that they should have to give as much as one third to the government. The emperor told all who were dissatisfied to go to one side, and I think the number he mentioned, was twenty-three; all of whom he had beheaded immediately on the spot. Then turning on his heel, he said to the rest, he presumed they would be well contented to give one third of their labor to the government for the time to come.

Ferrand also proved a redoubtable rhetorical opponent. Dessalines's ire at the magical effect of Ferrand's proclamations against him may have been a measure of their effectiveness in rallying the Spanish to the French cause. Ferrand's popularity among the colonial Spaniards was attested to at the time. A letter from an American merchant in Santo Domingo claimed that "The Spaniards have a fondness for general Ferrand which borders on enthusiasm."[58] When the Haitians besieged the city of Santo Domingo, General Ferrand borrowed heavily from Dessalines's own rhetoric of vengeance against a cannibalistic conqueror, tarring his opponent with his own brush. His revisiting of Dessalinian metaphors bordered on pastiche:

It is here you ought to revenge the manes of your fathers, mothers, brothers, sisters, wives, children and friends, who are all perished by blood thirsty hands—by the monsters who surround us! It is here that you ought to shew what the valor of a chosen few are able to perform against a number of assassins! It is here where the field is chalked out for victory! Do not be frightened at those cannibals; [...]⁵⁹

The Colonial Powers Unite

In truth, though, none of these factors was significant in the outcome of this specific siege. The real reason for the defeat of the Haitians was the appearance on the scene of soldiers from the French navy. Ferrand's requests for help from Bonaparte in defending a French colony briefly prompted the French and Spanish naval forces to work together as one, where they had previously fought over their own jurisdiction. In the mid-spring of 1805, international observers noted signals of serious maritime preparations aimed at the defeat of the Haitians. Word arrived, again from a "gentleman in St. Thomas," that "a French and Spanish fleet of 17 sail of the line was seen off Porto-Rico, standing to leeward. It was supposed they were headed to St. Domingo."[60] The *Mercantile Advertiser* (New York) noted on April 19 that "the Rochefort squadron in the West Indies had sailed from Guadeloupe for St. Domingo, where it was intended to disembark two thousand troops as a reinforcement to those under General Ferrand." The British were supportive also. By May 8, 1805, the New York *Mercantile Advertiser* was reporting that "The garrison of St. Domingo under general Ferrand, at the date of our last advices, consisted of about 6000 French and Spaniards […] The Snake British frigate was cruising off there, and flags were frequent between her and the garrison."

When Dessalines returned to Haiti, following a scorched earth policy throughout his retreat, he issued his last major narrative-style proclamation, called the "Adresse de l'Empereur au peuple, à son retour du siège de Santo-Domingo" ("Address by the Emperor to the People, After His Return from the Siege of Santo Domingo"), dated April 12, 1805. In this narrative he bitterly recounted his disappointed expectations that the survivors of the first genocidal colonization of Hispaniola, the "indigènes" of Santo Domingo, would wish to be freed. He seemed to ascribe this fact to a kind of decadence, a now traditional submission to tyranny, among the first inhabitants/blacks of the island:

> Il était naturel de présumer que les indigènes espagnoles, ces descendants des malheureux Indiens immolés à la cupidité et à l'avarice des premiers usurpateurs de cette île, saisiraient avec avidité la précieuse occasion de sacrifier aux mânes de leurs ancêtres; mais cette espèce d'hommes avilis et dégradés, préférant aux douceurs d'une vie libre et indépendante, des maîtres qui les tyranisent, fit cause commune avec les Français.[61]

> (It was natural to presume that the Spanish indigenes, descendants of the unfortunate Indians immolated by the cupidity and greed of the first usurpers of this island, would avidly seize the precious opportunity to make a sacrifice to the manes of their ancestors. But this degraded and weakened species of men, preferring the tyrannies of their masters to the sweetness of a free and independent life, joined forces with the French.)

Those Spaniards who had participated in the "liberticidal works" of the French now shared the legacy of their crimes, he stated.

But Dessalines was aware of the real cause of his defeat. It lay in the arrival, "against all probability," of a French division consisting of three frigates and two brigs. He still could have defeated that division, he asserted; but he was keenly aware of Bonaparte's determination to use any means to meet his ends, and he was alert to the possible arrival of other assisting European forces. After all, he said, recent news from abroad had revealed him to an emerging consolidation of interests among the European cabinets. He resolved to return to what he now, for the first time, called "la partie haïtienne"[62] ("the Haitian part") of the island, rather than "the island of Hayti."

Ashes, Iron, Soldiers: Build Forts!

Startlingly, Dessalines used his knowledge of foreign affairs to assert that the specter of an upcoming "paix en Europe" ("peace in Europe") made it likely that there would be more attacks on Haiti. Run and build your most remarkable fortifications, he urged ("courez perfectionner ces fortifications que vos mains ont élévées"). Be ingenious, be audacious, in planning to meet "vos tyrans" ("your tyrants"). At the first firing of the warning cannon, let Haiti offer to their greedy gaze nothing but ashes, iron, and soldiers ("Au premier coup de canon d'alarme, que le sol d'Haïti n'offre à leurs regards avides que des cendres, du fer et des soldats").[63]

Dessalines was exactly right that the spring of 1805 heralded a new sense of unity among colonial and slave-holding powers. Enough of fighting each other to the point of empowering a nation of former slaves, various writers reflected, directly or indirectly. An article in the *Aurora* on March 9 explained benignly that in the Haitian Revolution, what might have looked like British aid to the blacks was really just a matter of annoying the French:

> When the British fleet blockaded the ports of that island [Haiti], during the existence of the French army under Rochambeau, it was not with an intention of serving the blacks, but solely for the purpose of distressing the French [...] The idea that England approves of a black empire at Hayti is just as preposterous [...] In *their courts of admiralty* the British have not yet recognized his majesty the Emperor Dessalines.

If the British were done with their attempts to cripple the French, another editorial in the *Aurora* on April 13 stated, "Britain would do more than connive at setting bounds to Dessalines, they would treat him as they do the Mahrattalis [*sic*] and all the world." Their purpose had never been, the editorial claimed, "to give *independence* to the blacks."

Death Foretold, "Under the Denomination of Brigand"

Although Dessalines's death late in 1806 resulted directly from conflicts with rival leaders and populations in Haiti, it should come as no surprise that premature—and false—news of his demise had begun to circulate in Europe and the U.S. as early as the fall of 1805. The New York *Commercial Advertiser* on October 9, 1805, noted "The Editor of the *Petit censeur* in his latest number announces as certain the death of his Imperial Majesty Dessalines, Emperor of Haiti." This information spread widely. On October 14, the Massachusetts *Independent Chronicle* provided uncanny detail, noting that Christophe would replace Dessalines, since Dessalines, unlike Napoleon, had renounced hereditary empire. Perhaps the most unjust aspect of this false rumor was that the *Petit censeur* had referred to Dessalines "under the denomination of *brigand*":

> The editor of the Petit Censeur in his last number announces as certain the death of his imperial majesty the Emperor Dessalines, under the denomination of *brigand*. It is presumed he will be succeeded by General Christophe; his majesty (departing in this instances from the direct line of conduct adopted by the Great Man [Napoleon] whose example and form of government were his model) not having caused the crown to be declared hereditary in his own family.

The *New York Gazette* on October 15 hastened to correct the erroneous reporting of Dessalines's death: "The report of the death of Dessalines, Emperor of Haiti, proves to be untrue." So did a domino chain of other U.S. papers afterwards, each with its own language for the brief retraction of the story.

Newspapers were more circumspect when the actual event did occur, on October 17, 1806. The South Carolina *City Gazette* on November 19 printed an "outlier" article titled "Kingston, (Jama.), October 18": "Information has lately been received in this city, that there is every probability that the mock Emperor of Hayti, has by this time been deprived, not only of his regal honors, but of his life [...]."

Postscriptum

For reasons that I will further elaborate in Chapter 4, Dessalines was becoming increasingly aware of his potentially fatal marginalization. Like many a Haitian leader after him, he contemplated the logistics of a secure exile before the fact. After the American trade embargo against Haiti was passed in late February of 1806, the Philadelphia *Aurora* reported on May 10, 1806, that Dessalines was trying to laugh off the new legislation as a temporary setback, asserting that as long as Americans wanted coffee, they would want trade with Haiti:

> Dessalines laughs at the law of Congress, interdicting the trade and in exulting and contemptuous language declares that "as long as he has a bag of coffee for a dollar, he will never want Americans ready and willing to buy them, in disregard of the laws."

The article concluded with a tantalizing detail: Dessalines, it reported, was said to have bought an American estate, outside of Philadelphia, in the case of what was delicately termed an "imperial bouleversement":

A Gentleman of this city is said to be Dessalines' correspondent and agent. It was mentioned at the Cape, by persons who had intercourse at the black court, that Dessalines had purchased an estate in Pennsylvania, outside of Philadelphia, in the event of an imperial bouleversement.

Might Dessalines's "America" have included Dessalines's life *in* America? This is currently a mystery, although it was widely reported in September of 1807 that Dessalines's widow, the resourceful Marie-Claire Heureuse Félicité Bonheur Dessalines, had inexplicably arrived in Wilmington, Delaware: "It is said, the wife of Dessalines, with a numerous suite, arrived at Wilmington, Delaware, a few days since."[64]

Dessalines's America was never a home for him, but it was a place where his radical proclamations were surprisingly at home. It was the place where Haiti attempted to awaken empathic and egalitarian responses from white postcolonial hemispheric neighbors, and had glimmers of success. It was in Dessalines's America that it became necessary to read race in declarations of independence.

Notes

1. French colonial correspondence cited by Léo Elisabeth in "Les Relations entre les petites Antilles françaises et Haïti: de la politique du refoulement à la resignation (1804–1825)," in *Haïti première république noire*, ed. Marcel Dorigny (Saint-Denis: Publications de la société française d'histoire d'outre-mer, 2003).

2. Cited in David Armitage, *The Declaration of Independence* (Cambridge, MA: Harvard University Press, 2007), 3.

3. Armitage, *The Declaration of Independence*, 11.

4. Ashli White, *Encountering Revolution: Haiti and the Making of the Early Republic* (Baltimore, MD: Johns Hopkins University Press, 2010), 13.

5. Jefferson Papers, Series 1, image 667, Manuscript Division, Library of Congress.

6. Gordon S. Brown, *Toussaint's Clause: The Founding Fathers and the Haitian Revolution* (Jackson, MS: University Press of Mississippi, 2005), 233.

7. White, *Encountering Revolution*, 164.

8. *Aurora General Advertiser*, March 28, 1804.

9. Tim Matthewson, *A Pro-Slavery Foreign Policy: Haitian-American Relations During the Early Republic* (Westport, CT: Praeger, 2003), 131.

10. Matthewson, *A Pro-Slavery Foreign Policy*, 119–34.

11. Thomas Madiou, *Histoire d'Haïti* (Port-au-Prince: J. Courtois, 1849), 3:99.

12. *Poulson's Daily Advertiser*, January 5, 1804.

13. Government-issued broadsides and correspondence from the very early independence period presented a challenge to the new government: how to record, distribute, and preserve this patrimony. Article 44 of the May 20, 1805 "Constitution impériale d'Haïti" noted the establishment of a position of "Secretary of State," who rather than a foreign policy chief would be a more literal secretary for the state's documents, responsible for "the printing, recording, and sending of the laws, decrees, proclamations and instructions of the Emperor for the purpose of public

relations." Le Baron Linstant de Pradine, ed., *Recueil général des lois et des actes du gouvernement d'Haïti, 1804–1808* (Paris: A. Durand, Pédone-Lauriel, 1886), 1:53. This secretary was charged with working "directly" with the emperor on correspondence, supplying him with the documents by courts and by foreign ministries. Prior to 1808, according to Linstant de Pradine, the decrees of the government were registered negligently and partially (*Recueil*, iv–v).

14. Madiou, *Histoire d'Haïti*, 3:99.

15. See B. Aimé's copy of a military proclamation by Dessalines, with the notation "Pour copie fidèle, signé Aime secrétaire. Prise dans la feuille de New York du 3 Mai et copié littéralement," Archives d'Outre-mer, F3, vol. 141, 545–6.

16. Toussaint Louverture, proclamation to his army on May 21, 1797, quoted in the South Carolina *City Gazette*, July 8, 1797.

17. Tuesday, February 14, "Importation of Slaves," *Abridgment of the Debates of Congress, From 1789 to 1856*, vol. 3 (New York: Appleton & Company, 1857), 131.

18. Madiou discusses the role of Captain Perkins in tensions with the Haitian military in January 1804 (*Histoire d'Haïti*, 3:126–7), and in correspondence with Dessalines over other maritime scuffles in September of 1804 (*Histoire d'Haïti*, 3:178–9).

19. Madiou, *Histoire d'Haïti*, 3:154.

20. Lady Maria Nugent, *Lady Nugent's Journal*, ed. Frank Cundall (London: Adam and Charles Black, 1907), 250.

21. I am very grateful to Julia Gaffield, a doctoral student in history at Duke University, for sharing this detail of her outstanding research in Kingston, which confirmed a part of the puzzle that had previously been featured in drafts of this chapter only in speculative form. This quote comes from "No. 1 Report from Edward Corbet esq, dated January 25, 1804," Jamaican National Library, 784 N, MS 72 Box 3.

22. Archives nationales, AF III 210.

23. See Justin Emmanuel Castera, *Bref coup d'oeil sur la presse haïtienne, 1764–1850* (Port-au-Prince, Haïti: Imprimerie Henri Deschamps, 1986).

24. The translation choice of "manes" again reflects the operative nineteenth-century sensibility.

25. Tim Matthewson, "Jefferson and the Nonrecognition of Haiti," *Proceedings, American Philosophical Society* 140:1 (1996), 22–48.

26. *Commercial Advertiser*, March 21, 1803.

27. Jean-Jacques Dessalines, "Proclamation ou sommation faite au Général qui commandait à Santo Domingo," February 8, 1804. This text is copied in the *Notes historiques de Moreau de Saint-Méry*, Archives d'Outre-mer, F3, vol. 141, 549–53.

28. *Recueil général des lois et des actes du gouvernement d'Haïti*, 1:13.

29. *Mercantile Advertiser*, January 1, 1806.

30. *United States Gazette*, September 22, 1804.

31. Emmerich de Vattel, *The Law of Nations; or, Principles of the Law of Nature, Applied to the Conduct and Affairs of Nations and Sovereigns* (Philadelphia: T. & J. W. Johnson and Co., 1867), vii.

32. Vattel, *Law of Nations*, viii.

33. Vattel, *Law of Nations*, 437.

34. James Stephen, *The Opportunity: Reasons for an Immediate Alliance with St. Domingo* (London: J. Hatchard, 1804), 47.

35. Vattel, *Law of Nations*, 119.

36. Vattel, *Law of Nations*, 541.

37. *Reports of Cases Argued and Determined in the Court of Vice-Admiralty at Halifax*, ed. James Stewart (London: J. Butterworth, 1814), 66.

38. Stewart, ed., *Reports of Cases*, 67.

39. Stewart, ed., *Reports of Cases*, 72.

40. Stewart, ed., *Reports of Cases*, 73.

41. Stewart, ed., *Reports of Cases*, 75.

42. Dessalines, "Proclamation qui relate un acte des colons, recommandant le général Rochambeau au premier consul," April 1, 1804, in *Recueil général des lois et des actes du gouvernement d'Haïti*, 1:18.

43. *Suffolk Gazette*, August 13, 1804.

44. *Pennsylvania Correspondent*, September 11, 1804.

45. Henry Adams and Earl N. Harbert, *History of the United States of America During the Administrations of Thomas Jefferson and James Madison* (New York: Viking Press, 1986), 663.

46. Quoted in the *New England Palladium* (Massachusetts), October 17, 1806.

47. Cited by Brown, *Toussaint's Clause*, 257.

48. *History of the United States of America*, 700.

49. *Aurora General Advertiser*, March 9, 1805.

50. *Aurora General Advertiser*, January 22, 1805.

51. Quoted in *Poulson's Daily Advertiser* (Philadelphia), April 11, 1805.

52. *Poulson's Daily Advertiser* (Philadelphia), April 11, 1805.

53. New York *Commercial Advertiser*, July 3, 1806.

54. The *arête* by Ferrand is published in the *Recueil général des lois et des actes du gouvernement d'Haïti* as piece no. 23, 1:39–41. It was also published in the Haitian *Gazette* and is reprinted in the *Gazette politique et commerciale d'Haïti, le premier hebdomadaire haïtien, créé après le premier janvier 1804* (Port-au-Prince: Bibliothèque nationale d'Haïti, n.d.), 62–64. I will be referring to the latter edition.

55. Emilio Cordero Michel, "Dessalines en Saint-Domingue espagnol," in *Saint-Domingue espagnol et la revolution nègre d'Haïti*, ed. Alain Yacou (Paris: Karthala, 2007), 416.

56. Michel, "Dessalines en Saint-Domingue espagnol," 422.

57. Michel, "Dessalines en Saint-Domingue espagnol," 432.

58. *American and Commercial Daily Advertiser* (Maryland), January 1, 1805.

59. *Political Observatory* (New Hampshire), April 27, 1805.

60. New York *Commercial Advertiser*, April 5, 1805.

61. *Recueil général des lois et des actes du gouvernement d'Haïti*, 1:36.

62. *Recueil général des lois et des actes du gouvernement d'Haïti*, 1:37.

63. *Recueil général des lois et des actes du gouvernement d'Haïti*, 1:38.

64. *Daily Advertiser*, September 14, 1807.

4

Reading Between the Lines: Dessalines's Anticolonial Imperialism in Venezuela and Trinidad

As 1805 slipped into 1806, the law of nations was proving inhospitable to new black nations; sovereign Haiti was being reframed as an eternal rogue colony. When Dessalines attempted to build Haiti's economic, military, and cultural strength through international trade, demographic development, and publication of state documents, increasingly the wider world received the new nation not as the triumph of right and a stunning innovation, but as an inherent subversion of the racialized power hierarchies that were the basis of Euro-American prosperity. *Could* a former colony survive as the first free black nation in an international sphere without seeking political safe havens and partners in trade, not just among slave-holding and/or colonized states that normally depended on racial segregation, but among fellow anticolonial states—anticolonial states that were not yet in existence? The specter of Haitian transnational subversion, of a Haitian attempt not just to declare independence but also to spread it to other nearby populations, was alarmingly plausible to European colonists and metropoles. It is also what is most difficult to trace in terms of actual evidence; unlike the philosophically stunning narratives Dessalines was disseminating throughout the U.S., this is a text one must read between the lines.

My paradigm of Haitian revolutionary literary history broadens in this chapter to include largely uninscribed "texts" as a part of the larger field of narratives by slaves and former slaves. These "texts" bridge the gap between printed genres like the Anglophone slave narrative or the carefully crafted literary and political self-representations of Haitian leaders in the Euro-American media, and the oblique evidence of the actual, planned, and rumored slave insurgencies that played out on the historical rather than the literary stage, like the planned insurrection of Denmark Vesey on the Carolina coast, which was believed to have been influenced by Haitian connections and models. Few documents represent the identities and intentions of participants in isolated insurgent movements, who generally depend on stealth for survival. A cracked mirror of statements, correspondence, legal documents, and journalism provides the eclectic inscription, from mostly hostile points of view, of their activities. There is a fine line between documentation of participants' intentions and the contiguous domain of slaveholders' fears and political exploitation of slave rebellion.

The abundant paper trail relating to the Haitian Revolution derives from its fundamental embeddedness within the French colonial army in Saint-Domingue, which had a highly developed communicative and record-keeping apparatus. The Oath of the Caiman Woods at the start of the Haitian Revolution, despite the contemporary echoes of its structures that I have shown in Chapters 2 and 3, is a ghost text that contrasts with the correspondence, decrees, and proclamations of the revolutionary participants in the *armée de Saint-Domingue*. Maroon leaders in the Haitian Revolution, in contrast to the black officers of the French army, also remain ineffably mysterious as thinkers and manipulators of political processes. Dessalines, through intermediaries, quickly mastered and exploited for his own purposes the print culture proper to the contemporary European military, legislative, and diplomatic spheres. But subversive rather than military and governmental tactics were not suited to the same communicative practices. Colonial agents would accuse Dessalines of specifically off-the-record strategies such as the stealth infiltration of revolutionary agents. This chapter presents an encounter with a silent narrative of subversion that also existed in the margins of the slave narrative in the U.S., but that is here international in scope. The fundamental justification for engaging with admittedly sparse evidence is simple: without it, any account of the "slave narratives" associated with Dessalines would remain incomplete.

The "Pan-American" Paradigm

Two anticolonial episodes beyond the borders of Haiti were linked to Dessalines within the span of a year and a few months, both related to the Spanish colonies. The first was an alleged covert inter-island emancipation plot sponsored or inspired by Dessalines, most concretely traced to Trinidad and an alleged defeated insurrection plot there by French-speaking slaves in December of 1805. The second was the month-long anchoring of Francisco de Miranda's crew in the harbor of Jacmel in the spring of 1806, en route to try to overthrow Spanish colonial control of Venezuela. Neither of these episodes yields easily to analysis and interpretation; on the contrary, the question of Dessalines's "internationalism," or "pan-Americanism," as this problem traditionally has been framed, is contentious.

Dessalines's major biographers, Berthony Dupont, Timoléon Brutus, and

St. Victor Jean Baptiste, present a united front in arguing for the plausibility of Dessalines's international engagement and outreach to colonized and enslaved populations. Dupont states that Dessalines pursued a transregional overthrow of the infrastructure put in place by colonial powers to maintain enslavement. It was, he claims, "une question de vie ou de mort [...] que le succès de la révolution haïtienne ne reste pas isolé"[1] ("a question of life or death [...] that the Haitian revolution not remain an isolated event"). Brutus concludes the first volume of *L'Homme d'airain* with this statement: "Le Fondateur ne songeait pas à calfeutrer son pays dans le creuset étanche et sterile de l'isolement. Il avait compris la vie internationale dans son sens véritable"[2] ("The Founder certainly did not think of buffering his country in the airtight, sterile crucible of isolation. He had grasped the full meaning of international life"). Brutus, in his volume on Dessalines's empire, introduces the "pan-American" trope, citing the Miranda episode in Haiti.[3] St. Victor Jean Baptiste, in *Le Fondateur devant l'histoire*, continued development of "L'idée pan-américaine," making frequent use of primary sources from the political and economic spheres, and training a keen eye on small significant details concerning Dessalines in the encyclopedic work of Thomas Madiou. Jean Baptiste argues forcefully for Dessalines's role as the founder of the "Oeuvre de solidarité panaméricaine" ("the great work of panamerican solidarity"), and his status as precursor to "l'indépendance de tous les états hispaniques"[4] ("the independence of all the Hispanic nations").

Historians of the Haitian Revolution, on the other hand, when they do reach into the independence era, have often viewed Dessalines's involvement in emancipation schemes beyond Haitian borders as strategically implausible within the geopolitical conditions of the colonial Caribbean at the opening of the nineteenth century. As Léo Elisabeth characteristically cautions, "N'exagérons pas l'action subversive du gouvernement d'Haïti"[5] ("We must not exaggerate the subversive activities of the Haitian government"). David Geggus, in his detailed assessment of patterns of slave insurrection and their causality between 1789 and 1815, all but rules out the significance of Dessalines's role in the transnational spread of rebellion, reasoning in part that "early Haitian rulers could not afford to provoke a maritime blockade by the slaveholding powers that would cut off their source of arms."[6] Geggus's basic point, that Dessalines would not have challenged another nation by sea with his actual army, is incontestable (with the caveat that numerous observers claimed at the time that the blockades were more a matter of dominant posturing than actual deterrence). But the stealth infiltration and piggy-back maneuvers that I discuss here were specifically designed not to trigger naval response.

The indirect and covert spread of Dessalinian anticolonialism is in many ways the obverse mirror image of the trade of "neutral" merchants, in that neutral trade in practice often offered a way around restrictions imposed by national governments and their military representatives. As Gordon S. Brown notes, the "Haiti trade" was one place where American merchants "had determined to defend their interest without support from the government," by "arming their ships against the illegal privateers" and sometimes, "engaging in combat with the proper French cruisers."[7] General Ferrand in Santo Domingo, in October of 1804, fumed that records found on neutral vessels recently seized by the French proved that "vessels coming from the rebel ports are very carefully and very regularly dispatched for the ports of Dominica, Tobago, St. Thomas, Curracoa, Jamaica, Havana, Baracoa, Santiago de Cuba, etc."[8]

These trajectories from Haiti all around the Caribbean were ostensibly unattached to national or ideological causes, representing capitalism in a pure evolutionary form, following profits with little heed of the possible revolutionary consequences of new partnerships. As J. Randolph, a member of the U.S. House of Representatives, would poignantly note in March 1806, the politics of black versus white empires were irrelevant to participants on the high seas of trade:

> As to the motives of the neutral merchant, they are out of the question. His object, no doubt, like that of every other trader under the sun, is gain. He, sir, is too often the mere euphemeron [sic], the butterfly of the day, who does not care one farthing whether you are at war with this or that nation, with England or with France, provided he can get good returns. His is to post his books and balance the ledger, and whether he deals with the subjects of a white emperour or a black one, of Bonaparte or Dessalines, 'tis all the same to him.[9]

The ideologically "neutral" motivations for an economic relationship between American merchants and the Haitians sometimes seemed to replace the relationship of white and black with the green of the dollar.

This circum-Caribbean neutral traffic offered potential extensions of the sphere of Haitian influence. Ferrand took drastic measures in the spring of 1805 to counter the implicitly revolutionary consequences of international trade with Haiti. The merchants, Ferrand stormed, were "those scoundrels, who maintain the rebellion in Hispaniola, by furnishing everything necessary to the rebels."[10] Ferrand astounded the mercantile world by declaring that "all individuals, whomsoever, found on board of any vessel or vessels, allies or neutrals, bound to any ports in Hispaniola occupied by the rebels, shall suffer death." Likewise, all individuals, allies or neutrals, coming out of any port occupied by the Haitians, would suffer death. Furthermore, any individuals found within two leagues distance of Haitian ports would suffer death. The goal of the measures was to "prevent all kinds of communication with the coast of Hispaniola occupied by the rebels." Communication with Haiti meant death!

American merchants were incensed at what was seen as piratical militarism on the part of France. Where was their own government to protect them?

> The French in the West Indies [...] not only capture and condemn vessels bound to the Island of Hayti (St. Domingo) which might be justified if the island is regularly blockaded and proclaimed such; but the vessels are taken by cruisers without commissions; cargoes sold without condemnation, and our shipping plundered at sea [...] Have we a government? [...] America [...] is pillaged by the enlightened government of France.[11]

Governments claimed to control the maritime game, but "communication" of all kinds, and battles to suppress it, showed how much went between the lines.

Dessalines's Empire of Liberty

Nor was the "communicative" influence of neutral trade unattached to an American ideology of New World extensions of anticolonial freedom. The notion of democratic imperialism suffused early American state identity, as Gordon S. Wood has shown. America was a "Hercules in the cradle," advancing toward destinies Jefferson described as "beyond the reach of the mortal eye."[12] Territorial expansion was justified by "the attachment to neutral rights, or freedom of commerce in war."[13] The U.S. was not beyond tacit support for kindred anticolonial projects. Alexander Hamilton, for example, had asserted to the American minister in Britain that the U.S. should be "the principal agency"[14] in Francisco de Miranda's project to liberate several South American colonies from Spanish colonial rule. Dessalines arguably shared this value of anticolonial empire. He did not judge the politics of conquest or invasion in all cases as a duplication of the colonial power stance that he abhorred.

It has been frequently observed that the Haitian Declaration of Independence weighs against any proto-colonial or neo-colonial exercise of Haitian authority in the Caribbean region. The Declaration exhorts, "Gardons-nous cependant de l'esprit de prosélitisme [...] laissons en paix respirer nos voisins. Qu'ils vivent paisiblement sous l'égide des lois qu'ils se sont faites" ("Let us be on our guard against the spirit of proselytism [...] and allow our neighbors to breathe in peace. They should be allowed to live peacefully by the laws they themselves established"). Dessalines cautions against aspiring to be "legislators of the Antilles," or letting the Haitians' glory consist in "troubling the repose of neighboring islands." The French alone are the target of any outward aggression, not the Haitians' other neighbors: "Paix à nos voisins, anathème aux français!" ("Peace to our neighbors, anathema to the French!")

Yet Dessalines also showed profound empathy for the suffering of other enslaved people. He most likely did not equate insurrections against slavery with models of colonial "conquest," but rather with the undoing of conquest, even if he saw the people who would be affected as his own future subjects. The May 1805 Constitution of Haiti decreed, in article 36, that "The emperor shall never form any enterprise with the view of making conquests, nor to disturb the peace and the interior administration of foreign colonies."[15] But the Constitution was published *after* the failed invasion of Santo Domingo, which strongly suggests that Dessalines did not believe this episode had contradicted the principle articulated in article 36. It was self-defense on the island of Haiti, not a spread of Haitian dominion.

With regard to Dessalines's feelings about the French colonies of Martinique and Guadeloupe, our best evidence comes from the "I have avenged America" proclamation of April 28, 1804.[16] It urged remembrance of "the catalog of atrocities committed against our species," including the Napoleonic reinslavement plotted "with the calmness and serenity of a countenance accustomed to similar crimes." Dessalines celebrated Louis Delgrès's unsuccessful 1802 revolt in Guadeloupe: "the brave and immortal Delgresse [*sic*], blown into the air with the fort which he defended, rather than accept their offered chains." Dessalines expressed the wish that he could emancipate the slaves not only of Guadeloupe but also of Martinique: "Unfortunate people! If only I could fly to your assistance, and break your fetters!" In effect, the very notion of avenging not Saint-Domingue, but *America* in a large sense—the Americas—suggests Dessalines's interest in a larger domain of decolonization.

Caribbean Communion in Trinidad

The first episode of alleged Haitian imperialist decolonization that I examine here begins in St. Thomas and concludes in Trinidad. In the early spring of 1805, a former creole colonist from Saint-Domingue, Roberjot Lartigue, now a French agent and commissioner in St. Thomas, was becoming increasingly alarmed about the potential subversion of colonial authority in the French Antilles by the Haitians. He suspected the migration of Haitian emissaries with a mandate from Dessalines to infiltrate slaves' workshops and social organizations. Roberjot Lartigue did not use a first name on his correspondence or publications, but he was probably the Félix-André-Charles-Alexandre Roberjot Lartigue who appears as a "rightful claimant" in the Saint-Domingue indemnity reparations.

According to his later reconstitution of the events, Roberjot Lartigue spent months in 1805 working to suppress a Haitian movement in St. Thomas to spread insurrection to the slaves of Martinique and Guadeloupe, a movement which instead resurfaced in an attempted insurrection in Trinidad. St. Thomas in 1805 clearly served as a hub of insider information about the Franco-Haitian conflict, to judge from the flow of news to U.S. papers from sources in St. Thomas. Roberjot Lartigue typified that colonial insider status. The extended Roberjot Lartigue family had been wealthy and prominent in the colonial treasury and as landholders, and they would figure prominently in the disbursement of reparations to former colonists from the indemnity payments made by the Haitians.[17] Lartigue was related to the Mlle Roberjot Lartigue, later the baroness Lallemand, who wrote a memoir of her revolutionary-era sojourn in Saint-Domingue, including her engagement to the son of Rochambeau.[18] Fascinatingly, the future Mme de Lallemand was also identified as a mistress of Toussaint Louverture.[19]

Roberjot Lartigue had served in an official role as a commissioner in Saint-Domingue's Club Massiac to prevent the entry into the colony of affiliates, of whatever race, of the abolitionist *Amis des noirs* in 1791–92.[20] He had, in effect, a background in policing (or attempting to police) the newly vulnerable French colonial power, and he epitomized the injured party of French colonial privilege.

Roberjot Lartigue's letter (in two personally signed copies) on the episode in question to the ethnographer M. L. E. Moreau de Saint-Méry has the disadvantage of being a retroactive reconstitution, dated August 25, 1814, of an original letter ostensibly dating from May 20, 1806. That correspondence had allegedly been seized by the Spanish during an investigative trip by Roberjot Lartigue to Trinidad ("J'ai eu ma malle et mes papiers saisis par les espagnols" ["My briefcase and papers were seized by the Spanish"]). The letter describes his role in the third person. A notation in Moreau's own hand documents the date of receipt of the letter as 1814. A longer pamphlet, the *Rapport*, in which Roberjot Lartigue provides a transcription of the letter to Moreau, was published in 1815.[21] The report also featured extensive correspondence from an array of weighty colonial officials of the 1805–1806 period, many of whom had detailed personal experience of Saint-Domingue, including General Kerverseau, "certifying" his allegations.

Roberjot Lartigue apparently waited until 1814 to (re-)initiate contact with Moreau and other colonial officials about this episode from 1805 and correspondence from 1806 for two reasons. Moreau had returned to France only recently, and the Roberjot Lartigue document is one of several narratives, like the narrative of the kidnapping of Henry Christophe's son that will be discussed in Chapter 5, that people from the Haitian colonial domain brought to his attention in 1814. The *Rapport* was also part of Roberjot Lartigue's campaign for a royal retirement pension from the newly restored Bourbon government of Louis XVIII based on his earlier meritorious service.

The plot alleged by Roberjot Lartigue unfurled after the defeat of Dessalines's army in Santo Domingo in the spring of 1805. Roberjot Lartigue alleges that Dessalines had sent emissaries to foster a club for Haitian blacks and *gens de couleur* in St. Thomas, who were supposed then to infiltrate French colonies and foment a Christmas insurrection in Martinique and Guadeloupe. The planned insurrection involved 14 "regiments," with the simultaneous goals of emancipating those colonies and establishing Dessalines as leader:

> Pendant que Mr Roberjot Lartigue a fait le service à St Thomas en qualité d'agent et en qualité de commissaire du gouvernement français, il a fait dissoudre et déporter de St Thomas un club de nègres et de gens de couleur qui étaient envoyér [*sic*] par Dessaline [*sic*], le chef des révoltés de St Domingue, afin de parvenir à passer dans les colonies françaises pour soulever la Martinique et la Guadeloupe; et au mois de décembre 1805 Dessaline [*sic*] expédia de St. Domingue des émissaires pour exécuter le projet monstrueux de descendre à la Martinique et à la Guadeloupe, d'y assassiner tous les habitans [*sic*], de brûler les villes, de soulever les nègres et les gens de couleur et d'y former 14 régimens [*sic*] s'en rendre maître et établir l'indépendance de ces deux colonies.[22]

> (During the years in which Monsieur Roberjot Lartigue served in St. Thomas as an agent and commissioner of the French government, he disbanded and deported from St. Thomas a club of blacks and persons of color who had been sent by Dessalines, the leader of the rebels in St. Domingue, in order to infiltrate the French colonies and to establish insurrection in Martinique and Guadeloupe; and in the month of December 1805 Dessalines sent emissaries from St. Domingue to carry out the monstrous project of going down to Martinique and Guadeloupe, assassinating the plantation owners ["habitans"], burning the cities, provoking insurrection among the blacks and the persons of color and forming 14 regiments, in order simultaneously to establish his own authority and the independence of these two colonies.)

In a second sequence of events described by Roberjot Lartigue, he, as agent and commissioner, rushed to inform the General and Judge of St. Thomas about the plot, asking authorities to prohibit commerce and communication with the "nègres révoltés de St. Domingue" ("the insurrectional blacks of St. Domingue"). He claimed that the Danish government then issued a decree to this effect on October 15, 1805, and also that many blacks were deported from St. Thomas.

Following the chronology of events in Roberjot Lartigue's narrative, in the next episode the deported Haitian emissaries found themselves unable to enter Martinique and Guadeloupe to carry out their plot. But they went to Trinidad in December, 1805, with purposes of establishing insurrection. Roberjot Lartigue wrote that their plan was soon discovered, because several black female merchants in the streets there sang, in order to foment the revolt of the blacks and the *mulâtres*, "Le sang des blancs est bon pour boire; la chair des blancs est bonne pour manger; (refrain): vive Dessalines" ("The blood of whites is good to drink; the flesh of whites is good to eat; [refrain] long live Dessalines"). Roberjot Lartigue noted that the British governor of Trinidad, Hislop (whom he and the letter writers in the report call "Isloop"), was warned, and had an assembly of merchants, blacks, *mulâtres*, and foreigners arrested and thrown in prison. Thirty leaders of color were eventually tried and beheaded, according to Roberjot Lartigue, and many others were deported or sentenced to other punishments. Roberjot Lartigue closes his narrative by recounting that he himself went to Trinidad after hearing of these events, and had a copy of the judgment made and sent to Moreau de St. Méry "so that he could publicize it as he saw fit"; but presumably it was during this visit in the early summer of 1806 that his papers were seized by the Spanish.

To what extent can we treat Roberjot Lartigue's report as credible? The self-serving and self-confirming nature of the witnessing in the report, combined with the retroactive constitution of the correspondence at its core, and finally the narrative's compression of linked events in St. Thomas, Trinidad, and Martinique and Guadeloupe into a period of time between October 15, 1805, and December of 1805, have led to skepticism among the majority of the small group of historians who have mentioned Roberjot Lartigue's claims at all. Léo Elisabeth says of this Trinidad narrative, "Lartigue fantasme" ("Lartigue is dreaming").[23] Robert Paquette also torpedoes it as rumor:

> No proof has been put forward to show that Toussaint Louverture, Dessalines, or Christophe attempted to extend black freedom beyond Hispaniola. [...] the supposed expedition sent in 1805 by Dessalines to Martinique and Trinidad seems fairly obviously based on a rumor spread by a French colonist.[24]

Geggus dismisses Dessalines's "supposed involvement in the 1805 Trinidad conspiracy" as "quite spurious."[25] Roberjot Lartigue is described by Régis Antoine as a mouthpiece of "la peur politique de la contagion révolutionnaire en direction des deux îles"[26] ("political fear of revolutionary contagion from Haiti to Guadeloupe and Martinique").

Elisabeth's ambivalence and restraint are belied by his surprisingly suggestive research findings. His reasoning for discrediting the evidence he himself presents seems to be that Roberjot Lartigue was simply the first link in a racist rumor chain: "Roberjot-Lartigue construit la thèse d'une offensive.

Le 13 septembre 1805, il s'en tient aux on-dit" ["Roberjot-Lartigue constructs the hypothesis of an aggression. On September 13, 1805, he is still restricting himself to 'They say'").[27] Yet he cites a range of archival correspondence from that fall concerning Haitian emissaries and their establishment of a subversive club in St. Thomas. This includes the following December 1, 1805, announcement by Kerverseau, the general who had taken Santo Domingo back from Toussaint Louverture's appointed leaders:

> Dessalines, leader of the Brigands in Saint-Domingue, has chosen the island [St. Thomas] as the most convenient in the Antilles for the establishment of a public club of *gens de couleur* [...] The agents of this club are seeking by all possible means to communicate to the workshops of the French colonies that this leader of the rebels whom they call the Emperor of Hayti [...] has taken measures to protect their revolt, if they wish to follow the example of the blacks of Saint-Domingue.[28]

In Martinique, Villaret Joyeuse, who had earlier contributed to the dissemination of Roberjot Lartigue's allegations, seemed to view them as sufficiently credible to take follow-up steps including seizing Haitian sailors on the crews of American vessels.[29]

Jean Fouchard, in "Quand Haïti exportait la liberté aux Antilles" ("When Haiti Exported Liberty to the Antilles"), refers to unpublished documents in the C8 A series of the Archives nationales that speak of "de nombreux petits bâtiments armés par Dessalines pour introduire dans nos îles sa doctrine, ses apôtres, et ses principes"[30] ("numerous small ships armed by Dessalines to introduce into our islands his doctrine, his apostles, and his principles"), as well as of the "arrestations d'agitateurs haïtiens à St. Thomas" ("arrests of Haitian agitators in St. Thomas").

José Luciano Franco and Nicolas Rey also refer to colonial sources from other national perspectives. Rey hypothesizes in his work on the *negros franceses*, "la Révolution haïtienne, victorieuse, cherchait désormais à s'étendre à l'ensemble du basin caribéen, pour protéger ses frontières, et disposer d'alliés sûrs dans la région acquis à sa cause"[31] ("the Haitian Revolution, victorious, sought henceforth to spread to the larger Caribbean basin, to protect its frontiers, and to have predictable regional allies, won over to its cause"). As Franco notes, there had been a late November 1805 arrest in Puerto Rico inspired by the warnings provided by French authorities about a Dessalines plot. The Puerto Rican Governor Montes, on November 30, 1805, had ordered the arrest of a "mulato francés de apellido Chanlatte"[32] ("a French mulatto by the name of Chanlatte").[33] There was a time lag in moving from Chanlatte's actual arrest to documented statements and eventually legislation based on the threat of Haitian antico-lonial emissaries in 1806. Franco notes that "The French government had announced to Madrid on September 3, 1806, that Dessalines had sent emissaries to the European colonies of the Caribbean to incite insurrection among the slaves. And it had signaled the fact that it had arrested some seditious agents on the island of St. Thomas."[34] Then, on September 14, 1806, the Spanish crown issued the following decree:

> It has come to the attention of the King that some emissaries of Dessalines have left Saint-Domingue to organize a slave revolution in the American Establishments of the European Powers; his Majesty wishes that all men of color coming from Saint-Domingue to the Spanish colonies be immediately arrested, and likewise the colonists with direct knowledge of said emissaries.[35]

Is it possible that one individual had succeeded in establishing international credibility through various levels of colonial administration and government for a spurious rumor? The colonial administration took seriously enough the rumor of a Dessalinian plot via St. Thomas that there were real ramifications for vessels believed to have subversive Haitians on board, and for merchants with supposed ties to Haitian subversion.[36] On April 28, 1806, the *Mercantile Advertiser* in New York wrote that "The Danes have by proclamation prohibited all trade and intercourse between the island of St. Thomas and the Empire of Hayti."

Some of the most intriguing documentation of the St. Thomas episode was articulated around this prohibition. Various articles noted that the British navy was helping to enforce the Danish embargo, rerouting numerous ships from Haiti to Tortola rather than St. Thomas. For example, on October 27, 1806, the New York *Mercantile Advertiser* noted that "Schr. [schooner] Maddox, from Philadelphia, for Laguira, and schr. General Eaton, from Hayti for St. Thomas, are sent into Tortola. –'The British cruizers [*sic*] on the Tortola station, will send in all vessels bound to and from Hayti.'" The *United States Gazette* in Philadelphia reported on November 28, 1806, "Seven Baltimore vessels sent into Tortola, on their passage from Hayti to St. Thomas, have been condemned—three of them ransomed since condemnation."

The reasons for this embargo could conceivably have had more to do with the Danish relationship to France than with the plot referenced by Roberjot Lartigue; its historical existence does not in itself confirm Roberjot Lartigue's story, but it confirms that people believed the story. General Ernouf had sent his own aide-de-camp, Lieutenant-Colonel Mouton,

> vers le Gouverneur danois, afin de prévenir du danger qu'il y avait de souffrir dans son île de pareils émissaires; que le Gouverneur Danois, ayant pris conseil de M. Roberjot Lartigue, fit arrêter et déporter ces émissaires

dont les machinations auraient à nouveau excité la révolte dans les colonies françaises.[37]

(to the Danish governor, to warn him of the dangers he faced from such emissaries in his island; and that the Danish governor, after taking Roberjot Lartigue's advice, ordered the arrest and deportation of these emissaries whose schemes would have reignited revolt in the French colonies.)

A mid-nineteenth-century history of Martinique would specifically refer to the movement of Haitian emissaries from Tortola, where they been deported, to Trinidad. The 1846 *Histoire de la Martinique* by Sidney Daney de Marcillac notes the distraction of the colonists from financial problems in 1806 by "le danger auquel venait de s'échapper l'île de la Trinité" ("the danger narrowly escaped by Trinidad"):

Des émissaires [de Saint-Domingue], partis de chez eux, s'étaient rendus d'abord à Saint-Thomas [...] Mais le gouvernement danois les en avait expulsés et ils avaient cherché un asile à Tortole, véritable repaire de pirates. De cette petite île, ils avaient jeté les yeux sur la Trinité où ils savaient que se trouvaient plusieurs ateliers composés de nègres de Saint-Domingue."[38]

(Emissaries [from Saint-Domingue], after leaving their home, had gone first to Saint-Thomas. [...] But the Danish government had expelled them and they had sought asylum in Tortola, a true pirates' lair. From this little island, they had set their sights on Trinidad, where they knew that there were several workshops populated by blacks from Saint-Domingue.)

It is important to note that the order of events in accounts like Daney's contradicts Roberjot Lartigue's account. Roberjot Lartigue stated that the events in St. Thomas preceded those in Trinidad, which occurred in December of 1805. But the historical record of contemporaneous journalism and some testimonials in Roberjot Lartigue's own report seem to point to the opposite sequence: that *after* the events in Trinidad, in the spring of 1806, commerce between St. Thomas and Haiti was made illegal by the Danish government, and suspicious players were diverted to Tortola. Yet the warnings by French colonial administrators cited by Elisabeth make it quite plausible that Roberjot Lartigue had been bringing allegations to French and Danish authorities since the fall of 1805, but that they were only persuaded to act forcefully in 1806, after the Trinidad events came to light. A "chicken or egg" conundrum lies at the heart of these episodes—did Haitian participants in the Trinidad plot, with no St. Thomas connection, arbitrarily and indirectly justify the ongoing rantings of a minor French colonial official in St. Thomas? Or did participants who were forced to leave St. Thomas then travel on to Trinidad, fulfilling Roberjot Lartigue's worst fears? In either case, it cannot be denied that French officials were already warning the Spanish government of Haitian malice afoot in the fall of 1805.

So what was the episode that seemed to justify Roberjot Lartigue's warnings—what really happened in Trinidad? U.S. papers published detailed accounts of a complex social organization in Trinidad, with proto-military hierarchies, structures referring to Martinique, Guadeloupe, and the Danish islands (as well as to English and Spanish labels of distinction), the taking of oaths, ceremonies involving communion-like structures, and creole songs that connected communion motifs of flesh and blood to violent insurrection. In early December of 1805, a slave woman reported to the authorities that the group was preparing a Christmas massacre. The newspaper accounts explain that authorities in Trinidad had not originally found the group's organization to be a cause for alarm, but that once "convoys" were reframed as "regiments," there was increasing evidence of subversive intentions. The authorities did not overtly link the events to an earlier plot in St. Thomas or, specifically, to Dessalines.

The most complete transcription of an article "From a Late Trinidad Paper" representing "Extracts from the minutes of his majesty's council" on "20th December, 1805," appeared in the *Mercantile Advertiser* on February 6, 1806. On December 10, 1805, information that a "plan of the most sanguinary nature was in agitation among some of the negroes of the colony" was brought before the lieutenant-governor and the council, who examined the evidence and deliberated from December 11 to December 18, "sitting to a late hour every day." Four black leaders—not the 30 noted by Lartigue—"were found 'guilty of attempting to excite an insurrection among the negroes of this colony,'" and subsequently hanged, beheaded, and exhibited on pikes.

The society had begun with convoys. The convoys, the article explains, had structured what "more properly may be called *societies* for the purposes of *dancing* and *innocent amusement.*" Within these societies, they had "adopted different degrees of rank such as *generals en chef, generals en seconde, ambassadors, colonels, aide-de-camps, majors, prime ministers, treasurers, grand judges, secretaries, alguazies.*"

But these convoys had morphed into "regiments," most of which had French names, such as "Macaque,"[39] "Sans-peur," and St. Georges; another was called "Cocorite."[40] These regiments were primarily located in the area of Carenage, with the exception of Cocorite, which extended "to the town and outskirts of it." They were affiliated with additional regiments, named "Martinique," "Guadeloupe," "La Fantaisie," "Marine," and "Danish." The earlier convoys, despite their involvement in "the administration of oaths" of a complex ritual nature, did not appear to the council "to have been concerned in the plot." The problem was the sudden evolution of the organization and orientation of the societies: "the change, which lately introduced itself in their institution, cannot be regarded with indifference." The most recent rituals and ceremonies were "perfectly unnecessary for promoting the original intention of the convoys."

These ceremonies involved "the administration of oaths (or as it was termed, of the *communion*), when the *crucifix*, *holy water*, and *holy bread* were used, imposing obedience to their kings, and attachment to their regiments." These rituals, combined with the "*barbarous expressions* lately sung by the *huckster negro women* and other slaves (proved by incontestable evidence), alluding to the approaching annihilation of the *whites*," led the council to feel "beyond a doubt that (the insurrection having once broken out) measures had not been neglected to prepare the minds of the slaves for such an event." The lyrics in question were in Creole:

> Pain c'est viande Béqué,
> Vin c'est sang Béqué;
> Nous va mangé pain Béqué;
> Nous va boir sang Béqué
> [refrain] St. Domingue

> [Bread is white man's flesh,
> Wine is white man's blood,
> We will eat Béqué bread,
> We will drink white blood,
> St. Domingue]

The authorities believed that the song constituted indirect evidence of a cultural preparation for violence ("to prepare the minds of slaves"). But the heart of the matter was that one of the prisoners confessed that "he was to join with his regiment those at the *Carenage*, on Christmas day, for the purpose of rising against the whites; that having effected their purpose there, they were to proceed to town, to set it on fire, after which a general massacre of the whites, and free colored people, and those blacks who refused to join the insurgents, was to take place."

An article in the New Hampshire *Political Observatory* on February 28, 1806, summarized the repression of the plot, concluding that "At the last dates, tranquility was restored; and the blacks in perfect subjection." This "perfect subjection" had been achieved as follows: "Four of the ringleaders, viz. Samson, king of the Macaque regiment, Baptiste, king of the Cocorite regiment and Carlos, a general-in-chief, were apprehended, tried, condemned, and sentenced to be hung, and were beheaded."

Historians of Trinidad and its musical traditions have expressed skepticism that what was brewing in December of 1805 was actual insurrection. Geggus argues that songs commemorating the Haitian Revolution circulated throughout the Caribbean: "From Jamaica to Trinidad, slaves celebrated in song the triumph of the Haitian insurgents."[41] William Piersen considers the communion-based song documented at the time to have been satire.[42] John Cowley cites E. L. Joseph's 1838 history of Trinidad, in which he suggested that "'the principal evidence in the case' came from 'a mad woman!'"[43] And yet Joseph, in his history, expressed confidence that the judges of the potential insurrection were convinced by the verbal evidence: "It seemed to have originated with some French and African negroes. I have inspected the papers of the courts-martial held on these people, and fully believe that their *judges* were convinced of their guilt."[44]

One of the most ambiguous elements of the case is that, as James Millette has documented, there was a major French-speaking population of color in the Carenage quarters of Trinidad in 1803; they accounted for 126 out of 150 men in 1803.[45] Millette observes that Trinidad in many ways resembled a French colony, with a hybrid population of slaves from the rainbow of French-speaking islands in the Caribbean, but not least from Rigaud's forces, defeated by Toussaint.[46] Spies and intrigue from French-speaking islands had been a concern for colonial authorities in Trinidad throughout the final years of the Haitian Revolution.[47] As Geggus notes, "The Spanish government, seeking to create a plantation economy, had developed the island primarily with French settlers."[48] Rigaud's soldiers were not the only group of blacks and people of color from the wrong side of a given military moment in the course of the Haitian Revolution to migrate to Trinidad: when Jean-François's group of "auxiliary" soldiers fled Santo Domingo, the next to largest group went to Trinidad. According to Geggus, however, "they were sent back to Santo Domingo."[49]

This immigration profile means that Trinidad did not need to import Haitian emissaries in order to have devised a complex French-speaking, Haiti-inspired society; these could have arisen naturally in their own environment. Conversely, Haitian emissaries would have found a fertile ground in Trinidad for communication and for the invocation of shared revolutionary knowledge. Elisabeth quotes a colonial prefect from the Lesser Antilles, Laussat, who on February 2, 1806, stated that "Trinidad est le refuge de tous les nègres échappés de St. Domingue et une vingtaine ont été pendus à Noël."[50]

Paquette raises the possibility that "Many Haitian individuals were no doubt willing to venture where Haitian governments feared to tread"[51] as justification for a conceptual framework of Dessalines-*era* Haitian activities rather than a Dessalinian plot per se. But the consistent print-cultural evidence of Dessalines's careful consideration of anticolonial and postcolonial political identities, policies, and institutions makes it imprudent to rule out a Dessalinian role—and above all through reasoning about "fear," since Dessalines, no matter how strategic, never manifested fear.

Roberjot Lartigue's narrative of a movement to send Dessalinian emissaries to sow insurrection in other parts of the Caribbean, piggy-backing on neutral commerce, is not something that can be definitively confirmed with presently known materials. Something akin to colonial hysteria undoubtedly influenced extrapolations from Saint-Domingue to a falling colonial house of cards elsewhere in the Americas, and Roberjot Lartigue may have been convinced for personal and cultural reasons that Dessalines was a menace to other colonial worlds like the one he had seen disintegrate. But there is no evidence against this rumored stealth expansion of Haiti's empire of liberty either. Where there is smoke, there may be fire—and here there would seem to be an unthinkable amount of smoke for a purely rumored fire. Dessalines, returning from Santo Domingo as we saw in Chapter 3 and urging his compatriots to be on the defensive, to build new fortifications away from the coast, may well have been looking for new mechanisms and modalities to avenge America. This was a secret narrative of the "brigand sovereignty" of former slaves. It was a narrative of the broader influence of the Haitian model, and a will to "reenact" the Haitian Revolution, as the *Columbian Centinel* (February 19, 1806) commented of the Trinidad events: "The infernal plot [...] was to re-act in this island the sanguinary scenes of *St. Domingo.*"

Before Bolívar: Miranda, Haiti, and Venezuela

The next and final episode to be examined here, that of the Miranda expedition in Jacmel, augments the still oblique evidence of Dessalines's participation in decolonization schemes that did not rely on formal and national military engagement, but on incendiary persuasion and insurrection plotted by small numbers of people navigating through international spaces, equipped with revolutionary texts and ideas. This episode also reflects the prestige Dessalines's proclamations had attained in the revolutionary world, and the revolutionary credibility of the Haitians in the creole Americas.

The episode opens with a surreal scene of anticolonial print culture on board a ship, the *Leander*, docked in Jacmel, Haiti, in the early spring of 1806. James Biggs, a crew member in Don Francisco de Miranda's expedition, later recounted:

> February 23rd. One side of the quarter deck is occupied by a printing press, at which several young men of that profession are busy in striking off the general's proclamations to the people of South America, and setting the types for printing our commissions.[52]

Miranda not only produced his *Proclamation to the Inhabitants of South America* while in Haiti, but he also, according to Karen Racine, invented a new flag of "Columbian" independence there, and several other documents of anticolonial revolutionary propaganda: "While in Haiti, the printers cranked out over 2,000 copies of five different texts destined for the inhabitants of the Venezuela coast and 'all parts of the world.'"[53]

The relationship between Miranda's expedition to decolonize Venezuela as a foundation for his imagined empire "Columbia," which would be led by a ruler called the "Inca," and the government of Dessalines is a complex story, but it is symbolized by Miranda's decision to launch his proclamations to the world from Haiti, the site of Dessalines's remarkable conquest of New World media spaces. Haiti—and Dessalines—are more meaningfully embedded in Miranda's project than scholars such as François Dalencour have allowed.[54]

Miranda, of course, had not arrived in Jacmel out of the void. The Venezuelan creole revolutionary had been shopping for a sponsor of his intended decolonization blitz on South America for many years. He had first applied for U.S. support through Alexander Hamilton in 1789. Although Hamilton was enthusiastic, President Adams considered it a possible violation of neutrality laws, and declined to lend support. But in November of 1805, Miranda, using the incognito of George Martin, came to the U.S. He contacted a grandson of former president John Adams, Colonel William S. Smith, who had a governmental role as the Surveyor of the Port of New York, to accompany him on his expedition. Smith, according to his later testimony at his trial, declined to participate unless Miranda should be able to secure the permission of the U.S. government. Miranda then went to Washington (apparently using the name "Molini" at this point), and was received cordially by President Jefferson and Secretary of State Madison. Smith said that in the outcome of the meetings, they declined to give Miranda a letter of service for fear of committing the government, but asserted that Miranda "was at liberty to go if he pleased."[55] Miranda had also persuaded Smith that he had the approval of the British government. It was Smith who then arranged for Miranda to be fitted out with ships, arms, and men by the major figures in the U.S. Haiti trade.

The merchants working with Miranda were also the impresarios of U.S. commerce with Haiti; they had excellent connections to Dessalines. Jacob Lewis, the American merchant and the captain of the ship referred to by Miranda's crew as the *Black Emperor*, had a privileged role in Haiti where he served as, in the words of St. Victor Jean Baptiste, "the representative of all the American firms for traffic in arms and munitions [with Haiti]."[56] Leslie Jean-Robert Paen notes Lewis's close association with the black emperor himself, Dessalines: "Americans engaged in commercial operations there had a protector in the person of the merchant Jacob Lewis, who had close ties to Dessalines."[57] Samuel G. Ogden was also an influential merchant, connected to the Haiti trade, U.S. abolitionists, and the government.

One can see the ideological links between Ogden and Lewis in the uproar that had greeted a dinner the two men hosted in June of 1805 with the aim of consolidating American solidarity and political networks around the Haitian cause. The lavish dinner took place onboard the ship the *Indostan* in New York harbor prior to departure for Haiti. The guests included "one hundred of the most respectable characters in the city"[58] and the last American Ambassador to London, Rufus King, as well as General Stevens. The *Aurora* of June 17, 1805, reported that the toasts on board the *Indostan* included this one: "The government of Hayti, founded on the only legitimate basis of all authority: the *people's choice*! May it be as durable as its principles are pure!" Lewis, Ogden, and Washington Morton in effect controlled external commerce in Haiti.[59] Lewis also had the ear of the Jefferson administration. Brown notes that Madison and Jefferson "had been listening to an American merchant named Jacob Lewis, who had for some time been urging there be some contact with Dessalines."[60] Dalencour points out in addition that Lewis had a strong relationship with Pétion; in fact, after Pétion later came to power, Lewis returned to establish his home and business in Haiti.[61]

When Miranda set out from New York on February 3, 1806,[62] he was aboard the *Leander*, a ship owned by Ogden, and captained by Jacob Lewis's brother, Thomas. In port, Miranda's association with these American brokers of Haitian power aroused much conjecture and suspicion, as did the sight of arms being loaded. The *Leander* had a crew of about 180 men, many of whom, it would later be revealed, had been recruited to participate on a journey of the U.S. mails to South America, reportedly at the behest of the U.S. government, not on a decolonization mission via Haiti; their attempts to escape once they learned the truth were a picaresque feature of the voyage. The successful escape of at least one of them led to a strange loop in the chronology of reporting about the enterprise, since he was back and providing his account to the press before the mission had ended. (A number of his fellow captives were not so lucky; I will discuss later their 1808 petition to Congress to relieve them from slavery in Venezuela.)

The connections forged by Smith with Ogden and Lewis should not give the impression that the Haiti destination was a logistical happenstance, however. Although there were pragmatic reasons for launching a quasi-military initiative from the Caribbean rather than the U.S. mainland, there were also longstanding ideological ties between South American liberation movements and Haiti, and there is considerable evidence that Miranda expected to recruit Haitian forces via Jacob Lewis.

The links between Haitian and Venezuelan independence projects go back to the French revolutionary era, when the Venezuelan *zambo libre* José Leonardo Chirino organized a slave rebellion in Coro in 1795. Chirino in previous years had often traveled to Haiti for commercial reasons with his boss, Talleria. The model of revolutionary activity in Saint-Domingue was of primary importance in Chirino's (unsuccessful) adaptation of French revolutionary ideals to an abolitionist insurgency in Venezuela.[63]

This precedent was followed by numerous "pan-American" connections between Haiti and Venezuela in the early Haitian independence. St. Victor Jean Baptiste argues that Dessalines's discussions with Venezuelan independence partisans had begun in 1804: "Because of this climate of emancipation created in the Americas by the triumph of indigenous armies [...] the patriots of Venezuela went to Dessalines on a diplomatic mission charged with receiving his support for the Independence of that country."[64] A businessman from Trinidad, referred to as Fitzwilliam, revealed the plan to the English authorities, after which the Spanish put a stop to the 1804 Venezuelan outreach initiative to Haiti.

This prehistory to the Miranda expedition is given far more texture in Paul Verna's *Pétion y Bolívar*. Verna recounts that Miranda's great fear concerning the Haitians was that they were the *invited* decolonizers of Venezuela, and would beat him to the punch. Miranda had written to Lord Melville in September of 1804 that "The only danger that I foresee is [...] if the revolutionary people of Santo Domingo (that your Lordship knows is already invited by unaware inhabitants of the coast of Caracas) gets the start before us, then this Plan becomes nugatory."[65] Miranda had, in the preceding days, conveyed a message to Fitzwilliam in Trinidad that "The projected alliance and connection between the Province of Venezuela and the negro government of St. Domingo will happen infallibly."[66] Trying to cover even more bases for securing British assistance in preventing the Haitians from getting to Venezuela first, Miranda also wrote to Pitt, again explaining the earlier Venezuelan proposition for a Haitian alliance.[67]

By 1805, the English governor Bertrand de Moleville had proposed a plan for Miranda to "win over Dessalines's support 'with money and gifts,' in order to obtain a corps of 5000 to 6000 men."[68] (Verna also documents that the French revolutionary Brissot had, back in 1792, recommended that Miranda invade the Spanish colonies with an army of 15,000 *mulâtres* from Saint-Domingue, whose valor had already been confirmed in the American and Haitian revolutions.) Although Miranda rejected this idea at the time, it appears to have been very close to what he set out to accomplish in the spring of 1806.

En route to Jacmel, a British vessel intercepted the *Leander*. Miranda produced letters of introduction, which, as Racine notes, gave a "firmer impression" of official sanction by at least the British and quite possibly also the American governments.[69] The *Leander* arrived in Jacmel harbor on February 18.

While in Haiti, did Miranda or his colleagues ever meet directly with Dessalines, as Beaubrun Ardouin recounted?[70] Or even with his designated representative, General Magloire Ambroise, as Madiou contended?[71] Or with no one related to Dessalines's government at all, as Geggus asserted?[72] Biggs notes that in late February, Miranda's envoys—Thomas Lewis and William Smith—were in Port-au-Prince for a considerable time, approximately ten days, in their errand to finalize arrangements to commission Jacob Lewis's ship *Black Emperor* and, presumably, to recruit troops, since it would not have been necessary to wait to see Jacob Lewis in Haiti just to commission the ship.[73] Madiou claims that Dessalines had instructed General Ambroise to allow Miranda "to recruit young Haitians."[74]

Some detailed and apparently informed accounts in the U.S. media went further, reporting that Captain Lewis met personally with Dessalines, not in Port-au-Prince but in the city of Dessalines. It was not, after all, necessary that Miranda himself meet with Dessalines for his expedition to meet with the government. The New York *Daily Advertiser* on April 26, 1806, recounts the meeting as follows:

> On the arrival of the Leander at Jacquemel, there was the appearance of the greatest secrecy, no one was admitted on board, nor no one, excepting captain Lewis, was permitted on shore, and as soon as he landed, set off to visit and report to the black Emperor of Hayti, at the new city of Dessalines, which is built in the mountains and strongly fortified, it being the determination of the Brigands, to burn all the towns on the sea shore, should the French ever attempt to invade the island again, and defend themselves in the mountains to the last.

It is known that Dessalines was not in Port-au-Prince during the time of Miranda's stay in Jacmel, so this detail of Dessalines's whereabouts is important. The city of Dessalines, in the department of the Artibonite, is between Port-au-Prince and Cap Haïtien. The long period of Lewis's and Smith's trip, with approximately seven days left unaccounted for, gave them ample time to travel to another region.

The *Leander*'s mission was guarded with such secrecy that it alarmed the Haitians, as noted in the April 26 *Daily Advertiser*:

> While Admiral Lewis was on his visit to the Emperor, the Negroes at Jacquemel became uneasy at the great secrecy observed by the Leander, and before his return sent a formal message to know their business, and made preparations to attack the Leander should their ambassador

not be well-received; but their messenger meeting a polite reception, an explanation given, their fears and anxiety subsided.

This secrecy was also frustrating and confusing to the crew of the *Leander*, including Biggs. None of the crew, other than the senior officers, was entirely sure of the ship's destination, or its relationship to the politics of the U.S. or Great Britain, but it was very clear to them that they were under surveillance by French and U.S. vessels. Biggs was reduced to going to the "coffee house" in Jacmel "in the hope of getting some further intelligence, for on board nothing is to be learned of any material circumstance, and our curiosity is discouraged as inconsistent with that confidence and secrecy which is necessary to be maintained by the principals in the expedition."[75]

But this secrecy was to a large extent irrelevant, since in the U.S. much had already been discerned and published about the Miranda expedition. In reality, the expedition was unfurling in two geographic regions and two chronologies: on the one hand, a public scandal, arrests, and a trial associated with Miranda's expedition in New York: and on the other hand, the Caribbean expedition itself.

Even before the arrival of the *Leander* in Jacmel, newspapers in New York and Philadelphia reported that Miranda's ship was "laden with arms and ammunition, and nominally destined for Jacqmel; but really for some of the Spanish possessions."[76] The *Aurora* (whose editorial staff may actually have been delighted at the convergence of the Haiti trade with U.S. political scandal) expressed its shock at having to report the connivance of the U.S. government:

> The New York Gazette insinuates that this expedition is undertaken with the secret connivance of our government. –Although the conduct of Spain to us would warrant any attack that our citizens would undertake; we must [...] say, that the government of the United States whenever it attacks an enemy, will do it openly and honourably, and not in such an underhand way.

The only possible explanation for a U.S. role in a covert attack on the Spanish colonies, the paper conjectured, was the following: "*Perhaps* the celebrated arms traders with Dessalines, the admirers of the empire of Hayti, may have descended to this infamy."

A likely U.S. role, official or unofficial, in the decolonization plot had in fact become a major political scandal by mid-February 1806, before Miranda even arrived in Jacmel. The secret of the Miranda expedition may have been safe from Biggs and the other crew members, but the political cognoscenti of the U.S. journalistic milieu were inflamed by the non-transparency of the U.S. government's dealings with Miranda. And they had considerable knowledge of the whole affair, thanks to communications by the Marquis Casa Yrujo, the Spanish Minister in the U.S.

On February 4—two days after the departure of the *Leander*—Minister Yrujo had written to warn the Governor-General of Venezuela and Caracas, not just of Miranda's expedition, but of mulatto forces waiting to join the expedition in Haiti. Yrujo's warnings were also sent to several other people, including Cevallos, the Spanish Minister of Foreign Relations. Yrujo's letter was not actually published in the U.S. media until June of 1806, but his charges were apparently well known in political and journalistic circles from at least early February when Yrujo first sent his warning. The details of the diplomat's letter are fascinating, because they reveal not only the expectation that Miranda would have access to a force of Haitian soldiers,[77] but specifically to *mulâtres*, under the command of Pétion, who were willing to leave because they were afraid of being massacred by the blacks. They were undoubtedly, as later accounts would suggest, "Spanish" men of color who had earlier migrated from Santo Domingo and were now weathering the storms of Dessalines's loss of that part of the island:

> [...] a captain Lewis sailed with two schooners for Port-au-Prince, near which place there was a position occupied by 2500 mulattoes, who on a former occasion, had promised him to ship themselves in a body, if he would procure a country for them to go to, as they were afraid of being massacred by the blacks; the mulattoes are under the command of one Pichon or Pétion.[78]

Based on this ministerial-level report, there were journalistic challenges to Jefferson's and Madison's involvement in the Haiti/Venezuela expedition. Samuel Relf, of the Philadelphia *Gazette*, published an open letter of "Serious Questions to Mr. Madison" on February 19, testing the Secretary's insistence that neither he nor the government was involved: "Did Miranda go to Washington about the middle of December last? Had he two long interviews with you? Did he not present you a plan of an expedition against the province of Carascas [*sic*]?" (Relf's widely published open letter was satirized in the *Censor*. "Number 6. Did not the president let general Miranda have a *large hunk* of the Mammoth cheese for consumption on his voyage, and to furnish him with *soldiers*, like the myrmidons of old, when he should want them to overturn the Spanish Empire in America?") Adams and Harbert, in their *History of the United States*, would conclude that before Relf's attack, the U.S. government had been willing to "shut its eyes" to Miranda's expedition, but that it then changed tack when it found itself compromised.[79]

For Jefferson and Madison, the outpouring of charges against them was a serious matter, with the potential to impact significantly on the standing of the U.S. with its European allies. These political anxieties were pivotal in the sudden passage, on February 28, of legislation against the Haiti trade that had previously been defeated several times. The issue of the Miranda expedition had crept threateningly, but unnamed, into congressional debates on Haiti trade:

> Had this Government ever furnished arms and ammunition, or done any other act in order to assist and encourage the people of St. Domingo in attacking the countries of their neighbors? I cannot conceive what subject that might have been before Congress during our present session [...][80]

Almost immediately after Congress passed the bill prohibiting intercourse with Haiti, warrants were issued in the case. The arrests of Ogden and of Colonel Smith of the Custom House, "and others," and the filing of their indictments by the Grand Jury of New York, were reported in the *United States Gazette* on March 3, with the scandalized comment that "Mr. Ogden's answers went *directly to implicate the government of the U.S. in the fitting out of the Leander.*"

In mid-March, Jefferson's Secretary at War, General Dearborn, would publicly deny the reports of the administration's collusion with Miranda, asserting that neither Jefferson nor Madison had met with Miranda, or had known of the expedition's purposes, and that once they did learn of the "hostile voyage," "suits were immediately instituted against the parties concerned."[81]

William Smith, from being a talented and well-connected citizen, was suddenly demoted to a prodigal grandson, an untrustworthy scoundrel. John Q. Adams introduced to Congress the petitions or "memorials" that Ogden and Smith had composed in April of 1806, which provide their accounts of the events, and which presented correspondence between Miranda and Jefferson, among others.[82] The memorials caused an uproar among the Democratic Republicans; in congressional records the documents were first listed as "rejected," then as "withdrawn," and then as "expunged" on April 21. The resolution for this historic precedent[83] of "expunging" documents stated

> That the charges contained in the memorials of S. G. Ogden and William Smith are, in the opinion of this House, unsupported by any evidence which, in the least degree, incriminates the Executive Government of this country; that the said memorials appear to have been presented at a time and under circumstances insidiously calculated to excite unjust suspicions in the minds of the good people of this nation [...]

What was so alarming in the correspondence in the memorials? Perhaps it was the cozy lyricism of Miranda's euphoric prediction to Jefferson that "Columbia" would soon come into being under the president's auspices:

> If ever the happy prediction, which you have pronounced on the future destiny of our dear Columbia, is to be accomplished in our day, may Providence grant that it may be under your auspices, and by the generous efforts of her own children! We shall then, in some sort, behold the revival of that age, the return of which the Roman bard invoked in favor of the human race:—
>
> "The last great age foretold by sacred rhymes
> Renews its finished course; Saturnian times
> Boil round again; and mighty years, begun
> From this first orb, in radiant circles run."[84]

Miranda's letter also referred to a history of Chile he had given Jefferson following an earlier conversation, documenting their ongoing dialogue.

Ogden and Smith were tried for complicity with Miranda and violation of neutrality laws beginning in April 1806, but as the *Atlantic Monthly* noted, "the heads of that Government, Jefferson and Madison, were indirectly on trial at the same time."[85]

In the meantime, the separate chronologies of the Miranda events in the U.S. and Haiti overlapped when the U.S. sent word of both the trade embargo and the warrants for the arrests of Ogden and Smith to Haiti post-haste. An article in the New York *Commercial Advertiser* recounted the arrival in Haiti of news of the U.S. commercial legislation on March 24: "By this vessel [the schooner *Victory*] information was carried out to Hayti of the passage of the act prohibiting intercourse with the island; the officers of the Haytian government discredited the intelligence, alledging [*sic*] that it was merely a stategem of the Americans to lower the price of coffee."[86]

Even if the news of the new embargo didn't disturb the government in Haiti, Jacob Lewis, literally en route from Port-au-Prince to join the Miranda expedition in Jacmel, was chilled to the bone by the arrests of his colleagues. This was not just a problem with a court of law, but also with Congress (the embargo), and with the president. He reversed course, and in the *Black Emperor*'s return to port whatever faint hopes the Miranda expedition might have had of succeeding vanished. Biggs reported that Jacob Lewis literally closed up shop in Haiti: "The law of Congress, prohibiting intercourse with St. Domingo [...] induces captain Jacob Lewis to remain, in order to close his business in the island."[87] Thomas Lewis had followed on his heels to Port-au-Prince, trying to persuade his brother to return to the plan, but to no avail:

The ship Emperor had sailed from Port-au-Prince to join the Leander, but after hearing at sea that the Government of the United States had prosecuted Ogden, she put back. Captain Lewis, of the Leander, had gone overland to consult with the officers of the ship Emperor, and to induce them to persevere in the expedition.[88]

The retreat of Jacob Lewis, which had the side-effect of saving the reputation of the United States government from the stain of trying to topple the Spanish Empire with help from the blacks of Haiti, was a blow to the collaboration of Miranda and future Haitian president Alexandre Pétion, whose long-term rapport had been documented by numerous sources. Biggs claimed that Miranda had been "under the protection of Pethion"[89] in Paris at the beginning of the French Revolution, when Pétion was a French military officer. Many American newspapers also published a brief biography of Miranda in the spring of 1806 featuring the Pétion connection from the Revolutionary era. The *New York Gazette*, on March 3, 1806, implied that Pétion had previously saved Miranda's life. During the French Revolution, Miranda was already testing out ideas of decolonization, and Nicholas Rey notes that Pétion in 1790 was involved in denouncing racist presuppositions around triangular commerce to the Assemblée générale.[90]

Pétion was ostensibly the key link in helping Jacob Lewis and the *Black Emperor* with the recruitment of (nominally) Haitian soldiers. As Biggs noted, a large and well-armed ship would indeed "be necessary, if much force is required for our undertaking, and no British vessel of war, as we apprehend, is engaged."[91] In other words, the *Black Emperor* would have had a role like a vessel of war, involving large numbers of soldiers. Various texts attested to the recruitment of thousands of Spanish-speaking *mulâtres*—transplants from the French army in Santo Domingo, or migrants to the new black nation—who were now fearful of becoming a targeted population in Haiti, and eager to accompany an expedition to overthrow Spanish possessions. The *Morning Chronicle* on April 5, 1806, published an "extract of a letter from a gentleman on board the Leander, dated Jacmel, March 1, 1806, received via Baltimore," mentioning not only the availability of these troops, but Dessalines's approval:

General Miranda has explained to us his plan [...] The general will get as many men as he wants; general Pétion at Port-au-Prince who has the command of 8,000 mullattos [*sic*], speaking the language of the people of the opposite coast, are all eager to accompany him, and the emperor of Hayti, gives every facility; and for myself, I believe Miranda will succeed—perhaps we may yet go.

On April 8, the *United States Gazette* seized upon this attestation with great eagerness because it supported its earlier contention that the Miranda expedition would involve Haitian troops:

> The statement, which we made more than a month ago of the primary object of the Leander, is literally confirmed. We then stated that she was first to proceed to one of the ports of St. Domingo, for the purpose of recruiting a sufficient number of mulattoes, and was then to proceed with them to the Spanish main together with other such vessels as could be brought into service.

A March 29 article in the *United States Gazette* gave similar information, but more specifically associated it with the *Black Emperor*:

> The ship Emperour, commanded by a brother of capt. Lewis of the Leander, sailed from New York some weeks before for Port-au-Prince, with pikes and other implements of war, similar to those shipped in the Leander, and with a considerable number of volunteers, with the intention, we understand, of debauching some mulattoes at Port-au-Prince, and of sailing with this reinforcement on the intended expedition.

All of these media claims lead us to a question that is currently unanswerable except by conjecture: When Jacob Lewis, informed by the schooner *Victory* of his colleagues' arrests and new legislation against intercourse with Haiti, turned back on his course to Jacmel, who was on his ship?

Not only was it pragmatically devastating for the Miranda expedition to sail with just a small American crew, many of whom saw themselves as victims of kidnapping, but it provided a major propaganda advantage for the Spaniards that the famed Haitian revolutionaries were not on board. The Spanish colonial government seized on the absence of black and mulatto forces on Miranda's expedition as evidence that he was not the chosen one, that he had been met with closed doors when he went as a supplicant to the revolutionaries of Haiti. A handbill posted in Caracas exulted in his apparent inability to recruit the Haitians: "On the 27th of April the self-supposed general Miranda, without any other protection than an indirect one from a government calling itself a friend to Spain, despised and rejected by the negroes and mulattoes of Jacmel, presented himself on the coast of the province of Caraccas [*sic*] [...]"[92]

This was wishful thinking and clever propaganda on the part of the Spanish, however, since the Haitians *had not* "rejected and despised" Miranda and his mission. The degree of intentional Haitian involvement in Miranda's project is evident in the anecdote of the role of the American captain George Kirkland in the expedition.

A former member of the American military, contributor to the *Washington*

Federalist, and, by all accounts, a man of exceptional literary education, Kirkland had "adventured to Hayti with a view, it is said, of offering his military talents to Dessalines," as the *Newport Mercury* (Rhode Island) recounted in an article on August 30, 1806. One can assume that these military talents were in part redactive. But rather than becoming the first of Dessalines's American secretaries, Kirkland instead joined Miranda in Haiti. James Biggs records his having first joined the crew in the harbor of Jacmel on March 27, just before the departure of the *Leander*.[93]

In the course of the Miranda expedition, although he had left the territory of Haiti, Kirkland did not lose sight of the goal of using his literary talents for Dessalines. He sent a shipboard dispatch on Miranda's progress, addressed to a contact in Haiti, with the specific request that the friend present the report to Dessalines: "We request you instantly to communicate our progress to his majesty the Emperor of Hayti. Tell him that the first intelligence which we shall have the honor to give him, will be dated from Carracas. [...] Vive l'Indépendance!"[94]

The missive was duly presented to officials in Haiti, and printed in full in the government's newspaper, the *Gazette politique et commerciale d'Haïti*, on May 22, 1806. From there, the Haitian newspaper issue appears to have been sent to U.S. newspapers, since editors there made comments such as the following: "The editor has been politely favored with the Political and Commercial Gazette of Hayti, of the 22d of May, containing the following highly interesting letter from General Kirkland, one of the Commanders under Gen. Miranda."[95] Interestingly, this edition of the *Gazette* does not appear to have survived in Haitian archives, since it does not figure in the recent anthology of the paper.

The New York *Gazette* describes the letter from Kirkland to Dessalines as follows:

> A newspaper has been received in town printed at Cape François, on the 22nd of May, which contains a letter from Gen. Kirkland (who went out with Miranda as Colonel) written to his friend at Hayti, and desiring him to shew it immediately to Dessalines. This letter is dated at Cumana, April 19, and informs that Miranda had made a successful landing, had taken St. Margaretta, Barcelona, and Cuman, that the inhabitants were flocking to his standard in great numbers [...] Miranda was hailed with enthusiasm by all ranks of people as their deliverer; a second Washington.[96]

The editorial staff of the New York *Gazette* had done some fact checking, and found several people who vouched for it being "the known style of Kirkland." Kirkland's missive, with its overt connection of the South American decolonization campaign to the logic and actors of the

Haitian independence, was reprinted as extensively as the November 1803 proclamation of independence by Dessalines, Christophe, and Clerveaux; it echoed throughout the towns of the eastern seaboard and into the South, as far as Kentucky.

Kirkland believed that he was seeing in Miranda's wake just what Dessalines had hoped to find in Santo Domingo and perhaps elsewhere: a transnational colonized collectivity rushing to claim its new postcolonial independence: "At every step we take, our army is increased by these illustrious unfortunates, who think that they behold, in the Generalissimo Miranda, a NEW WASHINGTON, who comes to reestablish them in the primitive state of liberty, which the barbarity of the Spanish had ravished from them."[97] After the capture of Miranda's ship the *Bacchus* by the Spaniards in Caracas, Miranda escaped on the *Leander* and made his way to Trinidad. A July 24 letter from a friendly observer in Trinidad, published in the *New York Commercial Advertiser* on August 20, reported, "If we can credit the reports from the Continent, the *Sovereign People* have, in a large measure, revolted, and Miranda will find little or no difficulty in obtaining the objects of his wishes—*Hail Columbia Happy Land!*"

Colombia Happy Land was not so happy for Miranda's captured American crew members, however, who would prove to be a legacy of the intertwined destinies of Miranda's ideals, the Jefferson presidency, the non-materialized Haitian troops, and controls on neutral commerce. In September of 1808, 36 crew members who had been on Miranda's expedition petitioned Congress for international assistance to liberate them from the slavery to which they were condemned in Cartagena. They claimed that Smith and William Armstrong had enlisted them as guards to the U.S. mails. They were brought onto the ship *Leander*, "owned by Samuel G. Ogden, and formerly in the St. Domingo trade."[98] As they explained to the congressional audience, they were surprised to find themselves taken from New York to Jacmel:

> your petitioners were carried to Jacmel, in the island of St. Domingo, where they were exercised in military duty, under the most arbitrary stretch of power, by Miranda and his officers. At Jacmel several attempts to escape proved abortive, from the vigilance of our oppressors, they having procured guards to be stationed in all the passes leading from Jacmel to other parts of the Island, where your petitioners might expect to receive aid and protection from their countrymen.[99]

The expedition ended in precisely the misery they had feared: in Caracas on July 12, 1806, ten of their colleagues were hanged and beheaded, and the rest of them were sentenced to eight to ten years of slavery in irons. They petitioned Congress because "on several occasions, they were told by William Armstrong, Thomas Lewis, and others, that they were sent out by the Government of the United States." The petition closed with a stunning accusation:

> Your petitioners cannot for a moment believe that the United States will suffer officers under her constitution to kidnap her citizens into expeditions and serviced fitted out and maintained by a foreign outlaw against powers with which she is at amity and peace.[100]

Congress filed a resolution for the President of the United States to seek the liberation and repatriation of the Miranda crew members. But the motion was not passed. With its defeat, possible renewed publicity around the alleged government involvement was quashed.

In the end, apart from this petition from the poor enslaved dupes of the Miranda expedition, there was little follow-up or commemoration of this moment when the U.S. tilted toward assisting in the emancipation of the Spanish colonies with the help of Haiti. But part of the lasting legacy of the episode is the likelihood that Miranda would not have chosen a Haitian point of departure—the land of his rivals in imagined revolutions—if he had not planned to draw on their magic. Why set off to Jacmel with printing presses and journeyman printers if Dessalines, the new emperor of independence proclamations, were not a figure of identification in the creation of a "Columbian" flag and independence documents? After all, as newspapers noted in the summer of 1806, "Among the Americans captured by the Spaniards in Miranda's schooners, were three or four young Printers, who were going out to propagate revolutionary principles in the Spanish colonies."[101] Revolutionary principles were not just a matter of technology. Miranda presumably saw Colombia at this point as something like a new Haiti, as an editorial in the *Salem Register* of May 8 noted: "Should such a work begin in South America, the consequences will probably be very extensive, and to the new government of Hayti will add many similar establishments in America."

Dessalines's anticolonial empire, as suggested in the ventures in Trinidad and Venezuela, is in the end not measurable in terms of territory gained for Haiti or even in expanded influence of the model of Haitian freedom. But we can trace it in terms of Dessalines's sustained challenge, by means of proclamations, commerce, and stealth tactics, to the world beyond Haitian borders to cope with a black nation within the collectivity of Euro-American nations. His anticolonial politics did not create new postcolonies in any direct sense, but they did *make readable* a question that has haunted histories of neo-colonialism: How can freed slaves, if truly freed, sustain their economic and political interactions with slave-holding nations that refuse to accept their sovereignty? As a November 9, 1805, editorial in the *New York Evening Post* queried, "What is the situation of Saint Domingo; and how is it to be considered under the law of nations?" Haiti had made it philosophically "arduous" to trace "the threshold between revolution and rebellion." This philosophical editorialist noted, "Success stamps as revolution what without it would be rebellion; and subjugation marks as rebellion what better fortune would have made a revolution." Dessalines's combined literary and tactical "communications" with other islands and the wider world brought Haiti fully into the scope of the challenges that would mark its modernity. He employed, to borrow the *Evening Post* editorialist's words, "all the labor of language and energy of eloquence"—even in those narratives in which we must read between the lines.

Notes

1. Berthony Dupont, *Jean-Jacques Dessalines: Itinéraire d'un révolutionnaire* (Paris: L'Harmattan, 2006), 355. Dupont briefly addresses the invasion of Santo Domingo (354–5) and the Miranda episode (355–6) in his argumentation.

2. Timoléon C. Brutus, *L'Homme d'airain: l'éveil d'une nation* (Port-au-Prince: Editions Presses nationales d'Haïti, 2006), 1:333.

3. Timoléon C. Brutus, *L'Homme d'airain: Du sang sur le trône* (Port-au Prince: Imprimerie de l'état, 1946), 2:272–86.

4. St. Victor Jean Baptiste, *Le Fondateur devant l'histoire* (Port-au-Prince, Haiti: Imprimerie Eben-Ezer, 1954), 239.

5. Léo Elisabeth, "Les Relations entre les petites Antilles françaises et Haïti: de la politique du refoulement à la résignation (1804–1825)," in *Haïti première république noire*, ed. Marcel Dorigny (Saint-Denis: Publications de la société française d'histoire d'outre-mer, 2003), 177.

6. David Geggus, "Slave Resistance in the Spanish Caribbean in the Mid 1790s," in *A Turbulent Time: The French Revolution and the Greater Caribbean*, ed. David Barry Gaspar and David Geggus (Bloomington, IN: University of Indiana Press, 1997), 15.

7. Gordon S. Brown, *Toussaint's Clause: The Founding Fathers and the Haitian Revolution* (Jackson, MS: University of Mississippi Press, 2005), 247.

8. New York *Mercantile Advertiser*, January 1, 1805.

9. March 6, 1806; quoted in the *United States Gazette* (Pennsylvania), April 14, 1806.

10. Baltimore *American and Commercial Daily Advertiser*, April 12, 1805.

11. Massachusetts *Repertory*, May 22, 1804.

12. Gordon S. Wood, *Empire of Liberty: The Statecraft of Thomas Jefferson* (Oxford: Oxford University Press, 1992), viii.

13. Wood, *Empire of Liberty*, 17.

14. Gordon S. Wood, *The Empire of Liberty: A History of the Early Republic* (Oxford: Oxford University Press, 2009) 265.

15. New York *Mercantile Advertiser*, July 13, 1805.

16. "Proclamation relative au massacre des français," in Le Baron Linstant de Pradine, ed., *Recueil général des lois et des actes du gouvernement d'Haïti, 1804–1808* (Paris: A. Durand, Pédone-Lauriel, 1886), 1:24.

17. M. J. Madival and M. E. Laurent, *Archives parlementaires de 1787 à 1860: recueil*

    complet des débats législatifs & politiques des chambres françaises, vol. 57 (Paris: Paul Dupont, 1884), 546.

18. "Saint-Domingue sous le Consulat, fragment de souvenirs de la générale Lallemand," *Nouvelle revue retrospective*, December 10, 1902, and January 10, 1903.

19. Jacques Cauna, "La Face cachée de Toussaint Louverture," in *Saint-Domingue espagnol et la révolution nègre d'Haïti (1790–1822)*, ed. Alain Yacou (Paris: Karthala, 2007), 311.

20. Léon Deschamps, *Les Colonies pendant la revolution: la constituante et la réforme coloniale* (Paris: Perrin et Cie, 1898), 53–5.

21. Roberjot Lartigue, *Rapport de la conduite qu'a tenue M. Roberjot Lartigue, au sujet de l'entreprise formée par Dessalines, pour soulever la Martinique, la Guadeloupe, et Marie-Galante, Certifié de MM. Le Lieutenant-générale-Gouverneur de la Guadeloupe et dépendences; le Général-Préfet colonial et le Général-commandant des troupes de la même île; le Colonel-commandant de la ville et arrondissement de St.-Pierre; le Grand-Juge de la Martinique; le Général-commandant en chef, Administrateur-général de Santo-Domingo; d'un Habitant, Officier de la Trinité espagnole; et le Grand-Juge de St-Thomas, Conseiller de Justice actuel de S. M. le Roi de Danemarck* (Paris: Dubray, imprimeur, 1815).

22. A letter personally signed by Roberjot Lartigue, with the heading "St. Thomas île Danoise, ce 20 mai 1806," but labeled in Moreau's hand in the upper margin as being dated 1814 (along with some other dating information that I have been unable to transcribe, possibly "Paris 25 [or 29?] août 1814"), is archived, along with a copy, also hand-labeled by Moreau, in the *Notes Historiques* of Moreau de St.-Méry in the Archives d'Outre-mer, F3, vol. 141 *bis*, 453–62.

23. Elisabeth, "Les Relations entre les petites Antilles françaises et Haïti," 184.

24. Robert L. Paquette, *The Lesser Antilles in the Age of European Expansion* (Gainesville, FL: University of Florida Press, 1996), 296.

25. Geggus, "Slave Resistance in the Spanish Caribbean," 15.

26. Régis Antoine, *La Littérature Franco-Antillaise* (Paris: Karthala, 2002), 110–11.

27. Elisabeth, "Les Relations entre les petites Antilles françaises et Haïti," 183.

28. Elisabeth, "Les Relations entre les petites Antilles françaises et Haïti," 185.

29. Elisabeth, "Les Relations entre les petites Antilles françaises et Haïti," 184.

30. Quoted in Jean Fouchard, *Regards sur l'histoire* (Port-au-Prince: Editions Henri Deschamps, 1988), 96.

31. Nicolas Rey, *Quand la Révolution, aux Amériques, était nègre* (Paris: Karthala, 2005), 151.

32. José Luciano Franco, *La Conspiración de Aponte* (Havana: Editorial Ciencias Sociales, 2006 [1966]), 11.

33. In different accounts of this same episode, the name Chanlatte is rendered as Chaulatte or even Chaulette, but the same variations show up around the name of Dessalines's secretary Juste Chanlatte. This Chanlatte or Chaulatte could possibly have been the former mulatto general Antoine Chanlatte from the French army in Spanish Santo Domingo, commander of the "Legion of Equality" or the "Legion of the West," the brother of Dessalines's secretary Juste Chanlatte. Although Antoine Chanlatte had returned to France in 1801 after his failed opposition to Toussaint Louverture, his strong ties to colonial Spain make him a natural for dealings with Puerto Rico. He died in France in 1815. However, it could also well have

been François Desrivères Chaulatte or Chanlatte, who was an emissary to South America under Pétion and Boyer.

34. Franco, *La Conspiración de Aponte*, 11 (my translation). This Spanish documentation of French arrests of Haitian agents on St. Thomas provides indirect documentation of Roberjot Lartigue's claims.

35. Quoted in Franco, *La Conspiración de Aponte*, 11 (my translation) and documented in José L. Franco, *Documentos para la Historia de Haití en el Archivo National*.

36. In Roberjot Lartigue's report, Michael Smith, who had been a judge in St. Thomas in 1805 and 1806, certified that Lartigue had "frequently" requested the help of the Danish police to prevent the communication of "aucun émissaire du malfaiteur" ("any emissary of the evildoer") [Dessalines] with the French Antilles. Smith did not mention anything about arrests or deportations, nor did he confirm an October 1805 Danish decree against traffic with Haiti. He did, however, testify that following general reports that the Haitians had sent their emissaries to Trinidad to incite insurrection, Lartigue had asked the Danish authorities to "défendre, dans les îles Danoises, le commerce avec les révoltés de St. Domingue" ("prohibit commerce from the Danish islands with the rebels of St. Domingue") and that this request "was granted." Smith would appear to be a reliable source on this matter since there were published records of such a decree in April of 1806. If news of the Trinidad insurrection had arrived in January of 1806, March legislation would have been a reasonable timeframe.

37. Lartigue, *Rapport*.

38. Sidney Daney de Marcillac, *Histoire de la Martinique, depuis la colonisation jusqu'en 1815* (Fort-Royal [Fort de France]: E. Ruelle, imprimeur du gouvernement, 1846), 4:210.

39. There was a Colonel Macaque in Saint-Domingue, a commander of the regiment of the same name, according to Madiou: Thomas Madiou, *Histoire d'Haïti* (Port-au-Prince: J. Courtois, 1847), 2:428.

40. Cocorite is a swampy area of Trinidad, adjacent to Fort George; it is also the name of a snake found in Trinidad.

41. Geggus, "Slave Resistance in the Spanish Caribbean," 14.

42. "At other times the New World satires became openly insurrectionary. In 1805 Trinidad a Mr. de Gannes de la Chancellerie was bathing in the river that ran through his plantation when twelve black women, balancing plantain baskets on their heads, came by on the path. Swaying their hips to the rhythm of the chac-chac pods they carried, the chorus of women offered up what was to him a blood curdling threat:

> Pain c'est viande beque [Bread is white man's flesh]
> Vin c'est sang beque [Wine is white man's blood]
> San Domingo!
> Nous va boire sang beque [We will drink white blood]
> San Domingo!

After other Trinidadian whites heard the same or similar songs foreshadowing an impending slave revolt, an inquiry was begun that resulted in both executions and severe punishments for the accused rebel leaders." William D. Piersen, *Black Legacy: America's Hidden Heritage* (Amherst, MA: University of Massachusetts Press, 1993), 63.

43. John Cowley, *Carnival, Canboulay and Calypso* (Cambridge: Cambridge University Press, 1998), 12.

44. Edward Lanzer Joseph, *History of Trinidad* (New York: Routledge, 1970), 220–1.

45. James Millette, *Society and Politics in Colonial Trinidad* (Trinidad: Omega Books, 1985), table 3, no pagination.

46. "As the Napoleonic Wars progressed and the revolutionary spirit grew, Trinidad began to look more and more like a French colony. [...] Royalists from St. Domingue and Guadeloupe were followed by republicans from Martinique, Grenada, St. Lucia and St. Domingue, to be followed still later by a predominantly coloured republican group contingent on the defeat of the coloured Rigaud by the ex-slave Toussaint." Millette, *Society and Politics in Colonial Trinidad*, 27.

47. Millette, *Society and Politics in Colonial Trinidad*, 94.

48. David Patrick Geggus, *Haitian Revolutionary Studies* (Bloomington, IN: Indiana University Press, 2002), 184.

49. Geggus, *Haitian Revolutionary Studies*, 184.

50. Elisabeth, "Les Relations entre les petites Antilles françaises et Haïti," 184.

51. Paquette, *The Lesser Antilles in the Age of European Colonial Expansion*, 296.

52. James Biggs, *History of Don Francisco de Miranda's Attempt to Effect a Revolution in South America* (Boston, MA: E. Oliver, 1811), 26. In further precisions, Biggs writes, "Several hundred of Miranda's proclamations are printed off. These manifestoes, addressed to the people of South America, as you would expect, declare his views and intentions with respect to their country [...] and what they are to do when their deliverers arrive" (29–30).

53. Karen Racine, *Francisco de Miranda, A Transatlantic Life in the Age of Revolution* (Wilmington, DE: SR Books, 2003), 160.

54. Dalencour's book puts the overwhelming emphasis on Pétion's role in the "libération de l'Amérique Espagnole." François Dalencour, *Francisco de Miranda et Alexandre Pétion* (Paris: Berger-Levrault, 1955), 223.

55. *The Trials of William S. Smith, and Samuel G. Ogden: for Misdeamenours* (New York: I. Riley, 1807), xxi.

56. Baptiste, *Le Fondateur devant l'histoire*, 99.

57. Leslie Jean-Robert Paen, *Haïti, Economie politique de la corruption: De Saint-Domingue à Haïti, 1791–1870* (Paris: Maisonneuve et Larose, 2003), 149.

58. Massachusetts *Repertory*, June 18, 1805.

59. Baptiste, *Le Fondateur devant l'histoire*, 282.

60. Brown, *Toussaint's Clause*, 249.

61. Dalencour, *Francisco de Miranda*.

62. This is the date provided by William Smith, *The Trials*, 101.

63. Gérard M. Laurent, *Six Etudes sur J. J. Dessalines* (Port-au-Prince: "Les Presses libres," 1950), 71–2.

64. Baptiste, *Le Fondateur devant l'histoire*, 241.

65. Paul Verna, *Pétion y Bolívar: Una etapa decisiva en la emancipación Hispanoamérica (1790–1830)* (Caracas: Ediciones de la Presidencia de la República, 1980), 141.

66. Verna, *Pétion y Bolívar*, 143.

67. Verna, *Pétion y Bolívar*, 143.

68. Verna, *Pétion y Bolívar*, 143.

69. Racine, *Francisco de Miranda*, 160.

70. Beaubrun Ardouin, *Etudes sur l'histoire d'Haïti* (Paris: Dezobry and Magdaleine, 1856), 6:242.

71. Madiou, *Histoire d'Haïti*, 3:269.

72. Geggus, "Slave Resistance in the Spanish Caribbean," 15–16.

73. Biggs, *History of Don Francisco de Miranda's Attempt*, 33.

74. Madiou, *Histoire d'Haïti*, 3:269.

75. Biggs, *History of Don Francisco de Miranda's Attempt*, 37.

76. *Aurora*, February 13, 1806.

77. According to William Robertson, Yrujo had given "a grossly exaggerated idea of the strength of the expedition, the number of men being given at twelve hundred." *Francisco de Miranda and the Revolutionizing of Spanish America* (Worcestor, MA: American Historical Association, 1909), 370.

78. New York *Morning Chronicle*, June 11, 1806.

79. Henry Adams and Earl N. Harbert, *History of the United States of America During the Administrations of Thomas Jefferson and James Madison* (New York: Viking Press, 1986), 736.

80. *Abridgement of the Debates of Congress, from 1789 to 1856* (New York: D. Appleton, 1857–1861), 11:363, February 20, 1806.

81. New York *Gazette*, March 17, 1806.

82. See the account in Edwin Anderson Alderman et al., *Library of Southern Literature* (New Orleans, Atlanta, etc.: Martin & Hoyt Co., 1909), 7:3212.

83. See Robert Luce on the procedural and legal importance of the expunging of the memorials, in *Legislative Procedure: Parliamentary Practices and the Course of Business in the Framing of Statutes* (New York: Houghton Mifflin Company, 1922), 528.

84. New York *Gazette*, May 24, 1806.

85. "General Miranda's Expedition" (May 1860), *The Atlantic Monthly* (Boston: Ticknor and Fields, 1860), 5:593.

86. New York *Commercial Advertiser*, April 21, 1806.

87. Biggs, *History of Don Francisco de Miranda's Attempt*, 39.

88. New York *Commercial Advertiser*, April 21, 1806.

89. Biggs, *History of Don Francisco de Miranda's Attempt*, 294 and 296.

90. According to Rey, Pétion had accused Europeans of relying on a concept of African underdevelopment to justify colonization; and he had defended "l'idée que la civilisation du continent noir vaut bien celle des blancs" ("the idea that the civilization of the black continent was the equal of that of the whites". *Quand la Révolution*, 209.

91. Biggs, *History of Don Francisco de Miranda's Attempt*, 33.

92. Reprinted in the Virginia *Enquirer*, July 8, 1806.

93. Biggs, *History of Don Francisco de Miranda's Attempt*, 48.

94. *The Connecticut Courier*, June 25, 1806.

95. New York *Sun*, June 21, 1806.

96. New York *Gazette*, June 16, 1806.

97. New York *Gazette*, June 16, 1806.

98. November, 1808, "Miranda's Expedition," in *Abridgement of the Debates of Congress, from 1789 to 1856*, 4:38.

99. *Abridgement of the Debates of Congress*, 4:38.

100. *Abridgement of the Debates of Congress*, 4:39.

101. *Salem Gazette*, July 29, 1806.

5

Kidnapped Narratives:
The Lost Heir of Henry Christophe
and the Imagined Communities
of the African Diaspora

What does it augur when kidnappings are part of the primal scene of postcolonial nation-building? In this chapter, I explore the emblematic nature of kidnapping in the African diasporan colonial encounter with the conditions of literary culture. I argue that the Middle Passage, as a founding history of forced migration, was strikingly revisited in the liminal and urgent representations of kidnappings in the families of Toussaint Louverture and Henry Christophe during the Haitian Revolution and independence. The chapter begins with a text that is perhaps the closest thing to a French slave narrative in the Haitian revolutionary tradition: the narrative by a former slave named Praxelles representing the kidnapping and death of the eldest son, Ferdinand, of Henry Christophe. It is an eyewitness missive from "black Paris" documenting the downfall of a privileged son of the Haitian Revolution under the defeat of the French in Saint-Domingue. I then move on to the complex narratives of the kidnappings and semi-captive exile of Toussaint Louverture and his immediate familial entourage, which span a period from the Directory to the middle of the nineteenth century. Invoking the work of Benedict Anderson to broach the intrusion of layers of African diasporan and Haitian revolutionary kidnappings into the relationship between novel and nation in the imagining of New World communities, I argue that the history of kidnapping points to a different model of narratives in Haitian revolutionary and early independence history: kidnapped narratives.

Kidnapping le petit Christophe

It tells us something about the "brigand" sovereignty of Haiti that Dessalines's successor, Henry Christophe, served as president and king of a nation in the western hemisphere without ever breathing a public word about the abduction and death of his firstborn son while under the tutelage of another Western government.

Ferdinand Christophe was sent to France by Henry Christophe in September of 1802 to be educated as a guest of the French government. The politics behind this arrangement are not easy to trace; there is little direct correspondence in which Henry Christophe discusses Ferdinand. As was evident in the case of Toussaint Louverture's bequeathing of his sons Placide and Isaac to France for their education, parental willingness to convey a child to France could mask complex negotiations with the French over autonomy on the part of black leaders in the colony. Christophe's willingness to send Ferdinand to France following the deportation of Toussaint and his family in the summer of 1802, and at a time when the blacks were locked in anticolonial hostilities with the French, seems very curious. It may have indicated a close collaborative relationship between Christophe and the French in that period, or it may have indicated, on the contrary, a profoundly tenuous relationship in which it was necessary to make a potentially sacrificial gesture of good faith.

Arrangements for Ferdinand's travels had begun in late 1801, prior to the dramatic rift between Christophe and the French upon the arrival of Leclerc's army in Saint-Domingue in February of 1802. These arrangements were discussed in a manuscript copy, minus the original signature, of a letter to Christophe that had been copied and returned unsealed to the Colonial Ministry before being delivered by General Leclerc to Saint-Domingue. The letter appears to have been from someone well connected to the highest ranks of French government; it may have been from General Boudet or possibly Bishop Mauriel. The date is 19 Brumaire year 10, or November 6, 1801. The letter is unctuously flattering of Christophe's "submission" to France, of his interest in Europeans who had been "mistreated" by Christophe's superiors (presumably an allusion to the deportations of Sonthonax and Hédouville by Toussaint), and his centrality to France's efforts to bring about the "restoration" of Saint-Domingue:

> [...] vous témoigniez de l'intérêt à mes frères d'Europe maltraités par d'autres [...] Tant de qualités qui vous distinguent, ne seront pas perdues pour mon pays en ce moment important; je l'ai donné à croire aux représentants distingués du plus puissant des gouvernements qui semble ne plus avoir qu'une affaire dans ce moment, la restauration de St. Domingue; l'on compte sur vos secours, mon cher général, pour le succès de cette enterprise; et la France que vous aimez ne sera pas trompée.[1]

> ([...] you demonstrate interest in the plight of my European colleagues who have been mistreated by others [...] These and other qualities that distinguish you will not be lost on my country at this important moment;

I have conveyed this to distinguished representatives of the most powerful of governments, which seems to have the single ambition right now of the restoration of St. Domingue; we are counting on your help, my dear general, for the success of this enterprise; and your beloved France will not be deceived.)

The letter also establishes a strikingly personal tone, praising Christophe not just as a military officer, but also as a good father and spouse. The missive closes, "Mes sincères compliments à votre épouse, mille caresses aux petits enfans; je vous annonce le mentor qui doit ramener Ferdinand" ("My sincere compliments to your wife, a thousand hugs to your little children; I will send information soon on the mentor who will accompany Ferdinand to France").

But in February, General Leclerc would be deeply disappointed by Christophe's public statement of his allegiance to Toussaint, his refusal to permit the French to disembark, and his strategic burning of Cap Français to prevent the French from appropriating its resources. The correspondence between Christophe and Leclerc reproduced in Prince Sanders's 1818 *Haytian Papers* documents this phase of Christophe's relationship with the French. Leclerc wrote from his ship in the harbor,

> I learn with indignation, Citizen General, that you refuse to receive the French squadron, and the French army that I command, under the pretext that you have received no orders from the Governor-General.
>
> France has concluded a peace with England, and its government sends to St. Domingo, forces capable of subduing the rebels; at least if any are to be found in St. Domingo. As to you, General, I confess it will grieve me to account you among them.[2]

Christophe answered, with lucid distrust of colonial rhetoric and intentions, "The very mention of rebellion is an argument for our resistance."[3] This eloquent riposte demonstrated Christophe's understanding that Leclerc's usage of the term "rebellion" inherently implied an authority in relation to which the blacks' autonomy could only register as transgression; it made revolution into rebellion.

Over the course of the following months, Leclerc became confident, rightly or wrongly, of his success in "detaching" Christophe and Dessalines and their troops from Toussaint. He wrote to Napoleon on June 6, 1802, that he had "mastered the mind of Dessalines,"[4] showing a fundamental lack of insight into the black leaders' abilities to engage in political maneuvering.[5]

Contemporary witnesses documented the black generals' awareness of the fine line they had to walk at all times. Christophe made a statement to Pamphile de Lacroix contextualizing his agreement to send Ferdinand as a calculated risk: "La révolte augmente parce que la défiance est à son comble. Si vous aviez notre épiderme, vous ne seriez peut-être pas si confiant que moi, qui remets mon fils unique Ferdinand au général Boudet, pour le faire élever en France"[6] ("The revolt is gathering force because defiance is at its highest point. If you had our skin, you would perhaps not share my confidence in sending my only son Ferdinand to general Boudet, to be raised in France"). Pamphile is not black, but Christophe is; Christophe knows better, he implies, than to accept this arrangement.

What had pushed him, then, to agree? Perhaps the fact that in September of 1802, Christophe himself was at risk of forced deportation to France. On September 16, a disgruntled Leclerc wrote to Napoleon, "Christophe, pour réparer la sottise qu'il avait faite de 's'unir aux noirs,' les a tellement maltraités qu'il en est exécré et que je vais vous le renvoyer, sans craindre que son départ fasse la moindre insurrection. Je n'ai pas été content de lui hier"[7] ("Christophe, to make up for the blunder of 'uniting with the blacks,' has mistreated them so severely that they detest him, and I am going to send him off to you without the slightest fear that his departure will trigger an insurrection. I was not happy with him yesterday"). Only a couple of weeks later, Leclerc, in a letter to Napoleon on September 26, notes that Christophe inspired slightly more confidence in him than Dessalines, and that "J'envoie en France son fils aîné qu'il veut instruire"[8] ("I am sending to France his oldest son, whom he wants educated"). The possibility remains that Ferdinand had become a substitute deportee, a token of Christophe's willingness to sacrifice his own autonomy. Leclerc made no further comments on Ferdinand's departure to France; the French general's last letter to Napoleon was dated October 7, 1802, and he died of yellow fever three weeks later.

It is against this complex backdrop that the ostensibly consensual—but undoubtedly pressured—transfer by Christophe of his son, Ferdinand, to Paris occurred in late September of 1802. The date of Ferdinand's departure was confirmed in a later attestation from the Division of General Security to the Ministry of the Interior: "Le sieur Lambert, mandé à la préfecture de Police, a déclaré que, dans le mois de frimaire an 11 [septembre 1802], l'abbé Collin, son parent, résidant alors au Cap Français, lui avait adressé le fils de Christophe, âgé de 10 ans, accompagné de la négresse Marie [...]"[9] ("Mr. Lambert, ordered to appear before the Police Prefecture, declared that in the month of Frimaire, year 11 [September 1802], his relative the Abbot Collin, who resided at that time in Cap Français, had sent him the son of Christophe, who was at that point ten years old, accompanied by the negress Marie [...]"). The "negress Marie" was the French-educated sister of Henry Christophe's wife, Mary Louise.

It was after the first year of Ferdinand Christophe's education in France at the Collège de Justice on rue de la Harpe that his story took a dark turn, leading to his internment in a state orphanage, La Pitié, and his eventual death there. This fatal detour from the ostensibly consensual educational plan has not been addressed in any detail in biographies of Henry Christophe. The story did eventually unfold, however, in a handwritten transcription of a verbal testimonial by a former slave from Saint-Domingue, Praxelles, in papers belonging to Moreau de St.-Méry. The manuscript has never been reproduced anywhere other than in an obscure 1913 article by George Servant.[10] Like the fragments of the memoirs of Toussaint Louverture that he had written out from memory and hidden in his headscarf to preserve his story, this mediated document is what I will call a "kidnapped narrative" that emblematizes the larger role of kidnapping in the African diaspora's entrance into the textual and print cultures of modernity.

Either Moreau de St.-Méry himself or an assistant transcribed Praxelles's statement in Paris in 1814, some years after the conclusion of the events in question. Praxelles, the wife of Charle Magne (a man whose name evokes the trend among slaveowners of naming slaves for mythological or grand historical characters), was a godmother to one of Henry Christophe's daughters. She was also linked to Henry Christophe's wife's sister, Mademoiselle Marie, who served as Ferdinand's unofficial guardian in Paris, by a social bond between the family of her previous owners and the previous owners of Mademoiselle Marie. Praxelles's narrative pieces together an intricate fabric of acts of witnessing in a Parisian community that included numerous freed slaves interrelated by their relationships (sometimes biological and sometimes legal and social) to white colonial families and to each other; these complex overlaid relationships are represented partly through the affiliations of previous ownership, and partly through the codes of racial categories and African ethnic origins. Sisters and brothers identified in the narrative are clearly often half-siblings, contextualized separately. The document traces the variable social and economic status of non-whites in Saint-Domingue and Paris, from the neighborhood of "Petite Guinée" or little Africa in Le Cap, to the alignment of Henry Christophe's sister-in-law with a certain Bishop Mauriel (discussed in Chapter 3) in allegedly helping to persuade Christophe to send his son to Paris. It is a fragmentary but fascinating glimpse into the lives of free blacks from Saint-Domingue in Paris under the Empire.

Praxelles's testimonial recounts that, shortly after the arrival in Paris of Ferdinand with Christophe's sister-in-law, Mademoiselle Marie, they are brought by their governmental contact, Lambert, to visit the Consul himself, Napoleon Bonaparte, in the Tuileries. After Bonaparte questions Mademoiselle Marie at length, Lambert has a private interview with the Consul. The next day, Lambert explains to Marie that the child will be taken to a school at some distance from Paris. She gives her consent on the condition that she accompany him, but wakes the next morning to find Ferdinand gone. His disappearance upsets her deeply. She protests with great emotion, and is subsequently interned in the notorious asylum of La Salpêtrière.

The details of what had happened to Ferdinand and Marie after their vanishing are then pieced together by a cast of witnesses consulted by Praxelles: an elderly female street-sweeper; a Madame de St.-Joseph, the sister superior who orchestrates sewing jobs for inhabitants of La Salpêtrière, including Mademoiselle Marie; and a female companion of Madame de St.-Joseph.

What follows is a transcription (with minor updating of spelling and punctuation) and translation of Praxelles's narrative in its entirety:

[Henry] Christophe est un nègre ou grif créole de l'isle St. Christophe. Il en a été amené par un Anglais son maître au cap Français à Saint-Domingue. Ce maître a tenu longtemps le Café de la Couronne dans la rue Espagnole où était Christophe.

Après l'incendie du Cap Christophe, devenu libre, a voulu épouser la femme qu'il a aujourd'hui. Elle est fille d'un nègre libre, riche, et considéré demeurant au Cap dans la petite Guinée dans le voisinage du Café de la Couronne. Ce père nommé Codary refusa Christophe qui eut sa femme après la mort de son père.

Cette femme avait une soeur qui avait appartenue comme la famille à une famille blanche du quartier Maurin qui leur donna la liberté.

Cette famille blanche ayant passé en France y emmena Bonaire, frère de Madame Christophe, ainsi que sa soeur qu'on appella en France Mademoiselle Marie.

Cette dernière fut élevée dans un couvent à Paris avec ses demoiselles de la famille de ses anciens maîtres.

Bonaire y épousa la fille négresse de Flore, négresse Arada de Madame de Bouroust appellée Cécile soeur d'Adelaide qui était aussi fille de Flore mais mulâtresse.

Bonaire et Mademoiselle Marie reparurent à Saint-Domingue lorsque le general Leclaire [Leclerc] y arriva aussi. De concert avec l'evêque Maurielle, ils engagèrent [Henry] Christophe à envoyer à Paris pour l'y faire élever son fils âgé d'environ dix ans.

Christophe le confia à sa belle soeur Mademoiselle Marie et l'evêque Maurielle lui donna une lettre de recommandation pour un M. Lambert qui était son meilleur ami et qui prendrait soin d'eux.

Mademoiselle Marie et son jeune neveu [Ferdinand] Christophe arrivèrent chez M. Lambert qui alors était clerc de M. La Marinière, juge de paix à la porte Sait-Honoré.

Les nouveaux arrives étaient chargés d'or, de bijoux et de marchandises que Christophe leur avait données avec profusion.

Très peu de jours après, Lambert conduisait l'enfant et Mademoiselle Marie aux Tuileries chez Bonaparte, il les reçut fort bien et questionna beaucoup Mademoiselle Marie.

Ceux-ci retirés, Lambert rentra chez Bonaparte et tous s'en revinrent ensemble chez Lambert.

Le lendemain Lambert dit à Mademoiselle Marie que Bonaparte voulait que le fils de Christophe fut élevé à soixante lieus de Paris. La tante dit qu'elle suivrait son neveu, mais le lendemain on fit partir l'enfant. A son réveil Mademoiselle Marie ne le trouvant plus, s'en montra très affligée. Lambert lui répondit qu'il avait voulu éviter de douloureux adieux et qu'il allait la mettre elle dans une maison à Paris où elle jouirait de tous les avantages qu'elle pourrait désirer.

En effet peu de temps après il la fit monter en voiture, lui fit prendre un paquet et alla la mèner à la Salpêtrière.

Mademoiselle Marie qui avait connu Praxelles (femme de Charle Magne) d'abord parce qu'elle est marraine d'une fille de Christophe et liée à la femme de Bonaire à cause des relations qui ont existé entre la Baronne Bouroust et la famille de la Barre, ancienne maîtresse de Praxelles, en avait été visitée avec son neveu lors de leur venu à Paris; elle fut donc fort étonnée de ne plus entendre parler et chercha vainement à en avoir des nouvelles.

Longtemps après, vint chez elle une vieille balayeuse du quartier qui lui dit que Mademoiselle Marie était à la Saplêtrière et qu'elle ne pouvait l'y voir qu'en usant beaucoup d'adresse et en feignant d'y apporter de l'ouvrage en couture à Madame de Saint-Joseph la supérieure.

Praxelles suivit l'indication, arriva à Madame de Saint-Joseph chez laquelle elle trouva Mademoiselle Marie, qui en l'apercevant se trouva mal, fondit en larmes et lui dit qu'elle était enfermée dans ce séjour sans pouvoir en sortir ni conférer avec personne.

Depuis Madame de Saint-Joseph et une autre personne de son sexe alla se promener au Jardin des Plantes, aperçut un jeune homme mis en faction à la porte de la Pitié. D'après ce que leur avait repété Mademoiselle Marie du fils de Christophe, elles avançaient vers lui en s'écriant "Voilà le fils de Monsieur Christophe." Le jeune homme tout joyeux dit "Oui, c'est moi." Mais aussitôt un homme qui était à la porte de la Pitié vint à Christophe, lui appliqua deux vaillants soufflets qui firent tomber son fusil, le fit tomber lui-même et l'obligea à rentrer.

Il fut impossible de l'apercevoir depuis, mais on sait qu'on le mit à travailler du métier de cordonnier qu'on exigeait qu'il apprit. Christophe s'y refusa toujours disant que son père l'avait envoyé en France pour y recevoir une belle education et non pour être cordonnier. On lui répondait comme on l'avait déjà fait le jour de la rencontre de Madame de Saint-Joseph qu'il était un petit brigand, fils d'un plus grand brigand qui massacrait des blancs de Saint-Domingue. Le jeune adolescent disait à son tour que père n'était pas un brigand, mais un ami de Bonaparte.

Cette réponse et le refus obstiné de travailler à la cordonnerie furent la cause que Christophe fut tellement battu qu'il eut plusieurs abcès dont il mourut. Quant à Mademoiselle Marie, abbreuvée de chagrins et de regrets, elle mourut à la Salpêtrière bientôt après son neveu.

A sa mort Lambert fit apporter dans cet hospice quelques vieilles hardes, un vieux goblet et un vieux pot d'argent et six piastres gourdes composant, disait-il, tout ce qu'elle avait laissé.

Pour lui-même, il ne tarda pas à acheter une très belle maison dans la rue des Champs Elysées qu'il a richement meublée. Il a aussi acheté une très belle terre, et il affiche partout un luxe dont il l est plus que probable qu'il est redevable à la mort du petit Christophe et à celle de Mademoiselle Marie.

Cela m'a été raconté par Praxelles elle même le lundi vingt-quatre October 1814.[11]

[Henry] Christophe is a Creole negro or *griffe* from the island of St. Kitts. He was brought by his English master to Cap Français in Saint-Domingue. This master was the longtime owner of the Café de la Couronne on Espagnole Street where Christopher worked.

After the burning of the Cap, Christophe, now free, wanted to marry the woman who is today his wife. She is the daughter of a rich and highly esteemed free black who lived in the Cap in Petite Guinée [Little Africa] in the neighborhood of the Café de la Couronne. This father, named Codary, turned down Christophe, who only was able to take his wife after her father's death.

This woman had a sister who had belonged, like the rest of the family, to a white family from the Maurin neighborhood who gave them their freedom.

This white family, having returned to France, brought with them Bonaire, the brother of Madame Christophe, and also Bonaire's sister, who in France was known as Mademoiselle Marie.

Mademoiselle Marie was raised in a convent in Paris with some young ladies from the family of her former master.

In Paris, Bonaire married Cécile, the negro daughter of Flore, Madame Bouroust's Arada negress. Cécile was the sister of Adelaide who was also a daughter of Flore, but a mulatta.

Bonaire and Mademoiselle Marie went back to Saint-Domingue when General Leclerc arrived there. Together with Bishop Murielle they convinced Christophe to send his son, who was about ten years old, to be raised in Paris.

Christophe entrusted the care of his son to his sister-in-law Mademoiselle Marie, and Bishop Murielle gave him a letter of recommendation for a Monsieur Lambert who was his best friend and who would take care of them.

Mademoiselle Marie and her young nephew Christophe arrived at the home of Monsieur Lambert who was then a clerk of Monsieur de la Marinière, a justice of the peace at the Porte St. Honoré.

The new arrivals came laden with gold, jewels, and merchandise that Christophe had given them in abundance.

Only a few days later, Lambert took the child and Mademoiselle Marie to the Bonaparte residence in the Tuileries, where Bonaparte received them very well and questioned Mademoiselle Marie at length.

When the child and his aunt had left Bonaparte, Lambert went in to see Bonaparte, and then they all went back together to Lambert's.

The next day, Lambert told Mademoiselle that Bonaparte wanted Christophe's son to be raised sixty leagues outside of Paris. The aunt said that she would follow her nephew there, but the next day the child had left. Upon awakening, Mademoiselle could find no trace of him, and was deeply upset.

Lambert answered that he had wanted to avoid a painful farewell and that as for Mademoiselle Marie, he was going to send her to an establishment in Paris where she would enjoy every advantage she could wish for.

And in fact, shortly afterward he had her get into a carriage, had a packet of belongings prepared for her, and escorted her to La Salpêtrière.

Mademoiselle Marie had known a woman named Praxelles, the wife of Charle Magne, firstly because Praxelles was the godmother of one of Christophe's daughters and secondly because Praxelles was linked to Bonaire's wife through the relationship between the Baroness Bouroust and the la Barre family, [the family of] Praxelles's former mistress. Praxelles had visited Mademoiselle Marie and her nephew upon their arrival in Paris; she was therefore extremely surprised to have no more word of them and sought in vain to have news of them.

Long afterward, an old female street-sweeper from the neighborhood came to see her and told her that Mademoiselle Marie was in La Salpêtrière. She told Praxelles that she would only be able to see her with great ingenuity, and that she should feign to bring sewing work to Madame de St.-Joseph, the mother superior.

Praxelles followed these instructions and visited Madame de St.-Joseph where she found Mademoiselle Marie, who, when she recognized her, collapsed and dissolved in tears, telling her that she was shut up in this place and could not go out or confer with anyone.

Later, Madame de St.-Joseph and a female companion were walking in the Jardin des Plantes when they saw a young man standing guard at the gate of La Pitié. Because of what Mademoiselle Marie had told them about Christophe's son, they went over to him, crying out, "Here is the son of Christophe." The young man joyfully said "Yes it's me." But in that same moment a man who was at the gate of La Pitié gave Christophe two powerful blows that made Christophe drop his rifle, and fall over, after which it was necessary for him to retreat inside.

It was impossible to catch a glimpse of him from this time forward, but it is known that they set him to learn the trade of shoemaking, requiring him to take it up. Christophe continually refused, saying that his father had sent him to France to get a fine education, not to be a cobbler. They responded the same way they had the day Madame de St.-Joseph saw him, telling him that he was a little brigand, the son of a bigger brigand who was massacring all the whites in Saint-Domingue; the young adolescent responded in his turn that his father was not a brigand, but a friend of Bonaparte.

This response, and his obstinate refusal to become a cobbler, were the reasons that Christophe was beaten so much that he developed several abscesses, of which he died.

As to Mademoiselle Marie, overwhelmed with grief and regrets, she died at La Salpêtrière soon after her nephew.

Upon her death, Lambert had some old rags, an old silver goblet and pot, and six piastres gourdes brought to the hospice, saying that this was all she had had left.

As for himself, he did not delay in buying a lovely house on the Champs Elysées, which he furnished richly. He also bought a lovely property and he displayed everywhere a level of luxury which he more than likely owed to the deaths of the little Christophe and Mademoiselle Marie.

This was recounted to me by Praxelles herself, Monday the twenty-fourth of October, 1814.

Praxelles's narrative collapses some elements of the chronology together, notably, Ferdinand and Marie's respective internments, which occurred not a few days after their arrival in the fall of 1802, but a year later. Official correspondence cited the admission to La Pitié of Ferdinand Christophe, by order of the Minister of the Marines and of the Colonies and of the Minister of the Interior, on December 23, 1803[12]—immediately after the surrender and evacuation of the French from Saint-Domingue.

The narrative also errs in the chronology of Mademoiselle Marie's death, which Praxelles attributes to heartbreak following the news of the death of Ferdinand. In reality, Ferdinand, aged twelve, was still alive and a prisoner of La Pitié on July 8, 1805,[13] when Mademoiselle Marie died in La Salpêtrière. The actual date of the death of Ferdinand Christophe is not known, although it is highly likely that it occurred prior to the political rise of Henry Christophe after the assassination of Dessalines in October of 1806. Death records from La Pitié (formally known as the "Hospice des Orphelins") from 1803–1809 were destroyed in a fire during the Commune.

Praxelles's testimonial also departs from other records in terms of some names. Lambert would state the name of the clergyman who assisted in arranging Ferdinand's voyage to Paris as the abbot Collin, whereas Praxelles cites the Bishop Mauriel (who was also known as Maurielle). Most biographers of Christophe cite his wife's maiden name as Coidavic, whereas Praxelles lists Codary.

And yet Praxelles's mediated narrative is the single known historical account of a shocking episode that is confirmed in the essential details of Christophe's aborted schooling and his involuntary removal by order of the French government, after the defeat of the French in Haiti, to a state orphanage where he was kept captive. It goes without saying that Ferdinand had relatives in both Paris and Haiti who were willing and able to take care of him. Praxelles was also correct in the basics of her story of the forced admission to La Salpêtrière of Henry Christophe's sister-in-law, Marie.

What Praxelles had no way of knowing was that the French government had documented—and denied—charges made by Ferdinand himself. Ferdinand brought a formal complaint that Lambert had appropriated his and Mademoiselle Marie's funds and belongings after the death of Mademoiselle Marie, precisely along the lines of the allegations in Praxelles's story (although according to the French records, Praxelles's account of Lambert's profit is greatly exaggerated).[14]

Ironically, officials in Paris responded to Ferdinand's accusations by alleging that they were keeping him captive to protect him from a plot to kidnap him. The alleged plot was explained in an explanatory note sent to the police prefect:

> On assure d'ailleurs qu'un capitaine américain, s'était chargé depuis peu d'enlever le jeune Ferdinand et de l'emmener aux Etats-Unis et de là à Saint-Domingue, mais que ce capitaine s'étant aperçu qu'il inspirait des soupçons était parti précipitamment sans avoir fait exécuter son projet. Ce dernier avis coïncide parfaitement avec la déclaration de la négresse Marie.[15]

> (We are informed that an American captain had taken on the responsibility a while ago of kidnapping the young Ferdinand and sending him to the United States and thence to Saint-Domingue, but that this captain, noticing that he had aroused suspicion, had left precipitously without carrying out his plan. This last piece of information coincides perfectly with the declaration of the negress Marie.)

Ferdinand's aunt, Mademoiselle Marie, from inside La Salpêtrière, had remained informed about international dealings concerning her nephew, enough to be able to confirm to her interrogators that an American charged with returning Ferdinand to Haiti had departed once he realized he was under surveillance.

When officials asked Lambert about his use of the funds mentioned by Ferdinand, they also took the occasion to request that he continue to take care to prevent the kidnapping of Ferdinand: "il devra au surplus prendre les précautions pour empêcher cet enlèvement"[16] ("he should furthermore take all necessary precautions to prevent this kidnapping").

Henry Christophe's eldest son had been sent to Paris for an education, and died there after the independence, protesting that he was not a little brigand, not the son of a bigger brigand. Praxelles's narrative is an integral part of the literature of the Haitian Revolution and independence.

Kidnapping the Louvertures

The kidnappings that ultimately determined the destiny of the Louverture family were roughly contemporaneous with the secret history that stands as a traumatic, ghostly structure in the life of Henry Christophe. It began with the semi-hostage status of Toussaint's eldest recognized sons, Placide and Isaac, during their French educations, and evolved with the deportation of Toussaint and his family. Toussaint died in prison; his family members died in exile, semi-captive, in France.

General Caffarelli, in the journal of his revolutionary-era dealings with Toussaint, said that Toussaint had told him that he had "onze enfants, dont six filles; il lui en reste trois légitimes et deux naturels"[17] ("eleven children, six of them girls; he had three surviving legitimate children, and two unrecognized ones"). The three children of his marriage that Toussaint described to Cafferelli were Placide (1780 or 1781–1841), Isaac (1781 or 1782–1854), and St.-Jean (1790 or 1791–1804).

The childhoods of Placide and Isaac become part of the historical record of the Republic in 1796, when Toussaint sent them, supported by the French government of the Directory in recognition of Toussaint's military service, to the Ecole de Liancourt in Rochefort, France, a school for military orphans and the sons of indigent colonists or soldiers. In 1797, the Louverture boys were transferred to the Collège de la Marche in Paris, when they were fifteen and fourteen years old respectively. This was an era in which the French education of prominent young sons of Saint-Domingue, whether white, of mixed race, or now, in the Revolutionary era, black, was an essential mark of privileged class status and social mobility. By sending his sons to France for their education, Toussaint was claiming their place in the ranks of the educated and cosmopolitan group that had always negotiated the economic and political relationships between colony and metropolis. Michel Roussier outlines the arrangement through which educational privileges for the sons of French officers in Saint-Domingue were expanded to include the children of black leaders.[18]

There is evidence of Toussaint's early idealism concerning the educational arrangement, and of his desire to have his sons, unschooled up to that point, educated in France. In April of 1799, the *Ancien moniteur* printed a touching paternal recommendation of his sons to the care of his secretary, now in France, who seems to merge in Toussaint's rhetoric with France itself:

Voyez mes chers enfants le plus que vous pourrez, donnez-moi de leurs nouvelles: vous savez combien je les aime, combien est tendre mon attachement pour eux. Donnez-leurs les conseils et les avis qu'ils doivent attendre d'un ami de leur père; qu'ils soient laborieux, et qu'ils s'attachent à se rendre dignes, par leur application, des soins et des bienfaits de la mère-patrie; ils mériteront par-là que je redouble pour eux d'attachement.[19]

(See my children as often as you can, give me news of them: you know how much I love them, how tender my attachment is for them. Give them the counsel and advice that they should expect from a friend of their father; let them be hard-working, and commit to making themselves worthy, through their diligence, of the care and kind attentions of the mother country; through such behavior they will deserve a redoubling of my attachment to them.)

But it is also likely that Toussaint kept his sons in France because the tensions following his deportations of Sonthonax and Hédouville made it necessary to show his good faith by keeping something very precious in the hands of the French government. Victor Schoelcher explained that Toussaint "ostensibly wanted to put to rest the Directory's suspicions concerning his attempts to put distance between himself and European envoys. How could an ill-intentioned father give up such precious hostages?"[20] In this fraught context, it is perhaps not surprising that the story of their education devolves into a story of multiple and disputed schemes to use them as pawns in the chess game between France and Saint-Domingue.

The Directory gave responsibility for Placide's and Isaac's formal and personal education to the Abbot Coisnon, with whom Toussaint corresponded regularly, with considerable warmth and respect. Coisnon in turn corresponded with the president of the Executive Council of the Directory, forwarding Toussaint's letters and reporting on the progress of his children.[21] This relationship between the Louvertures, Coisnon, and the French government shifted dramatically with the coming to power of Napoleon Bonaparte.

Tensions between Napoleon and Toussaint concerning the Louverture children begin to come to light in the curious story of a kidnapping plot uncovered by the French police in 1800. David Geggus summarizes this plot by a creole émigré in London, Pierre-Victor Malouet, as outlined in a letter by Malouet intercepted by the French police. As Geggus describes it, the alleged plot involved another black military leader from Saint-Domingue, Jean Kina, who was then in London:

Toussaint's children were at school in Paris, effectively hostages of the French government. If they could be kidnapped, Malouet reasoned, Toussaint might be willing to sever his links with France. The British government, he admitted, would never approve such a plan, but, he added, if the children could be got to Dover, he was sure their kidnapper would be rewarded and they would be handed over to Jean Kina and sent to Jamaica.[22]

Malouet's musings may not have been chimerical. As early as 1804, a biography of Toussaint stated that he and General Maitland had agreed to try to remove the boys from an educational arrangement in which they were effectively hostages. It is not clear whether the following quote refers to Malouet's plan specifically, or to some other dialogue between Toussaint and the English regarding the problematic status of the Louverture boys in France, and the obstacle it presented to movement toward independence in Saint-Domingue:

> One other express engagement of a most interesting nature, [that] General Maitland concluded with Tousant [sic], ... was, that he promised, if possible, to enveigle [sic] his two sons from those who had charge of their education, he went to Hamburgh [sic] for that purpose, and endeavoured to perfect his intentions by deputation, in vain: this disappointment became a source of anxiety for their parent, still he was satisfied with the attempt: had it succeeded, Tousant no doubt would have proclaimed the independence of that colony... these children were a barrier thereto...[23]

The French police found the alleged plot to be a convenient pretext to suppress all attempted repatriations of the Louverture boys. No matter how legitimate, attempts to bring Placide and Isaac back to Saint-Domingue were now reframed as kidnapping plots. When Toussaint himself sent two of his associates with a straightforward request to repatriate just one of his sons, the French police seem to have intentionally "confused" this paternal objective with the plot referred to by Malouet. Historians including Nemours have accepted the logic of police letters linking Malouet's plot to a subsequent "kidnapping plot" by two men from Saint-Domingue named Huin and d'Hébécourt who came to France to bring at least one of the Louverture boys back to their father. But in order to connect the two episodes, the police had to overlook a letter by Toussaint to Napoleon:

> Mes deux enfans, qui sont à l'institut national, m'ont écrit pour me demander la permission de retourner à Saint-Domingue, au sein de leur famille. Mon intention ne serait pas de les rappeller tous les deux à la fois, mais un des deux. J'ai un troisième fils plus jeune que ceux qui sont en France, que je désirais y envoyer, pour y recevoir un peu d'éducation. Celui qui restera sera le guide de son cadet et celui qui reviendra à Saint Domingue me donnera un peu de joye [sic] et de consolation, ainsi qu'à sa tendre mère. Je vous prie, Citoyen Consul, de fournir à l'un de mes deux

fils l'occasion de revenir auprès de moi, soit au retour du général Michel, soit au retour de l'adjudant général Huin [...] Je me repose sur vos—et sur votre tendresse paternelle.

(My two children, who are at the National Institute, have written to me to request permission to return to Saint-Domingue, to the bosom of their own family. My intention is not to bring back both at once, but one of the two. I have a third son, younger than the two in France, whom I would like to send there, to receive some education. The son who will remain in France will be his younger brother's mentor, and the one who will return to Saint-Domingue will give me and his tender-hearted mother joy and consolation. I beg you, Citizen Consul, to give one of my sons the opportunity to return to me, either in the company of general Michel, or in the company of adjudant general Huin [...] I depend on your care and paternal tenderness.)[24]

When Toussaint's emissary Huin, accompanied by d'Hébécourt, arrived in Bordeaux, he was placed under strict police surveillance as a potential kidnapper and denied all access to the Louverture boys. Police correspondence earlier had indicated that the Abbot Coisnon had communicated Toussaint's request for the repatriation of his son, but in later correspondence Coisnon denied that there had been such a request, and specified that he would guard the boys from any contact with potential kidnappers.[25]

The status of the boys as hostages was again confirmed when Placide was taken out of school to accompany a French military expedition in 1800–1801. The expedition was supposed to be headed for Saint-Domingue—a destination that the presence of the son of Toussaint Louverture might have seemed to confirm to observers,[26] but in fact Placide served as a military decoy.[27] Isaac explained that Placide had been on Admiral Gantheaume's vessel as "aide-de-camp to general Sahuguet, with the firm belief that he was going to Saint-Domingue, whereas, without suspecting it, he was actually being used to mask the true goal of a naval expedition bringing reinforcements to the army in Egypt."[28]

How did Placide and Isaac experience their relationship to the French government? Roussier has provided fascinating details both of conditions at the Ecole de Liancourt, which were fairly appalling,[29] and of the curriculum and student body at the Collège de la Marche, which gave the boys access to a broader world of letters. Isaac and Placide would have studied Latin, texts by Stern, Goldsmith, and Montagu, Lessing, and mathematical treatises by Legendre and Bezout.[30]

The botanist M. E. Descourtilz had apparently met Placide and Isaac at the Collège de la Marche prior to his travels to Saint-Domingue, which suggests that the boys were seen as important connections to that colony.

He wrote of his first encounter with Toussaint, "nous ne le vîmes qu'un instant pour l'embrasser au nom de ses enfans alors à Paris, au collège de la Marche, et lui remettre des lettres dont ils nous avoient chargés à notre départ de France"[31] ("we saw him just long enough to greet him on behalf of his children in Paris, at the Collège de la Marche, and to give him the letters the boys had put in our care before our departure from France"). Some historians believe that Placide and Isaac were treated as "guests" within the entourage of Napoleon. Isaac Louverture describes a meeting at which the Consul, who seemed to be meeting them for the first time, tries to persuade them of his positive intentions toward their father.[32]

Isaac clearly shared his father's initial idealism concerning the custodial role of France as a substitute father in his life. His new accomplishments came at the price of shame about his pre-French state as one of "barbarism." In his letter to the Minister of the Marine, seconding his father's request that he be allowed to return to Saint-Domingue, he wrote:

Les bienfaits de la mère Patrie envers ses enfants des colonies seront à jamais gravés dans mon coeur. Si Saint-Domingue fut notre berceau, la France est notre asyle assurable. C'est dans son sein que l'éducation a dévéloppé en nous ces germes précieux de talens, que la barbarie avait étouffée [...][33]

(The good deeds of the Fatherland toward its colonial children will be forever engraved in my heart. If Saint-Domingue was our cradle, France is our sure asylum. It is in her bosom that we have developed the precious seeds of talents that barbarism had previously stifled [...])

Isaac even wrote an epic poem to Napoleon in 1801, called "For the Day of Peace," which begins:

O toi dont la valeur commande à la victoire,
Et dont les grands desseins ont mérité la gloire,
Jeune et vaillant héros, l'éclat de la grandeur,
Du beau jour qui nous luit, augmente la Splendeur.[34]

(O thou whose valor commands victory,
And whose great designs merit glory,
Young and valiant hero, the brilliant grandeur
Of the shining day that illuminates us, augments your splendor.)

Isaac's identification with Napoleon would complicate not only his relationship with his father and with Placide, but also the attempts of historians to decipher the nature of the final episode in which the boys were used as hostages, because Isaac had absolute faith in his role as an emissary of Napoleon.

On December 20, 1801, Toussaint issued a proclamation, published in the United States as well as Saint-Domingue, in which he made the contested custody of his sons an issue of public record. The proclamation broached the rumor of an upcoming French invasion, cleverly publicizing it while appearing to condemn it as an incendiary rumor: "Evil-minded persons have circulated a report, that France will come with thousands of men to annihilate the colony and liberty."[35] Toussaint then chose in this widely distributed proclamation to raise the question of his sons' hostage status, again publicizing it and contradicting it in one fell swoop:

> You, who in order to kindle amongst us the fire of discord, ascribe to the French government liberticidal intentions and projects of destruction; who, to give it plausibility, confidently assert that government would not send me my children when I asked for them, because it intended keeping them as a hostage [...]

Toussaint's condemnation of the rumor of kidnapping is instantly belied, however, by his subsequent frank admission that, in fact, he has been unable to persuade France to return his children. Concerning Isaac and Placide, he wrote, "It is true, I have sent for my children, who are not yet arrived: but though I am very sorry for this delay, because I only asked for a property lawfully my own, I am nevertheless very far from entertaining the same thoughts as the malevolent do."

Napoleon had, of course, sent both Isaac and Placide on the French military expedition, presumably to use the boys to gain leverage over their father, although they publicly denied this. As Isaac recounts the events in his memoirs, Napoleon personally had outlined a plan for the boys to sail ahead of the expedition and convince their father of his honorable intentions.[36] In a proclamation delivered on February 10, 1802, and published in the *Daily Advertiser* on March 26, 1802, Leclerc asserted, "The French government wished for an opportunity of shewing their regard for General Toussaint, and they charged me to return to him his children. These youths should not be the victims of the misconduct of their parent, I sent them to him yesterday."[37]

Coisnon himself published an account of the meeting between the boys and their father in the *Moniteur*, in a letter dated February 20, 1802. Under Coisnon's escort, on February 7, the boys were sent first to their overjoyed mother in Marmelade, where they waited overnight until Toussaint could be summoned home. Toussaint, according to Coisnon, received not only his sons but Coisnon also with open arms. Coisnon then asked Toussaint to hear out the boys as "faithful interpreters of the First Consul and of the

Captain General of the colony." Only Isaac actually spoke, however, and Coisnon recounts that "Toussaint observed a studied silence while his son was speaking." What did Toussaint's studied silence mean as he listened to his son parroting the Consul's self-justifications? Coisnon simply notes, without explanation, that after the meeting, rather than leaving the boys with their father, he set off with "the young Toussaints" back to the French camp in the Cape.

This return of Isaac and Placide to the French army is the key point of contention in accounts of what had actually transpired during the meeting. Did this mean that the boys were in fact brought to Toussaint as hostages in a negotiation, and that he refused the proffered terms?

This is certainly the drama that many opponents of Napoleon Bonaparte saw as having unfolded in the meeting with Coisnon. As Antoine Métral described the scene in 1818, "Saint-Domingue's destiny, the liberty of the blacks, a new people, all depended in that moment on a father's heart."[38]

The boys were soon released to their father's care anyway, but the scene of their jeopardy was inscribed immediately in historical accounts. The 1803 British abolitionist tract *Buonaparte in the West Indies, or, the History of Toussaint Louverture, the African Hero* described the scene with anti-Napoleonic relish: "To take these youths from their studies, and send them out to catch their father, as you would catch a bird, by stripping her nest, and baiting a trap-catch with her young ones, seemed no doubt a bright thought to the Corsican."[39]

Leclerc did explain, in a detailed letter to the Minister of the Marine that was first published in France in March, that when he duly sent Toussaint his children, "I gave him to understand that I will take upon myself to receive his submission."[40] This letter is quite convincing evidence that Toussaint was given to believe that his children's return was at the price of his submission.

The government of Napoleon would never be able to convince numerous significant participants in the European intellectual domain that he had not destroyed a man who incarnated the virtue of the human attachment to liberty as something more precious than a beloved child. The children's passage to Saint-Domingue on the *Jean-Jacques* coincided with this Rousseauist symbolism.

The events of the final kidnapping of Toussaint himself, along with his immediate family, began to unfurl in the early June of 1802. Although Aimé Césaire would later suggest that Toussaint had sacrificed himself to the French for the good of Saint-Domingue,[41] Toussaint himself insisted that he had been taken by force. The kidnapped Toussaint was taken to the port of Gonaives and embarked on the ship *Le Créole*, from which he made the famous tree of liberty statement. The ship proceeded to the Cap, where he was transferred to the ironically named vessel *Le Héros* and joined by his wife; his two elder sons; his younger son, St. Jean; a niece, Louise Chancy;[42] a young female companion, Victoire Thusac (who was briefly identified by French police as Placide's fiancée, but subsequently as someone with no relation whatsoever to the Louverture family, despite the fact that Placide apparently refers to both Louise and Victoire as "mes cousines");[43] and a maid, Justine.

The kidnapping itself was never reported as such in the French papers in the summer of 1802. On July 19, in an item buried among other *faits divers*, the *Gazette de France* simply noted that "The vessels the Argonaut, the Hero, the Mont-Blanc, and the frigate the Precious, under the command of Counter-Admiral Magon, entered, on the 18th of this month, the harbor of Brest. Toussaint Louverture was on board the vessel the Hero with his family."[44]

Leclerc instructed the Colonial Ministry to shut Toussaint away deep in the interior of France: "Il ne faut pas que Toussaint soit libre, faites-le emprisonner dans l'intérieur de la République; que jamais il ne revoye Saint-Domingue"[45] ("Toussaint must not be free, imprison him in the depths of the Republic; he must never see Saint-Domingue again").

Leclerc himself also provided what was no doubt the earliest French account to qualify Toussaint's departure as a kidnapping, in a letter to Napoleon on June 11, 1802: "Toussaint is kidnapped. It is a great step, but the blacks are armed and I need forces to disarm them."[46] On August 25 he reiterated this point, with a tone of desperation rather than triumph: "It is not enough to have kidnapped Toussaint, here there are two thousand leaders to kidnap."[47]

Toussaint, as discussed in the introduction, launched into the writing of his memoirs to Napoleon.[48] Caffarelli reported that on his visit of September 27, he returned Toussaint's text with a few discouraging remarks: "I told him coldly that I had not seen anything of interest, that this text had taught me nothing, and I asked him for more positive and true avowals than those I had read and heard thus far."[49]

In September and October, Toussaint wrote several letters in his own hand, and these documents are precious records of his unmediated voice and his despairing contemplation of the problematic "humanity" of his captors. From the "cachote du for Gout" (dungeon of Fort Gout [sic]), Toussaint wrote to "Caffaréli," "Je vous pri de rafraichire la memoire de première Consul a mon negard... Vous mavet asuré que le premiere Consul et eu min et plus guste que personne"[50] ("I beg you to refresh the First Consul's memory with respect to me... You have assured me that the First Consul is human and more just than anyone"). To his wife, Suzanne, Toussaint wrote in September, "J'ai été malade an narrivant ici, mais le commandant de cet place qui et un homme umain ma porté toute les cecours possible... vous savé mon namitier pour ma famille et mon nattachement pour une femme que je chéris, pour quoi mavé vous pa donné de vos nouvel"[51] ("I was sick upon my arrival here, but the commander of this place who is a humane man gave me all possible help... You know my friendship for my family and my attachment to a wife I cherish, why haven't you sent me your news"). To Napoleon, Toussaint wrote "Je vous pri au nom de dieu, au nom de lhumanite de jai té un coudeuille favarable sur ma reclamation [...] mon père qui et aveugle presantement, ma montre les chemien de la vertu"[52] ("I beg you in the name of God, in the name of humanity to look favorably upon my request [...] my father who is blind at present has shown me the paths of virtue"). In deciding all these questions of the "eu min," the "umain," and of "lhumanite," Toussaint could only conclude that God had suffered a malady of vision.

On November 6 of 1802, one of the commanders of the Fort de Joux, Baille, reported to the Minister of the Marine and the Colonies that he had approached the prisoner and taken away "all the written and blank papers existing in his room... He seemed deeply affected by the removal of these papers..."[53]

The Louverture children and their associates faced similarly heartbreaking experiences. Placide Louverture had insisted on accompanying his father to prison, but this filial piety was rewarded not with his father's companionship but with a cell in the prison of Belle-Isle en mer. On the way to his internment at Belle-Isle, he wrote a letter to his parents from aboard the brig *Nayade* that exemplifies both the stakes and the impossibility of communication among a family scattered to different ships and harbors and prisons: "Je suis abord du brick la nayäde j'ignore quel est mon sort. Peut-être je ne vous verez jamais [...] Je vous donnerai mes nouvelles si je ne suis pas mort"[54] ("I am on board the brig *Naïade* my fate is unknown. Perhaps I will never see you again [...] I will send you my news if I am not dead"). How can one really convey that one is not dead to people one may never reach with one's reassurances? The letter's envelope says on one side, "A Monsieur Toussaint Louverture a Breste Departement du Finistere a Brest," and on the other side, "Ou pour remettre à Madame Toussaint Louverture a Breste" ("Or to be delivered to Madame Toussaint Louverture in Brest"), and on yet another area of the paper, "A Madame Toussaint Louverture a bord du vaisseau le heros" ("To Madame Toussaint Louverture on the vessel the Hero").

A police letter to the Minister of the Marine notes the arrival in Agen of six members of the Toussaint Louverture family, including Isaac, St. Jean, and Suzanne Louverture, Justine the maid, Louise Chancy, and Victoire Thusac. Victoire alone became separated from the group, apparently to meet an aunt, "La femme Minot," in Marseille. Police records note that although "Victoire Thusac, mulâtresse," was given a passport to travel to Marseille, her aunt was never found there. The police, while awaiting the arrival of Victoire—an arrival never confirmed in these documents—pledged to keep her and her contacts under close surveillance.[55] This young woman of color from Saint-Domingue, whose historical identity is as interesting as it is elusive,[56] then disappears from the public record.

The youngest member of the Louverture party in France was St. Jean Louverture, who died in Agen shortly after the Haitian independence in 1804. The eldest was Toussaint's wife, Suzanne, who died in 1816. Isaac Louverture later married his cousin Louise Chancy. Like Placide after his release from prison, Isaac and Louise lived a life of house arrest and poverty under Napoleon, and then of restricted movement and penury under subsequent regimes. The Ministry of the Marine described their restricted movement and penury as "suitable to the condition of free negroes and negresses [...]"[57]

Isaac's correspondence is notable for the number of times he applied to the French government for permission to travel to baths to treat a skin condition. Although Louise ultimately made one brief trip to Haiti to settle a small inheritance claim, neither son of Toussaint Louverture would ever succeed in setting foot on Haitian soil again, despite numerous applications for travel papers.

Isolated from the history into which they had been catapulted, Isaac and Placide became separated by rivalry and misunderstanding. In 1821 Isaac and Louise sued to prevent Placide from continuing to use the Louverture name because they believed his lighter skin was evidence that he was not Toussaint's son.[58] When they won the case, Isaac thanked his lawyers in Latin.[59]

Isaac and Louise had no children. Although Placide had one daughter with his French wife, the Louverture familial line faded into the provincial French *petit bourgeoisie* and never reconnected with the destiny of Haiti.[60] The destiny of the Louvertures, scions of the founding family of Saint-Domingue's black leadership, had been kidnapped from them.

Kidnapped Origins and Origins of Kidnapping

Kidnappings within the families of Haitian revolutionary leaders require contextualization within the mass kidnappings in the previous two centuries of the colonial slave trade. Kidnapping ("enlèvement" or "ravissement" in French) was the traumatic starting point of eventual creole or hybridized identity for the African diaspora in the Caribbean. It figures in virtually all family histories related to the New World angle of the triangular slave trade, and was a fundamental mechanism of the large-scale transnational movement of populations in the colonial era.

As Prosper Mérimée's 1829 story "Tamango" brutally shows, the movement of large populations through the Middle Passage involved individual African profiteers partnering with the system of the Western slave trade. Through these kidnappings, Africans were pitched from a world of shared languages, cultures, and genealogies to the near-absolute disruption of identity and representational structures in slavery, from which a new social existence could only emerge like a phoenix. In the context of ravished individual and diasporan trajectories, the politics of the inhabitation of space are porous, violent, chaotically opportunistic, traumatic, and metamorphic. They frame a zone of inscrutable relations between law and non-law, in which anthropological structures of exchange and sacralization of familial bonds are negated wholesale; a zone in which, in other words, the way that communities imagine themselves, from the family to the tribe to the regional geopolitical and linguistic entity, has been subject to the severe stress of arbitrary nullification.

The drama of kidnapping into enslavement was well documented by Western observers of the colonial system from the early phases of Caribbean colonial exploitation. J.-B. Labat, in his famous late seventeenth- / early eighteenth-century Caribbean travel narrative, cited four categories of Africans forcibly brought to the New World as slaves. The first three categories represented a minor proportion of slaves: wrongdoers, prisoners seized in local wars, and the personal slaves of princes who decided, or were compelled by necessity, to sell them. The fourth category, far and away the largest, consisted of those who were randomly kidnapped for their human commercial value: "those that they steal away, either by order or with the consent of princes, or by certain thieves, called merchants, who kidnap everything they can catch in the way of men, women, and children, and take them to a ship or a merchant's establishment, where they are marked with hot irons and put into chains for security."[61] Labat was in no way alone in his linkage of kidnapping and slavery. Among the many texts that protest kidnapping in the Atlantic slave trade are Willem Bosman's *Kidnapping, Enslaved, and Sold Away*, and John Newton's *Kidnapping and Retaliation*.[62]

And yet, in contradistinction to this specificity of kidnapping in the African slave trade in the post-Columbian New World, kidnapping as intercultural movement is also, paradoxically, arguably at the very foundations of what we regard as cosmopolitan civilization. The name "Europe" itself derives from a mythological scene of a sort of Europeanization by kidnapping. In the myth of Europa, the Phoenician princess of that name, wandering along a beach, was persuaded by Zeus, disguised as a snowy white bull, to ride upon his back. The ride turned into an abduction / ravishment, as Zeus carried the princess across the Mediterranean to Crete, where she became the mother of Minos, Lord of Crete. Norman Davies points out that among the connotations of Europa's ride is the movement of knowledge and reading practices from East to West, locating the cultural identity of Europe in a sort of kidnapping, ravishment, and familial merger of crosscultural influences: "Zeus was surely transferring the fruits of the older Asian civilizations of the East to the new island colonies of the Aegean," writes Davies. "Europa's ride provides the mythical link between Ancient Egypt and Ancient Greece. Europa's brother, Cadmus, who roamed the world in search of her [...] was credited with bringing the art of writing to Greece."[63] On a mythological level, the origins of European civilization lie not in a peaceful founding nationalist scene, but in this involuntary hybridization that evokes the tension between force and exchange in colonialism.

The sheer scale of the phenomenon of kidnapping in the modern colonial slave trade, and its overlap with the other forced and unforced migrations that have ceaselessly reshaped boundaries of ethnicities and other communities into diasporan trajectories, makes it a fertile testing ground with regard to Benedict Anderson's famous analogy between nation and novel in his book *Imagined Communities*.[64]

"Imagining" Kidnapped Communities

Anderson argued that, within the modern print cultural convergence of capitalism and technological dissemination, the novel highlighted a synchronic temporality that simultaneously characterized the nation's self-concept. In Jonathan Culler and Pheng Cheah's description, temporal mimesis in the novelistic narration overlapped with "the simultaneity that allows one to imagine a limited sovereign community beyond face-to-face relations."[65] Anderson's linkage of the cognitive and infrastructural foundations of nationalism to the structure of the novel recalls Erich Auerbach's conception of a humanist historical perspective that is fundamental to literary realism. In other ways it brings to mind György Lukács's theory of the essential relationship between literary realism and the "totality" of capitalism, a totality outside of which the social comes to defy imagination. In both these latter literary / historical paradigms, the styles of our narration of historical experience shape that experience, just as historical infrastructural conditions such as capitalism mold narrative styles.

If the nation finds a form of mimetic analogue in the novel, what kind of mimetic architecture might we associate with the kidnappings that launched African diasporan movement into the colonial spaces of modern Western nations? Can we use any such analogy to help us locate and read texts that do not conform to the Anglophone model of the slave narrative, but that nevertheless represent slaves and former slaves? How might consciousness of diasporan kidnapping challenge our acceptance of national parameters for African diasporan literary studies in various languages, and our expectations of the kinds of genre and other textual characteristics that shape our "symbolic mapping of external social space"? How might we begin, in other words, to schematize the coming to literary and national consciousness of the African diaspora at the beginning of national modernity?

Black Creoles—Out of the Frame

Anderson's focus on the "Creole Pioneers" of New World nationhood would seem to open the door to consideration of the colonial African diaspora generally, and of the first postcolonial black New World nation, Haiti. However, although Anderson mentions Toussaint Louverture and the Haitian Revolution, they are forcefully relegated to the role of contrapuntal anecdote, because his argument relies on the concept of a linguistic and genealogical continuity between the New World and the European metropoles as the backdrop for the new imagining of communities.

For Anderson, the newly independent nations in the New World in the period from 1776 to 1838 provide the evidence for the association between novelistic and journalistic print capitalism and the national imagination. Whether exemplified by "Brazil, the USA, or the former colonies of Spain," the "new American states of the late eighteenth and early nineteenth centuries" share for Anderson a crucial identity as places where "language was not an element that differentiated them from their respective imperial metropoles. All were shaped by people who shared a common language and common descent with those against whom they fought."[66] This sharing of a common language and descent meant that New World creole "printmen" could travel back and forth between colonial and metropolitan spheres, disseminating literature and shaping new imaginings of the nation. For Anderson, this mediation, more than any European factor, contributed to the metamorphosis of New World colonies like the U.S. into New World nations.

But "common language and common descent" is precisely what the Haitians did not share with the European metropoles. In the French Caribbean colonies of the New World in the Revolutionary era, the term *créole* was generally synonymous with *américain* ("American") and designated anyone born in the colonies, whether of African or European descent. By contrast, in Latin America the term *criollo*, often also translated as "creole," referred to those born in the Americas but of unmixed Iberian descent. The creole pioneers in forging the novelistic consciousness of the nation were not, and could not by this definition be, slaves. The nation-building role of the creole printmen depended, according to Anderson, partly on their attempts to consolidate autonomous communities in order to deflect the Enlightenment metropolitan interest in modifying—however minimally, to our eyes—abusive power over slaves. "Far from seeking to 'induct the lower classes into political life,'" Anderson writes, "one key factor initially spurring the drive for independence from Madrid, in such important cases as Venezuela, Mexico, and Peru, was the *fear* of 'lower-class' political mobilizations: to wit, Indian or Negro-slave uprisings."[67]

Not only had the New World colony of Saint-Domingue been built on the importation of kidnapped Africans, but its steady movement toward autonomy led to the phenomenon of Napoleonic kidnappings of prominent Haitians that is exemplary of a profound *discontinuity* in the "symbolic mapping of external social space" between Haiti's new literary voices and the Euro-American metropoles. That discontinuity did not exclusively take the form of silence and non-dialogue—it took the heteroclite forms of political proclamations, letters, memoirs of self-defense, testimonials, and, as I will show in the second section of this book, popular songs.

The strange ballet of trust and hostility between the former slaves of Saint-Domingue and the French government led to moments when, for Napoleon Bonaparte and his associates, one black leader or another seemed to be France's best and fondest hope for an ongoing colonial future in Saint-Domingue, even in cases where these leaders clearly had been involved in earlier violent conflict with the French colonial hierarchy. At other moments, when the primary fidelity of these black leaders to their own constituent communities became clear, the impetus on the part of the Napoleonic government simply to seize and sequester members of the Haitian revolutionary leadership or their families apparently became irresistible, resulting in kidnappings that recapitulated the abusive deportations of the Middle Passage. But these leaders were already decisively exploiting the self-representational opportunities of print culture; their political strategies and individual poetics of anticolonial identity were, as we have seen in the preceding chapters, blazing through the journalistic and political domains of the Western world. In the context of deportations and captivity, their self-representations emblematized the structures of kidnapped narratives.

How do documents such as the mediated testimonial of Praxelles, or Toussaint's published proclamation denouncing—and simultaneously confirming—rumors of the kidnapping of his sons, represent Haiti as a different kind of "creole pioneer," articulating a different kind of new nationalism—Revolutionary-era black postcolonial nationalism—in which the imagining of communities does not conform to the model established by Benedict Anderson? In effect, here nation is to novel as kidnapping is to mediated and disguised witnessing. These are liminal texts. The narrative by Praxelles was told by a witness for posterity, transcribed by a secretary or ethnographer. It represented the historical knowledge of people whose social existence could be effectively erased when struggles for autonomy created "race" conflicts, labeled at the time in terms of "brigands" and "massacres." The proclamation by Toussaint is one of many texts that show his distinctive strategic brilliance, melding the conciliatory and the subversive to outmaneuver his opponents; these mediated texts were disseminated extraordinarily broadly through journalism, and yet are only now being specifically credited to Toussaint as the political and literary texts of a major figure on the Revolutionary world political stage.

Kidnapped narratives of the African diaspora in the Revolutionary era lurk in archives, newspapers, records, and even quotations in other works, in the various forms of fragments, edited popular oral literature, and mediated political proclamations and correspondence. Its messages were sometimes, as in the memoirs of Toussaint, precisely kidnapped: contained and isolated. At other times, as in the proclamations and correspondence of Toussaint and Dessalines, they were a Western print culture sensation. They are a corpus that must be researched outside of the framework of the novelistic masterpiece of national literatures, or even of the slave narrative shaped and cultivated by abolitionist "printmen," despite abundant overlap with that genre. This diasporan literature by those whose common descent involves kidnapping gives us a new point of entry to exploration of the nation, as not just an imagined community beyond face-to-face interaction, but as an imagined community with unimagined participants, un-becoming slaves, critiquing their status as sovereign "brigands." Kidnapped narratives represent one part of the answer to Laurent Dubois's provocative question of how we might "write an intellectual history of the enslaved."[68]

Notes

1. Letter to Christophe, author unknown, labeled "Copie de la lettre écrite au Général Christophe, Remise décachetée au Ministre de la Marine pour être Portée par le Général Leclerc à St. Domingue," *Notes Historiques de Moreau de St. Méry*, Archives d'Outre-mer, F3, vol. 141, 494–5.

2. Letter from Leclerc to Christophe, 13 Pluviose year 10 (February 2, 1802), included in Prince Sanders [Saunders], *Haytian Papers 1818: An Address Delivered at Bethel Church. Philadelphia: 1818. A Memoir Presented to The American Convention or Promoting by the Abolition of Slavery. 1819* (Philadelphia, PA: Historic Publications No. 238, 1969), 21.

3. *Haytian Papers*, 25.

4. Letter from Leclerc to Napoleon, dated June 6, 1802, in Paul Roussier, ed., *Lettres du Général Leclerc, Commandant en chef de l'armée de Saint-Domingue en 1802, publiées avec une introduction par Paul Roussier* (Paris: Société de l'histoire des colonies françaises et Librairie Ernest Leroux, 1937), 161–2.

5. Leclerc's confidence in the eventual submission of the black generals to his authority, no matter how dubious when framed on the continuum of both Dessalines's and Christophe's inspired rejections of French authority, has often been taken at face value in colonial historiography. A typical example of this tendency to conflate Leclerc's interpretation with historical reality can be found in Charles W. Mossell's *Toussaint L'Ouverture, the Hero of Saint Domingo*, where the author trenchantly reflected "A traitor is always a traitor. After betraying Toussaint L'Ouverture, Christophe betrayed Leclerc as soon as the opportunity presented itself, and finally, under the influence of a treacherous spirit, took his own life." *Toussaint L'Ouverture, the Hero of Saint Domingo: Soldier, Statesman, Martyr, Or, Hayti's Struggle, Triumph, Independence, and Achievements* (Lockport, NY: Ward & Cobb, 1896), 271.

6. François Joseph Pamphile de Lacroix, *Mémoires pour servir à l'histoire de la révolution de Saint-Domingue* (Paris: Pillet aîné, 1819), 226.

7. Roussier, ed., *Lettres du général Leclerc*, 230.

8. Roussier, ed., *Lettres du général Leclerc*, 246.

9. Letter dated 13 Frimaire year 13 (August 31, 1805), Archives nationales, F7 6461.

10. George Servant, "Ferdinand Christophe, fils du roi d'Haïti, en France," *Revue de l'histoire des colonies françaises* 23 (1913), 217–32.

11. *Notes Historiques de Moreau de St. Méry*, Archives d'Outre-mer, F3, 140 *bis*, 89–93.

12. Documented in a letter dated July 9, 1805, Archives nationales, F7 6461.

13. Death Register, Archives de La Salpêtrière, n.29, fol. 51v.

14. Letters dated July 5, August 3, and August 9, 1805, Archives nationales, F7 6461.

15. Letter dated August 9, 1805, Archives nationales, F7 6461.

16. Letter from the Minister of the Interior to the Minister of the General Police, dated August 3, 1805, Archives nationales, F7 6461.

17. Cited in Alfred Nemours, *Histoire de la descendance et de la famille de Toussaint Louverture* (Port-au-Prince: Imprimerie de l'état, 1941), 11.

18. Michel Roussier, "L'éducation des enfants de Toussaint Louverture et l'Institution nationale des colonies," in Jacques Cauna, ed., *Toussaint Louverture et l'indépendance d'Haïti* (Paris: Editions Karthala, 2004), 207.

19. *Ancien moniteur*, April 1799, 639.

20. Victor Schoelcher, *Conférence sur Toussaint Louverture, général en chef de l'armée de Saint-Domingue* (Editions Panorama, 1966), 12.

21. In a letter dated 9 Nivôse year 7 (December 29, 1798), addressed to the president of the Executive Council of the Directory, Coisnon assessed the Louverture boys' academic strengths and noted that he "hastened to send on to him" a recent letter from Toussaint. Archives nationales, F7 6266.

22. David Geggus, *Haitian Revolutionary Studies* (Bloomington, IN: Indiana University Press, 2002), 146.

23. Anonymous, *The Life and Military Achievements of Tousant Loverture* [sic] (Baltimore: no publisher, 1804), 40.

24. Letter from Toussaint Louverture to General Bonaparte, First Consul of the French Republic, 10 Messidor year 8 (June 29, 1800), Archives nationales, F7 6266.

25. An unsigned report entitled "Les Enfants de Toussaint Louverture" on stationery from the Ministry of the General Police, 15 Vendémiaire year 10 (October 7, 1801), Archives nationales, F7 6266, noted that Coisnon had received orders from

Toussaint to return his children to him, but then concluded "This fact is absolutely false."

26. See "Les Enfants de Toussaint Louverture," Archives nationales, F7 6266.

27. The "simulated destination" of Saint-Domingue on this expedition was confirmed in the police report "Les Enfants de Toussaint Louverture," Archives nationales, F7 6266.

28. Isaac Louverture, *Mémoires d'Isaac Louverture*, in Antoine Métral, *Histoire de l'expédition des français à Saint-Domingue* (Paris: Karthala, 1985), 228.

29. Roussier, "L'éducation des enfants de Toussaint Louverture," 209.

30. Roussier cites an impressive essay on mathematics by Placide, and notes that both boys had, within a few years, "appris la langue française, l'histoire ancienne et moderne, l'histoire des arts, des lettres et des sciences et même l'art de la flatterie!" ("learned French, ancient and modern history, the history of the arts, letters, science, and even the art of flattery!" ["L'éducation des enfants de Toussaint Louverture," 216]).

31. M. E. Descourtilz, *Voyages d'un naturaliste* (Paris: Dufart, 1809), 2:71.

32. Métral, *Histoire de l'expédition des français à Saint-Domingue*, 229–30.

33. Cited in Roussier, "L'éducation des enfants de Toussaint Louverture," 231.

34. Cited in Joseph Boromé, "Louanges de Napoleon Bonaparte par un fils de Toussaint Louverture," *Revue de l'institut Napoléon* 133 (1977), 169.

35. New York *Evening Post*, 1802.

36. Métral, *Histoire de l'expédition des français à Saint-Domingue*, 229–30.

37. New York *Daily Advertiser*, March 26, 1802.

38. Métral, *Histoire de l'expédition des français à Saint-Domingue*, 58.

39. Anonymous, *Buonaparte in the West Indies; or, the History of the African Hero, Toussaint Louverture* (London: J. Hatchard, 1803), 2:4–5.

40. New York *Evening Post*, May 11, 1802.

41. "Toussaint accepted this role as martyr." Aimé Césaire, *Toussaint Louverture: La Révolution française et le problème colonial* (Paris: Présence Africaine, 1981), 313.

42. The Chancy family continued to be prominently connected to Haitian political power during the reign of Henry Christophe. We read in Baron de Vastey's account of the Christophe years that Eléonore Chancy, widow of André Vernet, Prince des Gonaïves, then married the king's nephew, Prince Jean, Duke of Port-Margot, and after his death, became the lady in waiting of the queen. Baron de Vastey, *Essai sur les causes de la révolution et des guerres civiles d'Hayti, faisant suite aux réflexions politiques sur quelques ouvrages et journaux français, concernant Hayti* (Sans-Souci, Hayti: De l'Imprimerie royale, 1819), 201–2.

43. Archives nationales, AF IV 1213.

44. *Gazette de France*, July 19, 1802.

45. Roussier, ed., *Lettres du général Leclerc*, 173.

46. Roussier, ed., *Lettres du général Leclerc*, 171.

47. Roussier, ed., *Lettres du général Leclerc*, 217.

48. "Toussaint Louverture au Fort de Joux (1802), Journal du general Caffarelli," *Nouvelle revue retrospective* 94 (April 10, 1902), 4. A photograph as well as a transcription of this text can be found in Roussier, ed., *Lettres du General Leclerc*, 349–50.

49. Cited in Alfred Nemours, *Histoire de la captivité et de la mort de Toussaint Louverture* (Paris: Berger-Lavrault, 1929), 242.

50. Toussaint Louverture, letter to Napoleon with a postscriptum to Caffarelli, 17 Vendémiaire year 11 (October 9, 1802), Archives nationales, F7 6266, 24.

51. Cited in Alfred Nemours, *Toussaint Louverture fonde à Saint-Domingue la liberté et l'égalité* (Port-au-Prince: Imprimerie du Collège Vertières, 1945), 92.

52. Toussaint Louverture, letter to Napoleon with a postscriptum to Caffarelli, 17 Vendémiaire year 11 (October 9, 1802), Archives nationales, F7 6266, 24.

53. Nemours, *Toussaint Louverture fonde à Saint-Domingue la liberté*, 89.

54. Letter from Placide Louverture to his parents, Archives nationales, AF IV 1213.

55. The General Commissioner of the police in Marseille wrote "Au Citoyen Grand Juge Ministre de la Justice" on 1 Frimaire year 12 (November 23, 1803) and noted that the prefect of Lot et Garonne had been authorized to deliver a passport to "Victoire Thusac, mulâtresse," to travel to Marseille. Her aunt had been sought in vain, however, and "La Police de l'arrondissement [...] n'a pas eu connaissance d'aucune femme portant le dit nom de Minot." The General Commissioner then had made the necessary arrangements to insure that when Victoire, who had not yet arrived in Marseille, did turn up there, she would not be allowed to leave the city, and her conduct and relations would be scrupulously observed. Archives nationales, F7 6266.

56. Victoire Thusac is a model of the multiple challenges of accounting for the roles of non-whites in the social world of the Louvertures. Jacques Cauna suggests that her patronym should really be spelled "Tussac," and that it showed her relationship to the plantation of the chevalier François-Richard de Tussac on Saint-Domingue. (See *Toussaint Louverture et l'indépendance d'Haïti, témoignages pou un bicentenaire* [Paris: Karthala, 2004], 126, n. 10.) Richard de Tussac (1757–1837) was a botanist from a wealthy French family with colonial holdings. His *Flore des Antilles, ou Histoire générale botanique, rurale, et économique des végétaux indigènes des Antilles* (written 1808, published Paris: Chez l'auteur, F. Schoell et Hautel, 1828) includes an account of Toussaint Louverture and the Haitian Revolution.

57. Cited in Jean Destrem, *Les Déportations du Consulat et l'Empire* (Paris: Chez Jean Maire, Libraire, 1885), 499.

58. Placide was obviously lighter-skinned than Toussaint and the other brothers, and it was commonly assumed that he was, as Isaac recounted, a child of a "premier lit" ("first relationship") of Mme Louverture with a *mulâtre* or white man. In a legal document certifying his arrival at the prison of Belle-Isle in 1802, he is described as "Placide, mulâtre, fils de Toussaint Louverture" (Nemours, *Histoire de la descendance et de la famille de Toussaint Louverture*, 118). Yet of the brothers, Placide is almost always represented as the son who most unswervingly identified with and supported his father, and he is sometimes described as Toussaint's favorite son.

59. J.-R. Marboutin, "Notes Historiques sur l'expédition de Leclerc à Saint-Domingue et sur la famille Louverture," *Revue de l'Agenais* 42 (1915), 85.

60. For a detailed discussion of the lives of the surviving Louverture family members in France, see Nemours, *Histoire de la descendance et de la famille de Toussaint Louverture*.

61. J.-B. Labat, *Voyage aux isles (Chronique aventureuse des Caraïbes, 1693–1705)* (Paris: Editions Phébus, 1993), 222.

62. These texts are anthologized in *The Atlantic Slave Trade*, ed. David Northrup (Lexington, MA: D.C. Heath, 1994).

63. Norman Davies, *Europe: A History* (Oxford and New York: Oxford University Press, 1996), xvi.

64. Benedict Anderson, *Imagined Communities: Reflections on the Origin and Spread of Nationalism* (London: Verso, 1983).

65. Pheng Cheah and Jonathan Culler, *Grounds of Comparison: Around the Work of Benedict Anderson* (New York: Routledge 2003), 6.

66. Anderson, *Imagined Communities*, 47.

67. Anderson, *Imagined Communities*, 48.

68. Laurent Dubois, "An Enslaved Enlightenment: Rethinking the Intellectual History of the French Atlantic," *Social History* 31:1 (February 2006), 3.

PART II

Authorizing the Libertine Sphere

6

Traumatic Indigeneity:
The (Anti)Colonial Politics of "Having"
a Creole Literary Culture

Let Haitian writers follow the example of American novelists;
let them learn to create an African, American, tropical, and
Haitian literature, and when the day comes that, still respecting
the French language, they discover originality [...] on that
day they will conquer in Europe the readers they lack in the
Antilles. [...] Let us pass quickly over Creole literature. Blacks,
we will say echoing many others, are big children.

Alexandre Bonneau, "Les Noirs, les jaunes,
et la littérature française en Haïti"[1]

Imitation is not so simple. [...] What is civilization, in the end?
Pastiche or copy. Everywhere. All civilization consists in an
exchange of imitations, more or less appropriate, intelligent,
and opportune.

Louis Joseph Janvier, *La République d'Haïti et ses visiteurs*[2]

Creating Diasporan Nationalism

From the Parisian Parnassus of the *Revue contemporaine* in 1856, the French
journalist and diplomat Alexandre Bonneau airily laid out the seemingly
impossible stakes of an original new Haitian literature. It would have to be
an Afro-American, tropico-Haitian corpus; in French, yet unlike French
literature; inspired by genius, but a genius other than the Haitian "genius for
imitation";[3] and certainly not in Creole, because for Bonneau it seemed safe
to say, after all, that blacks were "big children." The multiple "catch 22s" of
this pronouncement include the insinuation that Haitian writers were only

black if they wrote in *Kreyòl*, and that a local Creole and black literature, which would ostensibly qualify as Afro-American and tropico-Haitian, and thus as not purely imitative, was simultaneously impossible for racial reasons. Bonneau's less than helpful prescriptions echoed Gustave d'Alaux's 1852 warning that "it is not by imperfect or notably delayed imitations, it is by originality alone" that Haitian writers would "force their way in."[4] Such backseat driving would lead the Haitian writer Louis Joseph Janvier in 1883 to spend a substantial part of a 635-page treatise foaming at the mouth over the commentary provided by "visitors." For his defense of Haitian literature, Janvier had recourse to a French Romantic poet, Alfred de Musset, who was also frequently accused of being derivative. "Let us remind you of this, my clever fellow," says Janvier to his cultural opponent: "'Plant a cabbage, and you have copied someone.'"[5]

Notwithstanding the racism that structured Bonneau's article, he was far ahead of his time in foreseeing that for Haiti to qualify as "having a culture"[6] in Western modernity, it would need a literary corpus exemplifying what James Clifford calls "an authentic collective 'property.'"[7] The collecting of literature, through publication or archives, has in national modernity played an especially resonant role in the political dynamics of a kind of "possessive individualism"[8] on the scale of the group: collective narratives unfurling around the claims of proto-individual subjectivity and legal status. Jens Bartelson has noted the relationship of sovereignty to conceptions of a unified "self,"[9] a metaphorical selfhood strongly bolstered by the narrative subjectivities of print culture. Rosemary J. Coombe cautions that "despite the epistemological bankruptcy of the metaphors of possessive individualism, they have become the dominant metaphors of world political culture"; "subaltern groups and less powerful nations"[10] correspondingly have faced particular challenges in what Coombe aptly calls "managing mimesis."

In this second part of *Beyond the Slave Narrative* I assess the mimetic politics of having a literary culture—the issues involved in "managing mimesis"—in three areas of Saint-Domingue's cultural life during the Haitian Revolutionary era and early independence: 1) its emergent identity in the community of exiles from Saint-Domingue, 2) its complex casting of colonizing and colonized roles, and 3) the relation of its libertine culture to a local literary tradition.

Managing mimesis in the colonies, fundamentally geographically, legally, and culturally distant from the metropolitan identity source, has always been a complex affair. "Having a culture," as Richard Handler defined it with reference to possessive individualism, depends on an underlying sovereignty equated with the indivisible "liberty of an adult."[11] In this modern sense, it stands as an expression of sovereignty affiliated with metropole rather than colony, whose inhabitants, as former slaves or subordinates, had not been gifted with the liberty of Western adulthood. From a postcolonial standpoint it is obvious that the least sovereign collectivities are, inevitably, as culturally active as the most sovereign collectivities, but their cultural production has been collected and recognized by metropolitan cultures in very delimited ways.

The "possessive" metropolitan appropriation, in both textual and human form, of cultures attributed less sovereignty into a hegemonic and imperializing "art-culture system"[12] has been widely studied. Such collecting includes the exhibition and documentation of Saartjie Baartman, the so-called "Hottentot Venus,"[13] Barnum's *American Museum*,[14] the ethnographic exhibits of the *Exposition universelle* or colonial museums,[15] or "colonial literature" representing exoticist literature by colonists.[16]

The slave narrative was historically parallel to this earlier corpus of radically objectified others, yet different with regard to the autonomy of its colonized or enslaved narrative voices. This genre, from early on, managed to pierce the armor of racial hierarchy and legal interdictions to allow self-representation by members of the African diaspora, in large part through collaboration with white abolitionists. As Jeannine DeLombard notes, "the development of the slave narrative as a new genre of literature made African Americans' personal stories of slavery indispensable to the court of public opinion," despite the "charged interplay of literacy and its legal proscription."[17]

But much less work exists on cultural self-representation emanating from colonies prior to the establishment of a modern art-culture system, or in languages other than English. Critical constructs from the 1980s and 90s that have had their day in the sun, such as those by Handler and Clifford used here, or of Anderson and Chartier used elsewhere in this book, are useful in charting the modes of (anti)colonial production that have fallen through the cracks of scholarship on modern national print. In early modern rather than modern colonies, the collecting of cultural texts through technologies more durable and transportable than verbal or ritual transmission, or through possessions privately accrued by individuals, was more haphazard and rare than in Clifford's art-culture system, although this period did feature important, if not widespread, examples of the slave narrative. Its study necessitates consideration of paradoxes of suppressive coexistence and unacknowledged interculturation. It fundamentally complicates chronological narratives of a larger Western colonial and postcolonial history, rendering suspect the "before" and "after" of colonized and postcolonial subjectivities (as opposed to postcolonial institutional and interstate relations, which, as we saw in Chapter 4, are arguably more "real" in relation to earlier or non-colonial frameworks).

The accrual of exemplary texts representative of cultures of non-whites in colonial environments prior to the nineteenth century, such as the evolution and dissemination of the "Mami Wata" motif exhibited and documented by Henry Drewal,[18] rarely drew attention to itself as a form of cultural collecting on the model of national print cultures or museum cultures. Eighteenth-century Saint-Domingue, at the apogee of its economic power in a transitional moment between metropolitan monarchical and national cultures, had to tread delicately with regard to positioning itself as having a culture proper to its own space and time, despite the abundant evidence of its de facto cultural vitality, among non-whites, whites, and merged demographics. If one viewed Saint-Domingue as a synecdochic representation, a delimited satellite, of the French metropole, its failures to coincide with the original might be the source of a singular cultural identity, but only as subject to commentary and critique, not cultivation. Structurally, its most powerful stakeholders, the large property holders, were absent, delegating from afar the management of their properties; they represented a limited sovereignty by proxy. Saint-Domingue's least powerful stakeholders, the enslaved, were presumed to have little more personal sovereignty or direct self-representational capacity than the other property or *meubles* with which they were identified in article 44 of the *Code noir*. Nor would it have been easy to pinpoint the contributions of the maritime element, with its oceanic field and scale, in the complex equation of cultural identity between metropole and colony.

The numerous examples of vital local cultural life in eighteenth-century Saint-Domingue, from the theater tradition studied by Jean Fouchard, Robert Cornevin, and more recently Bernard Camier and Laurent Dubois, to the religious, healing, and artistic practices of the enslaved, to the publication of local newspapers and the founding of cultural groups such as the *cercle des Philadelphes*, were rarely archived and described in terms resembling those involved in "having a culture." Fundamentally, cultural *patrimoine* was assumed to be a product of *patrie* rather than *colonie* in the French Caribbean at this time; the word "culture" in early modern Saint-Domingue was generally employed as a synonym for agriculture.

The colonial relationship to having an individual culture changed dramatically in the Caribbean in the Revolutionary era. As Dubois has demonstrated, the potential applicability or non-applicability of new constructs of governance and reforms of civil status prompted profound consideration of the colonies' particular legal and cultural existence (from the kaleidoscopic and often mutually antagonistic vantage points of different groups within the colonial demographic). Saint-Domingue in particular, as the host site of the most extreme transformations of the Revolutionary Caribbean, saw the emergence of multiple new forms of cultural revindication and representation. The politically autonomous texts produced by former slaves who had ascended to positions of military and political leadership, as discussed in the

first half of this book, were a hallmark of new ways of "having a culture'"
in Saint-Domingue/Haiti.

From Exile to Collecting

A parallel burst of ethnographic acts of description, accompanied by the
collection of heteroclite local materials, appears subtly yet decisively different
from the previous centuries of colonial travel narratives. The Martinican-
born Saint-Domingue colonist M. L. E. Moreau de Saint-Méry is of course
the best known, and by far the most significant, of these voices, not only for
his 1797 *Description topographique, physique, civile, politique et historique de la
partie française de l'île de Saint-Domingue*, but for the voluminous resources
of the *Collection Moreau de Saint-Méry*, including the *Notes historiques* in the
Archives d'Outre-mer in Aix. Michel-Etienne Descourtilz, a physician-
botanist-ethnographer whose in-laws, the Rossignol family, were property
owners in Saint-Domingue, was active in fieldwork there from 1799 to
1803, and published his *Voyage d'un naturaliste* in 1809. S.-J. Ducoeurjoly,
whom Karol Weaver cites as "a resident of Saint-Domingue for more than
twenty years,"[19] published his own ethnographic description of the colony
in 1802, along with a Creole instruction booklet and an early eighteenth-
century medical description of Saint-Domingue by the colonial physician
Jean-Baptiste-René Pouppé Desportes.[20] The colonist and botanist François-
Richard de Tussac, who owned property in Saint-Domingue, was also active
in the field in this period and described Haitian Revolutionary events in his
1808 *Flore des Antilles*. These ethnographers overlap with the categories of
traumatized Revolutionary witnesses in Saint-Domingue anthologized by
Jeremy Popkin.[21] They also overlap, through the literary materials collected
by Moreau and to a lesser extent by Descourtilz, with the new phenomenon
of literary anthologization of popular Creole literature that is the subject of
the next chapter.

Before broaching the anthologies and textual collections discussed in
Chapters 7 and 8, it is important to note the works I have selected for
analysis here are marked by their positioning within "collected" artifacts
and texts relating to the lost indigenous culture of Hispaniola, the diasporan
experiences of slaves, and a colonial society that was in the process of
becoming a thing of the past. Creole literature, which had previously
flourished primarily as a verbal entertainment genre among non-whites
and between non-whites and colonists, began in the Revolutionary era to
be transcribed and imbued with complex claims concerning its authenticity and the relations of influence between different racial/class segments
of colonial society and their European and African genealogies. The
processes of recognition and collection of Creole literary artifacts in a

transitional period are foregrounded by a cultural poetics of a paradoxical indigeneity.

Diasporan dislocation had begun to be appropriated as an identity politics both by former slaves and former colonists in the Haitian Revolutionary era. In the 1804 Declaration of Independence, Jean-Jacques Dessalines promised a stable government to the "indigenous people" of the country abruptly renamed "Hayti" after the aboriginal Taino Indian name, "Ayiti," for the "highlands" of the island of Hispaniola. The incongruity of the adoption of an indigenous identification—previously used pejoratively by the French military—to consecrate the independence of Haiti can be measured by the dramatic non-indigeneity of the participants in the Declaration. As discussed in Chapter 5, those of African descent had familial histories of kidnapping and forcible relocation from their native lands to the Caribbean, and those of mixed heritage combined that African diasporan background with European colonial migration. White colonial families were divided between absentee landlords in Europe, newly migrated Europeans looking for a foothold in the colonial economy, and *créole* or Caribbean-born families of European descent. In the Haitian Revolutionary era, many white Creoles from Saint-Domingue became refugees or exiles on other Caribbean islands and, especially, in the United States. Many former slaves, like Henry Christophe who was born in either Grenada or St. Kitts, as well as colonists like Moreau de Saint-Méry, from Martinique, had also previously moved from island to island within the Caribbean. None of these groups provided convincing long-term models of cultural indigeneity.

The fate of the earliest inhabitants of the territory, the Taino Arawak Indians, who might be identified as literal *indigènes* despite their migration from the Andes to the Caribbean in the early centuries of the second millennium CE, provides no less negative a model of the relation of population to homeland. In the history of the island of Hispaniola, the subject of indigeneity is inextricable from that of genocidal extinction. In the half century following Columbus's first New World disembarkation, only two segments of the Taino population had survived in considerable numbers: women who had been taken as wives[22] by Spanish colonists, and men and women who had fled to an outlaw or maroon existence in the hills, often joined by maroon slaves. Other than these demographic traces of *métissage* between precolonial and colonial populations, there were at the time of the Revolution and the independence no societies of "indigenous" natives of Hispaniola.

In effect, the indigeneity chosen by Dessalines and other officers as a model for postcolonial independence was not just a paradoxical indigeneity but a traumatic indigeneity of lost homelands on the one hand, and vanished homeland populations on the other. It is striking that what J. Michael Dash calls "self-fashioning in nineteenth-century Haiti"[23] was *not* an attempt to *recreate* "Guinen," the lost Africa. Instead, it symbolized the dislocation of populations from aboriginal cultures as a defining event in identity for those subjugated by European colonialism in an era of New World imperialism extending from Columbus to Napoleon. What Dessalines and his cohorts at the Independence called the new *Empire de la liberté* ("Empire of liberty") was constructed on the oblique memory of the destruction of native status at the intersection of the extinction of local inhabitants and their replacement by kidnapped Africans.

Identity in the colony of Saint-Domingue had already been organized around a hierarchy of very limited indigeneity, rather than race or class alone. As noted in Chapter 5, in contradistinction to Latin American *criollo* identity, the prestigious "creole" category designated those who were born in the colonies and who were thus "native," regardless of whether their earlier origins were European or African.[24] Toussaint Louverture and Dessalines had been creole slaves rather than the less valued *bossale* slaves who were newly arrived from Africa (although Dessalines appears to have been among the least privileged ranks of creole slaves). Postcolonial independence was conceived not as an extension of that creole privilege, however, but as the redemption of traumatic indigeneity.

With this symbolism, Dessalines and his fellow officers were arguably exhibiting diasporan consciousness *avant la lettre*. Diasporas are characterized by forced population movements (the dispersal of populations into "spores" scattered elsewhere) that are often catalyzed by nationalist or imperialist aggression or exclusivity. As Robin Cohen notes, "dispersal from an original centre is often accompanied by the memory of a single traumatic event that provides the folk memory of the great historic injustice that binds the group together."[25]

Traumatic memories of historic injustice often unite diverse strands of diasporan populations into "imagined" communities. This diasporan community diversity is virtually inevitable because one defining element of diasporan formation is the scattering of an original group to more than one new location, with subsequent integration with other groups and later moves to and from the original diasporan location. Kim Butler confirms that the communities we recognize as diasporas, such as the Haitian diaspora in the United States, are characteristically diffracted by geographically, historically, and chronologically diverse migrational experiences. Similarly, the history of the slave diaspora in Haiti reflects a diverse population from an array of earlier African regional affiliations, splintered further in their distribution among numerous different New World colonies. If diasporan communities cannot be reduced to a pure ethnic group with a truly collective migrational history, epistemologies of diaspora must account for what Butler calls "the complexity of multiple identities, the salience of which at any given time is conditioned by sociopolitical exigencies."[26] For Butler, a community's manifestation of diasporan *consciousness*, responding to the need to forge an identity in the face of sociopolitical exigencies, is therefore one of the most consistently exploitable elements of diasporan definition. "While all diasporas may be 'imagined communities,'" writes Butler, "only communities imagined in certain ways are diasporas."[27] A community's consciousness of its diasporan roots, including traumatic memories of historic injustice as a catalyst for migration, is crucial to its diasporan functioning.

In the Haitian independence, painful collective memory of displacement was often inextricable from the formation of strategies of cultural empowerment, as it is in the new millennium. Butler writes,

> Narratives of diaspora once focused on oppression and displacement; today they focus on diaspora as a potential strategy of empowerment. The ability to harness that potential varies greatly from one diaspora to the next, and these differences are evident between different branches of single diasporas as well. Using the case of the African diaspora [...] the African example illuminates the vast difference in political options for recent emigrants from nation-states versus the slave-era dispersals from a generic continental homeland. To what extent is it possible to coordinate multiple types of strategies towards a collective transnational political agenda?[28]

Such strategies are traceable in many different eras; diasporas have been experienced and documented—imagined—since the book of Exodus and on into the farthest reaches of documented history. In the specific context of the African diaspora, Tiffany Ruby Patterson and Robin Kelley note the existence of other early examples of the constitution of black identity based on displacement and threats to indigenous communities:

> Of course, attempts to make sense of the African diaspora are almost as old as the diaspora itself. Dating back at least to Juan Latino in the sixteenth and seventeenth centuries, black writers and activists have often defined themselves as part of a larger international black community... Their political and cultural vision criss-crossed the Atlantic from the U.S. to Africa, from the Caribbean to Europe, sometimes incorporating the struggles of indigenous people in the South Pacific as well.[29]

The traumatic indigeneity formulated by Dessalines and his generals on the occasion of the independence was precisely such an early attempt to "make sense of diaspora." It signaled an identity of dispossession and a subsequent reconstitution of identity (and its related social hierarchies) on the basis of that dispossession, in contrast to identities constituted on the basis of possession. For former slaves who had only recently fought to emancipate themselves from their status as possessions, the absence of nationhood was, paradoxically, a source of symbolic power[30] in the founding of the new nation.

How did the members of the "indigenous army" even know of the Taino word for "highlands" ("Hayti") in the renaming of their new state? David Geggus asserts that knowledge of the pre-Columbian name—as well as of any other aspects of Taino culture—"probably derived from literary sources."[31] Perhaps the most prominent of those literary sources using the term "Hayti" for Hispaniola would have been Raynal's 1770 *Histoire* [...] *des Deux Indes*. The major exception to a literary route of transmission, according to Geggus, is the discovery of Taino archeological remains by slaves working in the fields. It is not possible to ascertain which officers at the scene of the Declaration might have had literary familiarity with Taino history (or, more broadly, with Caribbean and Latin American history); Colin Dayan claims that independence-era symbolism was also nuanced by reference to the Incas and Peru.[32] Intercultural contact, traversing the boundaries of French versus *Kreyòl* and alphabetization versus analphabetization, was facilitated by the secretarial and mediatic structures of the French army in Saint-Domingue, as increasing numbers of non-whites assumed major military roles. The Revolution in Haiti had created a syncretic political environment in which knowledge that would ordinarily be limited to an elite educational minority passed from group to group through verbal dissemination and dialogue.

One very particular, and exceptionally well-documented, catalyst for interracial verbal encounters in the Haitian Revolution, already noted in Chapter 1, was the existence within the Haitian insurrectional forces of French or Anglophone hostages, who later used the experience to generate historical or ethnographic narratives of the Haitian milieu. These accounts were published by the historian Nicholas Gros,[33] the English military officer Marcus Rainsford,[34] and the naturalist Michel-Etienne Descourtilz. A major Romantic-era novel devoted to the Haitian Revolution, *Bug-Jargal* (1826) by the French writer Victor Hugo, also contains exactly such an embedded prisoner scenario. The main character, a French colonist named Léopold d'Auverney, spends enough time in the camp of Jean-François to hear that leader's narration of his ideological perspective, to witness a Vodou political ceremony, and to be asked to serve as a secretary to correct a letter by the leaders of the revolt. That letter is an amalgam of apparently fictional statements and rearranged segments of an actual address to the National Assembly.

And throughout the Haitian Revolution, a colonial diaspora in the opposite direction took shape, made up of expelled or threatened colonists who resettled primarily in other Caribbean islands, or the United States. In obscure but significant documents, former colonists from Saint-Domingue reflected on their status as a new class of dispossessed wanderers, presciently addressed by Jean-Jacques Dessalines in the November 1803 proclamation of the independence of Saint-Domingue: "Landholders of Saint-Domingue, wandering in foreign lands [...]" Some whites, like Claude-Corentin Tanguy de la Boissière, initially a partisan of revolution in Saint-Domingue who then fell foul of Sonthonax,[35] began, from early on, to tie upheavals in Saint-Domingue to the alienated history of the Taino Indians, precisely as the former slaves would later do more explicitly. Tanguy's pamphlet, *Proposals for Printing a Journal of the Revolutions in the French Part of St. Domingo* (much of which was printed in English as well as French), began in March 1793 with an "exposition" of original indigenous trauma upon the arrival of the Europeans:

> No country has ever experienced more physical, moral and political revolutions than the island of St. Domingo.—Possessed at the arrival of Christopher Columbus, in 1492, by the mildest, the most ready, and perhaps the happiest of people, Spanish avarice, superstition and cruelty soon snatched it from its native soil, and after having murdered the unfortunate natives who had rescued themselves from shipwreck in which they *ought* to have all perished, they took possession of their land.[36]

A few months later, in August 1793, Tanguy and his fellow ex-colonist authors had been forced to flee Saint-Domingue themselves, and the proposed journal was no longer printed in Le Cap, but in New York. They described the colonial population in diasporan terms: "For two months now we have been spread out and disseminated in a foreign land," they reflected bitterly. In order to continue to identify themselves as a society, they had to disassociate territory from population: "It is not the territory that makes the society, but the men."[37] This articulation of creole diasporan consciousness demonstrates the multi-directionality of identifications with indigeneity and trauma during the Revolutionary era.

In the case of Descourtilz, his "collecting" of cultural artifacts that support a traumatic indigenous identification began with his vivid illustration of his introductory history of Hayti with Taino *zémès* or gods (see figure 9). Descourtilz had been informed of the existence of caves, some with indigenous names, in various regions of Saint-Domingue, inscribed with these figures. A colonist to whom Descourtilz was related by marriage, M. Desdunes-Lachicotte, owned a case of small sculptures of *zémès*, carved in hard materials including stalactite and basalt. While showing Descourtilz the collection, Desdunes-Lachicotte noted that the Indians also "printed the image of their Zémès on their bodies with the help of their nails which they never cut,"[38] in a practice of indigenous tattooing. The *zémès*, which include mask-like faces on frogs' feet, floating eyes in a tear-drop shaped image,

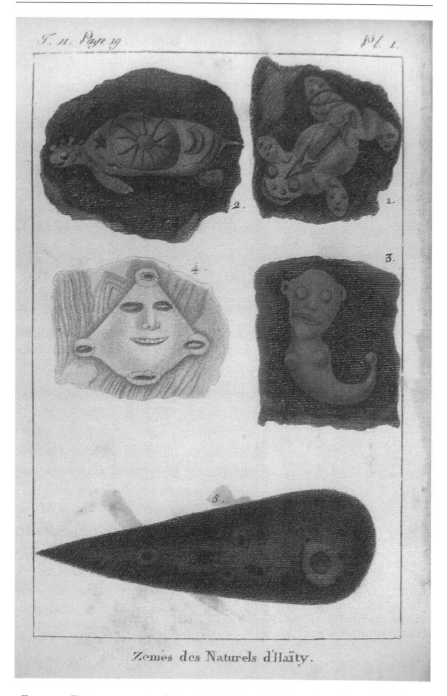

Figure 9. Plate representing Taino "zémès," probably based on the case of Taino sculptures Descourtilz had seen at the home of his host M. Desdunes-Lachicotte. *Voyages d'un naturaliste* (Paris: Dufart, 1809) 2:18.

mouth-like orifices at the corners of a face, and a sort of embryonic mermaid, present a haunting, disembodied, dislocated sense of the interhuman. The illustration is the only non-naturalist image in Descourtilz's three-volume work, signaling his high estimation of the collection's cultural importance.

Elsewhere in the *Voyage d'un naturaliste*, Descourtilz, like Moreau de Saint-Méry and Ducoeurjoly, engaged in minute description of the cultural practices, ranging from varieties of dance to varieties of suicide, that distinguished the various African diasporan groups represented among Saint-Domingue's slave population. In the context of these descriptions, Descourtilz presented what he identified as a Creole love song by two slaves, who are featured by name as the narrators within the song.[39] According to Descourtilz, Aza—a name familiar to us from the eighteenth-century French novel *Lettres d'une péruvienne* by Isabelle de Graffigny—was an Ibo slave owned by M. Pélerin, a colonist in the Cayes Saint-Louis. Aza was so melancholic at his separation through kidnapping from his beloved, Evahim, that he was unable to participate even in the "chica," a dance Descourtilz describes as involving the movement of the hips and lower back only, to the music of the *bamboula* (drums) and *banza* (flute). To Aza's great joy and amazement, at a later date his master bought another group of Ibo slaves that included Evahim and her mother. Gradually Aza taught Evahim the Creole he had learned, and put his expressions of love to the music of the "banza." Descourtilz transcribed and edited their poem, and set it to music of his own composition.

The song alternates between diasporan lament and diasporan rejoicing, savoring the contrast between separation and reunion. The quatrains of hexameter alternate a simple ABAB rhyme. The basic vocabulary, founded in the material rhythms of a slave's life, expresses the transition from despair to bliss through metaphors of life and death, work and languor, and above all through imagery of learning to taste the sweetness of fruit and sugar again.

Dialogue Créole—Aza et Evahim

(Creole Dialogue—Aza and Evahim)

Evahim

Aza! guetté com' z'ami toüé,
Visag' li fondi semblé cire!
Temps là! toué tant loigné de moüé!
Jourdi là, guetté moüé sourire!

(Aza! See how your friend's face
Melts into different expressions like wax!
Back then! You were so far from me!
Today, see me smile!)

Z'orange astor li douce au coeur,
Evahim plus gagné tristesse.
Toüé fais goûté n'ioun grand bonheur
A z'ami toüé gros de tendresse.

(Now the orange tastes sweet to my heart again,
Evahim is no longer sad.
You have made your friend, who is big with tenderness,
Taste a much greater happiness.)

  Aza

Quoir à moüé ci làlà crâsé!
Mon pas gagné quior à z'ouvrage;
A toüé nuit, jour mon té songé,
Cà fait li crâser davantage.

(My heart was crushed!
My heart was not in my work;
I dreamed of you day and night,
Which crushed my heart even more.)

Mon pas capab' souffri z'encor,
Mon té mouri loin de z'amie…!
Vla qu'Aza nien' place de la mort,
Dans quior à toüé trouvé la vie.

(I wasn't capable of more suffering,
I was dying far from my friend…!
Aza was in the place of death,
In your heart he found life.)

  Evahim

Bouche à toüé doux passé syrop!

(Your words are sweeter than syrup!)

  Aza

Baiser tien doux passé banane.

(Your kiss is sweeter than bananas.)

  Evahim

Dans mains z'ami i'ouquà de l'eau
Li soucré passé souc à canne.
Aï z'ami! toujours tout pour toüé:
Baï main sur quior!… li ça qu'échose!

(Cupped in the hands of my lover, even water
Is more sugary than sugar cane.
Oh, friend! Everything, always, for you:
Put your hand on my heart!... It knows there is something there!)

    Aza

Li broulé semblé quior à moüé!

(It burns like my own heart!)

    Tous deux

Crois ben piq' c'est pour même cause.

(You can bet it is for the same reason!)

It is of course possible that Descourtilz was trying to give a popular song of unknown origin a legendary allure by claiming that it revealed a simultaneously historical and emotional truth. In the first anthology to reproduce the text, Christophe Charles resolved the question of the author by labeling it "anonymous."[40] Descourtilz's historical details concerning Aza and Evahim as the putative authors of the song could have been confirmed or denied by living members of Saint-Domingue's former colonial community, however. Descourtilz admitted to heavy editing of the song, as I discuss in the next chapter, and this recasting of the overly "foreign" elements of the text accounts for the only partly authentic Creole flow of the text.[41]

The abundant contemporaneous testimonials of the taste and talent for poetic activity on the part of slaves and persons of color by writers such as Ducoeurjoly certainly suggests that whites frequently heard songs and lyrical work by slaves. Ducoeurjoly wrote that slaves' labor was always accompanied by music: "They are animated by song, and the beat becomes a general rule." But their musical aptitude was not limited to the context of work: "They are both poets and musicians. The rules of their poetry are not rigorous; they always bend to the music; they lengthen or shorten words as needed to mold them to the tune."[42] Ducoeurjoly associates Creole with a kind of primal poetic genesis, literally the birth of poetry from a pre-literary time: "Their compositions bring us back to the idea we might have of the birth of poetry in the first ages of the world."[43]

In the late Revolutionary and early post-Revolutionary period, exiled or refugee colonists turned their attention toward the collecting of artistic objects and literary documents expressive of popular culture in Saint-Domingue's libertine society and especially of social tensions and mobility around amorous or sexual relations between members of different racial categories. These collecting tendencies soon yielded unforeseen access to print or textual culture for popular materials that, despite their enduring anonymity, resonate with the mysteries of creative autonomy among culturally unempowered groups. At the same time, the traumatic indigeneity adopted as a post/colonial identity politics by the generation of independence leaders, contextualized through the singular intercultural dialogue on the history of the island of Hispaniola during the Revolutionary period, serves as a reminder that Haiti has always had a paradoxical status as a diasporan nation. The indigeneity that Africans had lost in the Middle Passage became a Haitian indigeneity that was always, to some extent, made up of loss, with an associated tradition of working with the symbolic power of that experience to build new foundations. Traumatic and paradoxical "indigeneity" during a period of Revolutionary rupture mobilized surprisingly diverse voices in the early Haitian project of "having a culture," voices which ultimately have survived colonial appropriations and codes of white immunity from the creolization of mimetic influence.

Notes

1. Alexandre Bonneau, "Les Noirs, les jaunes, et la littérature française en Haïti," *Revue contemporaine* (December 1856/January 1857), 112.

2. Louis Joseph Janvier, *La République d'Haïti et ses visiteurs (1840–1882): réponse à M. Victor Cochinat (de la Petite presse) et à quelques autres écrivains* (Paris: Marpon et Flammarion, 1883), 511.

3. Bonneau, "Les Noirs, les jaunes, et la littérature française en Haïti," 112. Bonneau's article was at once dramatically racist and yet also strikingly, even singularly for that time, detailed in its accounting for Haitian literature.

4. Gustave d'Alaux, "Les Moeurs et la littérature nègres," *Revue des deux mondes* 14 (April 1, 1852), 794.

5. Janvier, *La République d'Haïti et ses visiteurs*, 521. Janvier's fury at critiques of Haitian derivativeness prompted him to make brief but sophisticated defenses of the inevitability of mimesis that foreshadow the more sustained theorizations of "the laws of imitation" by Gabriel Tarde in France a decade later.

6. The expression "'having a culture'" received a considerable boost from Richard Handler's chapter of that name in *Nationalism and the Politics of Culture in Quebec* (Madison, WI: University of Wisconsin Press, 1988).

7. James Clifford, *The Predicament of Culture: Twentieth-Century Ethnography, Literature, and Art* (Cambridge, MA: Harvard University Press, 1988), 217.

8. C.B. Macpherson, *The Political Theory of Possessive Individualism: From Hobbes to Locke* (Oxford: Oxford University Press, 1962).

9. Jens Bartelson, *A Genealogy of Sovereignty* (Cambridge: Cambridge University Press, 1995), 32–3.

10. Rosemary J. Coombes, *The Cultural Life of Intellectual Properties* (Durham, NC: Duke University Press, 1998), 241.

11. Handler, *Nationalism*, 41.

12. Clifford, *The Predicament of Culture*, 215.

13. A number of recent resources are devoted to this collecting of the human "other." See, for example, Rachel Holmes, *African Queen: The Real Life of the Hottentot Venus* (New York: Random House, 2007); Barbara Chase-Riboud, *Hottentot Venus: A Novel* (New York: Random House, 2004); Clifton Crais and Pamela Scully, *Sara Baartman and the Hottentot Venus* (Princeton, NJ: Princeton University Press, 2008); T. Denean Sharpley-Whiting, *Black Venus: Sexualized Savages, Primal Fears, and Primitive Narratives in French* (Durham, NC: Duke University Press, 1999); and Bernth Lindsfors, ed., *Africans on Stage* (Bloomington, IN: Indiana University Press, 1999).

14. Rosemarie Garland Thomson's edited volume *Freakery: Cultural Spectacles of the Extraordinary Body* (New York: New York University Press, 1996) is a helpful introduction to this field, as is Benjamin Reiss's monograph *The Showman and the Slave: Race, Death, and Memory in Barnum's America* (Cambridge, MA: Harvard University Press, 2001).

15. The abundant scholarly corpus on this subject includes, besides James Clifford's important *The Predicament of Culture*, Tony Bennett, *Pasts Beyond Memory: Evolution, Museums, Colonialism* (New York: Routledge, 2004); Pieter ter Keurs, ed., *Colonial Collections Revisited* (Leiden: CNWS Publications: 2007); T. J. Barringer and Tom Flynn, eds, *Colonialism and the Object: Empire, Material Culture, and the Museum* (New York: Routledge, 1998), and Anne E. Coombes, *Reinventing Africa: Museums, Material Culture and Popular Imagination in Victorian and Edwardian England* (New Haven, CT: Yale University Press, 1997). A new field of multiform artistic praxis on the politics of exhibition and race is perhaps even more provocative in challenging spectators' instrumental consciousness; see, for example, *Fred Wilson: Objects and Installations 1979–2000*, ed. Maurice Berger, Jennifer A. Gonzalez, and Fred Wilson (Baltimore, MD: University of Maryland, 2001).

16. Manuals of "colonial literature" from the nineteenth- and twentieth-century colonial periods typically assumed that there were two possible figures of the colonial writer: literature produced "by a Frenchman born and raised in the colonies, or by a colonist who has lived there long enough to assimilate the spirit of the country." A third possibility, added as if as an afterthought, was "a native, writing in French, of course." Roland Lebel, *Histoire de la littérature coloniale en France* (Paris: Librarie Larose, 1931), 85.

17. Jeannine Marie DeLombard, *Slavery on Trial: Law, Abolitionism, and Print Culture* (Chapel Hill, NC: University of North Carolina Press, 2007), 109, 148.

18. Henry Drewal, *Sacred Waters: Arts for Mami Wata and Other Water Divinities in Africa and the Diaspora* (Bloomington, IN: Indiana University Press, 2008).

19. Karol Kimberlee Weaver, *Medical Revolutionaries: The Enslaved Healers of Eighteenth-Century Saint-Domingue* (Champaign, IL: University of Illinois Press, 2006), 49.

20. S. J. Ducoeurjoly's *Manuel des habitants de Saint-Domingue* (Paris: Lenoir, 1802) includes Jean-Baptiste-René Pouppé Desportes' "Médecine domestique de Saint-Domingue" (the author is also known as Pouppe-Desportes, Poupée-Desportes and other variations). Separately, Pouppé Desportes' *Histoire des maladies de Saint-Domingue* (Paris: Chez Lejay, 1770) had been published decades after the physician's death in 1848.

21. Jeremy Popkin, *Facing Racial RevolutionL Eyewitness Accounts of the Haitian Insurrection* (Chicago, IL: University of Chicago Press, 2007).

22. Emile Nau, a nineteenth-century Haitian historian, noted that a sixteenth-century

Spanish governor in Santo Domingo had enjoined colonists either to bring over Spanish wives or to marry their indigenous mistresses. *Histoire des Caciques d'Haïti*, 2 vols. (Port-au-Prince: Panorama, 1963), 2:13.

23. J. Michael Dash, *The Other America: Caribbean Literature in a New World Context* (Charlottesville, VA: University of Virginia Press, 1998), 43.

24. See Christopher L. Miller's reflections on the definitions and connotations of "Creole" status in the eighteenth and nineteenth centuries, *Blank Darkness: Africanist Discourse in French* (Chicago, IL: University of Chicago Press, 1985), 93–8.

25. Robin Cohen, *Global Diasporas: An Introduction* (Seattle, WA: University of Washington Press, 1997), 23.

26. Kim Butler, "Defining Diaspora, Refining a Discourse," *Diaspora* 10:2 (fall 2002), 193.

27. Butler, "Defining Diaspora," 193.

28. Kim Butler, "Multi-Level Politics in the African Diaspora: The Meta-Diaspora Concept and Mini-Diaspora Realities," in Gloria P. Totoricagüena, ed., *Opportunity Structures in Diaspora Relations: Comparisons in Contemporary Multi-level Politics of Diaspora and Transnational Identity* (Reno, NV: Center for Basque Studies, University of Nevada-Reno, 2007), 20.

29. Tiffany Ruby Patterson and Robin D. G. Kelley, "Unfinished Migrations: Reflections on the African Diaspora and the Making of the Modern World," *African Studies Review* 43:1 (April 2000), Special Issue on the Diaspora, 4.

30. Bourdieu notes that within the social "field of power," symbols are "the instruments *par excellence* of 'social integration': as instruments of knowledge and communication (cf. Durkheim's analysis of the festivity), they make it possible for there to be a *consensus* on the meaning of the social world, a consensus which contributes fundamentally to the reproduction of the social order." Pierre Bourdieu, *Language and Symbolic Power* (Cambridge, MA: Harvard University Press, 1991), 166.

31. David P. Geggus, *Haitian Revolutionary Studies* (Bloomington, IN: University of Indiana Press, 2002), 217.

32. "According to Madiou, Dessalines called the populations subject to his authority 'Incas or children of the sun,' memorializing the 1780 Inca uprising in Peru." [Colin] Joan Dayan, *Haiti, History, and the Gods* (Berkeley, CA: University of California Press, 1998), 22–3.

33. See Nicholas Gros, *Récit historique sur les événements qui se sont succédés dans les camps de la Grande-Rivière, du Dondon, de Ste-Suzanne et autres, depuis le 26 octobre 1791 jusqu'au 24 décembre de la même année* (Baltimore, MD: chez S. et J. Adams, 1793).

34. See Marcus Rainsford, *An Historical Account of the Black Empire of Hayti, comprehending a view of the principal transactions of the revolution of Saint Domingo; with its ancient and modern state* (London: J. Cundee, 1805).

35. See Frances Sergeant Childs, *French Refugee Life in the United States 1790–1800: An American Chapter of the French* Revolution (Baltimore, MD: Johns Hopkins University Press, 1940), 51–6.

36. Claude-Corentin Tanguy de la Boissière, *Proposals, for Printing a Journal of the Revolutions in the French Part of St. Domingo* (New York: no publisher, 1793), 8.

37. Tanguy de la Boissière, *Proposals*, 5.

38. Michel-Etienne Descourtilz, *Voyages d'un naturaliste*, 3 vols. (Paris: Dufart, 1809), 2:18.

39. Parts of the following analysis of the poetic dialogue between Aza and Evahim,

and also of the two poems from the *Idylles et chansons, ou essaies de poésie créole*, are translated from my article "Polyphonie sociale dans la poésie créole de Saint-Domingue (Haïti)," in *Langue et identité narrative dans les literatures de l'ailleurs (Antilles, Réunion, Québec)*, ed. Marie-Christine Hazaël-Massieux and Michel Bertrand (Aix: Presses Universitaires de Provence, 2005), 171–96.

40. Christophe Charles, *Anthologie de la poésie haïtienne d'expression créole*, 2 vols. (Port-au-Prince: Editions Choucoune, 1980), no pagination.

41. As Marie-Christine Hazaël-Massieux recounts, "On peut douter un peu de *l'authenticité* de la langue par rapport à la langue des esclaves de l'époque"; this inauthenticity plausibly derives from Descourtilz's revisions, however. *Textes anciens en créole français de la Caraïbe* (Paris: Publibook, 2008), 227.

42. Ducoeurjoly, *Manuel des habitants de Saint-Domingue*, 30.

43. Ducoeurjoly, *Manuel des habitants de Saint-Domingue*, 31.

7

Mimetic Mastery and Colonial Mimicry: The "Candio" in the Popular Creole (*Kreyòl*) Literary Tradition

In Revolutionary Saint-Domingue and early independent Haiti, side by side with the emergence of important political texts by (sometimes analphabet) former slave leaders working in tandem with secretaries, we find the documentation of Creole (*Kreyòl*) lyric poetry representing the experience of non-whites. This material aligns smoothly with contemporaneous descriptions of lyrical traditions by non-whites, but has often been identified as the work of colonists, who may more properly, in many cases, have been editors, co-authors, or print cultural mediators—"secretaries" of a different stripe—for the African diasporan creative verbal productions in which their society was steeped.

M.-E. Descourtilz was one of the few editors to have described such a process, in relation to the poem discussed at the close of Chapter 6:

> Comme je trouvai les idées de ces jeunes amans [*sic*] mal secondées par les expressions, et que l'air m'en parut insignifiant, je crus devoir [...] en faveur de la délicatesse de leurs sentimens [*sic*], concourir à les faire plaindre, et estimer des coeurs sensibles. C'est à cette considération que je rectifiai le mieux possible les paroles de leur entretien auquel j'adaptai un nouvel air de ma composition.[1]

> (As I found the ideas of these young lovers poorly articulated in the expressions they chose, and in the melody, which I found insignificant, I thought I should [...] to support the delicacy of their sentiments, make them lament, and give full emphasis to their sensitive hearts. With this in mind, I rectified as well as possible the words of their dialogue, to which I also adapted my own melody.)

Such processes point to the syncretic and halting trajectory of the emergence of this early phase of Haitian letters. It may seem to contrast starkly with the emergence of African diasporan literature in the Anglophone domain, but Robert Reid-Pharr has questioned the framing of "theoretical and historical practices" in African American literary studies to move from the eclectic and multilingual traditions of Africa and their diasporan adaptations to the apparent "Big Bang" of the slave narrative:

> There is perhaps no stronger impetus within the study of Black American literature and culture than the will to return, the desire to name the original, the source, the root, that seminal moment at which the many-tongued diversity of ancient West Africa gave way to the monolingualism of black North America. [...] Thus it should come as no surprise that our theoretical and historical practices so often work to reiterate a sort of "Big Bang" conception of Black American life and culture.[2]

In the mediated environment of texts representing African diasporan voices in Saint-Domingue in this period, Creole, a language spoken by all strata of society but associated strongly with blacks, became a particularly fraught and ambiguous field of textual representation. In this chapter I trace the mimetic claims associated with the emergence of this popular Creole poetry. I also introduce the male figure of the "Candio," who stands, mysteriously, at the center of early poetic explorations of Creole. The Candio stakes out the space of rivalries around potent uses of language; rivalries represented in terms of competition for women between field slaves and the most powerful speakers in the non-white social world, but also implicitly between white appropriators of Creole lyricism and their non-white rivals in the libertine cultural domain. The Candio is endowed with oddly simultaneous religious and sexual valences associated with his verbal activity, in a sort of hybridization of libertine, ritual, and creative life. His liminal social and literary position parallels that of the female figure of the *cocotte*, whose role I examine in the next and final chapter.

Creole Poetics in New York, 1804

In 1804, in New York, an anonymous "Colon de Saint-Domingue" ("Colonist from Saint-Domingue") published the first known collection of Creole poems, a series of seven amorous dialogues, primarily between slaves, called the *Idylles, ou essais de poésie créole*.[3] In 1811, a second edition of the *Idylles* was published in Philadelphia as the *Idylles et chansons, ou essais de poésie créole*, with five additional poetic texts that the author categorized as "chansons" or songs. The expanded contents of the 1811 version of the *Idylles* coincided with the anonymous author's revision of his own self-identification on the title page.[4] The "Colon de Saint-Domingue"[5] in 1804 had become "un Habitant d'Hayti"[6] ("an inhabitant[7] [or planter] of Haiti") by the 1811 edition. This change in authorial identity reflects the transformation from colonial to postcolonial identity, coinciding with the broadening of the span of materials in the collection.

The 1811 edition presents more mysteries of authorship than simply the colonial or "post"-colonial identity of the name on the title page. Did the colonist write the texts? In the preface, "On the Creole Language," he speaks of "offering" rather than of writing the texts in the *"recueil"* (collection or anthology) for an audience of fellow "colonists" (1804)—or, after 1804, fellow *"habitants* of the colonies" (1811). In the 1804 edition, there is no definitive way to ascertain whether there was a single author or multiple authors behind the idylls (since to date these texts have not been traced to other sources), let alone whether a single author might be the same person as the publisher of the texts. But the 1811 edition includes five additional poems or "songs," including a "Chanson Martiniquoise" ("Martinican Song") which seems to be a version of the still popular Lesser Antillean song "Pov' p'tit mamzelle Zizi" ("Poor Little Miss Zizi"), and a song simply called "Autre" ("Other"), which lists a series of localities from Martinique and Guadeloupe. The collection also includes a text called "Chanson créole" ("Creole Song"), which is a variation on the first published Haitian Creole poem, "Lisette quitté la plaine" ("Lisette Has Left the Plains"). "Lisette" was first transcribed by Moreau de Saint-Méry in his famous 1797 *Description* of Saint-Domingue; Moreau attributed the poem to the white colonist Duvivier de la Mahautière, in a period around the middle of the eighteenth century.[8]

When Edward Larocque Tinker, a specialist in Louisiana Creole, re-edited the 1811 edition in the *Proceedings of the American Antiquarian Society* in 1957, he appeared to be unaware that the "Chanson créole" was a variation on the earlier published poem "Lisette," just as he makes no mention of the existence of an 1804 edition of the *Idylles*. He did note that since all of the "chansons" were still popular "not only in Louisiana, but also through the French-speaking 'Isles sous le Vent,' as the West Indies are so poetically called," it was unlikely they had "originated in an ephemeral pamphlet in Philadelphia."[9] The fact that the "Chanson créole" was a variation on a song known from fifty or sixty years earlier confirms Tinker's intuition that at least the added material in the 1811 edition constituted something other than a single-author poetic collection. It points strongly to the 1811 *Idylles et chansons* as the first *Kreyòl* literary anthology, of unknown but probably popular and pan-Antillean origins. (Perplexingly, there was also an 1821 edition published in Cahors, France, in which the title had reverted to the *Idylles ou essais de poésie créole par un colon de St. Domingue*.)[10]

The False Transparency of Mimesis

The question then arises: if we cannot assume that a white male refugee from Saint-Domingue to the United States was the actual author of all of these texts, who did compose them? Tinker dismissed, with casual racism, the possibility that the songs could have been conceptualized by the "Negro mind."[11] Until very recently, even postcolonial theoretical models of colonial literary production have tended to harbor the assumption that white publishers of texts were the authors of those texts, and that colonized subjects were relegated to a role of mimicry.

In Homi Bhabha's paradigm of the politics of colonial textuality, the colonizer's authorial role connotes a mimetic or representational mastery that is synonymous with colonial mastery. The introduction of the book to the colonial scene reads as "the invention of historicity, mastery, mimesis," parallel to the "mode of civil authority and order."[12] In the twentieth century, the term "mimesis" was defined by Eric Auerbach and others as coterminous with "realism," and for Bhabha the mimetic interventions of the colonist impose a sense of a dominant original reality of European culture on the colonized. Bhabha's postcolonial usage of the term "mimesis" therefore denotes a realism that is more than a representational praxis: it is a transcendent authority of imperialist self-identity. In this model, cultural *hegemony* is the reality to which colonial representation is in thrall. Realism as technique merges with the privileging of imperialist reality as content. Print culture, as in "the book" or "the Word," is disseminated as the symptom or tool, the material politics, of that colonial reality. Colonial literature in this context would be an attempt to impose (literarily) a dominant cultural paradigm of the real on members of a subordinate culture.

Edouard Glissant, in *Le Discours antillais*, similarly theorizes that a sense of exclusion from the real is a trait of colonial heritage for non-white Antillean inhabitants: "All mimesis presupposes that what is represented is the 'true real.' When it is brought to bear on two realities, one of which is devoted to the reproduction of the other, the tenants [of the subordinate reality] in this operation consider themselves to be living a permanent unreality. This is the case for us."[13] Glissant does not believe that published work representing the voices of non-white populations could have existed in the colonial period. In his chart of the "Process of literary production" in the Caribbean, he categorizes the entire period of 1765–1902 as a period of "Creole oral literature (following patterns of life)" contrasting with "Béké literature denying the real country" and "Exotic elite literature."[14] These separate categories imply that elite "*béké* literature" such as "Lisette quitté la plaine" had no overlap with the oral tradition and was incapable of representing "the patterns of life" of the "real" country.

Within this scenario of colonial mimesis as the literary imposition of European hegemony, the role of the colonized subject is circumscribed to mimicry rather than creation, consistently with V. S. Naipaul's celebrated trope of the colonized "mimic man."[15] Yet for Bhabha this mimicry is in itself a creative act in a limited sense: coming "after the traumatic scenario of cultural difference," it reads simultaneously as the "'other scene' of *Enstellung*, displacement, fantasy, psychic defense, and an 'open' textuality."[16] The colonized subject parodies/imitates the dominant colonial identity, tracing through the "low mimetic literary effects" of mimicry a space of Lacanian "camouflage."[17] The imitative camouflage of the mimic man protects him from colonial power while nevertheless rendering the workings of that power visible and therefore representing that power.

In a postcolonial rather than a colonial Caribbean context, Glissant advocates a parallel deconstructive combat against an imposed mimetic reality effect: "the transparency of false mimesis must be wiped out in one blow,"[18] to be replaced by a social, traumatic, and opaque Creole counter-mimesis. This Caribbean "anti- (or counter-) poetics" resists "expression that is positive and semiotically straightforward,"[19] mimetic in a tradition honoring a transcendent reality and affiliated with modern national print cultures. The refusal of mimesis in Glissant's counterpoetics can also be seen as a re-adaptation of mimesis to a social rather than a purely artistic plane. It is a poetics of relation modeled on an experience of history that is at once unfathomable and unavoidable, symptomatic of the historical unconscious of "slavery as a struggle with no witness."[20]

Such logical presuppositions that the voices of slaves left no concrete historical traces have also left their mark on representational praxis in contemporary Francophone literature with historical subject matter. Régis Antoine, in *La Littérature franco-antillaise*, has described the literary techniques used by Francophone writers who want to represent slaves from the colonial period but believe that no literary records of early non-*béké* experience exist. "For a very long time in these territories there would only be one recognized voice: the colonial voice," Antoine notes; Franco-Antillean literature is now preoccupied by "the search for lost voices."[21] On the one hand, the figures of the native Amerindian and the *bossale* (African-born slave) or the creole slave, on the plantation or in a state of *marronnage*, are undergoing a profound "literary rehabilitation."[22] But on the other hand, to attempt to reconstitute their utterances would be to engage in what Antoine calls a "fantasy mimesis."[23]

Contemporary Caribbean writers try to avoid this fantasy mimesis, according to Antoine, by representing the "semi-aphasia of locutors."[24] This occurs notably in terms of "speech pathology," so that fictional maroon or insurgent slave characters proffer "sounds down in the back of their throats," and "incoherent propositions."[25] The laconic maroon occasions the replacement of a "mimesis of fantasy" with a mimesis of aphasia that symbolizes the pathological exclusion of the slave from print culture.

From the figure of the mimic man to the trope of a mimesis of aphasia, postcolonial schemas of literary voice thematize the impossibility of the slave's participation in print culture. But the existence of an early Creole poetic anthology necessitates reconsideration of the literary and historical record on the possible transversal production and circulation of *oraliture* among the different social layers of colonial society, leading to publication, by *békés*, of materials of hybrid origins.

The attempt of expatriated colonists, fleeing the anomalous defeat of Napoleon's army by former slaves, to popularize the Creole heritage of their former dominion necessitates an adjustment of Bhabha's theoretical grid. When "the book" is not an export from the metropolitan culture to a colony, but rather a souvenir of a pre-Revolutionary colonialism, written in the Creole vernacular of plantocratic society, is colonial mastery still aligned with mimetic mastery as in Bhabha's paradigm? How do historical factors specific to the discursive zone of French Caribbean colonialism, notably the social evolution of the Creole contact language and the positioning of all speaking subjects within the parameters of the slave economy, affect the equation of colonial and mimetic mastery?

In contrast to postcolonial tropes of mimesis as an imposed colonial reality effect, authorial production in colonial Creole literature generally is aligned with *artifice* and a resounding *inauthenticity*. In Élodie Jourdain's 1956 formulation, early Creole literature was a game of colonists eager to "tease a black muse."[26] For Jourdain, at least in the context of early Creole print culture, the colonist's ties to Creole were as artificial as the slave's ties were authentic. She hypothesized that side by side with the development of a spoken or sung Creole literature, there was "written Creole, first by whites, then by the 'mixed bloods' of French culture, each group trying, in all sincerity, to get under the skin of an exclusively Creole speaking storyteller or poet."[27] Written Creole in this account is an attempt to embody a purer Creole identity, a presumably illiterate and non-French-speaking subject. The *béké* author of Creole literature in the colonial era is a mimic man of a different color: a colonist mimic man.

The text that most bears examination in the *Idylles et chansons* of these questions of mimetic mastery and the colonial mimic man is the "Chanson créole," not only because it re-presents "Lisette quitté la plaine," but because of its thematization of poetic language as both a seductive and a threatening force in colonial society. Since it is impossible to assess the significance of the variations included in the "Chanson créole" without reading the poem against its model, I will begin by presenting the version of "Lisette quitté la plaine" transcribed by Moreau de Saint-Méry.

Moreau published "Lisette" as a defense of the Creole language. He contextualized it as a well-known Creole song by a prominent colonial citizen that would allow the French reader to "see whether the creole language is actually an insignificant and desultory jargon."[28] The poem consists of five stanzas of eight lines, each of seven syllables (a verse form particularly associated with songs), with a rhyme scheme of ABABCBCB, DEDEFEFE, etc. Moreau provided a poetic rather than literal French translation of the poem, which glosses over linguistic puzzles[29] in the text that impede interpretation of its content. I am including my own purely literal English prose translation after each stanza. (I use purely literal translations because a more poetic translation has the disadvantage of layering the Western class connotations of lyrical enunciation over the Creole; an attempt to recreate a distinctly different lyrical voice would risk imposing racialized mimicry. These are challenges amply worth tackling in a text devoted to translation, but here my primary goal is to make transparent the basic units of vocabulary.)

Lisette quitté la plaine,
Mon perdi bonher à moué
Gié à moin semblé fontaine,
Dipi mon pas mire toué.
La jour quand mon coupé canne,
Mon songé zamour à moué;
La nuit quand mon dans cabane,
Dans dromi mon quimbé toué.

(Lisette has left the plains,
And I have lost my happiness
My eyes seem like fountains,
Since I have not seen you.
During the day when I cut sugar cane,
I think of my love;
At night when I am in my bed,
In my sleep [my dreams] I hold you.)

Si to allé à la ville,
Ta trouvé geine Candio
Qui gagné pour tromper fille
Bouche doux passé sirop.
To va crer yo bin sincere
Pendant quior yo coquin tro;

C'est Serpent qui contrefaire
Crié Rat, pour tromper yo.

(If you go to the city,
You [will] find young Candios,
Who have with which to deceive girls,
Mouths [words] sweeter than syrup.
You are going to believe them to be very sincere,
When their hearts are [actually] too tricky;
It's like the Snake that pretends
To cry Rat, to fool them.)

Dipi mon perdi Lisette,
Mon pas souchié *Calinda*
Mon quitté *Bram-Bram sonnette*
Mon pas batté *Bamboula*
Quand mon contré l'aut' négresse,
Mon pas gagné gié pou li;
Mon pas souchié travail pièce:
Tout' qui chose a moin mourri.

(Since I lost Lisette,
I haven't thought of the *Calinda*.[30]
I have given up the *Bram-bram sonnette*.[31]
I haven't played the *Bamboula*.[32]
When I meet the other negress,
I have no eyes for her;
I don't think of work at all:
Everything that is something to me has died.)

Mon maigre tant com' gnon souche
Jambe à moin tant comme roseau;
Mangé na pas doux dans bouche,
Tafia même c'est comme dyo
Quand mon songé toué, Lisette,
Dyo toujour dans jié moin.
Magner moin vini trop bête,
A force chagrin magné moin

(I am thin as a stem,
My leg is like a reed;
Food isn't sweet in my mouth,
Even Tafia [alcohol] is like water.
When I remember you, Lisette,
Water is [tears are] always in my eyes.

My manners have become too stupid,
From the manner of my grief.)

Lisett' mon tandé nouvelle,
To compté bintôt tourné:
Vini donc toujours fidelle.
Miré bon passé tandé.
N'a pas tardé davantage,
To fair moin assez chagrin,
Mon tant com' zozo dans cage
Quand yo fair li mouri faim.[33]

(Lisette I have heard the news,
You count on returning soon,
Come back then still faithful.
Seeing is better than hearing.
Don't wait any longer,
You have caused me enough grief,
I am like a bird in a cage
When they make it die of hunger.)

Symbolizing Slavery

The poem is narrated by a male slave, but it transposes the experience of captivity and starvation ("Mon tant com' zozo dans cage") from the slave culture of the plantation to the psychology of love. This colonial poem about slavery therefore has the paradoxical task of making slavery aesthetically pleasing. In Western poetry, enslavement is one of the conventional figures used to symbolize the plight of the lover. It is possible that even in a society of literal slavery it retained this figurative value, in which case one could surmise that it had an additional function of distracting listeners from the brutal reality of slavery.

The ethical valence of such a gesture would vary prismatically in relation to the array of possible originators of the poem. If the poem originated with a slave owner, in other words, such as the putative author, the colonial administrator Duvivier de la Mahautière, then the metaphor of the slave might psychologically displace the mastery of the master to the desired mastery of the lover. It would thereby "free" the master from the more ethical "cage" of slave ownership. Conversely, if the poem originated in slave culture, it could have served as a poetic redistribution of the power to enslave away from the master and into the hands of the beloved. In this sense the slave might figuratively free himself or herself from literal enslavement by conceptualizing enslavement as an affective submission between social equals.

In "Lisette quitté la plaine," although the narrator's figurative starvation is caused by Lisette's absence, his metaphoric captivity is blamed not just on a *belle dame sans merci*, but on an unidentified "them," presumably representing actual slave owners ("When *they* make it die of hunger" [my italics]). Both Lisette and the narrator are vulnerable to this outside plurality and its capacity to override the relations between lovers. Nevertheless, the narrator is far more distressed by the vulnerability of his amorous subordination than by his literal enslavement.

"Lisette" involves a metaphorical use of the slavery that was brutally omnipresent in reality to conceptualize less literal tensions of human dominance and subjugation. As noted in Chapter 1, Susan Buck-Morss has theorized that Hegel's dialectic of lordship and bondage, long understood as a philosophical abstraction, was rooted in his fascination with the events of the Haitian Revolution. "The actual and successful revolution of Caribbean slaves against their masters," Buck-Morss theorizes, "is the moment when the dialectical logic of recognition becomes visible as the thematics of world history."[34] "Lisette" shows an inverse movement from reality to the figurative, an unexpected willingness to abstract from a position of master or slave in the colonial economy to that of shackled lover.

The dynamics of the identification with slavery, which as noted above could reflect whites or freed *mulâtres* "passing" literally as slaves, or slaves' representations of their own concerns, are greatly impacted by the meaning of the mysterious term "Candio" in the poem. The Candios (the term refers to a plurality, also described as "yo," "them") are presented as a linguistic threat to Lisette's fidelity to the narrator. The narrator of the poem is afraid that if Lisette has gone to the city (perhaps to a marketplace to sell the produce from her own small garden plot or to engage in transactions for her master), she will meet young Candios who will seduce her with their sweet language and displays of counterfeit vulnerability. Who are these Candios?

The Candio

The eighteenth-century term "Candio" is rendered as "*freluquet*" or "fop" in the translation of "Lisette" included by Moreau de Saint-Méry.[35] This gives the target group for the narrator's fears the vaguest possible racial or social identification. Yet the capitalization of Candio in the poem would seem to indicate that the term was a name for a recognizable group of people. Fortunately, in a rare text, *De la Danse*, he provided a far more targeted description: "on dit à Saint-Domingue d'un africain ou nègre créol, occupé de plaisir, et chérissant sur-tout la danse, qu'il est *Candiot*"[36] ("In Saint-Domingue we call any African or creole Negro occupied with pleasure, and above all cherishing dance, a *Candiot*").

This definition of a male involved in the world of sensual pleasures is not unrelated to a well-known definition of the Candio in the work of the naturalist M.-E. Descourtilz, a Creole speaker and a close observer of Creole life during the later years of the Haitian Revolution, who included a gloss on the word in a footnote to his 1809 *Voyages d'un naturaliste*. "On les appelle *Candiots*" he says: they were the class of "petit maîtres" ("little masters") among the "nègres créoles,"[37] meaning the slaves who had been born in Saint-Domingue and were therefore correspondingly more privileged than the *nègres bossales* newly arrived from Africa; "petit maître" also has connotations of dandyism. The Candios, or "Candiots" (elsewhere also rendered as "canguio"), by this definition, were a kind of category of mimic masters. Descourtilz, who describes only one such "petit maître," named "Joseph," found him to be a "caricature" of his type,[38] and ridicules him for his mismatched, ragged finery. He also mocks him precisely for the characteristically extreme popularity of the Candios with women: "One can judge [...] the indolence of these favorites of love, and the dominance they have over their mistresses."[39]

The romantic dominance of the Candio runs throughout different explanations of the term, but is associated with a variety of different social functions. Drouin de Bercy, in his 1814 *De Saint-Domingue*, describes the Candio in tandem with two other specialized male figures, the "Caprelata" and the "Don Pédro," all three of whom are very successful with the ladies.

Le Nègre Candio ou Docteur est ainsi appelé, parce qu'il s'habille avec plus de soin que les autres; il est entreprenant, libertin, et se fait entretenir par les Négresses; c'est un faiseur d'embrassas, qui, par ses motions, par son bavardage et par sa conduite indiscrète, occasionne souvent du trouble sur les habitations, ou dans les danses de Nègres, appelées Calinda.[40]

(The black Candio or Doctor is thus designated because he dresses with more refinement than the others; he is entrepreneurial, libertine, and is supported by the negresses; he is a troublemaker, who, by his gestures, his talk, and his indiscreet conduct, often raises trouble on the plantations or at the slave dances, called Calindas.)

The "Caprelata" or "caprelateur" is given an equally negative description by Drouin, but as an idler devoted to the making of amulets and fetishes, also called *caprelatas*; he wears a headdress of feathers and shells. The Don Pédro circulates through plantations at night to see "his women"; he likewise wears unusual head covering, and is often employed as a footman, a cart driver, or shepherd. Pierre Pluchon associates both the Caprelata and the Don Pédro with "les personalités du vaudou haïtien" ("the personalities of Haitian voudou"), and notes the possibility that the Candio also "doit ses succès féminins à un pouvoir occulte" ("owes his success with women to occult powers").[41] Karol Weaver accounts for the "caprelateur" as a "magician who makes magic charms" as a medical technique and concludes, "one of the major medical techniques provided by enslaved practitioners of medicine, the creation and distribution of amulets, became a significant part of the vodou ritual."[42] Drouin de Bercy's use of "Docteur" as an alternative title for the Candio suggests some similar honorary medical/magical status.

For Gustave d'Alaux (sometimes identified as the pen name for Maxime Reybaud, who had served as French Consul in Port-au-Prince) in 1852 there was no question but that the Candio was a *griot*-style storyteller, with a strong ceremonial role. His improvisational performance would begin with rhetorical questions to his rapt audience, or supply answers to their riddles: "Pourquoi les crabes n'ont-ils pas de tête?" etc. "*Cé bon kior crabe qui la cause li pas gagné tête* (c'est le bon coeur de la crabe qui est la cause qu'elle n'a pas de tête)"[43] ("Why don't crabs have heads? They have too much heart"). D'Alaux describes the Candio as responding to each "interpellation" in turn, "giving the *because* for each *why*."

Alexandre Bonneau, a peripatetic scholar/journalist/foreign service member, in 1857 also signals the identity of the Candio as an African *griot*, troubadour or "zamba." In addition to improvising verbally, the Candio makes fetishes, such as the "maman-bila"; they are also proud and rakish seducers:

> Nous avons perdu nos trouvères et nos troubadours, comme la Grèce de Periclès avait perdu ses rhapsodes; mais l'Afrique a conservé ses griots, et Haïti ses sambas ou zambas qui cumulent les doubles fonctions de l'improvisateur et du sorcier, passant leur vie à fabriquer des manman-bila, à conjurer les mauvais esprits, à évoquer les morts et à composer, séance tenante, des chansons ou des contes. Comme improvisateurs, ils portent surtout le nom de *candio*, dont notre mot *fat*, pris à la fois dans sons sens vulgaire et considéré dans son étymologie, rend parfaitement la double signification; car on appelle aussi candio l'homme qui, fier de ses avantages extérieurs, ne doute de rien, est toujours satisfait de lui-même et fait le roué devant les femmes.[44]

(We have lost our trouveres and troubadours, just as Pericles' Greece had lost its rhapsodists; but Africa has conserved its *griots*, and Haiti its sambas or zambas who have double functions as improvisers and sorcerers, passing their time making maman-bilas, conjuring evil spirits, evoking the dead, and, during assemblies, performing songs or stories. As improvisers, they are known above all as Candios, of which our word "swell," taken in its popular sense and considered etymologically, renders the double meaning perfectly; for they also call Candios the man who, proud of his appearance, confident in every way, is always self-satisfied and struts around before the ladies.)

The figure of the Candio is actually an international presence in the African slave diaspora, and turns up in various New World locations in the nineteenth century. An ethnographer in French Guyana, M. L. Fournereau, recounted that among the "Polygoudoux"—identified as one of four black tribes, perhaps maroons, living along the banks of the Maroni and its tributaries—the Candio presided over elaborate religious ceremonies, involving verbal improvisation, dance, and the profound respect of ceremonial participants:

> Au milieu du tumulte de toute cette mouqueterie, le nègre qui préside la fête (*candio*) apparaît, l'air impassible et majestueux, vêtu d'une longue robe en indienne rouge [...] A côté du candio, se tient une jeune fille portant un parapluie pour l'abriter des ardeurs du soleil. Une autre jeune fille le conduit par la main gauche, tandis que de la droite elle tient un mouchoir. Des femmes suivent en chantant. [...] Sur le seuil de la porte du sanctuaire se trouve une femme, choisie par le candio pour la circonstance. [...] Une vieille femme se détache de la foule et va féliciter le candio. Il se découvre, lui pose son chapeau sur la tête et l'invite à danser avec lui. Le délire s'empare de tous [...][45]

> (Amid the tumult of all this shooting into the air, the negro presiding over the event (the Candio) appears, impassive and majestic, draped in a long robe of crimson calico [...] A young girl stands by the Candio, shading him from the ardent sunshine with an umbrella. Another young girl leads him by the left hand, holding a handkerchief in her other hand. Women follow, singing. [...] At the doorstep of the sanctuary awaits a woman chosen by the Candio for the occasion. [...] An elderly woman steps out of the crowd and goes to congratulate the Candio. He removes his head covering, places it on her head, and invites her to dance. The crowd goes wild [...])

This remarkably detailed account of a voudou-like religious ceremony involving an African diasporan tribe of French Guyana, certainly not influenced by the dominant ethnographic accounts in Haiti, is of great interest but raises many questions concerning the geographical and linguistic trajectory of this group, and the source of the continuity between the role of the Candio here and in the accounts given by d'Alaux and Drouin de Bercy. Had slaves from Saint-Domingue migrated elsewhere? Or is there an African source for the term that reappeared in various sites of African diasporan culture, such as the Mande trope of the "koundjo" that emerges in Afro-Creole New Orleans in the nineteenth century?

In nineteenth-century New Orleans, Lafcadio Hearn and George Washington Cable were both popularizers of the Candio, to different effects. Hearn recounted to folklorist Henry Edward Krehbiel in the 1914 *Afro-American Folksongs* that *koundjo* or *counjai* was at the base of the term, and that it referred to a dance: "My quadroon neighbor [in New Orleans], Mamzelle Eglantine, tells me that the word *Koundjo* (in the West Indies *Candio* or *Candjo*) refers to an old African dance which used to be danced with drums."[46] This meaning of "Koundjo" is not the dominant valence found by Krehbiel, who found a very Saint-Domingue-like Creole song (translated by Cable into an African-American dialect) describing not a dance but an irresistible Afro-Creole seducer:

> In zou' in zène Criole Candjo,
> Bell passé blanc dan dan là yo,
> Li té tout tans apé dire,
> 'Vini, zamie, pou'nou rire.'

> One day one young Creole Candio,
> Mo' fineh dan sho'nuff white beau,
> Kip all de time meckin' free,
> 'Swit-hawt, meck merrie wid me.' [47]

In a conventional English translation:

> One day a young creole Candio,
> Far finer than all whites in those parts,
> Began wheedling on and on,
> 'Come on, my friend, let's have fun.'

This Louisiana "Criole Candjo" is "bell pass' blanc," more handsome than the whites. Krehbiel justifies this different meaning for the term *koundjo*, which Hearn had associated with a dance, by hypothesizing that the dandy's race-transcending appeal lies in the fact that he is a *beau valseur* ("fancy waltzer").

But *koundjo* provides what may be the most useful African etymological trace for this diasporan term, even if there is little documentation for Mamzelle Eglantine's claim (via Hearn) that it was a dance rather than a person. The Mande world in West Africa features a cult of a *koundjo* or fetish, as described in *Entretiens avec Bala Kanté*: "C'est comme un objet de djinn, sous forme d'objet de djinn. C'est mon [fétiche] Koundjo, j'en fais la préservation"[48] ("It's like a *djinn* [spirit being] object, in the form of a *djinn* object. It's my *Koundjo* [fetish], I take care of it").

A related Mande world derivation was claimed by George Washington

Cable in Louisiana, in a kind of amalgam of other sources he had encountered. In *Les Grandissimes*, translated as *Creoles and Cajuns*, he described the magnetic song of his Candio character Bras-Coupé in New Orleans' Congo Square in 1803 as a relic of a Bambara chieftain's song:

> The singers almost at the first note are many. At the end of the first line every voice is lifted up. The strain is given the second time with growing spirit. Yonder glistening black Hercules, who plants one food forward, lifts his head and bare, shining chest, and rolls out the song from a mouth and throat like a cavern, is a *Candio*, a chief, or was before he was overthrown in battle and dragged away, his village burning behind him, from the mountains of High Soudan... He is of the Bambaras, as you may know by his solemn visage and the long tattoo streaks running down from the temples to the neck [...][49]

Cable portrayed the regal Candio, very similar to the romanticized African chieftain found in French works such as Victor Hugo's *Bug-Jargal*, as unable to tolerate degradation: "He is a candio—a prince. If I whip him he will die."[50] Loading nearly all possible resonances of the Candio in the same characterization, he also portrays Bras-Coupé as a ladies' man ("she loves her *candio*") and a bewitcher, a maker of grigris.[51]

The Candios seduce with their fine language, but their language is imbued with African magic, medicine, and stories. They are masters among non-masters, and (perhaps for that reason) "troublemakers." Their pretensions strike colonial observers as absurd and comical, but they are, for male slaves and masters alike in matters of the heart, rivals.

In "Lisette quitté la plaine," the narrator of the poem seems to fear that Lisette will be seduced by these masters within the group of non-masters in colonial society. He specifically fears that their spoken discourse that will prove especially seductive. The first poem printed in Creole therefore makes linguistic competition parallel to sexual competition. From the various definitions cited above one can see a range of hypothetical bases for this linguistic prowess: these "swells" were also poets and masters of ceremonies; they had the magic not only in their words but in their fetishes and charms; and they "translated" African religious and cultural values to a New World audience.

In effect, the male slave's perceived linguistic and sexual rivalry with Candios whose roles emblematize socio-ethnic ambiguity mapped around a triangle of libertine, religious, and literary qualities in effect symbolizes the plight of the Creole poem itself. It must navigate the myriad hierarchical positions associated with Creole culture and its troubling but frankly esteemed creative power on the one hand, and the elite discourse of European print culture on the other. Ineke Phaf views this as a common motif throughout the Caribbean: "The erotic element converges with the linguistic factor in mediating between the European and Creole languages."[52]

Creole Camouflage

The ambiguity of a class of masters within the slave class recapitulates the encompassing nature of the rubric of creole identity, which included all "Americans," as they often were called, *born* in the islands, regardless of race. The fact that no term designed to easily distinguish white from black was widely used in colonial society is all the more interesting given that the racially clear term *béké* did already exist. It was spelled "béqué" in three rare early nineteenth-century examples, one in the lyrics of the alleged Trinidad slave insurrection plot discussed in Chapter 4, and the others in correspondence written by Marceline Desbordes-Valmore[53] and a Caribbean-themed short story by Pétrus Borel.[54] But the term "creole" was almost invariably used instead, despite its lexical undoing of racial logic in the midst of an indelibly racially hierarchized colonial society. It therefore provided a politically and ethically ambiguous camouflage with regard to enslavement or slave ownership for the creole "mimic man." This camouflage makes it difficult to discern who was imitating whom in creolophone letters. Whose language was more seductive, that of the "black muse" or the *béké* master? Or the Candio in his role as a kind of wizard of a mimic master?

Contrary to Jourdain's reference to an "authentic" Creole speaker defined as neither white nor *mulâtre*, Creole was spoken by established colonial inhabitants from all social environments. Albert Valdman describes the "generalized use" of Creole as the "colonial vernacular" in Saint-Domingue, citing Moreau de Saint-Méry's statement that "It is in that language [...] that Creoles [of all colors] like to converse and Negroes do not use any other language among themselves."[55] George Lang proposes that questions of authentic and inauthentic Creole usage should be replaced by more nuanced consideration of variations in milieu and speaker, as in Reinecke's categorizations of "settler's Creoles," "plantation Creoles," and "trade jargons."[56]

Creoles are an outgrowth of the pidgins that are categorized as "contact languages," meaning a discourse that evolved for purposes of communication among the disparate elements of populations in colonial mercantile and plantation societies. Since a contact discourse derives from extended contact among people with no shared linguistic background, it sounds like something of an *Esperanto*. Yet it evolves, as John Holm explains, "when they need some means of communication, perhaps for trade, but no group learns the native language of any other group for social reasons that may include lack of trust or close contact."[57] A contact language thus paradoxically evolves in some kind of relation to *a refusal of close contact*. In plantation society, the strict exclusion of the social substrata from forms of institutional acculturation such as education or religious observance prevented those at the bottom of the social pyramid from simply adopting the institutionalized European languages of power. In a paradoxical chiasmus, this language that begins with a refusal of close contact ultimately becomes metonymic of identity in a larger sense. As an identity marker, it collapses together the different identities (with the exception of *bossale* slaves or new European arrivals) on which colonial hierarchies were based.

Lang has theorized that the unusually direct social involvement of speakers in the *development* of Creole language for purposes of mediation gave it a prestige different from that associated with the imperceptible evolution of the languages of established nation states and print cultures. This prestige, which Lang calls "creolophilia," disappeared once abolition put an end to plantocratic society as nurtured by the Atlantic slave trade. "Often overlooked," Lang writes, "is that creolophobia, which affects Creole speakers themselves, emerged after, not before, emancipation: in other words that creolophilia, which drives the Creole literatures, is a sort of throw-back to the period of Creole genesis, when Creoles were positive poles of attraction, the focus of a creative and collective enterprise."[58]

The capacity of colonial Creole identity to camouflage the violence of slavery under a rubric of all-inclusiveness can make the idea of colonial literary creolophilia about as socially acceptable as necrophilia. It is arguably to avoid complicity with this camouflage that postcolonial critics have tended to apply the term *béké* to colonial Creole literature, as in Glissant's formulation of "*béké* literature denying the real country."[59] Critical insistence on colonial *béké* literature as unmediated by voices of alterity has the effect of contextualizing slavery, as in the prototype of the laconic maroon, as a sort of *hors texte* that language, and especially colonial Creole language, is incapable of representing.

Yet early Creole poetry such as the two versions of "Lisette" most likely originated in a racially hybrid setting worthy of the ambiguous seductions of the Candios. "Lisette," as Perry Arthur Williams notes, is an example of a popular sentimental genre sung by *cocottes* or female "mulatto entertainers" to their mistresses in colonial Saint-Domingue, as I will discuss in the next chapter. The linguistic and seductive powers of the "Candios" are in turn paralleled by those of female courtesans.[60] Other sources support this idea of omnipresent lyrical production in Creole, not least Moreau's *Notes historiques*, which include several hastily transcribed Creole poems and songs, none of them associated with named authors. Justin Girod-Chantrans, in his 1786 commentary on the popular culture of slaves, spoke disparagingly of creole composers who would spontaneously develop and sing languorous songs, repeated for hours, with "l'amour" as their ordinary subject.[61] Lang links the sentimental songs sung by the *cocottes* to the European tradition of the pastourelle, "a genre defined by its ambiguity as an expression of courtly love across normal feudal social relations. The pastourelle is also typically caught between high and low dialects."[62] Yet even measured by the "ambiguity" of what Lang refers to as "normal feudal" social relations, the chaotically intersecting lives of sexuality, cultures of religion and medicine, and hierarchies of power on the plantations of Saint-Domingue present a significant deviation from models of social and sexual exchange in analyses such as those by Claude Lévi-Strauss or Luce Irigaray. The Candio is in a position of extreme social hybridity. The slave who was a little master resists classification as much as the female troubadour, black or mulatto, slave or freedwoman, singing to the mistress with whom she might have been in sexual competition.

Given the omnipresence in colonial social life, according to Moreau's descriptions, of an abundant poetic *oraliture* generated by slave or mulatto classes, the authorial attribution of "Lisette quitté la plaine" to de la Mahautière becomes, to say the least, more convenient for Moreau than convincing. Moreau was, after all, engaged in defending the Creole language against criticisms that it was a desultory jargon.

Performing "Lisette"

The example of the variation included in the 1811 *Idylles* suggests the metamorphosis of "Lisette" through a popular performance tradition, which again points to popular origins for the text. And yet there is no particular reason to assume that the poems transcribed by colonists were directly or uniquely produced by slaves, people "of color," and *affranchis* alone. The culture of the production and reception of such songs was polyphonic, dialogic, and literally *métissée* or en route to *métissage* through sexual contact among different members of the colonial hierarchy, as I will outline in the next chapter. White colonists preparing Creole *oraliture* for publication may have felt that the difficulty of even settling on an orthography for this primarily spoken language, let alone fitting songs to French versification, was an authorial process in relation to which they did not see fit to acknowledge the origins of their material. There is one striking early example in which a convincing case has been made for white authorship of a text on exactly the themes found in the "Lisette" tradition, as I outline in the conclusion to this chapter, however.

The version of "Lisette" in the 1811 *Idylles* is in most substantial ways consistent with the version traditionally ascribed to de la Mahautière, yet it cannot be considered a reprint. The casual nature of changes in spelling, grammatical agency, and the specific ordering of elements suggest unintentional deviation from an original version either over the course of repeated performances or in someone's aural memory of the song.

Two of the original eight-line stanzas are broken into quatrains, but the rhyme scheme is preserved. Here it is not Lisette who will meet young Candios, but the narrator himself who has met them: "Mo conté Jeune Candios." The account of the slave's former preferred activities, dancing the *calinda* and playing the *bamboula* and the *bram bram sonnette* are now reduced to the former two only, in reverse order. Replacing the *bram bram sonnette* is the metaphor of the narrator's new muteness, "Bouche à moi tourné muette," which contrasts directly with the sweet talk ["bouche dous passé sirop"] of the Candios, showing a deepening of the original symbolism.

None of these changes represents a profound alteration from the text published by Moreau, yet taken together they unmistakably form a variation on the "original" text. It is in the last two lines of the song that one dramatic change occurs between this version and the earlier one. Rather than identifying himself as a starving bird in a cage, the narrator now identifies himself as the aggrieved party and enjoins Lisette to remember him, identifying himself by name. Here is the entire poem:

Chanson créole

Lizette toi quité la plaine,
Mo perdi bonheur à moi,
Gié à moi tourné fontaine,
Dipi mo pa miré toi.

(Lisette you have left the plains,
I have lost my happiness,
My eyes have turned into fountains,
Since I have not seen you.)

Laut' jour quan ma coupe cane
Mo songé zamour à moi,
La nuit quan mo dan cabane
Dan Dromi ma songé toi.

(During the day when I cut sugar cane
I think of my love,
At night when I am in my bed
In my sleep [my dreams] I think of you.)

Laut' jour m'alé à la ville
Mo conté Jeune Candios,
Yo gagné pour trompé filles,

Bouche dous passé sirop.
Yo van semblé to sincere
Pendan yo coquin trop,
Cé couleuvre qui contrefaire,
Crié à rat pour trapé yos.

(The other day I went to the city
[where] I met young Candios,
They have with which to deceive girls
Mouths [words] sweeter than syrup.
They are going to seem sincere to you
When they are [actually] too tricky,
It's like the snake that pretends
To cry rat in order to catch them.)

Dipi mo perdi Lizette,
Mo pa batte Bamboula,
Bouche à moi tourné muette,
Mo pa dansé Calinda.
Quan mo miré l'aut' Négresse,
Mo pas gagné gié pour li,
Mo pas songé travail piece,
Toute qui chose à moi mouri.

(Since I lost Lisette,
I haven't played the Bamboula,
My mouth has [words have] become mute,
I haven't danced the Calinda,
When I see the other Negress,
I have no eyes for her,
I don't think of work at all,
Everything that is something to me has died.)

Mo maigre tan comme yon boi
Jambe à moi tan comme Rosau,
Mangé pa dous dan bouche à moi,
Tafia même cé comme dio.
Quan moi songé toi Lizette
Dio toujour dan gié moi,
Magnière à moi vini trop Bette[63]
A force chagrin magnié moi.

(I am thin as a stick,
My leg is like a reed,
Food isn't sweet in my mouth,
Even tafia [alcohol] is like water.

When I remember you Lisette,
Water is [tears are] always in my eyes,
My manners have become too stupid,
From the manner of my grief.)

Lisette mo tandé nouvelle,
To comté bientot tourné;
Vini donc toujour fidelle
Miré bon passé tandé,
Na pas tardé davantage,
To faire mo assé chagrin,
Si coeur à toi pas volage
To doi souvenir Colin.

(Lisette I have heard the news,
You count on returning soon;
Come back still faithful
Seeing is better than hearing,
Don't wait any longer,
You have caused me enough grief,
If your heart isn't fickle,
You should remember Colin.)

The final lines of this version constitute a kind of *envoi*, in which the narrator identifies himself as "Colin." The fact that "Colin" is one of the few masculine names to rhyme with "chagrin" makes it less likely that a given masculine performer of the song would identify himself personally at the end of the performance in an appeal to his audience, and more likely that in the popular imagination Lisette's fictional lover had come to be known as a specific named character in his own right; Colin was also a very popular name in the French lyrical tradition.[64] This revised ending has the effect of reducing the psychological tension of slavery in the poem, as the subject-status of the narrator is revindicated precisely where in the earlier version the narrator had faded into the analogy of the caged bird. The narrator's initial fears that his lover will be seduced by the sweet talk of the Candios remains in this version, however. This suggests that the eroticization of different discourses associated with ambiguous subject positions within the Creole hierarchy continued to be a central concern of the poem.

The presence of different versions of "Lisette" in American francophone culture, apparently introduced through the large waves of immigration by colonists and their extended households during the Haitian Revolution, is evident even late in the nineteenth century in Francophone literature from Louisiana. A version of "Lisette" in Tante Marie's novel on the Haitian Revolution, the 1892 *Le Macandal*, features minor spelling changes from the original but is clearly based on the version transcribed in Moreau de Saint-Méry's *Description* of Saint-Domingue.[65] In Alfred Mercier's *L'Habitation Saint-Ybars*, with its theme of complex social and familial relations among master and slaves in antebellum plantations, a mad woman sings the first stanza of the song, with extensive spelling changes and some syntactical changes from the version transcribed by Moreau.[66]

"Lisette" arguably is also a forerunner of a line of Creole poems later in the nineteenth century that take up the concerns of a black male narrator who fears he will lose his lover to sweet talkers. These poems, however, specifically identify the language of whites as a feared language of seduction, rather than a discourse of liminality within Creole hierarchies. In effect, they reflect a move away from the extreme hybridity of colonial Saint-Domingue and into a more binary view of black and white relations.

In 1819, Marceline Desbordes-Valmore, the white French woman poet who had spent a few months stranded in Saint-Barthélemy and Guadeloupe during the revolutionary upheavals associated with Napoleon's re-imposition of slavery in 1802, published a poem in a French and Creole hybrid called "Tournez, tournez cher'belle." In this poem a male narrator describes his fears that his lover, "Betzi," will be seduced by the language of whites. I will present only the stanza that specifically coincides with the concerns of the narrator in "Lisette." (The poem is so grammatically ambiguous as to be in effect undeterminable; my "literal" translation here is simply a model of one series of awkward possibilities.)

"Betzi"

Toi gagne doux langage,
Z'ami toi connais blancs
Pour traper fille sage,
Gagner tout doux serments.
Quand bouche à toi souri,
Coeur toi songer trahi,
Si moi bay toi tendresse,
Toi va changer maîtresse,
Moi languir dans tristesse,
Et loin toi va souffrir;
    Et puis, et puis,
Dans chagrin moi bientôt va mourir.[67]

(Your language is sweet,
[But] your friend knows that whites,
In order to trap good girls,
Have very sweet promises.
When your mouth smiles,

Your heart thinks it is betrayed,
If I give you tenderness,
You will change [into a] mistress,
I will languish in sadness,
And far away you will suffer;
    And then, and then,
In grief I will soon die.)

The first poem written and published in Creole by a known black Haitian poet (as distinct from poems published in the text of critical commentary by others), the 1884 "Choucoune" by Oswald Durand, also connects with this tradition of male linguistic/racial anxiety. Here is the stanza in which the theme appears:

Gnou petit blanc vini rivé:
P'tit barb' roug', bel' figur' rose,
Montr' sous côté, bell' chivé...
—Malheur moin, li qui la cause!
Li trouvé Choucoun' joli,
Li parlé francé, Choucoun' aimé-li...
Pitôt blié ça, cé trop grand la peine.
Choucoun' quitté moin, dé pieds moin lan chaîne![68]

(A little white[69] arrived:
Little red beard, lovely pink face,
A watch at his side, lovely hair...
Of my unhappiness, he is the cause!
He found Choucoune pretty,
He spoke French, Choucoune liked him,
Better to forget that, the pain is too great.
Choucoune left me, my two feet are in chains!)

As evidenced by the first Creole anthology, the *Idylles et chansons*, and its relationship to both earlier and later poems in the "Lisette" genealogy, early Creole poetry is haunted by a self-reflexive intertextuality (poems imitating poems) about intervocality—people being threatened or seduced by the language of others.

Contact Literature

In the *Idylles et chansons*, a (descendant of) a contact language is the medium for a *contact literature*: oral literature in contact with print culture, the Candio in (indirect) contact with the *cocotte*, the colonist "mimic man" in (indirect) contact with the slave "mimic master." And yet this contact literature does not declare itself as such. If colonial "authors" were actually imitating and transcribing songs that they had heard from slaves and other classes in between those of slaves and masters, how are we to evaluate the politics of their simultaneously recuperative and anonymous role as "mimic men"?

In Bhabha's paradigm of the colonized mimic man, imitation has many creative virtues. Echoing and ironizing the colonial "reality effect," it introduces an element of difference structured by "displacement," "fantasy," and "psychic defense": it is a vehicle of "open textuality."[70] It resembles Glissant's construct of an anti- or counter-poetics to combat "the transparency of false mimesis."[71] And yet the potentially useful camouflage provided by the colonized subject's mimicry of the colonist takes on a different political valence when it camouflages slave ownership.

In the 1811 *Idylles et chansons*, a large part of what is lost to history is precisely the identificatory apparatus supported by the print culture of nation states—authorial identity, the specific culture of production and reception, traces of the economic life of the text, etc.—but what remains is nevertheless *voice*. The problem with that voice is that, unlike the mimicry on the part of the colonized in Bhabha's paradigm, it does not make the workings of power visible. Like the term *créole*, the colonial publication of early Creole literature veils colonial identities.

Roger Chartier's work on the cultural uses of print culture in early modern France supports the idea that even outside of creole society, print culture is marked by a certain "creolized" hybridity of authority and interlocutive relationships, of free play in the origins and appropriation of cultural capital. Chartier rejects the convention of neatly exclusive relationships "between specific cultural forms and particular social groups."[72] He discredits the perception that "the various cultural groups in a given society are sufficiently pure, homogeneous, and distinct to permit them to be characterized uniformly and unequivocally."[73] Chartier also insists on the role of print culture even among the unalphabetized who witness and hear, through others' readings, the messages of texts such as *affiches* (including legal and political procla-mations). Chartier's paradigm is obviously radicalized if one applies it to the colonial culture of slavery. And yet how can one not entertain such a possibility in relation to the historical period of the Haitian Revolution, when even Napoleon Bonaparte had a proclamation issued in Creole, presumably for literate readers to share with crowds of unalphabetized, Creole-speaking listeners? Chartier argues that in the "'popular' use of print, the spoken word mediated for the written word."[74] In early Creole poetry, the printed word mediated for the spoken/sung word: *oraliture* made it into print.

The postcolonial theoretical and literary models of the silence of slaves cited in the first part of this chapter arguably assume that popular oral traditions only began to be transcribed in the twentieth century because of the dehumanizing nature of slavery. The dismissal of early Creole literature as a vehicle for the expression of slave culture is logical in relation to the trauma of slavery. After all, as with the history of the Holocaust, the history of slavery is so traumatic as to provide a working model of what trauma *is*. Part of the definition of trauma provided by theorists such as Cathy Caruth is its inaccessibility to conscious expression, despite its repetitive manifestation as psychic or cultural evidence. One could theorize further that in the twentieth century, the perceived authenticity of inexpressible traumas such as slavery has come to provide a working model of what *authenticity* is. Guaranteed precisely by its failure to be articulated, the trauma of slavery provides a colonial metaphor for a failure of mimesis that is at the heart of the ethical tension of the representational endeavor.

Early Creole literature suggests that trauma itself cannot tell, or prevent the telling of, the whole story of lives lived under even singularly traumatic conditions. The very concept of *oraliture* in the colonial Caribbean sphere attests to the resilience of voice and to the prestige of different voices—not least the unsettling prestige of the African voice, as outlined in some accounts of the identity of the Candio. The 1811 edition of the *Idylles et chansons* problematizes the conventional chronological separation of the discursive realms of Creole orality and *béké* print culture because it points to an early manuscript or printed circulation of oral texts. Whether one responds to the idea of a colonial Creole contact literature with "creolophilia" or "creolophobia" depends to some degree on whether one believes contact literature can express forms of "contact" not completely regulated by colonial social control. Certainly the "Colon de Saint-Domingue," who became the "Habitant d'Hayti" after fleeing the Haitian Revolution, had witnessed the loss of colonial control over creole contact. The *Idylles et chansons, ou essais de poésie créole* inaugurated a conscious Creole literary tradition, one in which competition with charismatic (sexualized and sanctified) popular voices is paramount.

Trading Places

The free circulation of literary ideas, tropes, and aesthetics beyond groups by which they were generated or inspired goes without saying, and one of the most interesting representations of the Candio occurs in a rare popularly styled Creole theatrical text that has been associated with a colonist author through a relatively detailed sequence of references from the time of its first performance. The text in question is a popular Creole opera, *Jeannot et Thérèse*, an "opuscule négro-dramatico-lyrique"[75] ("Negro-dramatic-lyric opus") based on Rousseau's opera *Le Devin du village* (*The Village Soothsayer*), and its parody in provincial dialect, *Les Amours de Bastien et Bastienne*. It was written by a "Sieur Clément," well-known to Moreau de Saint-Méry, and was performed in Cap Français in 1758 and at various later dates. *Jeannot et Thérèse* has been studied by Bernard Camier and Marie-Christine Hazael-Massieux,[76] Marie-Christine Hazaël-Massieux,[77] and Bernard Camier and Laurent Dubois.[78] The opera makes a clear reference to the motifs of the city Candios' seductive speech in "Lisette quitté la plaine," but inverts their gendering.

In Clément's Creole version of the Rousseau opera, apparently performed in blackface,[79] the black *devin* character, a *caprelata*-like voudou "magician" named Papa Simon, provides (for a price) a voudou charm, an *ouanga*, for a young woman, Thérèse, who has come in tears to beg his help in regaining the affections of her Candio lover, Jeannot. Like Simon, who goes to lengths to identity himself as not being in the prestigious category of the native-born creole, Thérèse and Jeannot appear to be black rather than of mixed race, based on allusions to the economic and class mobility represented for them by the *mulâtresse* who tries to buy Jeannot's affections, and the *mulâtre* (also identified as white) who puts on airs and tries to pay for Thérèse's love. Thérèse only wants Jeannot, but Jeannot, like Lisette, in effect has left the plains.

As the *devin/caprelateur* Simon chides Jeannot, "Jeannot moi tandé nouvelle / trop longtems toi fair candio"[80] ("Jeannot I have heard the news / you have been playing this Candio role for too long"). These verses redeploy the first verse of the last stanza of "Lisette": "Lisette mon tandé nouvelle / To compté bintôt tourné" ("Lisette I have heard the news / You are planning to return soon"). Papa Simon has confirmed to Thérèse the reason for her lover's long absence in the city: a rich *mulâtresse* is keeping him.

> Vous pa conné c'est mulâtresse
> Qui gagné beaucoup la richesse
> Qui tienbé li dans cap, dans pi que vous paie voir li
> Li metté li comm' blanc la ville
> Manchett feston calin in pille
> Silla qui payé ben c'est premier yau servi[81]

> (You don't know it's a *mulâtresse*
> Who has a great deal of wealth
> Who is keeping him in the Cap, since you last saw him
> She has him all turned out like a white man from the city
> Sleeve cuffs, festoons, and hugs galore
> The one who pays best is the first served)

Although Papa Simon agrees to make the fetish to charm Jeannot to come back, in effect the real magic is making the rakish Jeannot aware that

Thérèse, in her turn, is being courted by a simpering, Pierrot-like *mulâtre*, who has offered her "gros l'argent" ("big money"). Jeannot correspondingly asks for Papa Simon's help to win Thérèse's affections back, and the *ouanga*, with the "Dahomey" chant so intriguingly analyzed by Camier and Dubois,[82] is delivered. It appears that the magic has much less effect than the spirited accusations and ripostes exchanged between the two lovers. Jeannot can, in Candio fashion, try to talk his way out of his infidelities ("Li pé ben parlé si li vlé"[83] ["He can speak well if he wants"]), but Thérèse has had it. As Thérèse reminds him directly, if the "white" pays her, she will look even more flamboyant than Jeannot, and everyone will call her "Madame": "Moi le flambé passé toy / tout monde va heler moi / madame"[84] ("I will seem to blaze more than you / everyone will call me / madame"). Jeannot counters that next to his rich *mulâtresse*, her white will seem stringy ("cheche" [chiche]). But clearly he does not mean to return to the city woman: he threatens that if she trades another boy for him ("changer garçon"), he will go maroon to the end of his days: "jouq moi mouri moi alé marron"[85] ("I will go maroon until I die"). The inescapable ending, of course, is the scene in which Jeannot, Simon, Thérèse, and all the "nègres et nègresses" ("negroes and negresses") happily assemble to see them "ben marié"[86] ("well married").

Jeannot et Thérèse represents an important and influential "marriage" of French and Creole language and plot material, with a remarkably frank portrayal of libertine culture, including the surprising detail of the *mulâtresse*'s financial leverage over desirable men. Although the Candio here is a "swell" in only the limited sense of the sweet-talking, seductive black man, rather than in the more extended valences of later definitions, the groundwork is established for this libertine mastery to extend into different areas of mobility with regard to colonial power: speaking well and looking good bring access to the city and to mixed-race privilege, and become a significant element of negotiated power in non-white social hierarchies. Blacks' social imitation of mastery and mastery of social imitation becomes a recurring theme of colonial literary production, with rivalries over popular creole expression underwritten by the libertine rivalries in which economic and racial upper classes are not always the winners.

Notes

1. M.-E. Descourtilz, *Voyages d'un naturaliste à Saint-Domingue* (Paris: Dufart, 1809) 3:135.
2. Robert Reid-Pharr, "The Slave Narrative and Early Black American Literature," in *The Cambridge Companion to the African American Slave Narrative*, ed. Audrey Fisch (Cambridge: Cambridge University Press, 2007), 137.
3. The *Idylles et chansons* add to the body of nineteenth-century texts published in languages other than English in the United States recently anthologized in *The*

Multilingual Anthology of American Literature: A Reader of Original Texts with English Translations, ed. Marc Shell and Werner Sollers (New York: New York University Press, 2000).

4. John Garrigus has kindly pointed out that an *habitant*, even one earlier defined as a "colon," could be a person of color. This is possible. My own intuition, however, is that in the U.S. context where these texts were published, people of color in the Saint-Domingue exodus were not defining themselves with the terminology and particular stance of confidence of this *colon/habitant*. Moreau de Saint-Méry, in his *Voyage aux Etats-Unis d'Amérique, 1793–1798* (New Haven, CT: Yale University Press, 1913), which includes material dating later than 1798, emphasized the "abject status" of the "hommes de couleur libres" (67) in the U.S., noting that they were treated better than slaves primarily in that no one had a legal right to beat them. He emphasized that their relationship to the white "class" was limited almost entirely to the libertine interactions of women of color with white men—interactions which, despite the luxury of the women's clothing, seemed to have more of an overt character of prostitution than they had in Saint-Domingue (325). I also feel that the preface is the least likely place for a person of color to have presented his project without the slightest gloss on his social context. In the collection of poetry by poets of color in New Orleans in 1845, *Les Cenelles*—admittedly a very different context—the preface referred to the importance of education to overcome "the position in which fate has placed us," and some such allusion is arguably characteristic of prefatory remarks by non-whites in publications in early nineteenth-century America. However, the *colon/habitant*'s anonymity technically could veil not only a male of color, but a female also.

5. Anonymous, *Idylles, ou essais de poesies créole, par un colon de Saint-Domingue* (New York: Hopkins and Seymour, 1804), 3.

6. *Idylles et chansons, ou essais de poésie créole par un habitant d'Hayti* (1811), reprinted in Edward Larocque Tinker, "Gombo Comes to Philadelphia," *Proceedings of the American Antiquarian Society* 67.1 (April 1957), 55.

7. Besides the more general literal meaning of "inhabitant," the term *habitant* often denoted a property owner in Saint-Domingue. The racial valences of the term are unstable, since an impressive proportion of Saint-Domingue's planters were people of color in the period leading up to the Revolution, and yet the category was generally associated with whites, in the same way that "plantations" in the U.S. context conjure slave-based agriculture rather than agriculture itself.

8. M. L. E. Moreau de Saint-Méry, *Description topographique, physique, civile, politique et historique de la partie française de l'isle Saint-Domingue* (Philadelphia: Chez l'auteur, 1797), 1:65.

9. Tinker, "Gombo Comes to Philadelphia," 53.

10. It would be intriguing to seek out refugees from Saint-Domingue in the population of Cahors. *Idylles ou essais de poésie créole par un colon de St. Domingue* (Cahors: Combarieu, Imprimeur de la préfeteur, 1821).

11. Tinker, "Gombo Comes to Philadelphia," 53.

12. Homi K. Bhabha, *The Location of Culture* (New York: Routledge, 1994), 108, 107.

13. "Toute mimésis suppose que ce qui est représenté est le 'vrai réel.' Quand elle porte sur deux réalités dont l'une est vouée à reproduire l'autre, il ne peut manquer que les tenants de l'opération se considèrent comme vivant un irréel permanent. C'est notre cas." Edouard Glissant, *Le Discours antillais* (Paris: Gallimard, 1997), 774.

14. Glissant, *Le Discours antillais*, 95.

15. See V. S. Naipaul, *The Mimic Men* (London: Penguin, 1967).

16. Bhabha, *Location of Culture*, 85.

17. Jacques Lacan, "The Line and the Light," in *The Four Fundamental Concepts of Psychoanalysis*, trans. Alan Sheridan (London: Hogarth Press and the Institute of Psycho-Analysis, 1977), 99.

18. "La transparence de la fausse mimesis est à dépouiller d'un seul coup." Glissant, *Le Discours antillais*, 803.

19. Édouard Glissant, *Caribbean Discourse: Selected Essays*, trans. J. Michael Dash (Charlottesville, VA: University Press of Virginia, 1989), 162.

20. Glissant, *Caribbean Discourse*, 231.

21. "Il n'y aura longtemps en ces territoires qu'une voix reconnue: la voix coloniale." Régis Antoine, *La Littérature franco-antillaise: Haiti, Guadeloupe et Martinique* (Paris: Karthala, 1992), 13.

22. Antoine, *La Littérature franco-antillaise*, 22.

23. Antoine, *La Littérature franco-antillaise*, 27.

24. Antoine, *La Littérature franco-antillaise*, 27.

25. Antoine, *La Littérature franco-antillaise*, 28.

26. Elodie Jourdain, *Du Français aux parlers créoles* (Paris: Klincksieck, 1956), 230.

27. Jourdain, *Du Français aux parlers créoles*, 230.

28. "Je vais rapporter une chanson bien connue, qui fera voir si le langage créol est un jargon insignifiant et maussade. Elle a été composée, il y a environ quarante ans, par M. Duvivier de la Mahautière, mort Conseiller au Conseil du Port-au-Prince." Moreau de Saint-Méry, *Description de Saint-Domingue*, 1:65.

29. The transcription of Moreau de Saint-Méry's handwriting offers many enduring puzzles. In 2002 I first presented my work on the Creole poems found in Moreau's *Notes Historiques* and in the *Idylles et chansons* to linguist Marie-Christine Hazaël-Massieux, who edited one of my first articles on this Créole literature in *Langue et identité narrative dans les littératures de l'ailleurs* (Université de Provence-Aix, 2005). She has since published transcriptions and linguistic annotations of all these texts, and an exhaustive array of other Creole texts from the era, in the very useful anthology *Textes anciens en créole français de la Caraïbe* (Paris: Editions Publibook, 2008). Her anthology indirectly highlights the different uses of these texts by linguists and literary scholars. While my goal is to transcribe the texts in such a way as to be able to decipher their meaning, and thus to be able to use them as literary and cultural texts, her goal is primarily to document linguistic occurrences in their historical unfolding, generally without furnishing translations or using them for broader purposes of literary and cultural analysis. She proffers minute differences between her transcriptions and mine as corrections. As examples, her rendition of Moreau de St. Méry's manuscript of "Lisette quitté la plaine" features the word for "young" (*jeune*) as "gënne," whereas I read it as "geine"; I transcribed the pronouns "me" (*moi*) as "moué," whereas she read it as "moé." This comes down to a visual judgment of these handwritten manuscripts; certainly "moué" was a commonly used spelling at the time, as in this quote from M.-E. Descourtilz's contemporaneous *Voyages d'un naturaliste* (Paris: Dufart, 1809), 2:453: "Toi puni moué, moué puni toi astor!"

30. Descourtilz defines "le calenda" as "une danse nègre consacrée à célébrer les funerailles: elle est extravagante et fort indécente." *Voyages d'un naturaliste*, 3:274 n. 1.

31. The *Bram-bram sonnette* is a belt decorated with bells.

32. Moreau de Saint-Méry gives this description of the *bamboula* and its role in the *Calenda*: "To dance the *Calenda* the blacks make two drums from, when possible, whole pieces of hollow wood. One of the ends is covered, and over the other end they stretch a sheepskin or goatskin. The shorter of these drums, which is sometimes made from a very wide bamboo trunk, is called the *Bamboula*. A black straddles each drum and hits it with his wrist and his fingers, but slowly on one drum and rapidly on the other." [Pour danser le *Calenda*, les nègres ont deux tambours faits, quand ils le peuvent, avec des morceaux de bois creux d'une seule pièce. L'un des bouts est couvert, et l'on étend sur l'autre une peau de mouton ou de chèvre. Le plus court de ces tambours est nommé *Bamboula*, attendu qu'il est formé quelquefois d'un très gros bambou. Sur chaque tambour est un nègre à califourchon qui le frappe du poignet et des doigts, mais avec lenteur sur l'un et rapidement sur l'autre.] *Description de Saint-Domingue*, 1:44.

33. Moreau de Saint-Méry, *Description de Saint-Domingue*, 1:65–6.

34. Susan Buck-Morss, "Hegel and Haiti," *Critical Inquiry* 26 (summer 2000), 852.

35. Moreau de Saint-Méry, *Description de Saint-Domingue*, 1:66.

36. I quote here from an excerpt of the book. M. L. E. Moreau de Saint-Méry, "Danse. Article extrait d'un ouvrage" (Philadelphia, PA: Printed by the Author, 1796), 60.

37. Descourtilz, *Voyages d'un naturaliste*, 3:192 fn. 1, 188.

38. Descourtilz, *Voyages d'un naturaliste*, 3:92,

39. "On jugera […] l'indolence de ces favoris de l'amour, et quel empire ils ont sur leurs maîtresses." Descourtilz, *Voyages d'un naturaliste*, 3:194–5.

40. Drouin de Bercy, *De Saint-Domingue: de ses guerres, de ses révolutions, de ses resources, et de moyens a prendre pour y rétablir la paix et l'industrie* (Paris: Chez Hocquet, 1814), 175.

41. Pierre Pluchon, *Vaudou, Sorciers, empoisonneurs de Saint-Domingue à Haïti* (Paris: Karthala, 1987), 113.

42. Karol Weaver, *Medical Revolutionaries: The Enslaved Healers of Eighteenth-Century Saint Domingue* (Urbana, IL: University of Illinois Press, 2006), 125.

43. Gustave d'Alaux, "Les Moeurs et la littérature nègres," *Revue des deux mondes* 14 (April 1, 1852), 788.

44. Alexandre Bonneau, "Les Noirs, les jaunes, et la littérature française en Haïti," *Revue contemporaine* (December 1856/January 1857), 119.

45. M. L. Fournereau, chef des travaux publiques à la Guyane, "La fête des Polygoudoux," *Revue d'ethnographie* 3 (1885), 124–31.

46. Henry Edward Krehbiel, *Afro-American Folksongs: A Study in Racial and National Music* (New York: G. Schirmer, 1914), 116.

47. Full transcription with musical score, Krehbiel, *Afro-American Folksongs*, 118–20.

48. *Entretiens avec Bala Kanté: Une Chronique du Manding au XXème siècle*, ed. Jan Jansen and Mountaga Diarra (Boston: Brill, 2006), 51.

49. George Washington Cable, *Creoles and Cajuns: Stories of Old Louisiana* (New York: Doubleday, 1959), 375.

50. Cable, *Creoles and Cajuns*, 24.

51. Cable, *Creoles and Cajuns*, 37.

52. Ineke Phaf, "Republican Code, Working Conditions, and Cross-Cultural Hybridity in the literature of Surinam and Cuba," in *A History of Literature in the Caribbean*, ed. A. James Arnold (Amsterdam: John Benjamins, 1997), 3:387.

53. In 1833 Desbordes-Valmore wrote a note to the actor Mélingue that included the phrase *Vous va baï lettre à pitit Béqué soldat qui rapporté li, vous tende?* ("You will give the letter to the little *béké* soldier who will bring it back, you hear?"). Marceline Desbordes-Valmore, *Oeuvres poétiques de Marceline Desbordes-Valmore*, ed. Marc Bertrand (Grenoble: Presses Universitaires de Grenoble, 1973), 2:772. Srinivas Aravamudan suggests the etymological origin of *béké* in an African loanword in colonial Jamaica, "buckra," present as early as Aphra Behn's 1688 *Oronooko* as "backereary," and adapted into French-based Creole as *béké*.

54. Pétrus Borel, "Three Fingered Jack," in *Champavert: contes immoraux* (Paris: Phébus, 2002), 93.

55. Albert Valdman, "Creole, the Language of Slavery," in *Slavery in the Caribbean Francophone World*, ed. Doris Kadish (Athens, GA: University of Georgia Press, 2000), 154.

56. George Lang, *Entwisted Tongues: Comparative Creole Literatures* (Amsterdam: Rodopi, 2000), 8.

57. John Holm, *An Introduction to Pidgins and Creoles* (Cambridge: Cambridge University Press, 2000), 5.

58. Lang, *Entwisted Tongues*, 104.

59. Glissant, *Caribbean Discourse*, 95.

60. Perry Arthur Williams, "La Fontaine in Haitian Creole: A Study of *Cric? Crac!* by Georges Sylvain" (unpublished Ph.D. thesis, Fordham University, 1972), 29.

61. Justin Girod-Chantrans, *Voyage d'un Suisse dans différentes colonies d'Amérique, pendant la dernière guerre, avec une table d'observations météorologiques faites à Saint-Domingue* (Paris: Chez Poinçot, 1786), 189–90.

62. Lang, *Entwisted Tongues*, 159.

63. The capitalization and spelling change from "bête" to "Bette" could possibly indicate that this was a wordplay on a woman's name, creating a couple consisting of "Bette" and "Colin" in the last line.

64. This transition from an unnamed first-person narrator to a first-person narrator who identifies himself by name late in the poem would occur between early and later versions of Oswald Durand's "Choucoune" as well.

65. Si to allé la ville,
    Ta trouvé jeine Caudio
    Ki gagnin pou trompé fille
    Bouche dou pacé siro.
    To va cré, yo bin sincère;
    Pendant quior yo coquin tro,
    Cé sarpan ki contrefaire
    Crié rat pou trompé yo.
    Tante Marie, *Le Macandal: episode de l'insurrection des noirs à Saint-Domingue* (New Orleans: Imprimerie George Müller, 1892), 59.

66. Lisett' to kité la plaine,
    Mo perdi bonhair à moué;
    Ziés à moué semblé fontaine,
    Dépi mo pa miré toué.
    Jour là can mo coupé canne.
    Mo chongé zamour à moué;
    Lanouitt' can mo dan cabane,

Dan droumi mo tchombo toué.

Alfred Mercier, *L'Habitation Saint-Ybars ou maîtres et esclaves en Louisiane* (New Orleans: Imprimerie Franco-Américaine, 1881), 31.

67. Desbordes-Valmore, *Oeuvres poétiques de Marceline Desbordes-Valmore*, 2:619.

68. Jourdain, *Du Français aux parlers créoles*, 269.

69. The expression "petit blanc" denotes a socioeconomic category: a white from the petit bourgeoisie, rather than one of the established planters. The expression here compounds other rather comical descriptions of whiteness, in what is arguably a satirical take on the allure of the white man for non-white women.

70. Bhabha, *Location of Culture*, 85.

71. Glissant, *Le Discours antillais*, 803.

72. Roger Chartier, *The Cultural Uses of Print Culture in Early Modern France*, trans. Lydia Cochrane (Princeton, NJ: Princeton University Press, 1987), 3.

73. Chartier, *The Cultural Uses of Print Culture*, 3.

74. Chartier, *The Cultural Uses of Print Culture*, 345.

75. Cited by Marie-Christine Hazaël-Massieux in *Textes anciens en créole français*, 128.

76. Bernard Camier and Marie-Christine Hazael-Massieux, "Jeannot et Thérèse de Clément. Un opéra-comique en créole au milieu du XVIIIème siecle," *Revue de la société haïtienne d'Histoire et de Géographie* 215 (2003), 135–66.

77. For historical notes on the linguistic aspects of the play, see Marie-Christine Hazaël-Massieux, "A propos de Jeannot et Thérèse: une traduction du *Devin du village* en créole du XVIIIe siècle?" *Creolica*, http://www.creolica.net.

78. Bernard Camier and Laurent Dubois, "Voltaire et Zaïre, ou le théâtre des Lumières dans l'aire atlantique française," *Revue d'histoire moderne et contemporaine* 54:4 (December 2007), 36–69.

79. Camier and Dubois, "Voltaire et Zaïre," 53.

80. Hazaël-Massieux, *Textes anciens en créole français*, 139.

81. Hazaël-Massieux, *Textes anciens en créole français*, 136.

82. Camier and Dubois, "Voltaire et Zaïre," 51.

83. Hazaël-Massieux, *Textes anciens en créole français*, 136.

84. Hazaël-Massieux, *Textes anciens en créole français*, 147.

85. Hazaël-Massieux, *Textes anciens en créole français*, 145.

86. Hazaël-Massieux, *Textes anciens en créole français*, 148.

8

Dissing Rivals, Love for Sale: The Courtesans' Rap and the Not-So Tragic Mulatta

Mulâtresses are in general much less docile than mulattoes, because they have claimed for themselves, over most of the Whites, an empire founded on libertinage.

Michel René Hilliard d'Auberteuil, *Considérations sur l'état présent de la colonie française de Saint-Domingue*[1]

Sex, Politics, and Manuscripts

In the rabbit hole of libertine sexual relations in slave-holding societies, white and black disappeared into one another. Frederick Engels' precept on the production and reproduction of "immediate life," with its "twofold character," meaning "on the one hand, the production of the means of existence, of food, clothing, and shelter and the tools necessary for that production; on the other side, the production of human beings themselves, the propagation of the species,"[2] has long been applied to the problem of the exchange of women, or what Luce Irigaray called "Women on the Market." In slavery, where the exchange of human beings as goods was not veiled by sentiment or familial consent, the obvious potential for the sexual use of human goods—a kind of "abuse value" overlapping with the Marxian "use value" of the human commodity—had the predictable yet paradoxical repercussion of bringing those defined as persons and those defined as things into the same colonial family. The category of the *mulâtresse* became iconic[3] as a subversive chess piece on the board of colonial race relations. Darcy Grimaldo Grigsby analyzes the condensation of myth and meaning involved: "The Mulatta incarnated empire; she was its sign because she was its product."[4]

This is the "productive paradox" of creolization, as Doris Garraway notes in *The Libertine Colony*: "the notion that a common culture may be constructed in a social system marked by asymmetrical power relations and the threat of violence."[5] For David Geggus, the exploitation of female slaves was facilitated by the conjunction of their comparatively small numbers and their lack of "legal personalities": "the paucity of females in both the white and the black communities in Saint Domingue evidently put the sexual favors of slave women at a premium. Lacking legal personalities, female slaves were exceptionally vulnerable to rape, and sexual harassment by whites occasionally extended to the most vicious sadism."[6] It is in this context that one can most aptly cite Antoine Métral's haunting critique of courtesan arts: "They covered their chains with a few flowers [...]"[7]

Women's sexual vulnerability, however, was simultaneously a nexus of mobility: "slave women were able to use their sexuality to obtain material advantages from whites, free coloreds, and fellow slaves, and sometimes to gain their freedom. Female slaves were manumitted more than twice as frequently as males."[8] (As noted in the previous chapter, however, the literary adventures of the "Candio" also trace important possibilities for mobility on the part of the black male in libertine society.) Manumission or other forms of social mobility originating in libertine commerce paralleled the power of revolt, according to Barry Gaspar and Darlene Clark Hine: "Collective slave resistance in the form of revolt was often aimed at the attainment of freedom ultimately, that is to say, freedom from white ownership and rule, but many slave women were able to obtain their individual freedom through other means."[9] Even in the colonial period, as Jean-Philippe Belleau has noted, some writers, like Justin de Girod-Chantrans, expressed the observation that for white men, libertine relations with non-white women inevitably caused slaves and women of color to appear "much closer and more respectable."[10]

In this chapter I move beyond the rich field of existing analyses of libertinage in slave-holding societies to chart libertinage as a key catalyst for the establishment of a popular Creole (*Kreyòl*) literary tradition, through black and mulatta women's often overlapping roles as entertainers for white women and as concubines for white men. Libertine relations became a subject of lyrical culture, both veiling and unveiling triangulated bonds across class and race lines. The mediation of these texts by transcribers and collectors reflected a complex re-evaluation of the *mulâtresse*'s incarnation of empire, to paraphrase Grigsby. From the courtesan as the "sign" and "product" of colonial hierarchies and their lascivious deconstruction, we move to her role as a narrative voice of the singular relations with which a whole society was identified. (Authorial mechanisms are suggested by contemporary commentators, but elude documentation, as do the dates of the composition of most of the texts I will analyze here, although the Revolutionary and post-Revolutionary window of their *collection* is verifiable.)

Popular Creole texts in which female voices narrate tensions around libertine activity are a rare early inscription of the experiences or perspectives of non-white women in slave-holding societies. They manifest what even colonists at the time, like Hilliard d'Auberteuil in the opening quote above, noted was a form of "empire" or power over white men. The "danger" presented by the *mulâtresse* to "the colony's social hierarchy and hence, to the stability of the slave regime," as Yvonne Fabella observes, lay in their provocative challenges to both "racial *and* gender hierarchy."[11] This literary corpus also reveals the tensions among different groups and classes of women at least as much as between women and men, however. For Thavolia Glymph, if the domestic sphere was a site of power for women, "it was also and therefore a struggle *between* women."[12] The rivalry between white and non-white women for the attentions of men in libertine societies was a potent force, and Girod-Chantrans, in Belleau's summary, traced white women's cruelty to their exclusion from the sphere of socially permissible interracial unions.[13]

The "courtesan poetry" analyzed in this chapter is, like the political texts analyzed in the first part of this book, another literary inscription of the process of unbecoming slaves, of discovering a public space of choice and power negotiations around the politics not of colony or nation, but shared bodies and affect. Their politics are of a different sort, aligned with Gayle Rubin's enduring comment that "Sex is always political. But there are also historical periods in which sexuality is more sharply contested and more overtly politicized. In such periods, the domain of erotic life is, in effect, renegotiated."[14] In the historical period of late colonial Saint-Domingue and the Haitian Revolution, the interracial renegotiations of the field of capital had profoundly unsettled the hierarchies of colonial identity—even as they also fragmented the field of revolutionary revindications.

The "tragic mulatta" figure critiqued by Sterling Brown in 1933 as a "woebegone abstraction"[15] is supplanted in this small collection of poems by the courtesan as a resilient and strategic evaluator of the social and economic fields, defending libertine entrepreneurial praxis, promoting her own charms and savvy, and "battling" rivals in wars of words reminiscent of rap.

Indigo Blues: Courtesan Diversity

The frequently re-adapted poem "Lisette quitté la plaine" is, by its lyrical concerns with the complexities of amorous relations, exemplary of a popular sentimental genre sung by *cocottes* or female "mulatto entertainers" to their mistresses in colonial Saint-Domingue, as Perry Arthur Williams notes.[16] The combined linguistic and seductive powers of the *cocottes* rival those of the Candios. Pierre de Vaissière, who like Williams is quoting the bulk of his evidence from the unpublished *Notes historiques* of Moreau de Saint-Méry, provides more detail on the tantalizing category of the *cocotte*, such as the astonishing degree of cultural and familial entanglement between the class of mistresses, the class of *mulattas*, and the class of female slaves:

> Dès lors, plus que toutes autres, elles [les maîtresses] sont fatalement livrées à cette influence noire dont j'ai dit les pernicieux effets. Avec leurs négresses domestiques ces femmes vivent sur le pied de la plus étrange familiarité. [...] La cocote est la confidente de toutes les pensées de sa maîtresse (et cette confiance est quelquefois réciproque), confidente surtout de ses amours. On ne quitte pas la cocotte; on couche dans la même chambre, on mange et boit avec elle, non à table ou aux repas, mais au moment où l'on savoure ces ragouts créoles, où la familiarité semble mêler un sel de plus, dans les endroits privilégiés et loin de la vue des hommes.[17]

> (From then on, more than anyone else, they [the mistresses] are fatally given over to this black influence and its pernicious effects. With their domestic negresses these women live on the basis of a most peculiar familiarity. [...] The cocote is the confidant of all the mistress's thoughts (and sometimes this confidence is reciprocal), above all concerning her love life. They never leave the cocote; they sleep in the same room with her, eat and drink with her, not at the table during meals, but at those moments when they savor those creole stews, to which familiarity adds spice, in the privileged quarters of the house and far from the eyes of men.)

In this interracial domestic environment, women from radically different positions in the socio-racial hierarchy shared Creole songs.

Often, as noted in the introduction, they shared much more than Creole songs: the very young *cocotte*, who might be mulatto or black, was sometimes the mistress (in the sense of lover) of the husband (or another male relative) of the mistress of the house. Moreau describes, under the rubric "Cocotes, gens de couleur" ("Cocottes, people of color"), the contradictions and tensions associated with this often double role of the *cocottes* as libertine associates to a male in the household and companions/entertainers to the women, as well as intermediaries in the white women's own libertine adventures. Moreau also states that the sharing of beds was a "dangerous condescension" on the part of "des personnes coupables" ("guilty persons"), a clear insinuation that the "teaching" relationship of the *cocotte* to her mistress could involve amorous intimacy between women of different races. His description of a pervasive antipathy between the different classes of women is belied by this account of the profound intimacy in which they lived; or rather, it challenges one to imagine a context in which a generally professed disrespect and dislike for courtesans on the part of white women masked interdependent social lives, and sometimes deep personal involvement, only to flare up around latent personal conflicts.

> Les femmes blanches ont, en effet un grand éloignement aux colonies pour les femmes de couleur, dont elles imitent apparemment les manières voluptueuses et dont elle font quelquefois leur institutrices en lascivité […] En effet, presque chacune d'elles à une jeune mulâtresse une quarteronne et quelquefois même une jeune négresse dont elle fait sa *cocote* […] C'est de cette entourage de femmes de couleur, dont les unes sont quelquefois les maîtresses de leurs maris, de leurs frères ou de leurs fils, que les créoles attendent le plus souvent toutes leurs distractions.[18]

> (White women in the colonies have a great disaffection for the women of color, whose voluptuous manners they nevertheless imitate, sometimes going so far as to make them their tutors in lasciviousness. […] In effect, nearly everyone of them has a young mulatta, a quadroon, or sometimes even a young negress serving as her *cocotte* […] It is from this entourage of women of color, some of whom are the mistress of their husbands, brothers, or sons, that the creole women generally derive their leisure amusements.)

White women's "amusements" were the Creole lyrics about the same amorous world that haunted the women's mutual dependence.

Moreau distinguishes the *cocotte* from the figure of the non-white *ménagère* or domestic manager, who was often a mistress integrated into the colonist's household. The *ménagères* "live with a white, in whose household, under the rather ill-fitted name of *manager*, they have all the functions of a spouse, without being necessarily inclined to assume the responsibilities of such a position."[19] As Laurent Dubois points out, Moreau spoke from experience; he had had a *ménagère*, Marie-Louise Laplaine, to whom he allocated money and slaves just before his eventual marriage to a white woman.[20] The enslaved mother of the French general Alexandre Dumas was another example of a *ménagère*.[21] The *ménagère* may normally have been older than the *cocotte*, and generally served a single man.

The *cocotte* likewise contrasts with the courtesan, despite the overlap in libertine occupations, because the courtesans "have their own lodging."[22] As independent city inhabitants, the courtesans formed, in Belleau's words, a core of the "urban bourgeoisie" of Saint-Domingue.[23] Moreau contextualizes courtesan status as a "necessary evil" to which mulattas, and also female slaves, are often "condemned," despite the social and moral ills of this "illegitimate commerce."[24] Courtesans had many different class positions, from vulnerable prostitutes to wealthy celebrities, as did their European counterparts, based on their renown, familial standing, and other factors.

The courtesans' activities were high-profile affairs. In the *Description de Saint-Domingue*, Moreau asserted that "la plus grande publicité accompagne leurs actions"[25] ("great publicity surrounds their every action"). This is documented in his *Notes* by anonymous poems, in various people's handwriting, about the role of courtesans in the civic arena of Saint-Domingue. A poem called "Chanson pour les Mullatresses [*sic*] du Cap" ("Song for the Mulattas of Le Cap") satirizes the courtesans' dismay at police action, possibly police enforcement of legislation (prompted by the jealousy of white women) forbidding courtesans to wear certain articles of clothing:[26]

> D'où vient donc la tristesse
> Des pauvres mulâtresses   bis
> Elles gémissent sans cesse
> Et soupirent tout bas ah ah
> La police traîtresse
> Avec impollitesse
> Leur coupe au ras des fesses
> Rubans et falbalas ah ah[27]

> (Whence this melancholy
> Of our poor mulattas   [refrain]
> How they groan
> And sigh and moan oh oh
> The treacherous police
> With consummate impoliteness
> Have trimmed their ribbons, frills and flounces
> To the level of their bottoms oh oh)

In this fascinating long poem, a key is given at the bottom of the page, identifying by their full names the courtesans mentioned only by surname in the stanzas. For example, among the mulattas "pleurant à la journée / négligeant leur appas" ("crying all day long, / neglecting their charms"), "on reconnaît à peine / la belle Madelaine" ("you would hardly recognize the lovely Madelaine"); in the key, Madelaine is identified as "Madelaine Coudoyan."

This celebrity status was to some degree transferable to metropolitan environments, if we can believe an account by Roger de Beauvoir in his 1856 *Aventurières et courtisanes*. This book, devoted primarily to French courtesans, recounts the eighteenth-century anecdote of "la belle Isabeau" (also called "la Duthé[28] de Saint-Domingue"), a "mulâtresse du Cap, qui faisait alors grand bruit à Paris"[29] ("a *mulâtresse* from the Cap, who made a great splash in Paris"). She was welcomed into the company of the court in Versailles and treated with kind condescension by a particularly famous courtesan, the *maîtresse-en-titre* of Louis XV, Madame DuBarry.

Moreau was intrigued by local justifications of the courtesan's trade, however, not only in terms of the effects of the "torrid" climate on white male physiology and psychology, but in terms of women's acculturation also. He points out that female slaves were in many cases accustomed to a culture of polygamy (recast in a different form in Saint-Domingue, as simultaneous polygamy and polyandry), and that they could make a better life for themselves and their children through their libertine commerce with whites. As for the mulattas, too distant from Africa to be directly conditioned by its marital customs, concubinage provided them with both freedom and pleasures. Moreau implies that libertinage gave them not only freedom from slavery or work on plantations, but also freedom from the constraints of marriage: "Tout porte les femmes de couleur à fuir le mariage et à se livrer à ce concubinage lucratif, qui satisfait mieux leurs inclinations voluptueuses, et auquel elles doivent leur liberté"[30] ("Everything leads women of color to flee the route of marriage and give themselves over to lucrative concubinage, which better satisfies their voluptuous inclinations, and gives them their freedom"). In effect, in Moreau's description, courtesans were condemned to their chosen liberty.

Moreau's fellow citizens were concerned about his *exposé* of libertine culture. He preserved in his notes a homely "Epigram" "To Mr. Moreau de St. Méry, on the occasion of an essay he plans to write on the social mores of Saint-Domingue." The text is an important trace of pressures exerted against the publication of texts on libertinage. (It also shows the range of degrees of literacy, and perhaps some variety of dialect, in French at the time.)

Epigramme

A m. Moreau de St. Méry, à l'occasion d'un essay sur les moeurs de St. Domingue qu'il projette

Vous qui rendes nos loix à la lumière
Gardés vous bien d'y produire nos moeurs;
Non que n'ayés le talent nécéssaire,
Mais le pouvés mieux employer ailleurs.
Las! Nous avons si peu de bonnes ames,
Qu'un people entier est en butte à vos traits;
Et que surtout vous allés à jamais
Déshonorer nos plus honnestes femmes.[31]

(Epigram

To Mr. Moreau de St. Méry, on the occasion of an essay he plans to write
on the social mores of Saint-Domingue

You who bring our laws to light
Should be careful about reproducing our mores;
Not that you lack the necessary talent,
But you could use it better elsewhere.
Alas! We have so few good souls,
That an entire people is the butt of your observations;
And above all you will forever
Dishonor our most honorable women.)

The "chansons créoles" ("Creole songs") scattered here and there in
Moreau's *Notes historiques*, and also quite clearly represented in the *Idylles et
chansons* discussed in Chapter 7, seem to be either examples of the *cocotte*'s
verbal arts, or texts from the city life of courtesans. In effect, the work of
courtesans in the colonial era was divided between the city, where they lived
quite independently, and the *habitations* or plantations; the lyrical songs I
will analyze in the different sections of the following literary analysis reflect
this duality of the *cocotte* or the courtesans' respective libertine situations.

A good starting place for this corpus is the song (previously mentioned
in the introduction) narrated by a courtesan explaining the dynamics of the
sexual market to a less experienced—and recalcitrant—younger colleague.
There are two versions of this song in Moreau's *Notes historiques* (partially
cited by François Girod[32]); one is written in Moreau's hand (which I will
refer to, in order to be able to distinguish the two texts, as "Na rien qui
dous"), and the other in an unknown hand (which I will refer to as "Zabet").
"N'a rien qui dous" seems to be based on a textual fragment—a small piece
of paper with the first words of several verses—in the same unknown hand
responsible for transcribing the "Zabet" text, as if Moreau had asked for
a knowledgeable source to help in reconstituting a known song. These
documents collectively point strongly to an oral tradition known by persons
capable of helping Moreau to assemble notes on the corpus—and to potential
imperfections in the accuracy of the transcriptions.

Although prior to my readings, this key element of the text had remained
unidentified, both versions use, as a symbolic model for the discussion of
libertine economies, the indigo plantations on Saint-Domingue, where
indigo plants were grown for use in the distillation of dyes in the workshops.
Abundant water was necessary for the cultivation and processing of indigo,
and the poems compare the water required by indigo planters (colonists) to
the money and financial transactions necessary to the successful cultivation

of libertine independence. The courtesan's work in the city is contextualized as being on an entirely different plane from the labors of the *indigoterice*, the female worker (presumably always a slave) on the indigo plantation. The poem thus suggests a kind of transition from the status of laborer to a more entrepreneurial career, in which resources are mustered from a position of the master's "natural" needs.

In "Na rien qui dous," the narrator discusses the conditions of a courtesan's life. It is pretty sweet life, she asserts, almost as sweet as a procurer's life, even if procurers take away much of what is rightfully theirs. Since plantation managers and various administrative authorities were also known as "procurers" in Saint-Domingue, the narrator could thus complain of exploitation by procurers—meaning pimps—in a discourse veiled as the problem of the exploitation of enslaved plantation workers.

> Na rien qui dous tant comme la ville!
> Vini bouger coté moin[s],
> N y en a dans morne, ma chere!
> Azinque deux métiers qui doux.
> Sila procureur yo fait l'ote la ce quin à nous.

> (Nothing is as sweet as the city!
> Come over here by me,
> There is nothing this good in the countryside, my dear!
> Likewise, there are two trades that are sweet.
> The procurer takes away what is properly ours.)

Contrasting with the courtesans and procurers in their cushy jobs is the poor female indigo worker, the *indigoterice*, who, when she does not have rain for her industrial processes, must "roulé" ("roll") continuously. What element of the indigo cultivation and processing sequence yields the activity signaled by this motif of "rolling"? "The most ordinary method for preparing indigo consists in steeping the plants, especially the leaves, in water, running off the infusion, and allowing it to ferment without contact with air, then precipitating it by means of agitation with air," recounts an 1881 *New York Times* article on "Old Indigo and the New (History of the One and the Nature of the Other." In factory contexts, the indigo was placed in "large vats of water," with a ratio of "one volume of leaves to six of water," and after a standing period of ten hours, the liquid is "agitated by the paddles of 10 to 12 natives for about two hours." Something related to the agitation of the fermented liquid with paddles is likely the onerous activity referred to in this poem, and in "Zabet," as "rolling." However, given the reference to shortages of water, it could also be that if there was not enough standing water, the leaves had to be agitated in some way during the fermentation process. Indigo is likely to have been a particularly visceral example of hardships contrasting with the life of the courtesan because it does not smell good; in addition to "true blue" staining, workers may have been identifiable by the odor peculiar to their trade.

> Tous digoteris qui sans la pluie
> Yo roulé toujour sencése... (bis)

> (Any indigo worker who doesn't have rain
> They roll without cease... [refrain])

The narrator's young interlocutrice in the poem apparently had given away her love for free, a serious taboo. How, the older courtesan protests, does she expect to gain status? The market of women is psychological: thus, to be valued, one must first make others pay. Making whites pay should be easy, the advisor contends. And the psychology of payment for valuable services actually protects women, she points out, since without it, they risk being beaten ("raussé," "rossé")—whether by procurers or clients is not specified.

> Comment toi vlé gagner cote?
> Si tos pas gagner largent
> Yo vas dit, femme la li sotte
> Li pas connait fair paiyer blanc
> Femme qui sote cé comme sa yo fair
> Yo raussé yo, sa fait nou piquié
> Comment toi vlé gagner côte
> Si tos pas gagne[r] largent?
> Yo vas dis femme la li sôte
> Li pas connait fai paiye[r] blanc[33]   fin

> (How do you expect to gain status?
> If you don't earn money
> They will say that woman there is an idiot
> She doesn't know how to make whites pay
> Women who are idiots, that's what they do
> They [men] beat them, which makes us pity them
> How do you expect to gain status
> If you don't earn money?
> They will say that woman there is an idiot
> She doesn't know how to make whites pay)

In the second version of this song in the *Notes historiques*, "Zabet," there are fewer details given on the financial and social mechanisms of prostitution-like libertine activity, and more details on the liminal social lives of courtesans in a more refined class context. The narrator here gives her advice to Zabette, who has not caught on that she should give up her own lover and take on a generous and rich lover. The term used in this poem to describe lovers, "dombo," seems to be of African provenance.[34] It was cited by Justin de Girod-Chantrans in his 1785 *Voyage of a Swiss*, in the context of a Creole lamentation of a female slave to her lover, whom she calls her "dear dombo," that she had not chosen to be unfaithful to him but had been raped by Zéphir.[35] Ducoeurjoly defined it as the Creole term for a concubine or lover, of either sex, with this example: "C'est dombo à ly"[36] ("It's his/her lover"). The use of the term, like the use of the term "Candio" in "Lisette" and *Jeannot et Thérèse*, signals the lexical field of the non-white world, and the hybrid ethnic and cultural world of the courtesans.

The narrator gives an example of how to "make whites pay": by the gift of a "Portuguese," a colonial coin valued at approximately ten *livres*. The work of the courtesan, which here is identified in a triumphal sense as the "rolling" disparaged in relation to indigo in "Na rien qui dous," is legitimated through analogy with planters' needs:

N'a pas-sé Zabet ma chere
Prend-Dombo pour samitié
Fille qui sotte comme ça y a faire
Aussi y-a faits nous pitié
Comment to vlé gagner cotte
Si to pas gagné d'argent
Yo va dire Zabet la sotte
Qui pa conné faire payé blanc

(It is not enough Zabet my dear
To take a Dombo for friendship
That's what the stupid girls do
And so we pity them
How do you expect to gain status
If you don't make money
They will say Zabet is an idiot
Who doesn't know how to make whites pay)

To take a lover for love is to court abandonment, she chides. If she is left by her stingy lover, she will be no better than an *indigoterice*, an indigo worker.

Faut prend gnion dombo qui riche
Qui ba toy tout ça to vlé
Car si quine a moy-te chiche
Ben vite nous cété brouillé

Quand mo vlé yon portugaise
Tout suite li couri bas moy
To resté la tant comme gnion niaise
Bandonné! Di go te ris a toy

(You have to take a lover who is rich
Who will give you everything you want
If a lover of mine was stingy
It would be over between us very fast
When I want a Portuguese
He runs to get it for me
You are sitting there like a ninny
Abandoned! You indigo worker, you)

The courtesan's need for money is no different from the need of indigo workers and planters for water, she implies. But where the planters are dependent on the elements, the courtesans have a much more reliable resource at their disposal: themselves. As long as they proceed intelligently, they will never be in drought. "Just roll like me," she urges the young courtesan; "you will have everything you want." "Rolling" here has clearly transitioned from a verb describing onerous activity in indigo processing to a verb with gleefully masterful and illicit connotations.

Tout digoterie sans la pluye
Pa gagné gnion brin digo
Tout sabitant san chource
Criée sech pour canne a yo
Nous gnioune pas gagné misere
Pis-que nous toujours pres roulé
Roulé tant comme moy ma chere
To va gagner tout ça to vlé[37]

(An indigo farm without rain
Will not make a drop of indigo.
Colonists without wells
Cry that it is dry for their sugar cane.
[But] we are not going to live in [such] misery
Because we're always ready to roll;
Roll like me, my dear;
You will have everything you want.)

These two poetic texts are quite remarkable in their detailed defense of what Moreau had conventionally described as the courtesans' "illegitimate commerce."

In contrast with the savvy *mulâtresse's* confidence, however, other songs underscore the affective and sensual bonds between the mistress and her lover, and the sadness of being replaced. The courtesans' indigo blues were sometimes the stain of despair:

Comment, vous quite moin[s] comme ca?
Songe[z] zamis! Na point tans comme moins,
Femme qui jolie.
Vous connai[s] moins gagner tous plains talens qui dous;
Sila vous vas prend—li pale bon pour vous,
Vou va regretté moins toujours.[38]   (bis) fin

(What, you're leaving me, just like that?
Think about it friend! There is no woman out there
As pretty as I am.
You know I have many sweet talents;
The one you are taking on—she will not be good for you,
And you will regret me always. [refrain]   End)

A Poetry of Tight Corners: The Cocotte

Returning to the domestic space and cast of characters of the plantation and the more "junior" (and perhaps fairly privileged) female companion, the *cocotte*, we find that rather than championing her libertine activity, the *cocotte* has a tightrope to walk. Like the Candio, the *cocotte* is in a position of almost unimaginable social hybridity. The slave who was a "little master" resists classification as much as the female troubadour, black or mulatto, singing to the mistress with whom she might have been in sexual competition. In the anonymous Creole anthology the *Idylles et chansons*, published both in 1804 and 1811 in the U.S., one poem features an extended lyrical dialogue between an *habitant* (planter) and the young girl who tends to his wife. The planter defends his desire, and the *cocotte* at least initially defends her fidelity to his wife.

In the poem, a man named Mozyre, apparently the master of a property, laments having introduced his lover, Louloute, probably a *mulâtresse*, into his home in the role of companion and servant to his wife, Melanie. Melanie is clearly conscious of the threat posed by this young rival, and keeps Louloute busy fanning her and chatting. Mozyre has virtually no access to Louloute thanks to Melanie's jealous domination of the young woman's time. Complicating the situation further, Melanie is Louloute's godmother. From a contemporary perspective, the idea of a white mistress serving as godmother to a woman of color in the colonial era can seem surprising, but people of color working in colonial households were often related to their white masters. In a nineteenth-century Louisiana novel by Alfred Mercier, an author sufficiently conscious of the colonial heritage of Saint-Domingue to include within the novel a variation on the poem "Lisette quitté la plaine," we find an evocation of this custom of white masters serving as godparents to the children of house slaves, some of whom were the offspring of various white males in the household.[39]

In the first of the two poems, Mozyre expresses his frustration at seeing his mistress become his wife's *cocotte*. In the colonial era, the local Creole spoken in Saint-Domingue retained the French distinction between "tu" and "vous" forms in the second person, a distinction which later disappeared in Haitian *Kreyòl*. Colonial documents show whites using the Creole equivalent of the more informal "tu" form to address blacks or persons of mixed race, whereas the latter used the formal "vous" in dialogue with whites. Here Mozyre uses the "tu" form with Louloute, who responds with "vous," demonstrating her consciousness of his superior social rank.

Idyll III

Dan caye-moi ça to te vini faire!
Bond-ié, pour qui Mélanie hélé toi!
Mo té bén di, cé pour gagné misére;
Dampui jour lá to trop chagriné moi.

(What is it that you have come to do here in my house!
My God, why is Melanie calling you!
I told you truly that this would compound our misery;
From the day you came here you have grieved me too much.]

Gié-moi partout io suivre toi dan caye;
Si to parlé toujour m'apré 'couté :
Tan ça to fai baï Mamsél l'embraye,
Tan ça to di fai quior-moi 'pré sauté....

(My eyes follow you everywhere in the house;
When you speak, I am always listening:
Like the gestures you use to give Mamzel shade,
What you say keeps my heart pumping...)

Si to vini quand moi gnon dan la salle,
Sitôt li là pour tendé ça nous di.
Li bén conné çaça ié gnon rivale,
Et bel gié toi doi faire li frémi...

(If you come into a room when I am in it,
Immediately she is there too to catch what we say.

She knows very well what a rival is,
And your beautiful eyes must make her tremble…)

Li pa v'lé baï monde à connaitre,
Mai mo bén sur li té voudré caché
Ca malgré toi mouchoir laissé paraitre…
Et que gié moi toujour conné cherché.

(She doesn't want to let anyone else know this,
But I'm quite sure she would like to hide
What your bodice reveals despite that kerchief…
And which my eyes can always make out.)

Ahd-ié, Zami, cé gnon tro gran contrainte;
Allé plitôt; nou va toujour contré;
Ca mo senti mo va dir-li san crainte,
Ca to caché to va capab' montré.

(Good Lord, friend, this is too great a constraint;
Go, rather than this; we will always find ways to meet;
Then I will say what I feel without fear,
And you will be able to show what you hide.)

Mais ça moi di! Non, n'a pa 'lé Louloute;
Si to parti gié moi va trop crié.
Tan comme moi to doi souffri san doute;
Mai gnon instant peu faire tout 'blié…

(But what am I saying! No, don't go, Louloute;
If you leave my eyes will cry too much.
You must be suffering as much as I am;
But a brief moment could make us forget all this…)

Guêté moment Mamsél allé la messe;
Guêté moment tout monde apré filé :
Ca io volor avec un peu d'adresse
Vau passé ça io prend quon io v'lé.[40]

(Watch for the moment when Mamzel goes to mass;
Watch for the moment when everyone is leaving;
That which one can steal with a little skill
Is worth more than what one can take at will.)

In the beginning of the second poem in this series, "Croux marraine" ("On My Godmother's Grave"), Mozyre reacts with anger and astonishment at Louloute's rejection of his libertine argument. Louloute defends her relationship with her godmother, and Mozyre mocks her for her naïve trust in the power of that relationship to protect her from Melanie's jealous vengeance. Finally, Louloute promises to yield to his seduction, and in order to prove her sincerity, swears on the cross on her godmother's grave.

Croux marraine ("On My Godmother's Grave")
Idyll IV
Mozyre and Louloute

Mozyre

Qui ça to di?... Mo pa capab' craire
Parole-là sorti dan bouchi toi.
Comment, Zami, malgré tout ça mo faire,
To di comça que to pa 'le ba moi ?...

(What are you saying?... I can't believe
Those words came out of your mouth.
How can it be, friend, after everything I have done,
That you say, just like that, that you're not going to give me?...)

Louloute

Ahd-iè! Mouché, vou fai moi trop la peine!
Io pa jamai voir gnon choye comça :
Vou pa conné Mamsél cé Marraine?...
Travail cilà ça pa travail...

(My God! Sir, you're causing me too much pain!
They will never see things like that:
Don't you know that Mamzel is my godmother?...
That kind of work is not work.)

Mozyre

    haba!
T'apré joué; tout ça cé gnon vié conte.
Es que to peur batême là gâté?
To va bén dup' si to v'lé couté
Tout ça io di pour ba toi mauvai honte.
To pa conné tout cé Marraine là
Coutumé fair leurs embarra
Côté Filleul', côté Commère,
Parce que io pa gan' pour plaire
Ca jeune fie peu gagné.

(Bah!
You must be joking: all that is an old wives' tale.
Are you afraid your baptism will be spoiled?
You'll be duped if you listen
To what they say to give you false shame.
You know the things that godmothers
Are in the habit of doing to cause trouble
For goddaughters, for best friends,
Because they can't please
The way young girls do.)

    Louloute

Ca pa li que mo doi craigné ?
Qui monde encor...

(Maybe she isn't the one I should fear?
Let's see, who else...)

    Mozyre

    To fé la Sage!
Ca to va faire quan t'a vié?
Laissé là tout ce radotage;
Quan io jeun' com'toi, quan io gagné bel gié,
Io doi quiémbé l'aut' langage.

    (Quite the virtuous performance!
What will you do when you're old?
Drop all this foolish talk;
When you are young, with beautiful eyes,
You should keep to an entirely different kind of language.)

    Louloute

Mo pa gnon bel, mo conné ça mo-ié;
Mo conné-tou ça mo gagné pour faire :
Mo pa v'lé cherché misére :
Ca io va dir si io conné
Que mo vini vou détourné
Côté cila...

(I'm not a beauty, I know what I am;
I know, too, what I have to do:
I'm not looking for trouble:
What will they say if they know

That I have turned you away from her
Like that...)

    Mozyre

To bien peureuse!
Qui cilà qui va soupçonné
Que mo prend toi pour amoureuse?
N'a point personne qui voir nous.
Fau pa comça faire la scrupuleuse.
Es que to pa 'lé plus heureuse
Que mo prend toi plitôt qu'un vié jaloux
Qui va toujour gagné mine boudeuse?

(You're such a scaredy cat!
Who is going to suspect
That I am taking you for a lover?
No one sees us.
Don't pretend you are the scrupulous type.
Wouldn't you be happier
To have me take you than some jealous old man
Who would always be frowning?)

    Louloute

Mo t'a prend vou, si ça pa té pêché.

(I would have you, if it weren't a sin.)

    Mozyre

Astore là to faire la dévote!
Ma foi, Bond-ié va bén souchié
Si to vini sa matelote!
Mai d'abord que to fé la sote,
Conte caba : n'a pas jamai cherché...

(And now you're pretending to be devout!
My faith, as if God really cares
If you become his *matelote*[41] or not!
But since first you are going to be a ninny,
We'll call it quits: I will never seek...)

    Louloute

Ahd-ié, Mouché! Vou pa té doi faché.

Tendre plitôt Mamsél allé la plaine.
M'a 'suré vou...

(Good heavens, Sir! You shouldn't get angry.
Wait instead for Mamzel to leave the plains.
I assure you...)

Mozyre

Mo doi conté sur toi?
Ca va bén sur ça to promettre moi?...
(Can I count on you?
Is it absolutely sure, what you are promising me?...)

Louloute

Oui, mo di vous...

(Yes, I tell you...)

Mozyre

Juré-li...

(Swear it...)

Louloute

Croux marraine!

(By the cross on my godmother's grave!)

The keen insights of the male partner in the dialogue into the potentially false and self-serving nature of conventional morality is counter-balanced by the young *cocotte*'s acute awareness of the safety zones of interracial social structures, in a virtuosic *pas de deux* of libertine consciousness.

The editor of the *Idylles et chansons* apparently saw no incompatibility between the politics of sexuality in courtesan society and the love lyric. Idyll 5 is a lovely little song of tender desire. More aptly, it is a lyric on desire and the poetic process: just as the beloved's kiss is always *something else*, something sweeter than the moisture in the rose, it is also something more than what the beloved gives. In the impossibility of fulfilling desire, the lover discovers the poetic sequence, in which pleasure-turned-to-pain yields "What I say"—poetry—and that is pain-turned-to-pleasure...

A BAGOE

Ca pas baisé mo prend sur bouche toi;
Cé douss sirop, cé miel, cé suc la rose,
Et cependant li gagné l'aut chose
Qui dousse encore passé ça to ba moi...

Baisé cilà pa 'lé jamai suffire;
Quior moi plifort tourmenté dan désir:
Dan ça to baï plaisi tourné martire,
Dans ça mo di... douleur tourné plaisir...

(That is no kiss I take from your lips;
It is sweet syrup, honey, the sap of the rose,
And still it is something else,
Sweeter still than what you give me...

That kiss will never suffice;
My heart is all the more tormented by desire;
In what you give me, pleasure becomes a martyrdom,
In what I say... pain turns into pleasure...)

Lisette Talks Back

As noted in Chapter 7, a considerable part of the early Creole lyrical tradition in Saint-Domingue unfurls in dialogue with the cornerstone "Lisette quitté la plaine." In the Creole version of the Rousseau opera *Le Devin du village, Jeannot et Thérèse*, there is some gender role reversal around "Lisette," reworking the male slave's fear that Lisette will be seduced by the Candios in the city as the female slave's fear that the Candio will himself be seduced by the *mulatta* courtesan in the city. This example in itself shows a striking capacity for flexible identifications and projections in Saint-Domingue's libertine society around the capital represented by desired bodies. The two poems in Moreau's *Notes historiques* organized around the indigo worker analogy also show a sophisticated slippage between ostensibly polar identities, from plantation procurer to procurer as pimp, and from indigo slave to the courtesan claiming equality of needs with the planter. The dialogue between Louloute and Mozyre in the *Idylles et chansons* likewise leaves the listener ping-ponging back and forth between the mental processes of the seductive master and the prudent *cocotte*. The Creole poems and songs scrawled in Moreau's *Notes historiques* include a startling poem that makes a fitting conclusion in this series. It is called "Chanson créole," with a subtitle in French: "Réponse de Lisette à son amant" ("Lisette's Response to Her

Lover"). Given the poem's comically belligerent tone, however, a more apt subtitle might be "Lisette Talks Back."

In this poem, Lisette herself is the narrator, and none too pleased by her lover's infidelities with a woman in town. It is important to note that this poem is one of two very different versions transcribed by Moreau. From the oblique relationships of expressions between the two, and the evidence of erasure and correction, it seems clear that he was struggling to recapture a song from popular verbal culture. The great difficulty of translating this piece may correspond to faulty transcription by Moreau;[42] for that reason, I am limiting my citation to the first two stanzas. What comes through, however, is that this is a poem of "dissing" or "signifying"; Robin D.G. Kelley expands the list to include "capping, sounding, ranking, bagging"[43] as terms for this form of verbal contest, which many ethnographers have equated with "a black male form of ritual insult" with ancient origins. As Kelley argues, however, the notion that "the dozens" is a male genre—a gendered genre—is probably a product of the framing of ethnographic methodologies by gendered expectations: "evidence suggests that young women engaged in these kinds of verbal exchanges as much as their male counterparts, both with men and between women. And they were no less profane."[44] "Lisette Talks Back" would seem to be the earliest example of female-narrated dissing in the New World African diaspora.

Quand to allé à la ville
To mété chapeau carré
Pendant quior moin dans tristesse
To va songé pour vanté.
Si to rencontre la belle
To va fair' yé doux pour li,
Pis' to trouvé li si belle
He bin! To na qua prend li.[45]

(When you go to the city
You put on your fancy square hat
While my heart is mired in sadness
You are all about showing off.
If you meet the beauty
You will make eyes at her,
Since you find her so beautiful
Well then! Go get her.)

Taille à li semblé gaulette
Visage li semblé moineau
Li maigre com' bois cot'lette
Bonda li c'est paquet zos.

Li pas teni dents dans bouche
Tété li c'est blan cochon
Gié à li magner' louche
li bête passé mouton.

(She is like a beanpole,
Her face is like a plain sparrow's
She is thin as a Cutlet tree[46]
Her butt is no more than a packet of bones.
She has not a tooth in her mouth,
Her tits are like the sugar cane trash we feed the pigs,
She is cross-eyed,
And dumber than a sheep.)

By contrast, Lisette herself has apple-red lips ("Lèv à moin rouge tant com' pomme"), white teeth ("Dentz mon blanc"), lovely manners ("belle magner") and she sings like a bird: "Mon chanté tant com zozo." Her breasts jiggle and stand upright: "Teté moins bougé debout," and she has claims—unfortunately illegible—to make about her "bounda" (behind) too. "I don't seem to be lacking *candios*" ("Mon pas lé manqué *canguio*"), she reminds him, and, obliquely, "mon gagné canal / D'yo pas lé manqué li" ("I have a canal / And no shortage of water for it"). Memorable Lisette! Speaking so powerfully on her own behalf, she makes it impossible to imagine an early black Atlantic sphere without a vigorous tradition of female popular verbal arts.

This same spirit passed on to New Orleans, where the freed man of color Camille Thierry transcribed the Creole "Lament of an Aged Mulatta" that seems to leap onto the page as recorded speech. The narrator remembers libertine Saint-Domingue with resounding nostalgia.

Regrets d'une vieille mulâtresse
Ou
Le Désespoir de Sanite Fouéron

Miré! Quand mon té Saint-Domingue,
Négresses même té bijoux;
Blancs layo té semblé seringue,
Yo té collé derrière à nous.
Dans yon ménage
Jamain tapage,
L'amour yon blanc, c'était l'adoration!
Yo pa té chiches,
Yo té bien riches,
Yon bon bounda té vaut yon bitation!...
Temps-là changé, nous sur la paille,

Nous que z'habitants té fèté...
Avant longtemps yon blanc pété
Va hélé nous canaille!!![47]

(Listen! When I was in Saint-Domingue,
Negresses were just like jewels;
The whites there were ninnies,[48]
They were always after us.
In a household,
Never any fighting,
The love of a white meant adoration!
They weren't stingy,
They were very rich,
A good ass was worth a plantation!
Times have changed, we are sleeping on straw,
We, whom the planters celebrated...
Before long a lower-class white
Will be calling us riff raff!)

The power of the "bounda" had been enough to rearrange hierarchies, she asserts, giving women a kind of economic power normally associated with colonists' status. And in fact the end of the poem, with its scathing reference to "blans petés," *petits blancs*, lower-class whites, stands as a challenge to white supremacy. It is an important marker of a libertine ideology in which race was not the same thing as class, and the racially unempowered could move into empowered class space. The sexual politics of courtesan poetry in late colonial Saint-Domingue and early independent Haiti speak above all to this unexpected chance to change places, to unbecome what one had never consented to be. These sexual politics are fraught with internal violence, deceit, and trauma, and threaten to nullify identity-based group political revindications—and yet they yield a fluidity of identification that is at the heart of metaphor. Haitian courtesan poetry makes that metaphorical power a property of Creole, and Creole poetry a form that, along with the Anglophone slave narrative and francophone political proclamations, distinguishes early black Atlantic literary history.

Notes

1. Michel René Hilliard d'Auberteuil, *Considérations sur l'état présent de la colonie française de Saint-Domingue* (Paris: Grangé, 1776).
2. Frederick Engels, *The Origin of the Family, Private Property, and the State*, ed. Eleanor Leacock (New York: International Publishers, 1972), 71–72.
3. This iconic status brought with it considerable mythification, with the *mulâtresse* representing the libertine courtesan, whereas women of mixed race were certainly

not always courtesans, and courtesans were black as well as of mixed race. Representations of the ethnic or racial identity of courtesans as a demographic are based on colonial ethnographic syntheses, not on detailed sociological examination of data: it is certainly not impossible that some white women were essentially living off courtesan activity, without being characterized as courtesans. The issue of homosexual libertine activity in Saint-Domingue remains, to my knowledge, veiled, although it is hard to imagine that a libertine society did not involve same-sex activity, within master–slave relations as well as within the market for sexual services; future research may well challenge conclusions like this one by David Geggus: "[Women's] slavery thus had a psychophysical dimension that male slaves did not experience, so far as is known" ("Slave and Free Colored Women in Saint Domingue," in *More than Chattel: Black Women and Slavery in the Americas*, ed. David Barry Gaspar and Darlene Clark Hine [Bloomington, IN: Indiana University Press, 1996], 265). Sexualized torture practices in slave punishments are a particularly accessible axis for future research on this conundrum.

4. Darcy Grimaldo Grigsby, *Extremities: Painting Empire in Post-Revolutionary France* (New Haven, CT: Yale University Press, 2002), 266.

5. Doris Garraway, *The Libertine Colony: Creolization in the Early French Caribbean* (Durham, NC: Duke University Press, 2005), 1.

6. Geggus, "Slave and Free Colored Women in Saint Domingue," 265.

7. Antoine Métral, *Histoire de l'expédition de Saint-Domingue sous le Consulat de Napoléon Bonaparte* (Paris: Fanjat aîné, 1825), 16.

8. Geggus, "Slave and Free Colored Women in Saint Domingue," 265.

9. *More than Chattel: Black Women and Slavery in the Americas*, ed. David Barry Gaspar and Darlene Clark Hine (Bloomington, IN: Indiana University Press, 1996), xi.

10. Cited in Jean-Philippe Belleau, "Ethnographic Voices in Eighteenth-Century Haiti," in *The Anthropology of the Enlightenment*, ed. Larry Wolff and Marco Cipolloni (Stanford, CA: Stanford University Press, 2007), 236.

11. Yvonne Fabella, "'An Empire Founded on Libertinage': The *Mulâtresse* and Colonial Anxiety in Saint Domingue," in *Gender, Race, and Religion in the Colonization of the Americas*, ed. Nora E. Jaffary (London: Ashgate Publishing, 2007), 112, 113.

12. Thavolia Glymph, *Out of the House of Bondage: The Transformation of the Plantation Household* (London: Cambridge University Press, 2008), 20.

13. Belleau, "Ethnographic Voices," 236.

14. Gayle S. Rubin, "Thinking Sex: Notes for a Radical Theory of the Politics of Sexuality," in *Culture, Society and Sexuality: a Reader*, ed. Richard Guy Parker and Peter Aggleton (New York: Routledge, 1999), 143.

15. Cited by Werner Sollors, *Neither Black Nor White But Both: Thematic Explorations of Interracial Literature* (Cambridge, MA: Harvard University Press, 1999), 224.

16. Perry Arthur Williams, "La Fontaine in Haitian Creole: A Study of *Cric? Crac!* by Georges Sylvain" (unpublished Ph.D. thesis, Fordham University, 1972), 29.

17. Pierre de Vaissière, *Saint-Domingue: La Société et la vie créoles sous l'ancien régime (1629–1789)* (Paris: Perrin et Cie, 1909), 314.

18. Moreau de Saint-Méry, *Notes historiques*, Archives d'Outre-mer, F3, vol. 139, 33.

19. M. L. E. Moreau de Saint-Méry, *Description topographique, physique, civile, politique et historique de la partie française de l'isle Saint-Domingue* (Philadelphia: Chez l'auteur, 1797) 1:94.

20. Laurent Dubois, *Avengers of the New World: The Story of the Haitian Revolution* (Cambridge: MA: Harvard University Press, 2004), 68.

21. Claude Ribbe explains the status of Dumas' mother: "C'est la maîtresse d'Antoine, sa ménagère. Rien d'étonnant à cela. La plupart des Blancs de l'île en ont une, même ceux qui ont amené leur épouse de France ou qui ont épousé une Blanche créole, c'est-à-dire, née sur l'île. Ils leur imposent leur ménagère et n'hésitent pas à s'afficher avec elle, ce qui est une dure épreuve pour la moins jalouse des femmes." ("She was Antoine's mistress, his manager. There was nothing unusual in that. Most of the whites on the island had one, even those who had brought their spouses from France or who had married a creole white woman, meaning a woman who was born on the island. White men imposed the managers on their spouses and did not hesitate to be open about their relationships, which severely tested even the least jealous of women.") *Alexandre Dumas: le dragon de la reine* (Monaco: Editions du Rocher, 2002), 12.

22. Moreau de Saint-Méry, *Description de Saint-Domingue*, 1:106.

23. Belleau, "Ethnographic Voices," 235.

24. Moreau de Saint-Méry, *Description de Saint-Domingue*, 1:106.

25. Moreau de Saint-Méry, *Description de Saint-Domingue*, 1:106.

26. [Colin] Joan Dayan discusses interracial tension around fashion dominance in *Haiti, History, and the Gods* (Berkeley, CA: University of California Press, 1995), 178–80.

27. M. L. E. Moreau de Saint-Méry, « Chanson pour les mullatresses du Cap », *Notes historiques*, Archives d'Outre-mer, F3, vol. 141 *bis*, 333–4.

28. The famous eighteenth-century courtesan known as la Duthé was described in numerous literary works, such as Edmond de Goncourt's *La Maison d'un artiste* (Paris: Flammarion, 1880), 2:49–50.

29. Roger de Beauvoir, *Aventurières et courtisanes* (Paris: Michel Lévy, Frères, 1856), 81.

30. Moreau de Saint-Méry, *Description de Saint-Domingue*, 1:106.

31. M. L. E. Moreau de Saint-Méry, "Epigramme: A m. Moreau de St. Méry, à l'occasion d'un essay sur les moeurs de St. Domingue qu'il projette," *Notes historiques*, Archives d'Outre-mer, F3, vol. 141 *bis*, 336.

32. François Girod, *La Vie quotidienne de la société créole* (Paris: Hachette, 1972), 102. This poem is also translated in abridged form in the indispensable anthology edited by Jean-Claude Bajeux, *Mosochwazi pawòl ki ekri an kreyòl ayisyen (Anthologie de la littérature créole haïtienne)* (Haïti: Éditions Antilia, 1999), 6. Bajeux seems to have used anthologies from the nineteenth and twentieth centuries as sources, rather than the manuscripts of the *Notes historiques*.

33. M. L. E. Moreau de Saint-Méry, « Chansons créoles, » *Notes historiques*, Archives d'Outre-mer, F3, vol. 139, 21–2.

34. I am grateful to Guy Horelle on the Bob Corbett list for the insight that in the *Kreyòl* particular to the Cap Haïtien region, the expression "Neg dombo" still exists and denotes someone especially well versed in social manners, as opposed to usage of the term "Neg Bosal," someone not well versed in social manners. ("Neg Bosal" of course also dates to slave culture, where it was a somewhat pejorative expression for an African-born, rather than creole [Caribbean-born], slave.) The "dombo" is particularly well versed in the art of love. In this sense, "dombo" appears to parallel that other mysterious term found frequently in colonial era

popular poetry, "Candio" or "canguio," as analyzed in Chapter 7. "Dombo" clearly has African origins, and although I cannot pinpoint a precise meaning that might have been transmitted to slave culture in Saint-Domingue, it existed in several forms in the Shona language in Zimbabwe. There was, notably, a Rezvi emperor, Changamire Dombo, also called "Dombo changa," who expelled the Portuguese from Zimbabwe in a successful early anticolonial movement in the seventeenth century. (See for example Peter N. Stearns and William L. Langer, eds., *The Encyclopedia of World History* [New York: Houghton Mifflin Harcourt, 2001], 394.) Guy Horelle notes that the term "Dombo changa," through what may or may not be coincidence with the Zimbabwean leader's name, in Haiti denotes a secret voudou initiation rite associated with Erzulie.

35. Justin Girod-Chantrans, *Voyage d'un Suisse dans les colonies d'Amérique* (Paris: J. Tallandier, 1980), 158.

36. S.-J. Ducoeurjoly, *Manuel des habitants de Saint-Domingue* (Paris: Arthus-Bertrand, 1802/3), 305.

37. Moreau de Saint-Méry, *Notes historiques*, Archives d'Outre-mer, F3, vol. 141 *bis*, 337.

38. Moreau de Saint-Méry, *Notes historiques*, Archives d'Outre-mer, F3, vol. 139, 21.

39. Consider the following dialogue from Mercier's novel: "'This characteristic custom astonishes you; yet it is very natural. These children [of mixed race] are born alongside our own, they share their games; each of them has one of my grandsons for a godfather, or one of my granddaughters as a godmother. They are submissive and loving; it would be impossible not to spoil them.' 'This gives me an entirely different perspective, answered Pélasge; I'm starting to see, between masters and slaves, affective ties that I had not suspected.'" Alfred Mercier, *L'Habitation Saint-Ybars* (Shreveport, LA: Les Cahiers du Tintamarre, 2003), 25.

40. Anonymous, *Idylles, ou essays de poësie créole* (New York: Hopkins and Seymour, 1804), 9–10 and 11–13.

41. In Haiti, a *matelote* is a woman set up in a second household, at times by mutual agreement with the man's first wife.

42. Marie-Christine Hazäel-Massieux, who struggled to assist me in editing this text in my 2005 article in her edited volume, has likewise concluded that this poem "indique bien comment se faisait la transmission orale" ("indicates the operations of oral transmission"). *Textes anciens en créole français de la Caraïbe* (Paris: Editions Publibook, 2008), 98.

43. Robin D. G. Kelley, "Looking for the 'Real' Nigga: Social Scientists Construct the Ghetto," in *That's the Joint! The Hip-Hop Studies Reader*, ed. Murray Forman and Mark Anthony Neal (New York: Routledge, 2004), 127.

44. Kelley, "Looking for the 'Real' Nigga," 128.

45. Moreau de Saint-Méry, *Notes historiques*, Archives d'Outre-mer, F3, vol. 140, 49.

46. "Bois côtelette" is a tree name found throughout the francophone Caribbean, synonymous with "bois carré."

47. Camille Thierry, *Les Vagabondes: Poésies américaines* (Paris: Lemerre, 1874), 22.

48. "Seringues" is ostensibly a palatalization of "serins," ninnies. However, as it is spelled in the poem it literally means "syringe," and with the idea of the whites being "stuck to their behinds," a latent scatological meaning here should be read as a *double entendre*.

Epilogue

This book has charted the emergence of a mediated Haitian literature composed of the texts produced by leaders of the Haitian Revolution, notably Toussaint Louverture and Jean-Jacques Dessalines, and lyrical representations of courtesans' experience that correlate to contemporaneous accounts of the popular *oraliture* of Afro-diasporic women. On the level of authorship, it is a tradition marked by striking slippage between conceptual voice, scribal or editorial practice, and French and Creole (*Kreyòl*). "Pure" categories of author and scribe undergo a mutual reconstitution in this corpus, one that parallels that of literature and politics in the textual arena, as well as that of master and slave in the Haitian Revolution. The French colonies did not, as noted in the introduction, yield a slave narrative; but Saint-Domingue/Haiti yielded one of the most prolific and meaningful bodies of early Afro-diasporic literature anywhere in the black Atlantic.

The material cited in this book only confirms the need for further scholarly work on an impressive scale. Consider our partial knowledge of the correspondence produced by Toussaint Louverture alone. The most voluminous anthology of his letters, edited by Gérard Mentor Laurent,[1] contains the Haitian general's correspondence with a single individual only, the revolutionary general and colonial governor Etienne Laveaux; based on three volumes of archival letters at the Bibliothèque nationale in France, it features more than one hundred often lengthy examples. Other correspondents with whom Toussaint had frequent and sustained exchanges included Napoleon Bonaparte, General Leclerc, Colonel Vincent, the French agents to Saint-Domingue (especially Commissioner Léger-Félicité Sonthonax), fellow military officers such as Jean-Jacques Dessalines, and his sons Isaac and Placide, as well as their tutor, Coisnon, in Paris. Beyond the Laurent anthology, Louis Marceau Lecorps provided an anthology of a small but significant sampling of Toussaint's correspondence relating to his negotiations with the American Consul in Saint-Domingue, Edward Stevens, between 1799 and 1800 in *La Politique extérieure de Toussaint Louverture*.[2] An important if slim recent anthology, edited by F. Nick Nesbitt, provides the most diverse representation yet of Toussaint's letters of any existing collection.[3] These existing anthologies, however important in themselves, only hint at Toussaint Louverture the epistolary producer.

Toussaint produced reams of correspondence to navigate diplomatic relationships, relay military plans, and justify his stratagems. A contemporary French general, François Joseph Pamphile de Lacroix, estimated that Toussaint was capable of answering, with panache, and even a kind of carnal satisfaction, between one hundred and three hundred letters and other military communications a day: "Le travail de cabinet, qui paraissait devoir lui être si étranger; cent, deux cents, trois cents lettres à répondre par jour, semblaient lui être des plaisirs aussi vifs que la satisfaction des sens pour le reste des hommes"[4] ("Deskwork, which should by rights have been so foreign to him—even up to one hundred, two hundred, three hundred letters to answer daily—seemed instead to yield for him the vigorous satisfaction that other men might find only in the pleasures of the senses").

Much of the revolutionary progress on the part of the insurgents between 1791 and 1804 arguably took place not on the battlefield, but in administrative collaboration between individuals and groups of different race and class backgrounds in the hybrid *armée de Saint-Domingue*, which splintered into the formal entities of the *armée indigène* ("the indigenous army") versus the French army only at the end of the conflict.[5] Within the shifting military collaborations that paradoxically characterized much of the Haitian Revolution, the scribal dimension was a primordial element. And in the eventual defeat of the French army by the indigenous army, the philosophical acuity and eloquence of the black leadership was an even more primordial element. Next to Dessalines's immoderate claim in the April 18, 1804 "I have avenged America" proclamation that the "irritated genius" of Haiti had summoned not only tempests and stormy seas but plagues like the yellow fever that decimated the French troops, one might make the more moderate claim that Dessalines's own irritated genius informed a formidable arsenal of words.

Did the black generals' letters and the courtesans' poetic claims ever meet in hybrid textual spaces? We do find an example of such a coincidence in one of the handwritten texts by Toussaint Louverture, a personal letter to a correspondent known only by the playful name *la reine de Sa ba*—the Queen of Sheba, or, in Toussaint's spelling, something like the "Queen of She ba." Toussaint's handwritten texts exemplify the kind of freedoms taken with the metropolitan linguistic model sometimes referred to in Haiti as a *français marron* or maroon French; language from the woods rather than the cities, from a zone of individual variation rather than national homogeneity, adaptation and eclecticism rather than uniformity and discipline. Toussaint not only worked in this literary language of his own, he played in it. Originating from Gonaïves in April of 1799, this letter addressed to the allegorical persona "bon sa mi" ("bon zanmi" in Creole or "bonne amie" in French), "accuser of the general and Queen of Sheba," reads as follows:

Gonaive ce 28 germinal an 7 tieme [April 29, 1799]
Toussaint Louverture

A bon sa mi, lacusateur du general et la rene
De Sa ba.

Je re su votre lettre avec tout la satis [faction] pocible, mon seul regre se davoir apri la maladies de la rene de Sa ba set tune creve ceur pou moi de voir une ci bone persone comme el et afligé, jan suis fache, je ne peuve vous se crire plu lon me devoire man peche, a mon re tour je vou repondré pour votre a fer par ticullée

Bon jour a tous vosa mis pour moi, anbrace votre père dour cément va loin et pasiance bai la force

Je vous de sire les meieur sante Salut a mi tier
Toussaint Louverture[6]

With French spellings it would read:

Gonaives, 28 germinal an 7
Toussaint Louverture

A bon zanmi, l'accusatrice du général et reine de Sa ba.

J'ai reçu votre lettre avec toute la satis[faction] possible, mon seul regret c'est d'avoir appris la maladie de la reine de Saba c'est un crève-coeur pour moi de voir une si bonne personne comme elle est affligée, j'en suis fâché, je ne peux pas vous écrire plus long mes devoirs m'empêchent, à mon retour je vou repondré pour votre affaire particulière

Bonjour à tous vos amis pour moi, embrassez votre père doucement va loin et patience bai la force

Je vous désire la meilleure santé Salut amitiés
Toussaint Louverture

Or in English:

Gonaïves, April 29 1799

To Good Friend, the Accuser of the General and the Queen of She ba

I have received your letter with all possible satisfaction. My only regret is to hear of the Queen of Sheba's illness; it is heartbreaking for me to see such a good person afflicted, I am very angry that it should be so, I cannot write longer now as my duties prevent me, on my return I will respond as concerns your particular affair

Greetings to all your friends, give your father a big hug, may you go far, and may patience give you strength,

I wish you the best of health, greetings and friendship,

Toussaint Louverture

In this artful, flirtatious consolation of a female correspondent who has taken him to task for his absence or silence, Toussaint reveals his delight in masquerade, in being the "general" counterpart to the Queen of Sheba, in feigning heartbreak while showing real tenderness. The secret subtext— "votre a fer par ticullée"—marks the space of intimacy. It is notable that he does not change his own persona—he writes his name at the top of the letter in normal print rather than his signature, playing at the forms of military correspondence, and taking pleasure in actually being, himself, a persona sufficiently remarkable that it needed no embroidering—the general.

Was this one of the fabled letters in a large correspondence with an array of mistresses found after Toussaint's kidnapping by the French? Pamphile de Lacroix attested to an ornate box filled with "des tresses de cheveux de toutes couleurs, des bagues, des coeurs en or traversés de fleches, des petites clefs, des nécessaires, des souvenirs, et une infinité de billets doux qui ne laissaient aucun doute sur les succès obtenus en amour par le vieux Toussaint Louverture!"[7] One might doubt such a conclusion because of the openness of Toussaint's tenderness with his correspondent's social entourage and even her father. And yet it may have been an example of Toussaint's close attachments to colonial families where discrete intimacies solidified protected status for the family as a whole, as would appear to have been the case for Madame Lartigue—and also, allegedly, Mademoiselle Lartigue— or for the Veuve Descahaux whose former home in Ennery Toussaint had come to occupy at the time of his deportation.[8] Such questions are hardly significant (although they could help us someday to understand the actual networks of collaboration between elite white and black families in the late Haitian Revolutionary context) compared to the marvel of Toussaint's use of the literary medium to engage in this tender transference across languages. A Creole culture crept into Toussaint's wording. "Pasiance bai la force," Toussaint encouraged his fond "accuser," using the Creole verb "bay" for "to give": "La patience donne la force."

A less direct but equally compelling representation of Dessalines's tender enthusiasms can be found in the historical prototype of the dancing Dessalines, Dessalines leaping irrepressibly like a Fon warrior of old. Military dignity could not prevent him from answering the call of the drums, and from loving a mistress, Couloute, celebrated for her dancing, leading to the creation of a dance, a *carabinier* related to the *meringue*, called "Dessalines vini voir Couloute danser." As Colin Dayan summarizes,

> Madiou and others recount Dessalines's notorious passion for dancing and women. His favorite mistress was the much-admired dancer Couloute, whom Dessalines met in Jérémie in 1800. The emperor's ardor for her inspired a celebrated and much popularized dance, the *carabinier* (a wilder, more energetic and undulating kind of *meringue*), which was accompanied by the chant: "The Emperor comes to see Couloute dance." At one particularly luxurious ball, when a dancing Dessalines leapt into the air and landed on his knee before Couloute, Christophe is reported to have remarked (loud enough for Dessalines to hear him): "See His Majesty! Aren't you ashamed to have such a *sauteur* [meaning both 'jumper' and 'temporizer,' or 'chameleon'] as our leader!"[9]

The figure of a dancing Dessalines, like that of Toussaint writing to the "Queen of She ba," shows the more personal side of a leader who could rarely afford to let his guard down.

At the same time that this book documents the autonomy, ingenuity, and boldness of texts from the Haitian Revolution, it documents the relentlessness of the threats that faced the new black nation, not least the threat of being redefined as a French colony. The lingering French colonial presence on the island of Hispaniola was all too real a factor in what one might call Haiti's failure to thrive. Was it humiliation that led Dessalines to gloss over the details of the multi-faceted warfare French general Louis Ferrand was still waging against Haitian commerce and independence from Santo Domingo throughout Dessalines's rule? Certainly when we read Dessalines's invective against the French, we should in part understand him to be railing against the general who issued, on March 17, 1804, the following call to French colonists to return to a French island of Saint-Domingue:

Aux Habitans Blancs
de l'île de Saint-Domingue, réfugiés
dans les Colonies voisines.

Citoyens, vous manquez de toutes espèces de ressources; et la partie de l'île de Saint-Domingue, occupée par les Français, vous en offre de nouvelles. Rentrez dans une Isle dont vous connaissez toutes les avantages, et que vous ne pouvez cesser de regarder comme votre Patrie. C'est à Santo-Domingo que vous êtes attendus. [...]

Les Gouverneurs des colonies voisines ont été invités, au nom du Gouvernement français, de procurer aux anciens Habitans de Saint-Domingue, les moyens d'arriver à Santo-Domingo.

Citoyens, ici vous n'aurez pas à craindre des événements pareils à ceux qui vous ont forcés de quitter l'île Saint-Domingue; et vous serez en état d'attendre que la France, après avoir rétabli la tranquillité dans cette Isle, vous remette en possession de vos propriétés. Vous vivez sous un Gouvernement paternel, dans un pays où les vivres sont en abondance, et où le commerce et la confiance font tous les jours de nouveaux progrès.

Santo Domingo, le 26 Ventôse, an XII de la République française.
Le Général, Commandant en chef, fesant fonction de Capitaine Général,

Signé,
L. Ferrand[10]

(To the white planters
of the island of Saint-Domingue, refugees
in the neighboring colonies.

Citizens, you lack all manner of resources; and the part of the island of Saint-Domingue occupied by the French can offer you new ones. Return to the island whose advantages you know so well, the island you cannot stop seeing as your Fatherland. You are expected in Santo-Domingo. [...]

The Governors of the neighboring colonies have been invited, in the name of the French government, to provide the former planters of Saint-Domingue with the means to reach Santo-Domingo.

Citizens, here you need have no fear of events like those that forced you to leave the island of Saint-Domingue; and you will be well-positioned to wait for France, after it has reestablished tranquility on the island, to restore your property to you. You dwell under a paternal government, in a country where supplies are in abundance, and where commerce and confidence progress further each and every day.

Santo Domingo, 26 Ventôse, year 12 of the French Republic [March 17, 1804].

The General and Commander in Chief, fulfilling the role of Captain General,
L. Ferrand)

Dessalines, whose alleged "ferocity" in the Haitian Independence has been critiqued from all quarters, in the early months of 1804 confronted not only the seizure of friendly commercial vessels from Haitian ports, not only international proclamations of the illegality of intercourse with the rebels of French Saint-Domingue, but an active policy of repatriation for white French planters. We know, from Dessalines's May 8 "Proclamation aux habitants de la partie Espagnole," that he considered the provocations of the "madman Ferrand" to be cause for an (unsuccessful) invasion, but to this day we fail to appreciate the degree to which Haiti's independence was, from the start, an independence denied.

This entrenched historical experience of threat in independent Haiti is especially important to keep in mind since the earthquake of January 12, 2010, which opened huge new ruptures—human and infrastructural, geological and inter-relational—in the Haitian landscape. A cataclysm of historical scope, the January 2010 earthquake nevertheless stands as one of a long chain of sudden reversals of terrain, conditions, expectations, and values in Haiti's trajectory. Perhaps unsurprisingly, there were observers who saw the Haitian Revolution itself as a seismic readjustment: Drouin de Bercy would comment, "Aux Antilles, au milieu des esclaves, la terre tremble au propre et au figuré" ("In the slaves' milieu, the earth shakes literally and figuratively").[11] And yet Michel-Rolph Trouillot's metaphor of the unthinkable[12] nature of the successful slave revolution in Haiti has proven to be less a diagnosis of unthinkability than a metonymy for our relentless desire to think past the impossible. This desire is precisely what characterizes the voices of the early Haitian literature explored in this book—even as the impossible was laid out in new yet familiar forms, stretching from the end of the colonial to its immediate return.

Notes

1. *Toussaint Louverture à travers sa correspondance*, ed. Gérard Mentor Laurent (Madrid: Industrias Graphicas Espana, 1953).
2. Louis Marceau Lecorps, *La Politique extérieure de Toussaint-Louverture; nos premières*

relations politiques avec les Etats-Unis, lettres de Toussaint-Louverture et d'Edward Stevens (1799–1800) (Port-au-Prince: Chéraquit, 1935). The anthology contains a 1798 letter from Toussaint to President Adams, lamenting a cooling of U.S./Saint-Domingue commercial relations.

3. F. Nick Nesbitt, ed., *Jean-Bertrand Aristide Presents The Haitian Revolution* (New York: Verso, 2008).

4. François Joseph Pamphile de Lacroix, *La Révolution d'Haïti*, ed. Pierre Pluchon (Paris: Karthala, 1995), 246.

5. Dessalines was using the title "Général en chef de l'armée indigène" in correspondence from November of 1803, such as his November 19 letter to the *Citoyens du Cap*, cited in the *Annual Register* (1804), 187.

6. Toussaint Louverture, letter to the "Queen of Sheba," Library of Congress, Miscellaneous Manuscripts Division, "Toussaint Louverture Papers," LC Control No. mm79005595. I am very grateful to my research assistant, Duke history undergraduate Andrew Walker, for finding this letter.

7. Pamphile de Lacroix, *Révolution de Haiti*, 304.

8. Jacques Cauna, "La Face cachée de Toussaint Louverture," in *Saint-Domingue Espagnol et la révolution nègre d'Haïti*, ed. Alain Yacou (Paris: Karthala, 2007), 201.

9. [Colin] Joan Dayan, *Haiti, History, and the Gods* (Berkeley, CA: University of California Press, 1995), 21.

10. This bilingual French and Spanish broadside was published in the city of Santo Domingo by the "Imprimerie de A. J. BLOCQUER.T [sic], Imprimeur du Gouvernement," on March 17, 1804.

11. M. Drouin de Bercy, *De Saint-Domingue, de ses guerres, de ses révolutions, de ses ressources, et des moyens à prendre pour y rétablir la paix et l'industrie* (Paris: Chez Hoquet, 1814), 199.

12. See Michel-Rolph Trouillot, "From Planters' Journals to Academia: The Haitian Revolution as Unthinkable History," *Journal of Caribbean History* 25 (1991), 81–89.

Index

The letter f indicates a figure and n an endnote